AN ARISTOCRACY OF CRITICS

THE COMMISSION ON FREEDOM OF THE PRESS

ROBERT M. HUTCHINS, *Chairman*
Chancellor, The University of Chicago

ZECHARIAH CHAFEE, JR., *Vice-Chairman*
Professor of Law, Harvard University

JOHN M. CLARK
Professor of Economics, Columbia University

JOHN DICKINSON
Professor of Law, University of Pennsylvania, and General Counsel, Pennsylvania Railroad

WILLIAM E. HOCKING
Professor of Philosophy, Emeritus, Harvard University

HAROLD D. LASSWELL
Professor of Law, Yale University

ARCHIBALD MacLEISH
Formerly Assistant Secretary of State

CHARLES E. MERRIAM
Professor of Political Science, Emeritus, The University of Chicago

REINHOLD NIEBUHR
Professor of Ethics and Philosophy of Religion, Union Theological Seminary

ROBERT REDFIELD
Professor of Anthropology, The University of Chicago

BEARDSLEY RUML
Chairman, Federal Reserve Bank of New York

ARTHUR M. SCHLESINGER
Professor of History, Harvard University

GEORGE N. SHUSTER
President, Hunter College

FOREIGN ADVISERS

JOHN GRIERSON
Former General Manager, Wartime Information Board, Canada

*HU SHIH
Former Chinese Ambassador to the United States

†JACQUES MARITAIN
President, Free French School for Advanced Studies

KURT RIEZLER
Professor of Philosophy, New School for Social Research

STAFF OF THE COMMISSION

ROBERT D. LEIGH, *Director*
LLEWELLYN WHITE, *Assistant Director*
RUTH A. INGLIS
MILTON D. STEWART

---

* Dr. Hu Shih was unable to participate in the work of the Commission after 1944.

† M. Maritain resigned February, 1945, to become French ambassador to the Holy See.

AN ARISTOCRACY OF CRITICS

Luce, Hutchins, Niebuhr, and the Committee
That Redefined Freedom of the Press

STEPHEN BATES

Yale

UNIVERSITY PRESS

New Haven and London

Published with assistance from the foundation established in memory of
Philip Hamilton McMillan of the Class of 1894, Yale College.

Yale University Press books may be purchased in quantity for educational,
business, or promotional use. For information, please e-mail sales.press@
yale.edu (U.S. office) or sales@yaleup.co.uk (U.K. office).

Set in Janson type by IDS Infotech, Ltd.
Printed in the United States of America.

Library of Congress Control Number: 2020935082
ISBN 978-0-300-11189-7 (hardcover : alk. paper)

A catalogue record for this book is available from the British Library.

This paper meets the requirements of ANSI/NISO Z39.48-1992
(Permanence of Paper).

10 9 8 7 6 5 4 3 2 1

To Clara and Charlotte

Contents

AN ARISTOCRACY OF CRITICS

Introduction

IN DECEMBER 1942, Robert Maynard Hutchins met Henry R. Luce for lunch at the Drake Hotel in Chicago. Hutchins, the nation's best-known educator, ran the University of Chicago. Luce, one of the nation's best-known publishers, ran Time Inc. Arm's-length friends since they first met as Yale undergraduates, both were cerebral, opinionated, and sharp-tongued, esteemed in some circles and abhorred in others. Out of their conversation that day would come the most extraordinary collaboration of American thinkers in the twentieth century, the Commission on Freedom of the Press. Hutchins and a dozen fellow intellectuals would investigate newsroom bias, distrust of the media, foreign and domestic propaganda, corporate domination of political discourse, a fragmenting and polarized electorate, hate speech, and demagoguery, as well as what we now call echo chambers, trolls, deplatforming, and post-truth politics. These problems afflicted the United States of the 1940s. Many of them afflict the United States of today.

Luce came up with the idea. Corporations, he told Hutchins, underwrite scientific research at the University of Chicago. What about a corporate-funded philosophical study? If Time Inc. provided the money, would the university convene a committee of intellectuals to rethink freedom of the press? No, said Hutchins. It couldn't be done. In subsequent encounters, Luce kept pushing. After a year, Hutchins agreed. The idea was audacious, but so were the men: Luce, proclaimer of the American Century, and Hutchins, anointer of the Great Books of the Western World.

Hutchins coined the grandiose name, the Commission on Freedom of the Press, and the two men recruited a group of intellectual superstars, including Reinhold Niebuhr, the foremost American theologian; Zechariah Chafee Jr., the preeminent First Amendment scholar; Archibald MacLeish, librarian of Congress and Pulitzer Prize–winning poet; Charles E. Merriam, a pioneering political scientist; William Ernest Hocking, an acclaimed philosopher; and Harold D. Lasswell, a propaganda expert and chief architect of the emerging field of media studies. Hutchins called them "some very eminent characters." All were men, and most were professors, but not the sort who devoted their careers to "the microscopic study of Byzantine mosaics," as Hutchins derided the gullies of academic specialization. These were foxes rather than hedgehogs, in Isaiah Berlin's terms, men who articulated and defended big ideas: Hutchins versus John Dewey on the ideals of education, MacLeish versus James T. Farrell on the duties of the artist, Merriam versus Friedrich Hayek on the role of the state, Niebuhr versus Merriam on the arc of history. These men left the college cloisters and worked for President Franklin D. Roosevelt, testified before Congress, charted the course of policy, and opined on matters cosmic and quotidian. They were leading figures in what Luce called the aristocracy of critics.[1]

Hutchins, one of the nation's most sought-after speakers, appeared twice on the cover of Luce's *Time*. His pronouncements made headlines. He championed isolationism before Pearl Harbor and world government after Hiroshima. He spoke out against greed in business, relativism in philosophy, electives in college, and physical exercise in leisure time. As his profile rose, many well-regarded Americans came to believe that the president of the University of Chicago ought to be president of the United States. Hutchins thought so too.

To Hutchins and others, it seemed an opportune moment to appraise the American media. Tabloids were pandering to the basest instincts of the crowd. Head-to-head newspaper competition was diminishing, and publishers were snapping up radio licenses. More and more media outlets were in the hands of fewer and fewer corporations. The corporations grew, but the political debate within the media didn't. Major news organizations ranged from

Colonel Robert R. McCormick's *Chicago Tribune*, with its far-right fulminations against FDR, to Luce's *Time*, with its center-right fulminations against FDR. President Roosevelt publicly complained about the press and privately plotted revenge through federal agencies, while his allies in Congress launched harassing investigations and threatened draconian regulations. Polls detected public animosity, too. In 1936, when researchers asked Americans which institutions were abusing their power, the press ranked number one, ahead even of bankers.

Newspaper publishers, for their part, acclaimed the press as an indispensable pillar of American self-government, a bulwark of democracy enshrined in the First Amendment not for its own sake but for the sake of the citizenry. (Whenever publishers gather together, said Harold Lasswell, expect to hear about bulwarks.) The Commission on Freedom of the Press, chaired by Hutchins, proposed to take the platitudes seriously. If the press is servant of the people, how's the service? After 17 meetings, 58 witnesses, 225 staff interviews, 176 documents, $215,000, and a lot of false starts and dead ends, the commission published its conclusions in a report, *A Free and Responsible Press*, in 1947.[2]

From the name, one might expect the Commission on Freedom of the Press to have championed a new birth of freedom. Instead it called for a new burden of responsibility, backed by a tacit threat of punishment. American journalists, according to *A Free and Responsible Press*, were doing a wretched job. With their sensationalism, sloppiness, bias, and outright lies, they were imperiling self-government, world peace, and human civilization. The report didn't recommend new restrictions, but it warned that Americans would not long tolerate such abuses. If the press didn't improve, its freedom would be curtailed. The First Amendment would provide no shield, for "the amendment will be amended."[3]

The heated criticism provoked a heated response. The *Wall Street Journal* construed *responsibility* as a code word for *censorship*. The commission's analysis reminded a writer at *Editor & Publisher* of the Star Chamber, the Associated Press's executive director of Soviet communism, and a reporter at Colonel McCormick's *Chicago Tribune* of "the late Adolf Hitler and the late Joseph Goebbels." Luce, perhaps miffed that Hutchins had barred him from commission meetings, disowned his brainchild. "Is this the best philosophy can do?" he scrawled across the manuscript. Hutchins, for his part, defended the report in public, apologized to Luce in private, and told an acquaintance that he hoped the body that produced the report would be remembered not as the Hutchins Commission but as the Luce Commission.[4]

For a while, it seemed that it wouldn't be remembered at all. In 1956, nine years after publication of *A Free and Responsible Press*, a University of Chicago Press editor recommended against a new edition, writing that the book is "best left unresurrected." Yet in the years that followed, it rose from the dead. According to Everette E. Dennis and Melvin L. DeFleur, *A Free and Responsible Press* ranks as "one of the most important documents in the history of American media." One scholar applies its teachings to news coverage of the post-9/11 War on Terror, another to "the disinformation dangers of the digital age." In a key First Amendment ruling, the Supreme Court quotes the commission's work and adopts its analytic approach.[5]

A Free and Responsible Press has outlived other books on the topic, outlived its authors, outlived even Time Inc., which was subsumed in a merger in 2018. Not bad for a slender volume published by an academic press, written by a committee of (mostly) professors, and completed so long ago that it's not just pre-internet but pre-television.

Understanding the Commission on Freedom of the Press, according to one member, requires "the three-dimensional picture—process plus result." Whereas the result, *A Free and Responsible Press*, is a media-studies classic, the process remains largely unknown: the meetings and memos in which towering intellects grappled with problems and groped toward solutions. "Expressions of principle were constantly in the air—proposed, beaten, surviving, or possibly reborn!" recounted William Ernest Hocking. The men discussed the crisis of liberalism in a postindividualistic age, the danger that pluralism will atrophy into nihilism, the tendency of overabundant liberty to undermine public order and lead to the constriction of liberty, and the limits of free will: "You are intelligent enough to know that you are not intelligent enough to act altogether voluntarily," said Reinhold Niebuhr. They contemplated the recondite and the banal: Kant and Hegel, Milton and Mill, Walter Winchell and "Little Orphan Annie." They deliberated over first principles: the hazards of an uninformed, misinformed, or disinformed electorate; the division of responsibility between elected nonexperts and unelected experts; the disconnect between the truth-seeking marketplace of ideas and the profit-seeking marketplace of media; and the distortions that emerge when certain facts get singled out, styled, and packaged into news stories. They pondered the value of diverse voices, too. What if God published a newspaper, Archibald MacLeish asked, and it printed nothing but truth? Why would we need any other media? The doctrine of free will, replied Hutchins.[6]

These men weren't necessarily suited to committee work. Hutchins was known for high-handedness in dealing with University of Chicago faculty. One commission member was notorious for pomposity, another for arrogance, another for hours-long monologues. Nonetheless, they shared a commitment to open, reasoned inquiry in pursuit of truth. In sometimes-intense discussions, they explored their realms of disagreement. Without surrendering their principles, many of them reevaluated and revised their policy views, especially on the intertwined issues of monopoly, ownership concentration, and antitrust law. Several described their work on the commission as exhilarating. Hocking called it "one of the greatest privileges of my life."[7]

In trying to fashion solutions, the members kept butting against a "hindrance," as Hutchins called it: the First Amendment. A couple of them wanted to rewrite the amendment—literally. Instead they ended up reconceiving it. They decided that, properly interpreted, "Congress shall make no law ... abridging the freedom of speech" sometimes means "Congress shall make law enhancing the freedom of speech." Though this concept is generally credited to Alexander Meiklejohn, the commission published it first. The deliberations prefigured other influential ideas, too. The members distinguished two types of liberty before Isaiah Berlin, sketched the philosophy of communitarianism before Amitai Etzioni, and advocated a right of media access before Jerome A. Barron. Hocking, in addition, sketched an approach for protecting speech from nongovernmental threats, which, had it been followed, might have helped defuse the anticommunist blacklists in the 1950s as well as the efforts to deplatform controversial speakers in the early twenty-first century.[8]

In the commission's final meeting, Charles Merriam suggested that its unpublished deliberations might outshine its soon-to-be-published conclusions. "I have been listening with open-eyed wonder at these arguments you gentlemen are making back and forth," he said, "but are we sharing these discussions with our readers?" They weren't. *A Free and Responsible Press* presents a ringing call to action, written in Hutchins's usual register, eloquent and graceful but also cocksure, Manichean, and brooking no dissent. It gives no hint of the two and a half years of debate that came before, the complexities, nuances, tensions, and trade-offs that prompted him to remark at one point, "I am very much distressed by the whole progress of this Commission's work, because I began with such a simple answer to all these questions." The richest explorations and explications got sorted, boxed, and buried in archives.[9]

Documentation of the chair's mismanagement got buried, too. Matters other than the commission took precedence for Hutchins: leading the Committee to Frame a World Constitution, selecting the Great Books of the Western World, figuring out the next stage of his career, and trying to restore tranquility to his raucous marriage. The Luce project fell behind schedule and surged over budget. The research staff descended into goldbricking and backbiting. *Variety* reported that commission members were irretrievably divided. At the last minute, Hutchins reengaged, negotiated some lingering disputes and papered over others, threw out half the report and rewrote the rest, and persuaded everyone to sign. A near fiasco turned into what MacLeish called a "human triumph."[10]

Though flawed, *A Free and Responsible Press* develops a more innovative, penetrating analysis of the press and its responsibilities than many contemporaries recognized, including Luce. In some respects, it's more apt today than it was in 1947. But the commission's most profound and prescient discussions have remained largely unknown.

I have two aims here. The first is the one described by Louis Menand in *The Metaphysical Club*: to understand "ideas in their own spirit—that is, to try to see ideas as always soaked through by the personal and social situations in which we find them." The history of

A Free and Responsible Press begins with the experiences and personalities of its authors, men molded by World War I, the Red Scare, the Great Depression, and the New Deal, as well as World War II and the dawning Cold War. The group included individualists as well as communitarians, isolationists as well as interventionists, New Dealers as well as a New Deal apostate, utopians as well as cynics, plus a longtime advocate of civil rights, a onetime advocate of eugenics, and a couple of genteel bigots. "Political science without biography," as Harold Lasswell wrote, "is a form of taxidermy."[11]

Materials in archives provide fresh perspectives. Only a handful of scholars have dug deep into the commission transcripts, memoranda, interview notes, report drafts, and correspondence. In addition to this official record, which is archived at four universities, I unearthed other materials, many of them previously unseen. Time Inc. opened its corporate files, including the typescript of *A Free and Responsible Press* with Henry Luce's exasperated marginalia, as well as his twenty-two-page critique of the report, which Hutchins pointedly omitted from the official record. I found Colonel McCormick's dark musings on the commission ("all part of a plot") in *Chicago Tribune* office files. Other archives contained comments on commission publications by Mortimer Adler (the report "out-areos the pagitica"), Walter Lippmann, and Arthur Hays Sulzberger, plus disgruntled reflections on the experience by two of the staff researchers, one of whom—the only woman associated with the project—later befriended Joseph McCarthy and urged the House Un-American Activities Committee to go after Robert Hutchins. "Mankind has thrown away most of its experience for lack of competent record-making," wrote Lasswell. Not in this case.[12]

My second aim is to consider the lessons of the Commission on Freedom of the Press in the context of our own era. Many of its concerns remain timely. Some, after a long latency, have flared up anew. In depicting news-media behemoths as threats to democracy, commission members used the same arguments as those commentators who now depict social-media behemoths as threats to democracy. Lasswell feared that Americans were being duped by unidentifiable propagandists, like the anonymous trolls on social media. Sounding like a critic of Facebook, Reinhold Niebuhr observed that "traditional and organic forms of cohesion" in society were being supplanted by "synthetic, mechanistic and artificial forms of togetherness."[13]

Commission members also worried that citizens were walling themselves off from ideas that differed from their own. *PM*'s left-wing subscribers, a researcher said, couldn't communicate with *Reader's Digest*'s right-wing subscribers. Egged on by partisan media, Americans were demonizing the opposition, fabricating conspiracy theories, and flouting Hocking's first commandment of intellectual morality: "listen to the other side." Niebuhr believed that an authoritarian demagogue might rise to power by exploiting the fragmentation and the rage. Others thought a greater danger was that voters, overwhelmed by the cacophony, would retreat from the public square. "The cure for distorted information may be more information," said Hocking, "but what is the cure for too much information?"[14]

This book chronicles the unprecedented, unparalleled, unlikely Commission on Freedom of the Press. Against the backdrop of World War II and the early Cold War, a committee of thinkers gathered around conference tables at the Waldorf-Astoria and the Biltmore, ate pricey meals, drank cocktails, smoked cigars, and ruminated over how to safeguard civilization from reckless journalism. Out of Henry Luce's half-baked notion and Robert Hutchins's slipshod execution emerged, miraculously, enduring truths about the media, freedom, and democracy.

CHAPTER ONE

Skunk at the Garden Party

I N THE TWENTY YEARS since the men first met as Yale undergraduates, Robert Maynard Hutchins and Henry R. Luce had flourished. Hutchins was the president of the University of Chicago; Luce was editor in chief of Time Inc. Their minds were wide ranging, their ideas unorthodox, their intellectual self-assuredness boundless. Each was accustomed to thinking himself the smartest man in the room, often with good reason. Each had reached the pinnacle of his field by age thirty and now aimed to leave a larger mark.

Yet in some respects, it was an improbable friendship. Hutchins was debonair, witty, always at ease; Luce, fidgety, humorless, never at ease. Hutchins was a liberal Democrat who voted Socialist in 1932; Luce, a moderate Republican. Before Pearl Harbor, Hutchins was a high-profile isolationist, Luce a high-profile interventionist. Though both were sons of Presbyterian clergymen, Hutchins professed indifference to religion—"I have succeeded in not thinking about these questions all my life," he told an interviewer—whereas Luce was a devout believer. "Almost thou persuadeth me to be a Christian," Hutchins once told him, "but not a Republican—that would be too expensive."[1]

When the men met at Chicago's Drake Hotel in December 1942, Hutchins was forty-three and Luce forty-four. Over lunch,

Hutchins talked about corporate-sponsored scientific research at the University of Chicago. (He was sworn to secrecy about the biggest research undertaking on the Midway, one sponsored by the government: the Metallurgical Laboratory, a branch of the Manhattan Project.) Luce proposed a different kind of sponsored research. If, he said, professors will research a scientific question for the Wrigley Company—Does chewing gum aid digestion?—then why not get them to research a philosophical question for Time Inc.: What is freedom of the press? He had in mind a modern-day restatement of freedom's foundations, in keeping with his conviction that the American press, in the American Century, was playing an unprecedented role in global affairs.[2]

As a college president, Hutchins devoted much time to fundraising. He once planned to seek $100,000 from fellow Chicagoan Al Capone; a colleague dissuaded him. Often he targeted Luce. "If you have money to throw away, throw it in our direction," Hutchins told him in 1929. The mendicancy would continue even beyond the grave: in 1982, fifteen years after Luce's death and five years after Hutchins's, the Robert Maynard Hutchins Center for the Study of Democratic Institutions would seek funding from the Henry Luce Foundation, unsuccessfully.[3]

Now, though, Hutchins brushed aside Luce's notion. A collaborative study of press freedom by philosophy professors, he said, would be impossible to organize.

If the University of Chicago can't handle such a project, Luce replied, philosophers in academia are useless.[4]

Henry Luce admired Robert Maynard Hutchins. Others were besotted by him. "He's one of the few men in the country with a cult," said their mutual friend and Yale classmate William Benton. Hutchins's ascent was meteoric. Born in 1899 in Brooklyn, he enrolled in Oberlin College, served in World War I, finished his undergraduate education at Yale, and went on to Yale Law School. Upon receiving his JD in 1925, he switched from student to instructor. Soon after, as the self-described "youngest and least offensive member of the faculty," he became dean. In 1929, age thirty, he was appointed president of the University of Chicago. Luce's *Time* called him "the youngest and handsomest big-university president in the land." Even the *Chicago*

Tribune, the wildly conservative newspaper run by the wildly eccentric Colonel Robert R. McCormick, swooned. "Chicago is going to like Robert Maynard Hutchins," the paper said, for he was "slender as an athlete," with "a man's sort of handshake" and the ability to "talk engagingly on anything from baseball to politics."[5]

Hutchins was a striking blend of brainpower and vainglory: almost six foot three, impeccably clothed—the American Tailors Guild included him on its best-dressed list—and uncommonly attractive. A University of Chicago colleague called him "handsome beyond my descriptive powers." The new university president favored a life of intellectual exertion and physical ease. He enjoyed detective novels, but to justify the pastime, he read them in German. Asked his views on exercise, he said he believed in it for others. He hadn't coined a line often credited to him—"The secret of my abundant health is that whenever the impulse to exercise comes over me, I lie down until it passes away"—but he shared the sentiment.[6]

In conversation, his default mode was sardonic. Justice James C. McReynolds once asked Hutchins, then dean of Yale Law School, if the professors taught students that Supreme Court decisions are nonsense. No, he replied; the students figure it out for themselves. On another occasion, when a woman remarked that her husband had been educated at Princeton, Hutchins corrected her: "You mean he *went* to Princeton." In the 1950s, Henry Ford II publicly accused him of exercising poor judgment as an officer at the Ford Foundation. Maybe so, Hutchins told reporters, but who built the Edsel? When allies said the quips made him seem flashy rather than substantive, wise guy rather than wise man, Hutchins acknowledged the concern. He told Luce, "Although I do not fancy the role of the Allen (Fred or Gracie) of Education—assorted wisecracks for all occasions—I admit that I have laid myself open to the characterization." But he couldn't help himself. He valued wit in others too, perhaps inordinately. William Benton accused him of keeping an inept business manager on the payroll because he knew how to write a limerick.[7]

On first arriving in Chicago, Hutchins effused over the fabulousness of the city while remarking privately that it was the ideal site for a university, a place so boring that professors had no distractions. Soon he began to make enemies. A great university must have either a great football team or a great president, he declared, and proceeded to eliminate the championship football program. Alumni protested the loss of football, and faculty protested other innovations. Hutchins dismissed the criticisms. Of alumni, he said that "no useful change could ever be made with their approval." As for faculty, "Every great change in American education has been secured over the dead bodies of countless professors."[8]

Hutchins upended the Chicago curriculum. Higher education in the United States, he believed, was divided between gentlemen's clubs and cow colleges. He envisioned a new kind of university, one dedicated to teaching students to think. A student could enroll after sophomore year of high school and get a Chicago BA after four years of general-education classes; those who wanted to specialize could stay on for a master's. Undergraduates all took the same core classes, because in Hutchins's view, a system of electives assumes that the uneducated can direct their own education, that they are wise in their ignorance. Although the content was rigid, the process was not. Students needn't attend lectures. Grades were based on comprehensive exams, which students could take whenever they felt ready, even before enrolling in the classes.[9]

The centerpiece of the curriculum was the Great Books of the Western World. Hutchins and Mortimer Adler—whom Hutchins called the Great Bookie—taught Great Books seminars at the university starting in 1930, tour de force presentations that attracted Orson Welles, Gertrude Stein, and other visiting celebrities. The university bookstore's best-selling author was Aristotle. Opposing the Hutchins model of education was John Dewey, who had spent a decade teaching at the University of Chicago around the turn of the century. An advocate of flexibility in the curriculum, he called the Hutchins approach elitist and reactionary. Hutchins responded that everyone can master the Great Books. "If we cannot give them all this education," he said, "we may as well drop the pretense of democracy." (His commitment seemed to falter in 1944 when he opposed the GI Bill of Rights. In the long run, everyone could master the Great Books, he now said, but universities weren't yet ready to teach the unwashed.)[10]

For a college curriculum, the Hutchins approach was singularly polarizing. *Washington Post* publisher Eugene Meyer sided with

Hutchins, while his wife, Agnes E. Meyer, sided with Dewey, her former professor and mentor. In the mid-1930s, their daughter, Katharine (the future Katharine Graham, *Post* publisher), got an A in the Hutchins-Adler Great Books seminar. Her father sent her $100. Her mother consulted Dewey and then took to the pages of the *Post* to liken Hutchins, with his conviction that he possessed universal truths, to Hitler. Dewey congratulated her on "a swell job."[11]

Hutchins's one-size-fits-all curriculum reflected his absolute faith in absolutes. "The man who says he must be free to say two plus two equals five," Hutchins said, "is not a liberal; he is a fool." Though leftist in politics, he was rightist in culture. The Great Books represented a radical return to tradition. A critic observed in 1948 that the curriculum "creates cultural isolation by emphasizing the ethnocentrism of the West." In 1949, Hutchins, collaborating with the conservative publisher Henry Regnery, founded a quarterly journal at the University of Chicago, *Measure*, which featured articles by T. S. Eliot, Russell Kirk, and Martin Heidegger, as well as Chicago professors Leo Strauss and Friedrich Hayek. A devout moralist, Hutchins often stated his positions with what one professor called a "theological penumbra" as well as palpable scorn for those who disagreed. The alternatives, as he framed them, were pellucid: his course of action or the apocalypse.[12]

Much as he denied it, Hutchins seemed to relish controversy. He was a *teacher*, he liked to say, and teachers are duty bound to speak truths that people don't want to hear. He planned to call his memoir *The Skunk at the Garden Party*. (He did publish a book called *No Friendly Voice*.) But his contrarianism rarely strayed far outside the mainstream. He was more wiseacre than bomb thrower, "the establishment's antiestablishmentarian," in the phrase of his friend and biographer Milton Mayer. After the *New York Times* called Hutchins a "foe of complacency," the journalist Meg Greenfield wondered whether "there isn't something a little bit complacent about being the foe of someone else's complacency."[13]

Along with promoting the Great Books, Hutchins inveighed against an obverse form of education, neither great nor bookish: vocational training. Vocational classes must be up-to-the-minute, whereas the Great Books are timeless. Vocational classes train graduates to chase "the Almighty dollar," whereas the liberal arts train graduates to recognize that there's more to life than money. "The notion that education guarantees a brighter social and economic future for the individual is illusory," he said; "the notion that education can lead to understanding, and that understanding is a good in itself, is not." Hutchins especially loathed journalism schools, "the shadiest education ventures under respectable auspices." All skills needed for the newsroom, he maintained, can be learned on the job. Chicago had no journalism school, and neither, in his view, should any other university. He seemed to take their very existence as an affront.[14]

Though not for everyone, the University of Chicago under Hutchins bewitched many. "We were awed," said the journalist Laura Bergquist, "not only by his good looks and charisma but by his ability to make you *think*." The political reporter David S. Broder remembered "an excitement of intellectual discovery" that "remains tingling in the memory." The philosopher and literary critic George Steiner wrote that Hutchins's "inebriation with excellence set ablaze every aspect of an undergraduate's day." The historian Gertrude Himmelfarb, who had a graduate fellowship at the university, said that "if you wanted to be an intellectual, Chicago was the place to be." "I still see that year as through a golden haze," wrote Himmelfarb's husband, the author and editor Irving Kristol, "and I have never met a Chicago alumnus of that period who does not see it likewise." Chicago isn't a very good university, Hutchins liked to say. It's just the best there is.[15]

If Hutchins sometimes treated students with "friendly disdain," as a reporter put it, he also addressed them as adults. In a commencement speech delivered in 1935, he warned the new graduates that they would soon feel tempted to compromise and conform. "My experience and observation," he said, "lead me to warn you that the greatest, the most insidious, the most paralyzing danger you will face is the danger of corruption. Time will corrupt you. Your friends, your wives or husbands, your business or professional associates will corrupt you; your social, political, and financial ambitions will corrupt you." He admonished the graduates to be strong: "Believe me, you are closer to the truth now than you ever will be again. Do not let 'practical' men tell you that you should surrender your ideals because they are impractical."[16]

By then, the *Chicago Tribune* no longer found Hutchins enchanting. Conservatives claimed that the faculty was chockablock with left-wing radicals, and the *Tribune*, along with William Randolph Hearst's *Herald-Examiner*, demanded an official investigation, which the Illinois legislature ultimately authorized. For Colonel McCormick, the university came to represent, as Milton Mayer put it, the "crème de la Kremlin."[17]

Although McCormick turned against Hutchins, another publisher remained an admirer. In the 1930s and '40s, Henry Luce published features about him, including two cover stories in *Time*; commissioned him to write an article for *Fortune*; and invited him to join the Time Inc. board of directors. In a publisher's note, *Time* said one reader got so tired of the University of Chicago ballyhoo that he canceled his subscription.[18]

Long before Luce's proposal, Hutchins pronounced on the shortcomings of American media. "We all take our opinions from the newspapers," he told the American Society of Newspaper Editors in 1930. "Indeed I notice that in spite of the frightful lies you have printed about me I still believe everything you print about other people." Partly he complained about the media because that's what intellectuals did. He lamented that newspapers seemed afraid to demand any mental effort whatsoever on the part of readers. Mass entertainment was even worse, with "the horrid antics of Milton Berle." He expected media consumers, like Chicago students, to strive to improve themselves—to choose *Troilus and Cressida* over *Amos 'n' Andy*, the *New York Times* over the *Daily News*.[19]

Hutchins's complaints were also based on convictions about the duties of teachers. He envisaged a division of labor between academia and media. Self-government, he believed, requires the application of timeless moral principles to up-to-date facts. The university supplies the principles; the newspaper supplies the facts. He cited the question, How do we achieve justice and freedom today? The university elucidates justice and freedom in all their complexity; the press elucidates today's circumstances in all their complexity. The University of Chicago was doing its job. Why weren't the newspapers? "You are educators," he told a convention of journalists, "whether you like it or not."[20]

Hutchins also needled the press because he needed it. He enjoyed telling reporters to stop writing about his youth, which served to remind them of his youth. He insisted that he took no notice of his coverage. When asked about a *New Yorker* profile of him, he maintained that he had no plans to read it. "I am afraid it will confuse me." In truth, he pored over such articles and kept lists of their errors in his files ("I have never worn a Brooks suit"). The articles were many, for he lived in an era when an intellectual could achieve the status of public figure. During his tenure at the University of Chicago, from 1929 to 1951, he was one of the most popular speakers in the country. He published articles in general-interest magazines, Luce's and others. Journalists solicited his views. He called for creating a federal Department of Education, raising income and inheritance taxes, adopting a system of compulsory old-age pensions, and eliminating tariffs.[21]

"No man could rise so high as President Hutchins has in half his life without causing the world to wonder what the second half may hold for him," said *Time*. Many people thought he was destined for national leadership. In 1932, he delivered what the *New York Times* termed a "spell-binding" speech to the Young Democratic Club, which provoked talk that he might get the vice presidential nomination. (He was too young, just thirty-three.) In 1936, the columnist Dorothy Thompson wrote that Hutchins belonged in the White House. Two years later, Sinclair Lewis, who was married to Thompson, endorsed him for the presidency. "He is actually such an anarchist," the novelist said in a speech, "as to believe . . . that the wisdom of Shakespeare, the Bible and Aristophanes still is higher than the wisdom of Dale Carnegie." For Hutchins to win the presidency would have surpassed even Woodrow Wilson, who spent two years as governor of New Jersey between Princeton and the White House. His sole qualification was his stewardship of the University of Chicago.[22]

Hutchins missed out on several opportunities to gain government experience. President Franklin D. Roosevelt asked him to join the leadership of the National Recovery Administration in 1934, and Hutchins arranged to take a leave from the university. But NRA board members threatened to resign en masse rather than work with the notoriously arrogant university president, and the offer vanished with no explanation. Hutchins's pride was wounded. In 1939, the president summoned him to Warm Springs, Georgia. Securities and Exchange Commission chair William O. Douglas was being nominated for the Supreme Court. Would Hutchins take the SEC position? "I said under no circumstances would I consider the job," Hutchins recalled. He yearned to join Douglas on the Supreme Court, but he refused to toady to FDR. The president noticed. When adviser Harold Ickes recommended him for a Court vacancy, Roosevelt said that "he had begun to have his doubts about Hutchins" because, according to Ickes's diary, "he hadn't heard anything from him for a couple of years." Ickes suggested Hutchins for other vacancies, but FDR always spurned him. After the president announced his candidacy for a third term in 1940, Hutchins launched an implausible crusade to become his running mate. Ickes considered him "an ideal candidate," but Roosevelt chose Henry Wallace instead. Justice Douglas later said that if Hutchins had taken the SEC job, he "could have had the vice-presidential nomination of the Democratic Party for the asking."[23]

In 1941, Hutchins became an outspoken isolationist, an America First backer though not a member. "As Hitler made the Jews his scapegoat," he said in one speech, "so we are making Hitler ours." To defeat a totalitarian state, the United States would have to become a totalitarian state; war would mark the end of democracy, freedom, capitalism, and not least, liberal-arts education. Isolationists ranged across the ideological spectrum, and Hutchins fashioned alliances of convenience, including one with the publisher of the *Chicago Tribune*. After Colonel McCormick testified before Congress in opposition to President Roosevelt's efforts to aid Britain, Hutchins complimented him for an "absolutely impregnable" argument. When Hutchins made a major antiwar speech, the *Tribune* gave it lengthy coverage on its front page. Ickes thought Hutchins sounded like an appeaser, which he attributed in part to "his very just resentment over the manner in which the Administration has treated him."[24]

Hutchins's first wife might have foreclosed a political career anyway. Maude Phelps McVeigh was born in New York in 1899. She met Hutchins after his return from war, and they married in 1921.

While he studied and then taught at Yale Law School, Maude got a degree from the Yale School of Fine Arts and began exhibiting and selling her sculptures and paintings. Later, she would go on to publish poetry and fiction as well.[25]

Like her husband, Maude was tall and attractive, and they made a glamorous couple, although, according to Robert's friend Thornton Wilder, they were actually "two rather lonely young souls." Both could be haughty and condescending, but Robert cloaked condescension in wit, whereas Maude came across, in Wilder's phrase, as "Marie-Antoinette-disdainful." Sometimes her rudeness was tactical—a shield, she claimed, against pressure to conform—while at other times, she misread her effect on others. In the 1920s, F. Scott Fitzgerald flirted with her in the Ritz Bar in Paris, and she either gave him a thumbs-down (her account) or belittled him (a witness's account). She thought it was all in fun, but she later heard that Fitzgerald had taken umbrage. She once asked a friend, facetiously but perhaps not altogether, how she could get people to love her.[26]

Upon arriving at the University of Chicago in 1929, Maude declared that she intended to continue her career as an artist. On that point, wrote one reporter, "she was almost bellicose." In 1932, she and Mortimer Adler collaborated on an art project to decouple form and meaning, which they called *Diagrammatics*. Maude produced spare sketches of heads, limbs, and mostly unclothed figures, which she said flowed from her subconscious. She stressed that the drawings were "non-representative" and therefore, even if they looked it, not necessarily human. Adler contributed brief passages, grammatical but meaningless, evoking particular genres. From "Prayer": "Blue art thou, O Last, and deeply to be raised; blue is thy pagination, and of thy fistula there is no wing."[27]

Along with a limited-edition book, the project spawned a live performance that the duo delivered in various Chicago venues. From the stage, Maude would announce at the outset that the presentation would "signify nothing and be of no consequence." She would then show slides of her drawings while Adler read his gibberish. In concluding remarks, she would say, "I hope I have not made myself clear." The Dadaist act went over well in arts circles, with one critic praising its "keen and impish wit," but a presenta-

tion to a women's group misfired when some in the audience suspected that they were the butt of the impish wit, being played for
suckers by snickering Midway sophisticates. The sincerity of the
two presenters was "extensively doubted," according to the University of Chicago student newspaper, the *Daily Maroon*, but Maude
insisted that *Diagrammatics* was serious art, not a put-on.[28]

Another contretemps arose a few years later. The Hutchins
family's 1937 Christmas card, sent to a thousand people, featured
Maude's sketch of a nude prepubescent girl in pigtails who was
holding a long candle in each hand. The figure closely resembled
their eleven-year-old daughter, Franja. Newspapers and magazines,
even *Time*, reprinted the work, provoking strangers to send Maude
censorious letters. Echoing her *Diagrammatics* performance,
Maude insisted that the critics were mistaken: the sketch on the
card wasn't a literal representation, so if it looked like Franja, that
proved it wasn't Franja.[29]

Maude was seldom seen on campus, and when she did appear, according to the *Maroon*, "she looks even more bored than her husband." She preferred Chicago's arts community, much of which
revolved around Bobsy Goodspeed. Goodspeed was president of the
Arts Club, which sponsored shows by Pablo Picasso, Salvador Dalí,
and Marc Chagall. She also hosted Chicago parties and dinners for
George Gershwin, André Maurois, and Gertrude Stein. Maude
Hutchins became a regular at the Arts Club, and she painted a portrait of Goodspeed. The arts circle and the University of Chicago circle intersected: Goodspeed's husband, Barney, was a university trustee
as well as a retired industrialist, a philanthropist, a Republican power-
broker, and, according to a 1934 letter from the French writer Bernard Faÿ, "the lover of the wife of the [university] president."[30]

Regardless of whether Maude had an affair—Faÿ's letters are
the only evidence—her marriage unraveled in the 1940s. Robert
Hutchins moved out in 1947, they divorced in 1948, and he married his former secretary in 1949.

Hutchins once likened his career to the history of the Byzantine
Empire: a speedy rise to power followed by fourteen centuries of
decline. He never ran for office. He said he had no interest in politics after having run a university, "the worst kind of politics that

any human being can experience." He did not join the Supreme Court, as he wanted, or become director general of UNESCO, as William Benton wanted. He left the University of Chicago in 1951 for the Ford Foundation and then its spin-off, the Fund for the Republic. "It's a nice job," he said of grant making. "You meet so many interested people." In 1959, he launched a think tank, the Center for the Study of Democratic Institutions, in Santa Barbara, California. In 1963, he spoke of his distaste for the historian and Kennedy aide Arthur Schlesinger Jr. He was "too glib, flashy, political, and ambitious," said Hutchins, perhaps forgetting that a few decades earlier, he too had been a young man on the make.[31]

"There was something about Hutchins that was bigger than anything he ever did," a colleague said. He promoted the Great Books without writing any lasting books of his own; mostly he published collections of speeches. If he revolutionized undergraduate education at the University of Chicago, he failed to anticipate the counterrevolution. After his departure, the university shook off many of his changes. Even football came back, though without the earlier levels of triumph. According to one loyalist, it was erroneous to call Hutchins the former president of the University of Chicago; he was the president of the former University of Chicago. He wondered if he ought to have stayed. He found that he missed the students, too. "I did not think that they were particularly bright," he told a correspondent in 1959, "but they did strike me as singularly strong and beautiful."[32]

Hutchins spent the rest of his life in Santa Barbara. (He died in 1977.) Encyclopædia Britannica's sales of the fifty-four-volume Great Books began to slump. The centuries of respect that consecrated a book in the 1930s execrated it in the 1960s. In 1964, a wildfire destroyed Hutchins's home in the hills above Santa Barbara, including all his books. His Center for the Study of Democratic Institutions splintered into acrimony, penury, and litigation. Invited to play himself in a dramatization of the Manhattan Project, he replied, "After playing myself for 61 years, I am bored with the part. I would consent to play Einstein or General Groves."[33]

In 1971, Hutchins had heart surgery, followed a few months later by removal of his bladder and prostate. When one of the surgeons promised to have him back on the tennis court in six weeks, he replied, "In that case, the operation is off." To Thornton Wilder, Hutchins called Santa Barbara the perfect place to recover from any illness other than boredom.[34]

With Wilder, his closest friend, Hutchins dropped his aloof irony. The long, handwritten letters in the Wilder Papers at Yale's Beinecke Rare Book and Manuscript Library show him at his most open, heart-felt, and, often, bleak. He wrote, "I find myself less & less interested in more & more things, especially people." When Wilder dedicated his 1973 novel *Theophilus North* to him, Hutchins's gratitude and affection were tinged with jealousy: "You are the authentic version of what I would like to have been—I don't mean literally or in detail, but essen-tially." He regretted having devoted so much of his career to adminis-tration. He spoke of regret, too, over having neglected his family and friends. Instead of *The Skunk at the Garden Party*, now he said his memoir should be called *Some Natural Tears*, a phrase from *Paradise Lost*. But he decided not to write it, because, he said, he couldn't bear to revisit the past. "It's all my own fault," he told Wilder in 1975, as the Center for the Study of Democratic Institutions was falling apart. "But I can't help wishing that it had turned out better."[35]

Hutchins did have faithful hirelings—two of whom, Milton Mayer and Harry S. Ashmore, wrote biographies of him—and a reputation, which he denied, for surrounding himself with syco-phants. He had a few lifelong friends, too, in addition to Wilder, particularly William Benton, an adman turned encyclopedia pub-lisher, politician, and philanthropist, and, less close than the others, Henry Luce.[36]

About Luce, Hutchins had mixed feelings. He liked him per-sonally, disagreed with him politically, and deplored his impact on media and culture. In a letter to Luce, Hutchins brought up his 1935 commencement speech, the one beseeching University of Chicago graduates not to abandon their high ideals. "When I said 'Time will corrupt you,' " he wrote, "I meant the magazine."[37]

CHAPTER TWO

Unlucky Crusader

ENRY ROBINSON LUCE SAID he became a journalist because it enabled him to "come nearest to the heart of the world." He was born in China, where his parents were Presbyterian missionaries, in 1898. (Later he would note that the foreign birth rendered him ineligible for the presidency.) As a student at Yale, he tried writing poetry but concluded that he could never be a first-rate poet, "so the hell with it." Instead, after graduating in 1920, he became a reporter. In 1922, he and a college friend, Briton Hadden, left their jobs at the *Baltimore News* to launch what they called a "news-magazine," which would organize, summarize, and simplify the events of the preceding week for "the illiterate upper classes, the busy business man, the tired debutante." After contemplating *Facts, Hours, Briefs, Destiny, Chance,* and the *Synthetic Review*, they decided to call it *Time*. The first issue was dated March 3, 1923. Hadden had just turned twenty-five; Luce's twenty-fifth birthday was a month away.[1]

Time developed a style all its own, with words lifted from other languages (*kudos, tycoon*) or invented (*cinemactor*), quotidian details ignored by other news outlets (a middle name, the color of a necktie), capitalized epithets ("Pundit Lippmann"), and uncharitable compound adjectives ("blubber-lipped"). The magazine featured sentences that were "twisted, ductile ... like a Modigliani woman," as Mary

McCarthy put it, such as "Forth from the White House followed by innumerable attendants, Mr. and Mrs. Warren G. Harding set out on a 1,500 mile journey to Alaska and return." As Wolcott Gibbs wrote in his renowned takedown, published in 1936 in the *New Yorker*, "Backward ran sentences until reeled the mind." The magazine's cofounder, the bubbly and antic Hadden, was responsible for many of the quirks.[2]

Luce was more standoffish than Hadden. If journalism brought him closest to the heart of the world, perhaps he never made it all the way. "I have had the reputation of not caring enough about 'people,' " he remarked to the philosopher William Ernest Hocking. He tended to prefer ideas. Though he revolutionized journalism, his greatest legacy, according to David Halberstam, may have been bringing culture to the masses. The first issue of *Time* featured articles on T. S. Eliot and James Joyce. In the 1920s and '30s, John Dewey, Alexander Meiklejohn, George Santayana, Franz Boas, and Lewis Mumford all appeared on *Time* covers, as did Robert Hutchins. After Hadden died in 1929, of a blood infection incurable in the pre-penicillin era, Luce started *Fortune* in 1930 and *Life* in 1936. *Fortune* was dominated in its early years by a claque of left-wing literary intellectuals that included Dwight Macdonald, James Agee, and Archibald MacLeish. Luce wanted *Life* to nurture "America's intellectual health," and each issue featured at least one upscale offering in literature or the arts alongside the fluff—as Macdonald put it, "nine color pages of Renoir paintings followed by a picture of a roller-skating horse." In the mid-1940s, Time Inc. began developing a highbrow magazine devoted to culture, though it never got off the ground.[3]

Luce and the *New Yorker* editor Harold Ross feuded from time to time. Wolcott Gibbs's article mocking Luce and his magazines was a fusillade. The two editors present a sharp contrast. Ross was a high school dropout whom Brendan Gill termed "aggressively ignorant." On one occasion, according to Gill, Ross shouted to colleagues, "Is Moby Dick the whale or the man?" By contrast, the historian Alan Brinkley calls Luce "an intellectual omnivore." Yet the *New Yorker* managed to be more intellectual than its editor, whereas Time Inc. magazines, by design, tended to be less intellectual than theirs. Luce sought the audience that Ross, in his prospectus for the *New Yorker*, famously spurned: "the old lady in Dubuque."[4]

Luce often pondered the relationship between the press, the public, and the First Amendment. "How are you going to regulate a free press?" he said in a letter to former president Herbert Hoover in 1937. "And if you don't regulate it, I can see nothing to rely on except private conscience. And if you will rely to some extent on the private conscience of editor-publishers . . . why not rely also on the private conscience of bankers, manufacturers, educators, etc.?" In 1938, President Roosevelt charged that greedy publishers were choosing private profits over public service. In a response published in the *St. Louis Post-Dispatch*, Luce credited FDR with raising important issues about media responsibility. "The time has come for a thorough-going public debate on the whole question of the position of the free press today," he wrote, "and I congratulate you on your contribution to it." The same year, Luce offered to pay the Columbia University School of Journalism to research public attitudes toward the press. The *New York Times* publisher Arthur Hays Sulzberger objected that such a study of the press—"what is wrong with it, and what should be done about it"—would be "dangerous." He may have thought that quantifying the press's unpopularity would only reinforce it. He may also have been angry over *Time's* reference in 1937 to "the Jewish-owned *New York Times*," which had prompted him to protest to Luce. In any event, Columbia pulled out, and the project died.[5]

Luce didn't need Columbia, the University of Chicago, or FDR to tell him that freedom of speech entails responsibility. He believed that the media must give citizens what they need, not what they want: "The people are to be served, not necessarily to be pleased." He resisted proposals to raise the price of *Life*, saying that working-class Americans needed the education it provided, and Time Inc. "has other purposes besides the maximizing of profits." To whom is a publisher ultimately answerable? Not the readers, the stockholders, or the board of directors. "I decided that my ultimate accountability," he said, "had to be to my Creator."[6]

According to Luce's onetime employee and longtime friend Theodore H. White, he was motivated above all by Christianity; money ranked second. He enjoyed the company of theologians and Christian philosophers such as John Courtney Murray, Paul Tillich, and two members of the Hutchins Commission, Reinhold

Niebuhr and William Ernest Hocking. He publicized them as well: Murray, Tillich, and Niebuhr all appeared on the cover of *Time*. Luce prayed, read the Bible, attended church, pondered God's will, and spoke of himself as a sinner. One friend called him the most guilt-ridden Gentile she had ever known.[7]

The Seventh Commandment appeared to give Luce particular trouble. Married to the former Lila Hotz since 1923, he had an affair with the playwright and journalist Clare Boothe Brokaw in 1934. When he talked of leaving his wife for her, Clare teased that her "little minister" would never do such a thing. But he did. In 1935, he married her, and she became Clare Boothe Luce. Later, as he was nearing sixty, Luce had a long affair with a woman half his age, Jeanne Campbell, granddaughter of the British publishing mogul Lord Beaverbrook. When Campbell referred to herself as Luce's mistress, he grimaced. "The son of a Presbyterian minister can't have a mistress," he told her. Clare affected lightheartedness. If Luce married Campbell, she told friends, she might marry Lord Beaverbrook and "become Harry's grandmother." John Courtney Murray stepped in as counselor, Jeanne Campbell began dating Norman Mailer, and the marriage survived.[8]

Luce was the "most powerful private citizen" in the United States, according to William Benton, a Yale classmate and friend who underwrote the final expenses of the Commission on Freedom of the Press. The media empire became a state within a state, presided over by the sometimes imperious "Il Luce." In the course of promoting American aid to Britain, Luce remarked that *he* had declared war on Germany in 1939; FDR needed to catch up. In "The American Century," published in *Life* in 1941, Luce, the son of missionaries, called on the United States to become "Good Samaritan of the entire world." Later, Time Inc. created a Post-War Committee to plan for the future—not the future of the magazine but that of the nation.[9]

Success spoiled Henry Luce. The scrappy striver became surly and charmless, a "self-conscious 'great man,' " according to Alan Brinkley. At a dinner for the *Time* staff, Luce told his guests, "I could fire any of you. . . . But I don't know anyone who can fire me." His style at times became domineering. In the late 1930s, at a meeting with leaders from business, academia, and law to talk about the defense of England, Luce insisted on discussing his moral quandaries as a publisher instead. "He would not drop the matter, and the rest of us became increasingly wearied," wrote one of those present. During Luce's affair with Campbell, she later said, "I couldn't get a word in edgewise." In conversation, Luce interrupted everyone, even the pope.[10]

Benton liked Luce but found him heavy-going and boorish. At one lunch, Luce cross-examined him on whether he believed in God. On another occasion, he demanded to know why Benton didn't read Time Inc. magazines. When the conversation turned to Eleanor Roosevelt, who had died a few weeks earlier, Luce declared that she would burn in hell.[11]

The poet and playwright Archibald MacLeish wanted nothing from Luce, and he felt free to speak his mind. The two grew close in the early 1930s, when MacLeish was *Fortune*'s most prolific writer. Luce sought his counsel on personal as well as business matters. After MacLeish resigned in 1938, Luce tried repeatedly to lure him back to Time Inc., without success. "I loved him very much," MacLeish said, "although I thought him wrong as hell much of the time." Their contact was infrequent; MacLeish rarely made good on his promises to Luce that they would get together. "The last person I'd think of to call was Harry," MacLeish told an interviewer. "He was so awkward to be with, so heavy-handed, so lacking in a sense of humor." On the page, though, the relationship could be almost intimate. "I wish you hadn't been so successful," MacLeish told Luce in 1938. "Because it's very hard to be as successful as you have been and still keep your belief in the desperate necessity for fundamental change. . . . I think you hate being rich. I think you hate being a pal of the people who want you to be their pal." Later, in 1949, Luce told MacLeish that they both were inclined to be crusaders. Sounding wistful at fifty-one, Luce wrote, "On the whole you have been much luckier (and deservingly so) than I have been in the fulfillment of this inclination." In 1958, MacLeish's play based on the Book of Job, *J.B.*, opened on Broadway. During rehearsals, MacLeish told the director, Elia Kazan, about Luce. Kazan was captivated, MacLeish recalled, by "this man whose wildest aspirations of himself and his country could swallow him up." The tragedy of Henry Luce, Kazan said, would make a great play.[12]

Luce kept trying to give his country what he thought it needed. In 1960, he decided that the United States lacked a sense of purpose, so he commissioned MacLeish, Walter Lippmann, and eight others to come up with one. When Luce concluded that Americans hadn't found contentment in prosperity, he delivered an address on the subject. "We have won all the marbles—and it just isn't enough," he told the audience. Because he believed Americans needed to recommit their lives to God, *Life* devoted an issue to Christianity. In the Cold War, *Sports Illustrated* filled a national need, too. "He gave me a forty-five minute speech," Robert Hutchins said, "about how he was starting a sports magazine because we had about seven years to annihilation and he wanted us to have a good time while we could." Perhaps Luce was mistaking his own yearnings for the nation's. He may have been the one in need of purpose, contentment, a deeper faith, a good time.[13]

Luce died in 1967. Hutchins didn't go to the funeral. His feelings about Luce were tangled, and after decades of asking him for money, perhaps he felt the beggar's grudge against the almsgiver. In a letter to Benton, he briefly reflected on Luce. "Of course he didn't enjoy life—much. A Presbyterian minister's son was not supposed to," wrote Hutchins, another Presbyterian minister's son.[14]

At lunch at the Drake Hotel in 1942, Hutchins dismissed Luce's idea of a corporate-sponsored, university-produced restatement of freedom of the press. Luce periodically raised the subject in subsequent meetings, and Hutchins continued to show no interest. Then, in fall 1943, the two men sat together at a board meeting of Encyclopædia Britannica. Rather than listen to the discussion, they began passing notes. Hutchins told Luce that the study of press freedom might be feasible. They passed more notes. "By the time the meeting was over," recalled Luce, "a scheme had taken shape in his mind."[15]

In a phone call afterward, Hutchins raised a few concerns. Luce asked why he was wavering. He replied that he was *thinking*, not wavering; business leaders needed to learn the difference. Although Luce had initially talked of it as a job for the University of

Chicago philosophy department, Hutchins said that they would need to look elsewhere, because "we haven't got the people." (He had clashed with the philosophy department for years.)[16]

Hutchins was ready to begin. "I will undertake—with proper financing—to organize a national group" to study freedom of the press. Luce told him to get started.[17]

Three years later, as the Commission on Freedom of the Press was completing its work, Hutchins would write, "I am sorry I ever met Harry Luce."[18]

CHAPTER THREE

Disillusionment in Democracy

LTHOUGH THE COMMISSION ON Freedom of the Press met during and just after World War II, its members were more influenced by the preceding decade, their perspectives molded by the Depression, the specter of totalitarianism, and widespread doubts about the future of democracy. A pioneer of journalism education articulated those doubts. Willard Grosvenor Bleyer, chair of the journalism program at the University of Wisconsin since 1912, had helped persuade many professors and administrators that journalism is a serious subject that merits the systematic attention of students as well as scholars, though nobody would ever persuade Robert Hutchins. In 1933, addressing the American Association of the Schools and Departments of Journalism, Bleyer sketched the press's prospects after the collapse of the United States government. "We may try some form of fascism," he suggested, "with the government attempting to save private business and industry by means of state socialism. When this fails, some form of communism is bound to follow." He predicted that publishers would do fine under fascism; communism, with "the workers ... in the saddle," would prove more challenging. Democracy's demise wasn't inevitable, but it was likely enough to require no detailed explanation.[1]

Bleyer had plenty of company in the early 1930s. "Democracy has collapsed as a philosophy," Rowland A. Egger wrote in the

American Mercury. "All over the world," the economist Henry Hazlitt wrote in *Scribner's*, "democracy as we have come to know it is in disrepute." From the heart of the American establishment, Columbia University president Nicholas Murray Butler told students in 1931 that dictators generally possess "far greater intelligence, far stronger character and far more courage" than the leaders of democracies. It was clear that he was referring to Benito Mussolini, whom he had met several times in Rome. Extolling dictatorship didn't tarnish Butler's reputation; three months later, he and Jane Addams shared the Nobel Peace Prize.[2]

Many of the doomsayers blamed the electorate. Some feared that democracy would degenerate into rule by angry mob. In one of the most talked-about books of the decade, *Revolt of the Masses*, translated into English in 1932, the Spanish philosopher José Ortega y Gasset warned of a "hyperdemocracy" controlled by "intellectually vulgar" masses. Henry Luce read the book and found it overly pessimistic but compelling; for a time, he quoted it in nearly every speech. Hutchins considered Ortega one of the greatest minds of the age. Under a different scenario for the implosion of democracy, confused citizens would misapprehend issues and elect bunglers, the economy would further collapse, and the people would welcome a strongman who promised to relieve them of self-government's burdens.[3]

In the 1930s, one future member of the Hutchins Commission, Reinhold Niebuhr, contemplated the electorate as angry mob and saw catastrophe. Another, Charles Merriam, contemplated the electorate as muddled masses and saw opportunity.

Of the Hutchins Commission's thirteen American members, four foreign advisers, and four staff members, Niebuhr remains the most prominent. New books appear almost every year about his life, his ideas, his influence, his friendships and feuds, even the "Serenity Prayer" attributed to him. Born in Wright City, Missouri, in 1892, he studied at Yale Divinity School, spent thirteen years as a pastor in Detroit, and in 1928 joined the faculty of Union Theological Seminary in New York. Two years later, he ran unsuccessfully for the New York State Senate as a Socialist.[4]

Niebuhr was prolific, producing 21 books of his own, chapters in 126 other books, and more than 2,600 articles. He devoted much of his writing to politics, power, and history. Hans J. Morgenthau in 1962 called him "the greatest living political philosopher of America." Andrew J. Bacevich considers Niebuhr's *The Irony of American History*, published in 1952, "the most important book ever written on U.S. foreign policy." Niebuhr's views were informed by Christian doctrine but not infused with it, or so it seemed to his many secular admirers, the so-called Atheists for Niebuhr. "Some of my friends," he remarked, "think I teach Christian ethics as a sort of front to make my politics respectable."[5]

Though Niebuhr was a leading public intellectual, he distanced himself from the intelligentsia. Intellectuals glorify reason, he said, but reason "is partly the servant and only partly the master of the interests and passions." The unschooled laborer who struggles to get by can perceive injustices unrecognized by the intellectual "whose eyes are too fat to see clearly and whose mind is too engaged by self-interest to think honestly." Niebuhr called for commitment to pursuing justice tempered by pessimism about achieving it. Too many intellectuals have pessimism without commitment, he said, and too many Christians have commitment without pessimism.[6]

Niebuhr also disparaged liberalism and its ever-upward narrative of human progress. An uncritical faith in the goodness of human nature, he believed, aggravated many social problems, and the faith was especially difficult to dislodge from liberals, who liked to think of themselves as shrewd and sharp-eyed. He mocked liberalism's pieties, including the certitude that the spread of education and enlightenment would bring an end to injustice and war. Politics is about *power*, he said, and liberals like to pretend otherwise. Niebuhr considered himself a realist. "I hate a thoroughgoing cynic," he said. "I don't want anyone to be more cynical than I am." Although he wrote in 1936 of "disillusionment in democracy," it's debatable whether he himself was subject to it; to become disillusioned, presumably, one must first have harbored illusions.[7]

Whatever the topic, Niebuhr's arguments often followed these lines: the situation is more complex than we recognize and the players more self-serving; our ideals point in different directions; any resolution will be shaky, incomplete, and provisional, based on exigencies of the moment; we must diminish our expectations and redouble our efforts, for "nothing that is worth doing can be achieved in our lifetime." He was partial to paradox and dialectic. "Man is mortal. That is his fate," he wrote in 1937 in *Beyond Tragedy*. "Man pretends not to be mortal. That is his sin." In *The Children of Light and the Children of Darkness* in 1944, he wrote, "Man's capacity for justice makes democracy possible; but man's inclination to injustice makes democracy necessary."[8]

During the 1930s, Niebuhr feared that the dispossessed and frightened members of the lower middle class, which he defined as the working class except for industrial labor, would rally behind a demagogue who preyed on their fears and pointed their anger toward scapegoats of different races and nationalities. In the event of another economic downturn, he said, this spirit of grievance would "undoubtedly express itself in fascistic or semi-fascistic terms." At times, he thought fascism in the United States was imminent. In 1933, he predicted that "the inexorable logic of history" would bring the Tribulation of capitalism's demise, the Armageddon of fascism, and finally the Millennium of socialism.[9]

Niebuhr waited for history's inexorable logic to play out. And waited. President Roosevelt's "amiable opportunism," he said in 1933, merely postponed the inevitable. "No final good can come of this kind of whirligig reform," he wrote in 1938. Gradually he concluded that democracy and capitalism were sturdier than he had thought. He left the Socialist Party in 1940 and backed FDR.[10]

Henry Luce considered Niebuhr a great philosopher. A *Time* senior editor said that the fast-talking Niebuhr was the only man able to "out-interrupt" Luce. Luce helped fund Niebuhr's journal *Christianity and Crisis*, published his articles in *Life*, and put him on the cover of *Time*. The admiration wasn't wholly mutual. Time Inc. magazines exemplified what Niebuhr called the "perpetual liturgy of self-congratulations about the vaunted virtues and achievements of the 'American way of life.' " Successful people believe that their status attests the superiority of their characters, he said, whereas it's often a matter of luck; "our fortune-favored nation has developed this habit with the greatest possible consistency." He excoriated Luce's "American Century" as an expression of "egotistic corruption" that is "remarkably similar to the Messianic errors castigated by Christ." Luce was a man of conviction, but on this topic, faced with this criticism from this critic, he backed down. "Very well, I acknowledge and confess and repent," he wrote in a private reflection. He went on to express his "admiration for Niebuhr and gratitude to him" for illuminating the "pitfalls and heresies" in "The American Century."[11]

On the Commission on Freedom of the Press, Niebuhr often spoke of tensions among competing social forces—individual autonomy versus community cohesiveness, freedom versus order, the dangers of untethered economic power versus the dangers of untethered political power. When it came to recommendations, he stressed the inadequacy of all options. "We are trying to find a way of mitigating the evils of a technical society," he said during a discussion of antitrust law in 1946, "without losing consciousness of the fact that there are some gains in this technical society. ... We don't have an answer and we are conscious of the fact that democratic life is like that; that you can't go too far trying to keep away from Scylla without shipwrecking on Charybdis. So we find a way in between." In another meeting, Niebuhr declared that "every alternative is really pretty bad."[12]

The alternatives didn't seem so bad to another member of the commission, a man who cherished the tenets of liberalism that Niebuhr scorned and who characterized democracy as "a constant drive toward the perfectibility of mankind."[13]

Charles Edward Merriam Jr. was born in 1874 in Iowa. After completing his doctorate at Columbia University in 1900, he joined the small political science department at the University of Chicago. Three years later, he helped found the American Political Science Association, a spin-off from the American Historical Association. Activist as well as theorist, a combination common among turn-of-the-century political scientists, Merriam served for six years on the Chicago City Council. "There seems to be no prejudice against you because you are a professor," a friend told him. "And that is saying a good deal." In 1911, Merriam ran for mayor as a Republican; he blamed his loss on fraud at the polls. (He later switched from Republican to Progressive to Democrat.) Along the way, he won the respect of Woodrow Wilson and Theodore Roosevelt. During World War I, he spent seven months heading the Rome office of the Committee on Public Information, better known as the

Creel Committee, where he worked to burnish the image of the United States. His tactics for winning over the hearts and minds of Italians included distributing illustrations of George and Martha Washington.[14]

In the 1920s, political science spawned what Merriam called "scientific politics." He believed policy making could be as nonpartisan, objective, and replicable as mathematics or biology. To critics who maintained that politics can never be fully rational, he responded that "it is difficult to trust the rational demonstration that all rational demonstrations are irrational." Several historians point out that Merriam's scientific politics actually amounted to scientific antipolitics, a promise of policy making purged of ideology, passions, pressure groups, and unpredictability. Raymond Seidelman posits that Merriam expected science to prove the validity of his Progressive beliefs, whereas Barry D. Karl thinks Merriam realized that public administration without politics is impossible; he just wouldn't admit it.[15]

In Merriam's vision, social and economic planners would displace "jungle governors"—that is, elected officials. Citizens too would be shunted aside to an extent, but they would be glad to surrender some voice in self-government in exchange for order, security, and a higher standard of living. Social planning, Merriam predicted in 1935, would usher in a "fairyland of achievement" free of "hunger, disease, toil and fear." The planners would control politics. They would control the economy. (Niebuhr considered unbridled capitalism oppressive; Merriam considered it wasteful.) They would even control reproduction. Through "scientific adjustments of individuals and groups," Merriam wrote, experts would determine "what sorts of creatures are to be born." Though wary of studies purporting to show racial disparities in intelligence, he embraced the fundamental tenets of eugenics. The state must produce ideal citizens, first by "forbidding certain unions" and ultimately by taking "constructive measures" consonant with "a science of social and political control."[16]

In 1929, President Herbert Hoover, engineer and technocrat, asked Merriam and other social scientists for policy proposals that would improve the well-being of Americans. The scholars replied that they lacked the data with which to formulate proposals. "We are all feeling around in the dark," they wrote, "never sure that the premises on which we are basing our thinking are going to sink out from under us when subjected to scientific research." Hoover directed them to assemble the data. With funding from the Rockefeller Foundation and research support from the Social Science Research Council, the President's Research Committee on Social Trends set to work on discovering and diagnosing social stresses. Merriam was the group's vice chairman.[17]

Hoover asked his question in prosperous 1929. In 1932, a very different time, he got his 1,568-page answer, *Recent Social Trends in the United States*. To reduce the risk of "violent revolution," the Research Committee called for economic planning of the sort "keenly appreciated by the Soviets." Although the committee maintained that it advocated planning as a general method but no particular policies, it did cite an "immediately urgent" necessity of "preventing individuals with undesired inheritable traits from having offspring." Scientists might lack a comprehensive understanding of heredity, the committee said, but "breeders of livestock have accomplished results without this information."[18]

In order to weaken party bosses, turn-of-the-century Progressives had entrusted some authority to experts, as in the city-manager system, but much of their reallocation of power strengthened the electorate in relation to politicians and parties—initiative, referendum, recall, direct primaries, popular election of U.S. senators. By contrast, Merriam and many other social scientists of the Depression wanted to shift power from electorate and politicians to nonpartisan experts. Walter J. Shepard, president of the American Political Science Association, wrote that citizens must cede authority to "an aristocracy of intellect and character," which would govern with "a large element of fascist doctrine and practice."[19]

Merriam believed that "the wisest kings and rulers were those who were advised by their wisest men." When asked, he advised. From 1933 to 1943, he served as a member of President Roosevelt's National Resources Planning Board (it operated under different names at different times). The board's first report, which Merriam helped write, promoted social planning and eugenics. The board also drafted a New Bill of Rights, with guarantees of food, work, security, and equality, as well as "rest, recreation, and adventure."[20]

In the mid-1930s, President Roosevelt asked Merriam for ideas on how to restructure the federal government. Merriam suggested that the Social Science Research Council undertake a study, but FDR preferred to keep it under his control. The president had in mind a three-man committee: Merriam's University of Chicago colleague Louis Brownlow, Columbia University political scientist Luther Gulick, and Merriam. But even though all three men supported FDR politically, he hesitated. What if he didn't like the report? Merriam told him not to worry. He would like it. With the help of twenty-six advisers, mostly academics, the Brownlow Committee worked in secret on a blueprint for a new federal government. Its final report, issued in 1937, called for streamlining the executive branch under greater presidential authority and expanding the civil service. The plan would augment presidential power, and it would extend New Deal policies by lodging high-level political appointees in permanent positions. Conservatives enlisted their own political scientists, from the Brookings Institution, to develop a competing plan with less power centralized in the presidency. The differences between the two plans undercut the argument that political science produces consistent, replicable results. Public opinion turned against the bill, especially after Roosevelt's Court-packing attempt, and the reorganization plan was defeated in 1938.[21]

Earlier, the members of the Brownlow Committee had faced a test. After reading a draft of the report, FDR told them it was wonderful. Just one thing: Could they add a recommendation that the president take control of the independent federal agencies? It was a decisive moment for Merriam and the others, scientists and truth tellers, unambitious and therefore uncompromising, in government but not of it. They acceded to the president's wishes. "Truth threatens power," Hans Morgenthau, the Niebuhr admirer, once remarked, "and power threatens truth."[22]

Most future members of the Commission on Freedom of the Press worked for FDR and his administration. They crafted presidential speeches, party platforms, industrial legislation, and tax policy, as well as plans to restructure the government. According to the columnist Marquis Childs, the reliance on intellectuals in policy making may have been the New Deal's most consequential innovation.

For many professors, being called to Washington was a heady experience. "What would *you* do, friend," wrote H. L. Mencken in 1936, "if you were hauled suddenly out of a bare, smelly schoolroom, wherein the razzberries of sophomores had been your only music, and thrown into a place of power and glory almost befitting Caligula, Napoleon I, or J. Pierpont Morgan, with whole herds of Washington correspondents crowding up to take down your every wheeze, and the first pages of their newspapers thrown open to your complete metaphysic? You would conclude at once, I fancy, that you were a very smart fellow, and it would be pretty hard for you to keep your head."[23]

Whatever Americans may have thought about the Brains Trust of the 1930s, they seemed to respect academics in the 1940s. In 1947, the year *A Free and Responsible Press* appeared, the National Opinion Research Center asked respondents to rank professions by their standing in society. With a score of 89, college professors came in fifth, behind Supreme Court justices (96), physicians (93), governors (93), and Cabinet members (92) but well ahead of newspaper columnists (74) and reporters (71). *Time* put intellectuals on its cover, including Robert Hutchins and Reinhold Niebuhr. On radio, NBC aired the weekly *University of Chicago Round Table*, with Midway professors discussing current issues and events with public figures.[24]

Whether in or out of government, many scholars in the 1930s and 1940s grew accustomed to answering questions far afield of their academic training. A psychologist worked on fiscal policy. A poet helped draft wartime censorship rules. A theologian foretold American fascism. An invitation from the president of the University of Chicago to reconceptualize freedom of the press was nothing extraordinary.

By the 1940s, Charles Merriam had moderated his views. He now prefaced "social planning" with the word "democratic." No longer did he refer to "jungle governors" or call for breeding better citizens. But he retained his faith in the "perfectibility of man" as well as his idealistic view of humanity's trajectory. In the long run, he said, peace will triumph over war, love over hate, intelligence over ignorance. Reinhold Niebuhr scoffed. In 1940, a few months after Germany invaded Poland, he reviewed Merriam's *Prologue to Politics* in the *Nation*.

"Surely our present crisis," he wrote, "is something more than a mere momentary backsliding ... in the general line of advance toward a completely rational society." He also considered Merriam deluded in believing that social science could ever be a true science, objective and value-free.[25]

The two men met for the first time at a meeting of the Commission on Freedom of the Press. Niebuhr was fifty-one, Merriam sixty-nine. Niebuhr was "brash, outspoken, vehement," according to his biographer Richard Wightman Fox, "strikingly unselfconscious in public" and "oblivious to social form." Merriam, according to a colleague, was "famous for his imperturbability." In the course of their conversation over dinner, Niebuhr's outspokenness overpowered Merriam's imperturbability. "I hope I did not frighten you by my emphatic utterances at the Wednesday night dinner," Merriam wrote Niebuhr afterward. "I was a little shocked by the shade of defeatism but, of course, this is a free country and there must be freedom of speech as well as press." Niebuhr replied, "It was partly the opportunity of meeting with people like you which attracted me to the Freedom of the Press Committee." He added an apology. "I am sorry I shocked you by my defeatism in regard to the drift of things. I hope you are right and I am wrong."[26]

The two did agree on some things. Both favored an expansive government and rejected laissez-faire economics. Both considered the mass media reckless and untrustworthy. On the last point, a lot of Americans agreed.

CHAPTER FOUR

Synthetic Dead Cats

M OST NINETEENTH-CENTURY CRITICISM of the news media amounted to little more than drive-by derision. In *Martin Chuzzlewit*, Charles Dickens invented New York newspapers named the *Peeper*, the *Sewer*, the *Stabber*, and the *Rowdy Journal*. In 1911, when Will Irwin searched for books about American journalism in the Library of Congress, he found "a few treatises on the making of newspapers, a few volumes of pleasant reminiscences, one interesting but incomplete and shallow history." Magazines of the day, he said, did feature the occasional denunciations of newspapers, written by "professors who, from their narrow cells, preach to an imperfect world counsels of perfection." Irwin went on to publish a fifteen-part series in *Collier's* that year, "The American Newspaper." After World War I came critical works by Upton Sinclair, Walter Lippmann, Oswald Garrison Villard, and Silas Bent, plus a cascade of books by former journalists, or so it seemed to H. L. Mencken. "Every time a disabled journalist is retired to a professorship in a school of journalism, and so gets time to give sober thought to the state of his craft," Mencken wrote in 1925, "he seems to be impelled to write a book upon its ethics, full of sour and uraemic stuff."[1]

More books appeared in the 1930s, some of them scholarly. In 1937, Leo C. Rosten published *The Washington Correspondents*, an opinion survey and analysis, based on the University of Chicago dissertation he had written under the guidance of Charles Merriam. Also in 1937, Herbert Brucker published *The Changing American Newspaper,* followed by Curtis D. MacDougall's *Interpretative Reporting* in 1938 and Sidney Kobre's *Backgrounding the News: The Newspaper and the Social Sciences* in 1939. Such books suggested, as the Hutchins Commission would later do, that the press was failing to keep pace with the complexities of modern life. Today's newspaper, wrote Brucker, must help readers make sense of "the WPA, sit-down strikes, fascism, dust storms, wars that are not wars, the A plus B theorem, silver nationalization, the Comité des Forges, import quotas, Father Coughlin, cosmic rays, nonintervention agreements to screen intervention, and unemployment." More partisan works appeared too. In the decade before publication of *A Free and Responsible Press* in 1947, Villard, Morris L. Ernst, Harold L. Ickes, George Seldes, and the Nieman Fellows at Harvard all wrote damning books about American journalism—two books apiece, in the case of Ickes, Seldes, and the Nieman group. Seldes also published a weekly newsletter of press criticism, *In Fact.*[2]

Criticism mushroomed in other venues as well. The Marxist magazine *New Masses,* the liberal New York newspaper *PM,* and the *Saturday Review of Literature* regularly evaluated press coverage. The *Nation* ran a series of articles on influential columnists and critics. A. J. Liebling began writing "The Wayward Press" in the *New Yorker* in 1945. The Nieman Foundation launched *Nieman Reports,* a journal of press criticism, in 1947. On radio, *Town Meeting of the Air* devoted several programs to journalism. *CBS Views the Press,* hosted by Don Hollenbeck, premiered in 1947; Robert Hutchins was a guest.[3]

Public disenchantment with the press seemed to grow during the Roosevelt years. In a poll in 1936, *Fortune* asked Americans to identify the worst abuser of power: the press, radio, bankers, veterans, or clergy. Editors expected the bankers to be ranked first, probably followed by the veterans. Instead, the press ranked as top power abuser, at 42 percent, followed by bankers, clergy, veterans, and finally radio. Much of the mistrust of newspapers seemed to rest on political grounds, especially a perceived bias against President Roosevelt and the New Deal. Villard wrote that FDR didn't just defeat Alf Landon in the 1936 campaign; he also defeated the publishers. In a 1939 poll, more than a third of Americans said that newspapers shouldn't be allowed to attack President Roosevelt. Many surveys found that people considered news and commentary more credible on radio than in newspapers. When FDR used radio to bypass journalists, the American Newspaper Publishers Association charged that the unmediated Fireside Chats were a propaganda tool that could pave the way to dictatorship. With critics of the press increasingly vehement and visible, *Editor & Publisher* warned its readers that their "every move is being watched." Wilbur Forrest, president of the American Society of Newspaper Editors, complained that "anti-newspaper literature holds the stage virtually without competition." He saw the press as the innocent victim of irresponsible left-wing criticism.[4]

President Roosevelt, meanwhile, viewed himself as the innocent victim of an irresponsible right-wing press. The oft-cited figure, repeated by FDR at a news conference in 1940, is that 85 percent of the nation's newspapers opposed him. Actually, according to the historian Graham J. White, most of the hostility came during election years; and even then, most newspapers took no editorial position. Roosevelt had supporters in the press, too. The publisher Ralph Ingersoll privately declared *PM* "150% for Roosevelt," and Dorothy Thompson backed FDR in her columns while writing campaign speeches for him on the side. But the fury of a few anti-Roosevelt newspapers stood out, none more sharply than the paper that George Seldes called an "Outstanding Enemy of the People" and Harold Ickes called "the rottenest newspaper in the United States": the *Chicago Tribune.*[5]

Critics dubbed Robert Rutherford McCormick one of the great minds of the fourteenth century. Born in 1880, he studied at Groton and Yale and served with the American Expeditionary Force in World War I, rising to the rank of colonel, a title he used for the rest of his life. McCormick was an Ivy Leaguer wary of higher education. The *New York Times* publisher Adolph Ochs once considered having the presidents of Harvard, Yale, and Princeton guide *Times* editorial policy. "I urged him very strongly against this," McCormick said. Later, the Colonel would describe the Hutchins Commission members as "pinko professors living off the money other men have made." Inconsistency, his biographer Richard Norton Smith points out, never troubled McCormick. When someone proposed adding a book section to the newspaper, he said no. "Readers of the *Tribune* don't read books." Yet during the Depression, the *Tribune*'s WGN aired highbrow radio shows produced by the Illinois Writers' Project. In his spare time, McCormick scoured the *Encyclopædia Britannica* for errors. Why, he asked *Britannica* publisher William Benton in 1945, did the entry on plumbing say nothing about Louis XIV's celebrated pipe from Versailles to the Seine?[6]

The Colonel's eccentricities were legendary. Offended by the capriciousness of English spelling, he tried to fix it. The *Tribune* denounced government "burocrats" and, later, the "totalitarian philosofy" of the Hutchins Commission. "No other publisher would presume to reinvent the English language," writes Smith, who goes on to say, "Whether the Colonel was brilliantly inventive or merely unhinged was a much debated topic around the *Tribune*." Either way, the voice of the *Tribune* was the voice of the Colonel. The newspaper protected McCormick's friends—he assured the *New York Times* publisher Arthur Hays Sulzberger that "nothing objectionable" to him "should appear in print in the Tribune"—and savaged his enemies. An isolationist, he especially despised the internationalist Henry Luce. In an article, not a column or editorial, the *Tribune* said that "Luce, who wields dictatorial power over his magazines and nurses imperialistic ambitions that vie with those of a Mussolini, was born in China but is not a Chinaman." McCormick also reviled everything British not named Winston Churchill. The Rhodes Scholarships, he maintained, were part of a plot to indoctrinate young Americans and turn them into undercover agents of their British spymasters. Above all, he loathed President Roosevelt. The New Deal, he believed, embodied "the spirit of the big red square in Moscow." Liberals spoke of the unemployed as the forgotten Americans; the *real* forgotten Americans, McCormick insisted, were the property owners. In 1936, *Tribune* operators answered the telephone with a countdown to the election: "Only 97 days left to save your country!"[7]

In the mid-1930s, Leo Rosten solicited Washington correspondents' views on American newspapers. Asked to name the most reliable paper, they cited the *New York Times* more often than any other. Asked to name the least reliable paper, they most frequently cited the *Chicago Tribune* or the Hearst papers. (The *Tribune* received one vote for most reliable. So did the *Daily Worker.*) When Rosten published his findings, the *Tribune* responded with a full-page ad lauding its Washington reporters and proclaiming that "in spite of fake statistics put out by reds and pinks, these men give you the real Washington news."[8]

The press, according to McCormick, serves a quasi-constitutional function. It uncovers and publicizes evidence of corruption in government and thereby operates as an external check on state power—hence the First Amendment. McCormick generously championed freedom of speech, including the rights of those with whom he disagreed. He financed the appeal of Jay Near, an anti-Semitic publisher in Minneapolis. In a landmark ruling in 1931, *Near v. Minnesota*, the Supreme Court held that prior restraints against the press are almost always unconstitutional. By one estimate, McCormick spent $3 million protecting press freedom between the mid-1920s and the mid-1940s, prompting Fred Friendly to call him the "Daddy Warbucks of the First Amendment." Under McCormick's expansive view, the First Amendment prohibits not just interference with newspaper content but also any government action that, in his words, would "unreasonably decrease the return from publishing." Sulzberger thought he was overreaching. The First Amendment, he wrote, "seems to me . . . to refer to the spirit and not to our bodies. We are after all business enterprises, and our bodies are correctly subject to all the ills to which flesh or other industry may be heir." For McCormick, body and spirit were one. He and the American Newspaper Publishers Association sought exemptions from rules governing collective bargaining, the minimum wage, maximum hours, child labor, false advertising, Social Security, and antitrust, but the courts generally enforced Sulzberger's distinction. "The publisher of a newspaper," the Supreme Court said, "has no special immunity from the application of general laws."[9]

Colonel McCormick viewed the National Industrial Recovery Act of 1933 as a particularly catastrophic breach of media autonomy. Drafted in part by the future Hutchins Commission member John

Dickinson, the NIRA directed industries to establish self-regulatory codes, to be vetted by the government. McCormick deemed the law an invitation to dictatorship and an unconstitutional regime for licensing the press. In a news conference, President Roosevelt scoffed that McCormick was "seeing things under the bed." Grudgingly, newspaper publishers drafted the required self-regulatory code, but they included a caveat stating that they did not "consent to the imposition of any requirements that might restrict or interfere with the constitutional guarantee of the freedom of the press." The president and his aides resented the insinuation that they were trying to subvert the Constitution. In a testy statement approving the code, Roosevelt dismissed the provision on press freedom as "pure surplusage" with no legal effect. His administration would protect freedom of expression, he said, but "not freedom to work children, or do business in a fire trap or violate the laws against obscenity, libel and lewdness." General Hugh S. Johnson headed the agency in charge of implementing the NIRA, the National Recovery Administration. In a speech, Johnson said that when he took the job, he knew "the early applause would cease and soon the air would be full of dead cats." He had no objection to "really honest and substantial dead cats," he said, but "most of these dead cats are synthetic," especially "the one about the freedom of the press."[10]

Roosevelt may have endured more abuse from the press than any president since Andrew Jackson, as the historian Sally Denton writes, but FDR also nursed grievances toward the press and a hunger for vengeance that went unmatched until Richard Nixon and Donald Trump. According to the White House aide Raymond Moley, animosity toward newspapers was Roosevelt's "oldest grudge." In 1937, when the president praised radio and newsreels for keeping the public informed, he pointedly left out newspapers. He charged *Time* with "stocking the arsenals of propaganda of the Nazis to be used against us," referred to columnists as "an unnecessary excrescence on our civilization," and pretended to confer an Iron Cross on John O'Donnell of the *New York Daily News*. Some of the president's subordinates weighed in as well. Secretary of the Interior Harold Ickes, a close friend of Charles Merriam's, denounced the press in two books and many speeches, and he called on Congress to investigate corruption and abuse of power in the newspaper industry.[11]

FDR was lucky in his media enemies. The loopy accusations advanced by Colonel McCormick and the newspaper publishers' organization enabled the president to dismiss all his opponents in the press as loopy. They also drew attention away from FDR's eagerness to use federal power to reward friends in the press and, especially, to punish enemies. McCormick may have imagined many machinations and conspiracies, but when he said in 1942 that "the administration is out to get the *Tribune*," he was right. FBI agents installed wiretaps on the phones in the newspaper's Washington bureau. After hearing rumors that McCormick had exaggerated his World War I exploits, the president ordered the War Department to send over his records. The *Tribune* began having trouble getting newsprint from its Canadian paper mills. Ickes tried to persuade FDR to have the Canadian government shutter the mills on the ground that the *Tribune* was lending aid and comfort to the enemy. Although that didn't happen, the War Production Board did impose quotas on the supply of newsprint. It let other Chicago newspapers exceed their quotas but not the *Tribune*. In 1945, the Colonel told Robert Hutchins about the newsprint situation, thinking that it might interest the Commission on Freedom of the Press. It didn't.[12]

The administration also investigated the *Tribune* for criminal prosecution. A few days before Pearl Harbor, at a time when the president insisted that he had no intention of getting involved in the European war, the *Tribune* revealed secret contingency plans to invade the Continent. The FBI investigated the leak, and Ickes urged that the newspaper company be prosecuted for treason, though nothing came of it. After the Battle of Midway in 1942, the *Tribune* implied, accurately, that the United States had broken the Japanese code. FDR considered sending Marines to Chicago to occupy Tribune Tower. The Justice Department appointed a special prosecutor, who recommended dropping the case, but Roosevelt overruled him. Ultimately, the grand jury voted not to indict the paper. In addition, at FDR's urging, the Justice Department considered charging the *Tribune* with sedition, based on a wartime content analysis conducted by Harold D. Lasswell under the supervision of Archibald MacLeish, both future members of the

Hutchins Commission. No prosecution took place, but when Radio Tokyo quoted McCormick's charges of incompetence in the American war effort, FDR in a Fireside Chat condemned "bogus patriots who use the sacred freedom of the press to echo the sentiments of the propagandists in Tokyo and Berlin."[13]

Then there was what the journalism historian Margaret A. Blanchard calls the administration's "highly personal and political" antitrust case against the Associated Press. In 1941, with the president's encouragement, Marshall Field III launched the proadministration *Chicago Sun*. (Field also financed the proadministration *PM* in New York.) Under the wire service's bylaws at the time, an Associated Press member often could prevent competing papers from getting AP service. The *Chicago Tribune* vetoed the *Sun's* application to join the AP. The president discussed the issue with Field, after which the Justice Department launched an investigation. FBI agents questioned Colonel McCormick and other AP board members, leaving some feeling strong-armed. The administration filed a civil antitrust suit against the AP and threatened to prosecute board members for criminal violations if they didn't back down. In a meeting, the antitrust enforcer Thurman Arnold told Colonel McCormick that the goal of the investigation was to seek his indictment. The antitrust case was justifiable—the Supreme Court ruled that the AP had violated antitrust law—but not the threats or the president's involvement.[14]

The administration contemplated using the law against others in the press, too. In 1935, journalists mocked the National Recovery Administration economist Irene Till over a ponderous study of milk production. Three years later, she had an opportunity to get even. Working at the Justice Department in 1938, she advocated a major antitrust investigation of "the control of editorial and news policy." Because the press had become big business, she wrote, "the public cannot expect to get impartial stories." A federal investigation was especially appropriate now that "the industry is under general suspicion by the public." Thurman Arnold rejected the recommendation, and it appears that it never reached the attorney general. In 1940, George Seldes's newsletter criticized FDR's record on labor. The White House directed J. Edgar Hoover to investigate him. In the broadcast field, the president leaned on the

independent Federal Communications Commission to bar newspapers from owning radio stations. "Will you let me know when
you propose to have a hearing on newspaper ownership of radio
stations," he asked Federal Communications Commission chair
James Lawrence Fly after the 1940 election. Fly acceded to the
president's wishes and opened an investigation. The agency held
hearings in 1941 and 1942 but took no action. Roosevelt also
sought to protect his supporters. When Fly launched an investigation of the NBC and CBS radio networks, which were largely
friendly to the administration, FDR tried to quash it.[15]

Threats also came from the president's allies, notably Senator
Sherman Minton, a Democrat from Indiana. Publishers, Minton
said, "would not scruple to throw this country into fascism rather
than surrender their privileges." He introduced a bill to criminalize
the knowing publication of falsehoods, with a penalty of up to two
years in prison. He also proposed a Senate investigation of inaccuracy in the press. In addition, as chair of the Senate Select Committee on Lobbying, he subpoenaed Western Union for telegrams
to and from prominent FDR critics, including the publishers Frank
Gannett and Colonel McCormick.[16]

From McCormick's perspective, Senator Minton, Chairman
Fly, Assistant Attorney General Arnold, and especially President
Roosevelt all threatened the First Amendment. But they weren't
the worst. The worst, McCormick believed, were "those academic
thinkers who desire the government to control, regulate and regi-
ment the press in order to obviate some imagined or comparatively
insignificant evil"—people, in other words, like the members of the
Commission on Freedom of the Press.[17]

CHAPTER FIVE

Highest Intellect Ever

THOUGH LESS RANCOROUS THAN in the 1930s, relations between the press and the government remained testy in the early '40s. Public hostility toward the press endured as well. In polls, about a third of Americans said that newspapers shouldn't be allowed to criticize the government, even in peacetime, or to endorse political candidates.[1]

"Some time ago Bob and I came to the rather obvious conclusion that this whole business of 'the Freedom of the Press' needed an airing," Henry Luce wrote in late 1943. "We came to the equally obvious conclusion that nothing was being done about it." So he and Robert Hutchins were convening a committee in the hope of "rethinking for our times the 'fundamentals' of freedom." They invited about a dozen scholars and public intellectuals to meet at the University Club in New York on December 15.[2]

To chair the group, Luce and Hutchins wanted Learned Hand, a legendary federal judge on the U.S. Court of Appeals for the Second Circuit in New York. They hoped that the seventy-one-year-old judge might be planning to step down from the court; he could chair the commission in retirement. Judge Hand attended part of the December 15 meeting; but he turned out to have no plans to retire, and he declined to become a member. Justice Oliver Wendell Holmes had once advised him to avoid "hot spots," he explained, and he doubted "at the present moment that there is a much 'hotter spot' than the freedom of the press." Though he didn't mention it, he had landed at the center of the hot spot two months earlier, on October 6, 1943, by ruling that the Associated Press had violated antitrust law; the case was headed to the Supreme Court. With Judge Hand unavailable, Hutchins agreed to take the chairmanship of, as he dubbed it, the Commission on Freedom of the Press.[3]

Hutchins and Luce chose a dozen men as members, with Hutchins as thirteenth. Five had ties to the University of Chicago. Charles E. Merriam was the nation's preeminent political scientist as well as a former Roosevelt adviser. The communications researcher Harold D. Lasswell had been a student of Merriam's and a member of the Chicago faculty; now he ran the Experimental Division for the Study of War Time Communications, based at the Library of Congress. Beardsley Ruml, a psychologist and the former dean of social sciences at Chicago, served as treasurer of R. H. Macy & Co., and he chaired the Federal Reserve Bank of New York. The anthropologist Robert Redfield had succeeded Ruml as dean of social sciences. The economist John M. Clark, formerly of the University of Chicago, now taught at Columbia.[4]

Three men from Harvard joined the commission. The law professor Zechariah Chafee Jr. was the leading First Amendment scholar of the day. Arthur Schlesinger Sr. specialized in American history from the colonial period through the nineteenth century; Hutchins had tried to lure him to Chicago. The emeritus philosophy professor William Ernest Hocking was a Christian metaphysician accustomed to tackling big topics; a few months earlier, *Life* had published his article "America's World Purpose."[5]

Hutchins and Luce chose two other Christian thinkers, both from New York City. Reinhold Niebuhr taught at Union Theological Seminary; Luce considered him one of the great minds of the time. Luce wanted an American Catholic for the group, so Hutchins recruited Hunter College president George N. Shuster, the former managing editor of *Commonweal*.[6]

Hutchins and Luce also selected two Roosevelt-administration officials, one former and one current. John Dickinson, a University of Pennsylvania law professor and the general counsel of the Pennsylvania Railroad, had held two sub-Cabinet positions in the mid-1930s, assistant secretary of commerce and assistant attorney general. Archibald MacLeish, a poet and essayist, had been librarian of Congress since 1939; he had also publicized military preparedness as head of the Office of Facts and Figures. Since leaving the government, Dickinson had turned against the New Deal, whereas MacLeish venerated Roosevelt.[7]

Four foreign advisers were selected to sit in on the meetings but not sign the final report: the French Catholic philosopher Jacques Maritain, the German-born philosopher Kurt Riezler, the Chinese philosopher and diplomat Hu Shih, and the Scottish-born documentary maker John Grierson. Hu and Maritain left the commission by early 1945.[8]

The thirteen American members of the commission were a relatively homogeneous lot. All were white males. (One woman later served as a staff researcher.) Schlesinger was Jewish on his father's side, Shuster was Catholic, and everyone else was Protestant. All were academics or former academics except MacLeish, and he had spent a year running the Nieman Foundation program for journalists at Harvard. (He would permanently join the Harvard faculty in 1949.) Most were affiliated with elite institutions. When they talked of adding a new member to the commission in 1945, Niebuhr observed that one candidate, the Kansas State University president Milton S. Eisenhower, would bring "academic sanctity," but, according to the minutes, "this was questioned by Shuster who pointed out that the college was in Kansas." Hutchins and Shuster were not merely professors but college presidents. Dickinson had been rumored to be a candidate for the presidency of Princeton in 1933, and in 1949, Niebuhr would be considered for the Yale presidency. Politically, Niebuhr was a Socialist-turned-Democrat, Merriam a Republican-turned-Progressive-turned-Democrat, Hocking and Shuster Republicans who backed FDR, and Ruml a Republican who, according to a profile of him in the *New Yorker*, almost always voted for Democrats. Only Dickinson, a former New Dealer, was shifting rightward. Homogeneous or not, though, they were not necessarily suited to committee work. Dickinson was notoriously pompous, Redfield arrogant, Lasswell long-winded, Hutchins imperious.[9]

Unlike the New York intellectuals of *Partisan Review*, who maintained a principled distance from the American establishment, the Hutchins Commission members occupied its very center. They were "bookish men of action," in the media historian Brett Gary's phrase. Most had ties to the Roosevelt administration. From offices at MacLeish's Library of Congress, Lasswell conducted content analysis of media for government agencies. Merriam had served on the National Resources Planning Board as well as the Brownlow Committee on restructuring the executive branch. Clark had been a member of a federal committee to evaluate antitrust law and a frequent expert witness before Congress. Redfield had been a consultant to the War Relocation Authority, which oversaw the internment of Japanese Americans. Schlesinger served on a federal advisory committee on war records. Shuster wrote propaganda speeches for the Office of War Information to broadcast to Germany. An activist outside government, Niebuhr, the commission's only New York intellectual, cofounded the Union for Democratic Action and its successor, Americans for Democratic Action. It seems that only Hocking had no significant political experience.[10]

Hutchins and Luce discussed several other candidates but decided not to invite them, including Hutchins's Great Books ally Mortimer Adler, FCC chair James Lawrence Fly, ad maker Raymond Rubicam, and several members of the judiciary in addition to Judge Hand: Supreme Court Chief Justice Harlan Stone and Justice William O. Douglas, as well as federal appellate judge Thurman Arnold, who, as assistant attorney general, had filed the antitrust case against the Associated Press. Hutchins also suggested asking Walter Lippmann to join the commission; but Luce decided he would rather not include any members of the working press, and Hutchins agreed. Hutchins later gave several reasons. If the group included a newspaper person, then radio, magazines, newsreels, and other media would demand representation. He also contended that "adequate criticism of an activity cannot come from within that activity." In addition, he doubted that the news industry was too recondite for intelligent outsiders to comprehend. (Six months into the project, Luce reversed course and said the commission ought to add two members from the working press; but Hutchins resisted, and Luce didn't push.)[11]

The final composition of the group pleased Luce and Hutchins. Luce said that the members had "probably the highest average of intellect ever to constitute a Commission." Hutchins deemed them "some very eminent characters."[12]

The historian Arthur Schlesinger Jr., whose father was a member of the Hutchins Commission, once proposed a taxonomy of intellectuals. The Analyst seeks to comprehend and diagnose society: Thorsten Veblen. The Activist tries to solve social problems by influencing or joining the government: Felix Frankfurter or, a few years later, Schlesinger himself. The Prophet takes the longest view, articulates the biggest ideas, and serves as "the setter of goals, the peerer beyond distant horizons, the interpreter of the future to the present": John Dewey. Finally, the Gadfly is "the chronic critic and perpetual irritant—in short, Mencken." On the Hutchins Commission, Merriam, Lasswell, Chafee, and several others were Analysts. Merriam and Lasswell worked in government, but except for Merriam's involvement in Chicago electoral politics early in the century, they got little public attention; they were what the historian Richard S. Kirkendall calls "service intellectuals." MacLeish was an Activist who engaged in the partisan fray from high-profile positions in the Roosevelt administration. Niebuhr and Hocking were Prophets—profound and innovative thinkers. Hutchins, too, was a Prophet, albeit one with a penchant for gadfly quips. During much of the commission's tenure, unfortunately, he turned his prophetic gaze elsewhere.[13]

Before the public announcement of the Commission on Freedom of the Press, Luce and several of his Time Inc. colleagues met with most of the men in New York on December 15, 1943, and February 2, 1944. Hutchins later counted them as commission meetings, but at the time, he insisted that they were merely preliminary discussions. He wanted to be free to add or drop members, though in the end he didn't.[14]

Hutchins said the project aimed to answer three questions: "What society do we want? What do we have? How can the press . . . be used to get what we want?"[15]

Luce provided context. According to the minutes, he said he wanted to clarify the obligations of editors and to enhance public understanding of the press's role. Freedom of the press faced no immediate danger, he said, but he worried about the future. "What are the foundations of our freedom? Are they being strengthened or weakened?"[16]

Niebuhr set forth one of his characteristic paradoxes. The uncensored expression of diverse views, he said, can cleave a society. Free expression can thus engender disorder, which in turn imperils freedom. "What should be done," he asked, "if freedom accentuates conflict to the point where the fact of freedom cannot be accepted?" Luce was impressed.[17]

With input from Niebuhr and a few others, Hutchins drafted a statement of fundamental principles to guide their analysis. A free society, he wrote, is one with the greatest possible political participation by all citizens. Such a society is desirable because "it most nearly corresponds to the basic needs of human nature," including the rational, spiritual, and social needs. Without free expression, a free society is impossible. But the scope of freedom must be defined in terms of its service to a free society. As Niebuhr had observed, a free society can be imperiled by too much freedom, not just by too little.[18]

The University of Chicago announced the Commission on Freedom of the Press on February 26, 1944. The two-year inquiry would evaluate the performance of the American press and examine all types of limitations on free expression, "whether by governmental censorship, pressures of readers or advertisers, the unwisdom of its own proprietors or the timidity of its managers." No working journalists would be members, but editors, reporters, and others associated with the media would be invited to appear and "give testimony." Luce told *Editor & Publisher* that the commission would operate with complete independence.[19]

Editor & Publisher asked prominent editors what they thought. Most were unconcerned about the exclusion of journalists. The *Chicago Times* editor Richard J. Finnegan said that "no man should judge his own case." Harold Sanford, editor of the *Rochester Democrat and Chronicle*, said the commission need not include a journalist, but he thought professors were overrepresented. The *Los Angeles Times* managing editor L. D. Hotchkiss said that "outside of Walter Lippmann, I can think of no working newspaperman who could stand confinement with announced members of the committee for any length of time."[20]

One prominent journalist did view the Commission on Freedom of the Press with alarm. According to Hutchins, the *Chicago Tribune* publisher Robert McCormick told him there was no need for "a bunch of academic busybodies ... monkeying around" with the First Amendment. Freedom of speech needed no recalibration and "could only be damaged by their interference."[21]

After choosing the commission members, Hutchins faced one more personnel decision: hiring a full-time administrator and research director to manage the project. He asked the executive committee—Harold Lasswell, Reinhold Niebuhr, and Beardsley Ruml—to suggest candidates. The committee recommended Lasswell's friend Robert D. Leigh, a political scientist and the founding president of Bennington College, who was running the Foreign Broadcast Intelligence Service at the Federal Communications Commission. Hutchins hired him. It was a decision he would come to regret.[22]

Leigh in turn hired three researchers. Ruth A. Inglis was completing her PhD in social economy and social work at Bryn Mawr. She had studied movie regulation in the late 1930s as a researcher on the foundation-funded Motion Picture Research Project, directed by Leo Rosten. Later she grew close to the husband-and-wife communications researchers Paul F. Lazarsfeld and Herta Herzog. Lazarsfeld agreed to collaborate with her on a book called *How to Study the Radio, Movies, and Press*, but they never finished it. The second commission researcher, Milton D. Stewart, had worked in 1942 and 1943 as a researcher for the Office of War Information, where he had met Lasswell. He too had worked with Lazarsfeld. While on the staff of the commission, Stewart occasionally wrote about the media for the radical magazine *Common Sense*. Llewellyn B. White, finally, had spent nearly twenty years as a reporter, columnist, foreign correspondent, editorial writer, and editor, including a two-year stint as national affairs editor of *Newsweek*. When Leigh hired him in December 1944, he was working for the OWI.[23]

The three researchers stood out, not just from one another but from the commission members. White was the only person with extensive newspaper experience. Stewart was the youngest person associated with the commission, twenty-two when he began. Inglis was the only woman. Although her scholarly credentials exceeded those of the other researchers, Leigh occasionally assigned her secretarial tasks. More than anyone else associated with the project, she ended up disputing its key presuppositions, methods, conclusions, and recommendations.[24]

Luce made one more personnel choice, assigning Eric Hodgins to act as the Time Inc. liaison to the commission. Hodgins had been one of the first writers and editors at *Fortune*, where he had worked alongside Archibald MacLeish; later he became the magazine's publisher. Now, as a corporate vice president, he oversaw public relations while keeping Time Inc. magazines in compliance with military censorship. As Time Inc.'s intermediary with the commission, Hodgins later wrote, "I was chore-boy" on "a $200,000 disaster."[25]

At first, Luce played an active role. He attended meetings, joined in discussions, and received memos. Later, in 1963, Hutchins told a correspondent that Luce "absented himself from further meetings, in the conviction that the commission should reach its own conclusions and that it should not labor under any impression that the donor was trying to influence them." In an interview in 1966, Hutchins gave a different account. "I wouldn't let Mr. Luce come into the meetings," he said, "because I didn't want anyone to think he had anything to do with the conclusions that we arrived at." Contemporaneous documents tell a different story. Hutchins thought Luce should be invited to meetings as an observer. When some of the others objected, Hutchins pushed back. "I think Mr. Luce might well be permitted to continue to attend the meetings if he wants to do so," he told Harold Lasswell. "He is being educated by them. This may be the chief result of his expenditure. I hate to deprive him of the opportunity unless you think his presence is embarrassing to the Commission." After other commission members sided with Lasswell, Hutchins gave in.[26]

Hutchins was no doubt eager to avoid a strained conversation with his patron, and he delegated the task. He phoned Eric Hodgins at Time Inc. before the commission's meeting in September 1944. "I have a difficult and possibly fatal assignment for you," Hutchins said, in Hodgins's recollection. Luce had to be kept away from the project he had devised and financed: "You've got to find some way of telling

Harry that when the Commission meets in New York he is invited for the dinner *only*. And that since he's putting up the money, when the Commission starts deliberating, he must not linger, as he has been doing." Hodgins presented the news as diplomatically as he could. He told Luce of "a slightly delicate matter but not a weighty one." Members of the commission believed that "although they profit very greatly from your presence at their meetings, they would have to turn the official frown upon it as being construable as an impropriety." Accordingly, the men wanted Luce to attend cocktails and meals but not meetings, including the meeting the following week. Luce wrote atop the memo, "will go for cocktails *only*." He underlined the word *only* twice.[27]

According to Hodgins, Luce was "terribly hurt." He knew he shouldn't be attending the meetings, but "he had found it so hard to resist." Later, William Ernest Hocking would speculate that Luce's displeasure with the commission's report stemmed, at least in part, from his exclusion. Having made possible these gatherings of intellectuals—his idea, his money—he felt entitled to be there.[28]

From the first exploratory gathering in December 1943 to the final one in September 1946, the Commission on Freedom of the Press met seventeen times, usually in hotels in New York City or Chicago. Most meetings extended over two or three days. "The continuous social contact had great value in enabling us to know each other well," said Zechariah Chafee. During breaks, the men set aside the fine points of press freedom and talked of other things. Food, cocktails, and cigars "put us in a good mood," Chafee said, ready to resume grappling with the issues Hutchins had raised at the outset: the society we want, the society we have, and the role of the press in getting what we want.[29]

CHAPTER SIX

Restless Searchlights

ISTORIANS OF JOURNALISM, ALEXANDER Woollcott wrote in 1933, someday would look back on "the Age of the Two Walters": Lippmann, "the patient pedagogue, attempting the Sisyphean task of teaching the American citizen how to think," and Winchell, "little brother to the sidewalk clowns." Members of the Commission on Freedom of the Press believed that American journalism was veering toward the wrong Walter. They wanted a press with higher aspirations, higher standards, higher brows, a press worthy of philosopher king Lippmann.[1]

Before Henry Luce and Robert Hutchins decided to exclude journalists, Lippmann's name appeared on lists of potential members. Both were fans. Lippmann made the cover of *Time* in 1931 and 1937, and Luce considered his *The Good Society*, which occasioned the second cover appearance, among the most important books of the generation. Hutchins offered Lippmann an endowed chair at the University of Chicago, but he turned it down because of his distaste for Chicago, teaching, a fixed routine, and "the pettiness of academic life."[2]

Lippmann was born in New York City in 1889. He attended Harvard, where he studied under George Santayana and Irving Babbitt, befriended John Reed, and joined William James for weekly teas. After contemplating a career as an art historian, he decided on journalism. He went on to become one of the founding editors of the *New Republic*, the editor of the *New York World*'s editorial page, and finally a columnist for the *New York Herald Tribune*, which touted him as "The Man with the Flashlight Mind." Along the way, his ideology shifted from socialism to centrism. The *Nation* judged him an unprincipled opportunist—a man "who began with a wealth of thought and ended with the thought of wealth." A more apt formulation, given Lippmann's backstage advice to presidents, might be that he was enraptured first by the power of ideas and then by ideas of power.[3]

Lippmann spent much of his life pondering how self-governing citizens can acquire the information and education they need. Like Charles Merriam, he believed science could help; the challenge lay in striking a balance between experts and voters. In *Drift and Mastery*, Lippmann argued in 1914, as Merriam would later do, that most Americans would be happy to let experts rule: "They don't want the responsibility. . . . They want to be taken in charge." The book's enthusiasts included Theodore Roosevelt and Oliver Wendell Holmes.[4]

Lippmann evaluated journalism as democracy's salvation in 1920 in *Liberty and the News*, much of which prefigures *A Free and Responsible Press*. "The health of society," he wrote, "depends upon the quality of the information it receives." Because the newspaper, "the bible of democracy," was failing to provide the information citizens needed, "the present crisis of western democracy is a crisis in journalism." As the Hutchins Commission would later do, Lippmann called on newspapers to hire better-educated reporters (the newsroom was "the refuge of the vaguely talented"), to act as common carriers, and to accept a duty of accountability to society. Also anticipating the commission, he said the press must reform for its own good; otherwise "Congress, in a fit of temper, egged on by an outraged public opinion, will operate on the press with an ax." Finally, he called for the creation of private organizations to evaluate misrepresentation in the press, which overlaps with the commission's principal recommendation. He undertook one such evaluation himself. With Charles Merz, Lippmann published a forty-eight-page supplement to the *New Republic* in 1920, sharply criticizing the *New York Times*' coverage of the Russian Revolution.

The *Times* took it seriously enough to assign a different reporter to cover the Soviet Union: Walter Duranty, who reversed the paper's stance from blind castigation to blind approbation.[5]

In 1921, Lippmann sent a handwritten note to Merriam at the University of Chicago, saying that Merriam's 1920 book, *American Political Ideas*, had been indispensable as he worked on his own book about the public mind. Lippmann's *Public Opinion*, published in 1922, has become a media-studies classic. James W. Carey calls it "the founding book of modern journalism." It's the work of a despondent democrat who had lost the hope expressed two years earlier in *Liberty and the News*. Lippmann now judged the information problems of democracy far too extensive for the press to solve. Governing requires steady illumination, wrote The Man with the Flashlight Mind, whereas the press by its nature is "a searchlight that moves restlessly about, bringing one episode and then another out of darkness into vision." Moreover, democratic theory presumes that citizens have "an appetite for uninteresting truths which is not discovered by any honest analysis of our own tastes." Elaborating on arguments from *Drift and Mastery*, he proposed delegating many political decisions to experts in "intelligence bureaus." He referred to nonexperts as "outsiders," akin to Merriam's "jungle governors."[6]

Lippmann acknowledged that he couldn't figure out how to end *Public Opinion*. Ultimately he concluded it by asserting that human virtue exists, despite the recent horrors of the Great War. "If amidst all the evils of this decade," he admonished readers, "you have not seen men and women, known moments that you would like to multiply, the Lord himself cannot help you." Reviewers noted that that sentence, the last in the book, leaves some loose ends. Merriam said that *Public Opinion* "points the way toward the new politics and the new social science that are now slowly taking shape," but "in the last chapter the author is plainly nonplussed, for . . . doubt seems to seize him." H. L. Mencken likened the book to near-beer: "I am full, but not at all satisfied." Lippmann's closing pages, he wrote, represent "a gigantic begging of the question, which, in plain terms, is this: how, *in spite* of the incurable imbecility of the great masses of men, are we to get a reasonable measure of sense and decency into the conduct of the world?"[7]

Over the years that followed, Lippmann tried various formulations for reconciling majority rule and expert authority. At one point, he suggested that officials ought to heed the views of the majority when those views are sound, but when the views seem misguided, the officials ought to follow the path that citizens *would* favor if they understood the situation. "The good," he believed, "is that which men would wish to do if they knew what they were doing." At another point, he urged scholars to stay out of government when public opinion is fluctuating, as he believed was the case early in the Depression. Only when attitudes stabilize, he said, can we "expect society to be guided by its professors."[8]

Though not invited to join the Hutchins Commission, Lippmann remained an offstage presence. He appeared on an early list of possible witnesses, but apparently he was never summoned. (The same is true of Mencken.) Commission members and staff discussed *Public Opinion* in meetings and memos. Although Merriam had praised the book upon publication, he now saw it as disconsolate and unhelpful. "I don't know any sadder picture than Mr. Lippmann's on public opinion," he told colleagues, "where he . . . discovered that the people did not know enough about anything to decide anything. . . . He went into a complete bog."[9]

The commission held a view closer to *Liberty and the News* than to *Public Opinion*. Although members believed that citizens ought to listen to experts, they didn't propose rule by experts. Those who had come close to doing so in the past, Merriam in particular, had moderated their views. Rather than sidelining voters so that experts could rule, they now wanted to bolster the expertise of the press so that voters could rule more effectively. The commission generally embraced "the democratic hypothesis," as staff director Robert Leigh put it: "if people have access to the facts and arguments, they will govern themselves more wisely than anyone can govern them."[10]

But the people *didn't* have access to the facts and arguments, because the press was shirking its responsibilities. Perhaps the press was no worse than before and no worse than the press of other countries, but according to the commission, new circumstances had made its shortcomings potentially calamitous. With the United States a global superpower, political decisions were more numerous, momentous, complex, and arcane—Americans must "make up their minds concerning the border conflicts and nationalistic and imperial demands in Transylvania, Singapore, Iran, Ecuador and Iceland." Misreckoning could spark a global war, even an atomic one. All in all, the United States was more powerful, which meant its citizens were more powerful, which meant its press was more powerful. "The more profoundly you go into the matter of adequacy of information we have to deal with," said Archibald MacLeish, "the more you are not sleeping at night."[11]

With the metaphor of a restless searchlight, Lippmann suggested that the press didn't pause long enough for voters to puzzle through issues. The commission was more worried about what the searchlight missed altogether. Members believed the "sum of . . . discontinuous parts"—the picture given by news coverage—"does not equal the whole." The selection of news distorted reality by emphasizing the aberrant over the normal, the new over the old, the nearby over the distant, and the conflict-ridden over the cooperative. Worst was the newsroom obsession with the negative. Editors devoted more attention to ax murders than to majestic public works like the Grand Coulee Dam. The commission wanted newspapers to cover "the lives of the great men of the past," "the friendly goodwill of our melting pot policy," the "increase of participation in music through the schools," and other news that would inspire as well as inform.[12]

When important facts did get into the newspaper, commission members believed that the norms and forms of journalism twisted them. "You get information turned into news by even the best reporters," said MacLeish. Journalists pared away complexity and replaced it with pizzazz. They concocted or overstated conflict for the sake of drama, especially in writing about government. The press "stirs up fights and controversies when there aren't any," said the former Roosevelt-administration official John Dickinson. William Ernest Hocking posited that journalists deploy cynicism to hide their ignorance. In his analysis, "the reporter should be a man of universal learning and understanding, and since he cannot be this, sophistication becomes his life-preserver." Hocking also blamed the press for the "disordered vanity and ambition" of celebrity culture,

in which publicity matters more than talent. In addition, he thought
the ceaseless clamor of news might erode the individual's capacity
for quiet reflection. "The press, by . . . its decisive, staccato presentation," he wrote, "adds to the difficulties of an emotionally shallowing age."[13]

Another problem was information presented out of context.
Commission members believed that "an account of an isolated fact,
however accurate in itself, may be misleading," or, as Beardsley
Ruml put it, "facts are not necessarily true." At the time, African
Americans appeared in the news disproportionately as criminals (as
Gunnar Myrdal pointed out in 1944) or as servants. Commission
members believed such depictions were fueling racist attitudes.
"One of the reasons for being oppressed," said Hutchins, "is that
you don't appear in the mass media." (The *New York Times* was addressing the problem. "If a Negro boy commits a hold-up," publisher Arthur Hays Sulzberger said in 1947, "we do not describe
him by race unless he escapes. . . . If a Negro scientist contributes
to human knowledge, we welcome the opportunity of calling attention to his race. It's as simple as that.") More broadly, descriptions
of race, ethnicity, nationality, age, and sex could reinforce the audience's prejudices. MacLeish and Ruml came up with a hypothetical
scenario: "Four Negro boys" rape and murder an elderly Italian
Catholic schoolteacher. During their arrest, an Irish policeman is
killed, orphaning his twelve children. "What standards of truth do
you apply in that kind of a case?" MacLeish asked during a meeting
in 1946. An article that merely recites the facts "produces symbolic
overtones . . . which are untruthful and considerably harmful."[14]

The men tried various approaches to stating the problem.
Hocking spoke of "the value scheme which enwraps information."
MacLeish drafted an admonitory version: "It is no longer enough to
report *the fact* truthfully. It is now necessary to report the *truth about
the fact*." Reinhold Niebuhr objected that there is no such thing as
the truth. Context is a matter of opinion. "It is a terrific problem," he
said, "what kinds of facts you select as representative facts."[15]

One of the commission's foreign advisers defended American journalism in general and yellow journalism in particular. Born in Scot-
land in 1898, John Grierson arrived at the University of Chicago in

1924, on a Laura Spelman Rockefeller research fellowship, to investigate immigration and civic education. While studying with Charles Merriam, he read *Public Opinion*. "Some of us noted Mr. Lippmann's argument closely," he said later, "and set ourselves to study what, constructively, we could do to fill the gap in educational practice which he demonstrated." Spending time in immigrant neighborhoods of Chicago, Grierson tried to figure out how newcomers became, in their own eyes and the eyes of their neighbors, Americans. He concluded that a powerful catalyst was "the yellow press at its yellowest," as developed by Joseph Pulitzer, Charles Dana, James Gordon Bennett, and "the greatest newspaper genius of them all," William Randolph Hearst. Yellow journalism, with its melodramatic storytelling, helped impart American attitudes, mores, and culture to immigrants, including those with shaky English. Sensationalist papers didn't just convey information, he said; they told simple, appealing stories, with eye-catching headlines. They gave workers what they wanted: diversion, not "heavy moralisms and stale preachments." Grierson thought Americans ought to take national pride in yellow journalism, "the most considerable contribution to democratic education in the last fifty years."[16]

Grierson left Chicago after eight months, planning to continue his research on the press and assimilation by interviewing journalists. In New York, he met Lippmann and told him about the project. Grierson said they "disagreed a whole lot" about the gloominess of *Public Opinion*, but he took Lippmann's advice to study films rather than newspapers, because box-office records were a metric for quantifying the impact of a movie. He gained access to a Hollywood studio's financial files but never published his findings. Instead, the experience deepened his interest in film. He wrote about movies for newspapers—in a 1926 review of *Moana* in the *New York Sun*, he was the first to apply the term *documentary* to a film—and then started directing documentaries in Britain and elsewhere. In 1939, he became the first film commissioner of Canada.[17]

On the Hutchins Commission, Grierson argued that sensationalism represents a solution to "the crucial problem set out by Lippmann." Dramatizing information "may twist a bit and exclude a bit," he said in a memo to colleagues in 1946, "but [it] has the justification of bringing stubborn material alive." He pointed out that his short documentaries were shown between Hollywood films in theaters. "If you have only eighteen minutes in which to do the job and are, not improperly, in competition with Betty Grable, only 'emotional symbols' will do it."[18]

MacLeish also objected to vulgarities of a second type: the gossip columns, sports, comics, advertising, and other frivolity interspersed with public-affairs news. This nonnews material diverts readers from important information, he complained, because fluff is "more tempting to the palate than the plain and simple fare of fact and thought." He believed that such material distorts the information marketplace: people will read a lying newspaper "if the funnies are funny enough, the gossip columns gossipy enough and the sports pages knowing enough." Again, Grierson dissented. "I feel rather less sympathetic than most to the atmosphere of indictment," he told colleagues, "not only because of the, to me, very exciting new things these media have given us, but because of the contributions they have made through this ragbag of entertainment." MacLeish viewed entertainment as mere "come-on stuff and sugar for the pill," said Grierson, "but dammit, it isn't." Entertainment can "make a technological society a human society."[19]

Charles Merriam said Grierson seemed to consider sensationalist newspapers "vulgar and democratic." Grierson didn't dispute the characterization. But he didn't manage to persuade the others, either.[20]

The Commission on Freedom of the Press adopted traditional frameworks for analyzing the press. Although staff researchers wrote books on movies and radio, the commission members concentrated on news media; and they assessed the contributions of news coverage to democracy in a straightforward fashion, without applying tools of literary or cultural criticism or the template of technological determinism. In these respects, the commission's approach differed from the approaches of Herbert Marshall McLuhan, as he then signed his articles, and Dwight Macdonald. In the mid-1940s, both of them published commentaries on popular culture, including McLuhan's "Dagwood's America" and Macdonald's "Theory of 'Popular Culture.' " Both also published analyses of the news media, including critiques of Henry Luce's magazines.[21]

The Hutchins Commission followed a traditional approach in another way, too. Before and after the commission, ideas for altogether-new forms of journalism have occasionally arisen. Some have been widely adopted, such as the Hearst-Pulitzer yellow journalism that John Grierson admired and the newsreel reenactments of events popularized by Luce's *March of Time*. Other innovations have proved less influential. One notion remained theoretical. In the 1890s, John Dewey and a reporter named Franklin Ford developed a proposal for *Thought News: A Journal of Inquiry and a Record of Fact*. According to a promotional circular, the publication would use "philosophic ideas . . . as tools in interpreting the movements of thought." It never appeared, perhaps because the two men conceived the project differently. Ford envisioned radical journalism that would help bring on a revolution, whereas Dewey envisioned a philosophy journal infused, he said, with "a little newspaper business." Another innovation was a precursor of the newsreel, a theater production called the living newspaper, with actors dramatizing actual events. It began in Italy around 1913 and later popped up in the Soviet Union, Austria, the United States, and elsewhere. Some productions were scripted, including the Work Projects Administration's Federal Theatre Project in the United States during the 1930s. Others were improvised by actors on the basis of the day's events. The material was generally taken from newspapers, though a troupe in Vienna sent actors into neighborhoods to gather information to be dramatized that evening. Media scholars starting in the late 1980s proposed another, more modest innovation: public or civic journalism, in which the press consciously sought to reengage citizens with public life. Some proponents cited the Commission on Freedom of the Press as an inspiration.[22]

The commission itself didn't suggest any revolutionary changes in the presentation of news. It proposed no new principles to guide journalism. Instead, it called on publishers and editors to live up to the principles to which they were already committed or at least claimed to be committed.

According to the constitutional scholar C. Edwin Baker, the Hutchins Commission esteemed the press partly as a watchdog on government. Actually, as the media historian Victor Pickard points out, the commission never endorsed a watchdog function. Although commission members spoke of an independent press as "our chief safeguard against totalitarianism," they didn't spell out what this role entailed for news coverage. Beyond a handful of remarks, they barely talked about investigative reporting, muckraking, or reformist crusades, and the remarks they made were often negative. Harold Lasswell called for less attention in the media to "deviation from high moral standards" and more attention to "constructive instances of goal-conforming conduct"—that is, more coverage of public officials who *aren't* corrupt. Commission members didn't view the press as an extraconstitutional check on state power, as Robert McCormick did at the time and as Vincent Blasi and Justice Potter Stewart would do later.[23]

With a couple of exceptions, the members of the commission believed the state posed little danger to the press in the United States. Several members believed that pressure groups, trying to manipulate news coverage through blandishments and boycott threats, endangered freedom of the press more than government did. Just as they deplored the fetishization of the First Amendment, most of the members deplored the demonization of the state. Government isn't "something alien," said Beardsley Ruml; it's "people acting collectively where they cannot do the job individually." Merriam declined to lend his name to a draft of their report that, he said, "states the anti-governmental position too strongly."[24]

Advocates of a watchdog press commonly trust voters and distrust government. H. L. Mencken distrusted everyone. In the 1930s, some of the commission members, Merriam in particular, had distrusted voters and trusted government. Now most were inclined to trust both. They anticipated many future developments in politics and the media, but the duplicities of Vietnam and Watergate weren't among them.

The men may have thought the federal government in the mid-1940s needed bolstering in a way it hadn't a few years earlier. Politics and policies were shifting. The wholesale critique of capitalism from the early 1930s, as Alan Brinkley notes, had been replaced by relatively modest proposals for fine-tuning the free market. Many New Deal agencies got shuttered. Congress cut off funding for the National Resources Planning Board, on which

Merriam served, after it began promoting a New Bill of Rights. In 1940, FDR had been adamant about having Secretary of Agriculture Henry Wallace as his running mate; in 1944, he dropped the left-wing Wallace in favor of the middle-of-the-road Senator Harry S. Truman.[25]

A sign of the changing times, as Matthew Jones points out, was 1944's surprise best seller, Friedrich A. Hayek's *The Road to Serfdom*, published by the University of Chicago Press. It sold three hundred thousand copies in the United States, became a Book of the Month Club selection, and received a long condensation in *Reader's Digest*. On a publicity tour, Hayek decried big government, not only Roosevelt's but also Hoover's. For once, Niebuhr and Merriam were in accord. Niebuhr called *The Road to Serfdom* "pretty close to pure nonsense," and Merriam called it "cynical and confused." When Hayek appeared with Merriam on *University of Chicago Round Table*, each accused the other of hating democracy.[26]

At a 1944 dinner honoring Freda Kirchwey, the editor and publisher of the *Nation*, MacLeish delivered a speech blending lamentation and mobilization. "When it was, precisely, that the blinds were drawn and the lights turned down on the morale of American liberalism, I should not undertake to say," he told the audience. "It was long enough ago in any case to produce a funerary and unventilated atmosphere in which hope goes out like a miner's candle. Liberals meet in Washington these days, if they can endure to meet at all, to discuss the tragic outlook for all liberal proposals, the collapse of all liberal leadership and the inevitable defeat of all liberal aims." MacLeish said that the American Left, "sure of itself and certain of its cause" in 1941, had become "faint-hearted, discouraged, and ready to admit defeat." He exhorted liberals to regain their confidence, even if "the political pendulum swings right."[27]

Other commission members also seemed disinclined to follow the political pendulum to the right. It fell to William Ernest Hocking to construct a philosophical armature consistent with their views—a theory of free speech predicated on trust in government.

CHAPTER SEVEN

The Glorious, Mischievous
First Amendment

"**I** AM COMING TO the meeting on Dec. 15, not too confident that I will be of any special use, but interested in the theme," William Ernest Hocking told Henry Luce in late 1943. The jaunty mystic of the Commission on Freedom of the Press, Hocking took the lead in what Charles Merriam called their "Remodeling of Freedom." In the process, he developed a fine-grained analysis of the functions of news media in democratic discourse, a complementary theory of free speech, the foundations of the constitutional theory of the positive First Amendment and of the philosophical school of communitarianism, and a proposal, admittedly quixotic, to amend the Bill of Rights.[1]

Hocking was born in Cleveland in 1873, the son of a homeopath. The family prayed each morning, and Ernest and his four sisters recited Bible verses. From an early age, he recalled, he felt "the possibility of an endless series of awakenings." At a Methodist revival meeting when he was twelve, he had a vision of "men like souls walking" in a "great procession of humanity." He began weeping. "Something happened to one," he wrote, "and after it had happened, one could never again be just the same."[2]

Another awakening occurred when Hocking was nineteen, working as a railroad surveyor to earn money for college. On a hot summer day, he walked the tracks between Aurora and Waukegan, Illinois. Every one hundred feet he made a chalk mark; every five hundred feet he painted a number. After getting to the number eighteen hundred, he slowed and contemplated every foot, pretending the numbers were years. "The imaginary living-through-past-time becomes as real an experience as the rail-painting, and far more exciting!" he recounted. "1865, 1870—suddenly 1873, my birth year: 'Hello! Hocking is here!' Every mark, from now on, numbered or not, is entangled with personal history." He walked on. "Very soon, 1892, *the present:* the painter's story and the actual story coincide: I paint the Now! From this point, memory is dismissed; it gives place to anticipation, dream, conjecture." On he went. "1900—where shall I be? 1950, fairly old, very likely gone. 1973, a hundred years from birth—surely gone: 'Good-by, Hocking!' I see myself as dead, the nothingness of non-being sweeps over me." Contemplating the dead Hocking, the living one realized that death "can be spoken of, *but never truly imagined.*" At the same time, he understood, as he had not understood before, the doctrine of the immortal soul. "May not the observing self be enduring, while the observed self drops away?" He spent the rest of the day "in a new lightness of heart," he said, "as if I had come upon a truth that was not to leave me."[3]

Hocking enrolled at Iowa State College in Ames to study civil engineering. There he read William James's *Principles of Psychology,* a work he found so remarkable that he vowed to get to Harvard and learn from the author. He dropped out of Iowa State, resumed working—this time as a teacher and principal—and after four years saved enough to enroll at Harvard in 1899. He studied under James, as well as Josiah Royce and George Santayana, while earning spending money by playing organ at Harvard Divinity School. After short stints teaching at Andover Theological Seminary, the University of California at Berkeley, and Yale, Hocking joined the Harvard faculty in 1914. In 1915, he and his wife, Agnes, founded the Shady Hill School when their son's school closed for renovations; the school continues to operate in Cambridge. One of their students, the writer May Sarton, became a lifelong friend.[4]

Time called Hocking "the last of the great American Idealists." During his lifetime, he ranked among the nation's most respected philosophers, though his prominence has faded, according to Bruce Kuklick, as academic philosophers have grown more specialized and withdrawn from public engagement. Hocking published 20 books and more than 250 articles, which addressed, in addition to religion and philosophy, ethics, law, political theory, education, and aesthetics. (His Hutchins Commission book on freedom of the press digresses at one point to denounce modern art.) Along with scholarly works, he published general-interest articles in the *Atlantic Monthly* and *Saturday Review* as well as Time Inc. magazines.[5]

Life can never be boring, Hocking once said, as long as new ideas await discovery. Not all of his ideas have aged well. Although he opposed Harvard president A. Lawrence Lowell's efforts to limit the enrollment of Jewish students in the 1920s, he also opposed civil-rights legislation in the 1950s and '60s. African Americans, he said in a letter to President John F. Kennedy in 1963, ought to stop pushing for desegregation and voting rights, because their demands were unfair to white southerners.[6]

Hocking's connection to Time Inc. began in 1941, when Whittaker Chambers came to see him in Cambridge. *Fortune* was planning a series of articles on the moral condition of civilization, and Hocking agreed to write the first installment. His "What Man Can Make of Man" appeared in *Fortune* in February 1942.[7]

After hearing about Hocking from Chambers and from the novelist Pearl Buck, Luce arranged to meet him. They dined at Hocking's Harvard Square house in June 1942. As the historian Robert Vanderlan points out, Luce developed occasional crushes on deep thinkers, and he was smitten with Hocking, a fellow internationalist with an abiding interest in religion. He called Hocking one of his "favorite intellectuals," told him that he loved talking with him, and closed one letter by referring to his Confucian respect for Hocking as teacher. Hocking, for his part, seemed to like Luce more than his magazines. In a letter to the editor, he said he was getting tired of *Time*'s habitual snideness. He chastised *Life* editors over the magazine's photos of female dancers that, he said, drew one's eyes to their crotches.[8]

At Luce's invitation, Hocking, who had retired from teaching, moved to New York in the mid-1940s, during the tenure of the

Commission on Freedom of the Press, to help develop a new Time Inc. magazine. *Measure*, sometimes called *Quest*, *Progress*, or simply *Magazine X*, was to be a culturally conservative survey of the arts, religion, and ideas, featuring such contributors as George Orwell, Lionel Trilling, T. S. Eliot, Reinhold Niebuhr, and Simone de Beauvoir. It was envisioned as more intellectual than *Harper's* but more mainstream than *Partisan Review*. Hocking worked alongside William S. Schlamm at Time Inc. The project stalled and finally died, to Hocking's bewilderment. Even so, he continued answering Luce's pleas for intellectual guidance. In the 1950s, the two corresponded extensively about the rule of law, a new interest of Luce's.[9]

Luce wasn't the only one to treat Hocking—"ineffably pink and serene, quietly glowing," in May Sarton's description—as a guru. Though he and Anne Morrow Lindbergh met only a few times, she sent him long, handwritten notes, candid, confessional, and tender. She said she considered him her spiritual father and often thought of him late at night, when she couldn't sleep. In her 1962 novel *Dearly Beloved*, she based a character on him. Clare Boothe Luce sent long letters too, more cerebral but no less adoring. "Do you know how dearly I love you, and how often I think of you?" she wrote. She was jealous of her husband: "Harry gets to see you quite often. I never do." In 1960, she told Hocking about her fascination with LSD. The "assertive, abrasive ego simply fades," she said, though she suspected that Hocking didn't need narcotics to efface his ego; "you live in a quasi-LSD world now." Both women obliquely referred to troubles in their marriages—"I have had much reason to be sad, worried, even heartsick in these last months," Clare Luce told him in 1960, after learning of her husband's affair with Jeanne Campbell—and the elderly Hocking pledged his love to both.[10]

Hocking's wife, Agnes, died in 1955. In 1960, he reconnected with Pearl Buck, whom he had met in 1931 (and who had told Luce about him). Hocking now was eighty-seven, and Buck was sixty-eight. They fell in love, writes John Kaag in *American Philosophy: A Love Story*, "two people—one at death's door—deciding to linger a bit longer in each other's company." After Hocking died in 1966, Buck wrote a novel based loosely on their romance, *The Goddess Abides*, which was published in 1972.[11]

Hocking's name appeared on the earliest Hutchins-Luce lists of potential members of the Commission on Freedom of the Press. The oldest member, seventy when it began, Hocking was tall and ruddy, with thinning hair, a white moustache, and a fondness for three-piece suits. He was courtly in bearing, puckish in humor, playful in ideas, and, according to Niebuhr, "prolix" in conversation. Though both approached philosophy as Christians, Niebuhr was a pragmatist and pessimist who talked of the darkness of human nature, whereas Hocking was a sunny idealist. When they appeared together on a radio program near the end of the war, Hocking urged Americans to forgive Germans; Niebuhr urged Americans not to consider themselves better than Germans. As for sin, Hocking liked to quote a swami he had heard in 1893 at the World's Columbian Exposition in Chicago: "It is a sin to call men sinners!"[12]

Hocking's commission book, *Freedom of the Press: A Framework of Principle*, is sometimes formal, sometimes folksy, and sometimes impenetrable. "Why cannot a report on free speech be written in simple, comprehensible language?" asked Erwin Canham, editor of the *Christian Science Monitor*. Hocking acknowledged the challenges. In the book, he warned readers to prepare themselves for a "long, schematic, and frequently tedious analysis." He also wrote his own blurb and insisted that the publisher use it: "As juicy as a steel rail. . . . Readers who do not care to try a hard job of thinking are advised to look elsewhere."[13]

Developing a theory of press freedom entailed many detours and reversals for Hocking. He advanced ideas, contradicted himself, changed his mind, changed it back again. But he remained steadfast in his belief that "the First Amendment is glorious—and potentially mischievous!"[14]

Hocking rooted his philosophy of free speech in a rejection of liberalism. Liberalism, with its suspicion of government, its deification of rights, and its "arrogant" individualism, might have suited the early years of American independence, but he thought its moment had passed. Now the tenets of liberalism were producing "dead citizens"—lazy, selfish, frivolous, uninformed, and unreasoning—who didn't deserve freedom. The community is greater than the sum of its citizens, he believed, and "a durably united community" is more important than extensive individual rights. Broadly speaking, this particular remodeling of freedom became familiar in the 1980s, when Amitai Etzioni and other communitarians argued for rebalancing community interests and individual rights. Hocking, though, went beyond the communitarians. He considered the state the people's master rather than their servant, and he saw rights, including freedom of speech, as the state's voluntary indulgences. Hutchins told him that his model "does not seem . . . strictly accurate" as applied to the United States, given the theory of popular sovereignty, but Hocking kept it in his book. His thralldom to state power and social unity led him to laud "the fierce idealism" of Russian and Chinese youth, "to whom the nation itself . . . has become the absorbing business of life." He praised fascist countries, too, for their success in eliminating "the hopeless politics of a swarm of venal party groups."[15]

Hocking said in his book that he was sidestepping the philosophical grounding of human rights. "We do not commit ourselves," he wrote, "to any of the traditional theories of right, such as the 'natural rights' theory. We are reviewing the problem." Actually, he rejected the theory, developed by John Milton, John Stuart Mill, and Oliver Wendell Holmes, that truth prevails in the marketplace of ideas. He accused Milton of lapsing into a "somewhat roseate-optimism," Mill of purveying "gracious poisons," and Holmes of reducing "to absurdity the agnosticism latent in toleration." Instead of the discovery of truth, Hocking embraced another instrumental justification, the belief that free expression fosters self-government. Like Hutchins and others on the commission, he held a civic-republican vision of democracy, in which citizens set aside self-interest and seek to advance the common good. Democracy, in this view, isn't a matter of simply counting the votes of isolated citizens; the citizens must come together and deliberate. But robust deliberation doesn't arise spontaneously, according to Hocking. Citizens may be selfish and closed-minded. They may be irrational or lazy. They may believe that propaganda is ubiquitous and truth unattainable, attitudes that erode the foundations of self-government. Or they may simply be overwhelmed. "The cure for distorted information may be more information," he wrote, "but what is the cure for too much information?"[16]

The self-government justification for free expression is commonly identified with the philosopher Alexander Meiklejohn (who, by one account, was disappointed not to be invited onto the Commission on Freedom of the Press). Meiklejohn's *Free Speech and Its Relation to Self-Government* appeared in 1948, a year after Hocking's *Freedom of the Press*. Hocking got there first.[17]

Hocking drew a distinction between negative and positive freedom, a concept that Isaiah Berlin would develop in 1958 in *Two Concepts of Liberty*. Negative freedom entails noninterference in the exercise of a right; positive freedom entails the resources needed to exercise the right. In the American tradition, almost every constitutional right falls in the negative category, by prohibiting government action. You have a First Amendment right to exercise your religion, a Second Amendment right to bear arms, and a Fourth Amendment right to be secure in your house, but these rights don't entitle you to a state-provided chapel or gun or house. A government that ignores you, under this model, cannot violate your rights. Positive freedom, by contrast, allows or even requires government to act in order to supply what is needed to effectuate a right. Hocking had long embraced the positive view. In 1925, he defined liberty as "the presence of the conditions which enable an individual to fulfill his will, namely, (a) absence of restraint; (b) availability of the necessary equipment."[18]

On a related point, commission members distinguished between freedom *from* and freedom *for*. Some of them meant merely that freedom is always exercised for some purpose. Freedom, Hutchins said in 1938, is not an end in itself; "we want to be free to obtain the things we want." Hocking, though, generally construed freedom *for* as a requirement that freedom be exercised for a specific purpose. He saw all rights as conditional. Each exists for a reason, and that reason limits its scope. Freedom of the press exists for the purpose of informing the public; therefore, when the press misinforms the public, it operates outside its freedom. Freedom *for* means, in part, duty, enforced by governmental or nongovernmental authority.[19]

The notion of positive freedom gained ground in the political rhetoric of the 1930s and '40s. During the 1932 presidential campaign, Franklin Roosevelt said that "every man has a right to life;

and this means that he also has a right to make a comfortable living," a formulation that Jonathan Alter terms "revolutionary." FDR
outlined the Four Freedoms in his 1941 State of the Union Address; fulfillment of two of them, the freedoms from want and from
fear, would require government action rather than inaction. The
National Resources Planning Board, with Charles Merriam as a
member, promulgated a New Bill of Rights in 1942, including
rights to food, clothing, shelter, education, work, and recreation. In
1944, Congress enacted a law recommended by the Planning
Board, the GI Bill of Rights, which conferred educational and
other benefits on World War II veterans. Under the positive theory
of freedom, the growth of government could be justified as advancing human rights, not just human wants.[20]

According to advocates of a positive theory of rights, the First
Amendment, by declaring that "Congress shall make no law ...
abridging the freedom of speech," implicitly calls on Congress to facilitate free speech. In their reading, the amendment declares free
speech so important that Congress must not abridge it, as the text
says, and must affirmatively promote it, as the text implies. This view,
too, is often ascribed to Alexander Meiklejohn, but Hocking articulated it earlier. The Supreme Court heartened advocates of the positive First Amendment in 1945, when it ruled that antitrust law
required the Associated Press to make its services available to all
would-be subscribers. Writing for the Court, Justice Hugo Black rejected the AP's argument that the First Amendment shielded it from
antitrust enforcement: "It would be strange indeed ... if the grave
concern for freedom of the press which prompted adoption of the
First Amendment should be read as a command that the government
was without power to protect that freedom.... Freedom of the press
from governmental interference under the First Amendment does
not sanction repression of that freedom by private interests." Some
commentators, then and later, construed this ruling as tacit recognition of the positive interpretation of the First Amendment. Hocking
thought it "enwraps the whole work of the press in a public interest
publicly guaranteed."[21]

Hocking, applying his conception of the positive First Amendment, favored the use of state power to improve the processes of
self-government in several overlapping ways. He envisioned rules to

foster public deliberation among citizens, rules to protect speakers from economic coercion, and rules to enhance the quality of public-affairs coverage in the news media. With regard to public deliberation, just as the untidiness of unregulated human reproduction once perturbed Charles Merriam, the untidiness of the unregulated marketplace of ideas perturbed Hocking. Politicians, he said, were pontificating rather than debating. Citizens too were shirking their duties. They must study issues, candidates, and events—"the news per se I am no longer free not to consume"—and listen with open minds to both sides, "the fundamental point of intellectual morality." Every game needs rules, he said, and proper rules improve the experience for players and spectators without favoring any side. To be effective and efficient, in his view, public deliberation must be supervised by the government. "The state cannot officially declare the truth," he said; "but its responsibility is to see that the truth has a fighting chance." The state should act as a moderator, reducing redundancy and distraction, ensuring that speakers are knowledgeable and accurate, and guiding the discussion toward a conclusion. He proposed a government Office of Communications, though he was vague on details. With this model of the state as moderator, he once again prefigured Meiklejohn, who in 1948 would liken public deliberation to a town meeting in need of a moderator.[22]

Whereas Hocking was mostly alone in musing on the shortcomings of public deliberation, the commission as a whole contemplated the second obstacle to effective self-government: efforts to silence speakers through coercive tactics. At the outset of the inquiry, this was a major concern. Hutchins wrote that the gravest threat to press freedom came from private organizations seeking to impose their views on media organizations. In an eighty-one-page memo, "Twentieth-Century Pressure Group Techniques in the United States," researcher Milton Stewart wrote that such groups sway the media through propaganda, intimidation, and boycotts. Commission members learned about several incidents, including boycott threats against the *New York Daily News* by Jewish groups, the *Louisville Courier-Journal* by Catholic groups, and the *New York Times* by followers of Father Charles Coughlin. Yet ultimately the commission had little to recommend, beyond urging citizens not to boycott the media.[23]

Hocking dove into the topic more deeply. Penalties for ideas, he wrote, are unavoidable "except in a moribund society empty of contending forces and beliefs." One who proclaims an unpopular idea must be prepared to suffer the consequences; the freedom to express an idea is no greater than others' freedom to condemn it. But opponents go too far when they try to suppress an idea rather than rebutting it and thereby subtract from the marketplace rather than adding to it. Threats of violence fall in this category, and the state must intervene; public order, said Hocking, is "the cornerstone of free expression." He believed that some nonviolent forms of pressure could be improper, too, though he acknowledged the difficulty of drawing distinctions. On the one hand, readers must be free to cancel subscriptions, investors to rescind financial backing, clients to take their business elsewhere, and everyone to express "irritability, stupidity, and intolerance." On the other hand, private authorities as well as state authorities can exert chilling effects and prevent ideas from being heard. Hocking concluded that the price imposed on an unpopular message must be proportionate, reflecting opposition to the idea rather than opposition to the expression of the idea. The state, accordingly, ought to protect a speaker from "types of harm not an integral part of the argument or relevant to the argument." It should prohibit threats, bribes, and other forms of coercion.[24]

In trying to protect speakers against private suppression, Hocking anticipated the First Amendment doctrine of the heckler's veto, which the Supreme Court first recognized in the 1960s. In jurisprudence, the doctrine generally bars the state from silencing controversial speakers solely on the ground that their messages may provoke violent responses from others. Hocking would have gone further, requiring the state to protect the speaker from some nonviolent reprisals as well as from violent ones—an affirmative obligation to foster freedom of speech and thus an application of the positive First Amendment. His approach, if implemented (and if ruled constitutional), might have lessened the impact of so-called private censorship in the years that followed, including the Hollywood and broadcast blacklists of the 1950s as well as pressures to deplatform controversial speakers in the early twenty-first century.[25]

Hocking's principal concern was the quality of news coverage, a concern that his colleagues on the Hutchins Commission shared.

Under the positive First Amendment, the citizenry has a right to truthful information, which, in Hocking's view, supersedes the speaker's right of free expression, at least where the speaker is a corporation disseminating facts relevant to self-government. The positive First Amendment might require government to enhance the quantity and diversity of speech in a content-neutral fashion, such as by releasing its own secret documents, building new auditoriums, stopping mobs from silencing speakers, prohibiting employers from firing workers on the basis of their speech, or limiting the size of media companies. More controversially, the positive First Amendment might require government to regulate the content of speech, by telling speakers what they must not say (even though they want to say it) or what they must say (even though they don't want to say it). Although the line between the two is often contestable, the AP ruling falls closer to the weak approach. It aims to foster diversity of speech and speakers by restricting the AP's choice of clientele, not its message.[26]

Hocking embraced the strong version of the positive First Amendment. Because "the god that is involved in our discussion is truth," he said, the community is entitled to "true knowledge of its world and true understanding of itself." News organizations perform indispensable democratic functions by acting as intermediaries between the people and the government. Media companies represent the government to the public, by publicizing government actions; and they represent the public to the government, by publishing commentaries about government actions. These functions make the press "an aspect of government itself," he said, so, like other parts of government, it must be subjected to checks and balances.[27]

Here, Hocking turned the usual argument on its head. Civil libertarians argue that government officials can't be trusted to regulate the press because of an inescapable conflict of interest: whether they remain in office may depend on how the press covers them. In this view, democratic discourse is so vital that the state must leave it alone. To Hocking, democratic discourse is so vital that the state must regulate it. He acknowledged the conflict-of-interest argument, but he maintained that the press isn't neutral, either. As big businesses, news organizations also have a stake in the outcomes of elections. Just as government officials want to keep their jobs, media executives want to keep their profits. Because everyone is tainted, there must be a "mutual checking process" in which the government monitors the press while the press monitors the government.[28]

In sum, according to Hocking, rights entail responsibilities; the press's right to publish entails a responsibility to serve the audience, which has rights of its own; freedom of speech can be endangered by private entities, including media organizations; and the government has a duty to facilitate the system of free expression, including, if necessary, through censorship—all of which adds up to the strong version of the positive First Amendment. In viewing corporate media as threats to freedom, and the government as potential champion of freedom, Hocking anticipated Meiklejohn as well as Thomas I. Emerson and Owen M. Fiss.

Zechariah Chafee was Hocking's sparring partner. They had known each other for decades. Chafee, also a Harvard professor, had been on the board of the Hockings' Shady Hill School, which he considered the best school he had ever known. On the commission, the two men agreed on many points. Both believed, as Chafee put it, that "speech should be fruitful as well as free." Both believed that the derelictions of the press were keeping some speech from being fruitful. Both believed that the press published lies, that publishers were biased in favor of business, and that the norms of news selection and presentation distorted reality. But they couldn't agree on a solution to the problems. They couldn't come close.[29]

CHAPTER EIGHT

The Right to Be Let Alone

I N 1916, AS ZECHARIAH Chafee Jr. prepared to teach his first classes at Harvard Law School, he sought to fill a gap in his understanding. What test did judges apply in deciding whether to issue an injunction prohibiting a defamatory utterance? In his legal practice, he had never followed developments in First Amendment law. "I was like most Americans, who, as the polls indicate, have no enthusiasm or even interest in the importance of free speech," he later said. "It is, I suspect, an acquired taste like olives." Digging into cases and commentaries, he acquired the taste.[1]

Chafee was born in 1885, in Providence, Rhode Island, the ninth generation of his family to live in New England. On his father's side, Thomas Chafee had arrived in the New World in 1635; his mother's side counted Roger Williams, the pioneering advocate of church-state separation, as an ancestor. Chafee studied classics at Brown, earned a law degree at Harvard, held an executive position in a family business, practiced law in Providence, and ran unsuccessfully for the Providence City Council. In 1916, he joined the faculty of Harvard Law School.[2]

In the *Harvard Law Review* in 1919, Chafee published an article that helped establish him as "the nation's first great scholar of free speech," according to his biographer Donald L. Smith. In "Freedom of Speech in War Time," Chafee argued for an expansive approach to the First Amendment. He favored the constitutional protection of speech until "close to the point where words will give rise to unlawful acts," a position supported, he said, by the intent of the Framers of the First Amendment as well as by the holdings of courts in pre–World War I cases. In 1920, Chafee published *Freedom of Speech*, which he revised in 1941. In the view of Mark DeWolfe Howe, his Harvard Law School colleague, the book "had more effect on the decisions of the Supreme Court of the United States relating to the Bill of Rights, and therefore on the liberties of the American people, than any other single work of legal scholarship."[3]

Chafee embraced dual justifications for free speech. First, he articulated a marketplace-of-ideas approach, watered down from Milton and Mill. Although the marketplace doesn't guarantee truth, it beats the alternatives. "Because of inevitable elements of friction, truth comes with greater imperfections and delays than we used to think," he wrote, "but if freedom be lessened it comes still more imperfectly and slowly." Second, he deemed free speech a precondition of democracy, with a focus on the necessity of deliberation among citizens. Like Alexander Meiklejohn, he stressed the need for unregulated public discourse about politics, but unlike Meiklejohn, he applied the rationale across the board. All speech contributes to self-government, he believed, so he rejected Meiklejohn's attempt to privilege political speech above nonpolitical speech. (Meiklejohn later adopted Chafee's view.) Combining the two theories, the marketplace of ideas and self-government, Chafee wrote of "a social interest in the attainment of truth, so that the country may not only adopt the wisest course of action but carry it out in the wisest way."[4]

For Chafee, the paradigmatic First Amendment case pitted the power of the state against the powerlessness of the dissenter, a framework reflecting the Red Scare, the Palmer Raids, and a panicky, reckless government. Unlike most of his colleagues on the Commission on Freedom of the Press, Chafee believed that distrust of the state is embedded in the First Amendment, and "we cannot get away from that." Censors always seek to silence the speech that offends or endangers those who are in power. Yet he took pains to distance himself from the radicals whose rights he defended, perhaps partly because, like Robert Hutchins, he hoped for a Supreme Court nomination. Radicals were "loud-mouthed, unattractive men," "hot-heads," "heedless and aggressive," "devoid of personal appeal." Their writing was "so wordy, shopworn, and vituperative as to make reading it a complete waste of time." But even false and pointless speech, according to Chafee, must be tolerated. It may bring attention to legitimate grievances, however deficient the proffered solutions. Restrictions on pointless speech also silence worthwhile speech—"the governmental attack on the loud-mouthed few frightens a multitude of cautious and sensitive men"—and can close people's minds. Censorship, he wrote, "produces an uncritical public opinion and intense satisfaction with one's own views." In this respect, "the real value of freedom of speech is not to the minority that wants to talk, but to the majority that does not want to listen." Like William Ernest Hocking, Chafee believed that free speech must serve the community. Unlike Hocking, he believed that it does so most effectively when individual rights are protected.[5]

Chafee was far from a First Amendment absolutist. "It is plain," he wrote in 1928, "that freedom of speech, despite the unqualified language of the First Amendment, cannot be regarded as an absolute right." Speech interests must be balanced against other social interests, albeit with a thumb on the scale in favor of speech. He defended the Espionage Act of 1917, which punished speech intended to undermine the U.S. military, though he believed that the courts had misconstrued it. He accepted content restrictions in broadcasting, including the controversial FCC Blue Book, which called for more stringent regulation of programming. He considered obscenity a problem to which "no solution yet offered is entirely satisfactory." He thought it might be a mistake to grant the press greater protection in libel law. He believed that the state could apply neutral business regulations to media organizations, the First Amendment notwithstanding; in a debate over the AP case in 1943, he declared that "speech can be stifled by private individuals or corporations," much as the Supreme Court would conclude two years later. He believed that witnesses were obliged to testify before the House Un-American Activities Committee and similar investigations.[6]

Chafee accepted the positive approach to freedom of speech in its lesser, content-neutral form. It's wrong, he believed, to view the state solely as the enemy of press freedom; it can also play important positive roles without regulating content, such as by providing auditoriums and other facilities, protecting unpopular speakers from hostile audiences, and policing the use of the broadcast spectrum. Most of the second volume of his two-volume book for the commission, *Government and Mass Communications*, was devoted to the government's role in enhancing free speech. But he stressed that this is a matter of policy rather than constitutional law. "So far as law goes," he wrote, "freedom of the press is only the right to be let alone."[7]

His biographer describes Chafee as reserved and aloof. Perhaps he was a snob; like Henry Luce, Hocking, and others associated with the commission, he longed for an American intellectual aristocracy. His standoffishness may have been magnified by the mental illness that clouded his family life. Suffering what was diagnosed as a nervous breakdown in 1936, he was hospitalized for nearly a year. His wife, Betty, had a breakdown in 1937 and spent two years in hospitals. Their daughter Nancy developed anorexia, and in 1941, their son Robert killed himself by standing in front of a train.[8]

When the Hutchins Commission began meeting in 1943, Chafee's reputation was at its peak, according to the legal historian John Wertheimer, but it plummeted after his death in 1957. The 1919 *Harvard Law Review* article that had established his reputation now upended it. The first major challenge came from the historian Leonard W. Levy. With financial support from the Fund for the Republic, a civil-liberties foundation devoted to fighting McCarthyism, Levy studied the historical record of the First Amendment's adoption. He concluded, contrary to Chafee, that the Framers had harbored a narrow view of the scope of free speech. Chafee had provided historical backing to a highly speech-protective interpretation of the First Amendment; now Levy took it away. The head of the Fund for the Republic—Robert Maynard Hutchins, who had been a foundation executive since leaving the University of Chicago in 1951—told Levy that the fund wouldn't publish his analysis of free speech, though it would publish his other research. Levy felt that his study of censorship was being censored because his conclusions were uncongenial. Fueled by "indignation at Hutchins and The Fund," he expanded his research into a book, *Legacy of Suppression: Freedom of Speech and Press in Early American History*, published in 1960. Levy rebutted many of Chafee's conclusions about the Framers' intent, though he later decided he had overstated his case.[9]

Subsequent scholars examined another part of Chafee's argument, an analysis of free-speech case law and commentary before World War I, and judged it not just mistaken but mendacious. Courts construing the Espionage Act starting in 1916 punished speech if it had a "bad tendency." Chafee maintained, inaccurately, that the bad-tendency test conflicted with the pre-1916 understanding of the First Amendment. To make the argument, he mischaracterized some cases, ignored others, and elided vital distinctions. His article "Freedom of Speech in War Time" is "devious," writes the legal historian David M. Rabban, "a work of propaganda" and "creative misrepresentation." Another historian, Mark A. Graber, charges that Chafee "suppressed or distorted evidence" and "manipulated historical facts." John Wertheimer writes that "Chafee the activist ordered a custom-tailored historical narrative to fit his public policy agenda" and "misrepresented the nation's past in order to improve its present."[10]

In Chafee's commission book too, he at least once omitted inconvenient evidence. He included long quotations from colleagues on the commission because, he said, "they express what I think right so much better than I could that I refuse to let them be lost." One quotation came from a memo by Reinhold Niebuhr, identified only as "one of our members," on the problem of concentrated ownership. Chafee deleted, without acknowledgment, the sentences in which Niebuhr endorsed the use of state authority to "prevent the centralization of exorbitant and irresponsible power" in media. In the original, Niebuhr disagreed with Chafee. After the excisions, the two agreed. "Deliberate press falsification by lies and omissions greatly concerned the Commission throughout," wrote Chafee, with perhaps a lack of self-awareness.[11]

Press critics of the 1930s and 1940s produced lengthy indictments of newspapers' shortcomings but a relatively narrow range of ideas for legal solutions. Most proposals concentrated on regulating the producer rather than the product. Some sought to reduce concentration of ownership in the media industry through antitrust enforcement, Federal Trade Commission regulations, or changes in postal rates or tax laws. Others sought to complement the for-profit press with nonprofit, endowed, or state-run media. Still others endorsed official investigations of the press. Senator Sherman Minton called for a Senate study of newspaper accuracy in pro– and anti–New Deal newspapers. Nothing came of that proposal, but Minton launched his own investigation of a magazine for farmers, *Rural Progress*, which he considered "unjustly critical of the administration." A handful of proposals called for regulating the content of newspapers. J. B. S. Hardman, editor of the *Advance*, published by the Amalgam-ated Clothing Workers of America, outlined an extensive regulatory regime: a Free Press Authority would license newspapers, ensure that they publish an adequate range of opinions, and halt the publi-cation of those that it deemed biased. Chafee called it "the most magnificent opportunity to fetter the press which has ever existed in English-speaking countries." More modestly, Minton in 1938 intro-duced a bill to criminalize knowing publication of falsehoods.[12]

Commission members believed that falsehoods in newspapers represented a major problem. Hocking spoke of "the lying press," presumably forgetting that the Nazi Party in the 1930s had applied the term—*Lügenpresse*—to its opponents in the media. According to MacLeish, journalists covering the United Nations Conference on International Organizations in 1945 reported one crisis after another in negotiations; MacLeish had been there, and, he said, no such crises existed. He considered a knowing propagator of lies "an enemy of the state." Researcher Llewellyn White complained that "the press, led by the Scripps-Howard papers, has inflicted upon the public a good many round lies" concerning the Office of War Information, where he had worked, including a report that the staff took a two-hour break for tea every afternoon.[13]

Hocking followed Senator Minton's approach: an editor who knowingly publishes falsehoods ought to be prosecuted. Stopping liars doesn't diminish free speech, he maintained; it enhances it. The strongest counterargument he could think of was that the workload would overwhelm the courts. White cheered him on. "Dynamite?" he wrote. "So, too, I rather imagine, was Jefferson's Act to Establish Religious Freedom. Is the Commission afraid to write history?" MacLeish also favored such legislation. Of the possibility that such a law might be abused for partisan purposes, he said, "Let's not get into a position where you can't defend society because you might step on a few toes." Hocking supported additional forms of regulation, too: an editor ought to be charged with fraud for misrepresenting authorship of an article, as when a press release is packaged as news; a publisher who presents advertising or other paid material as if it were unpaid ought to be charged with bribery; and journalists ought to be licensed. Chafee acknowledged "some pretty disquieting evidence about deliberate lying" in the press, but he maintained that it should be addressed not in a court of law but in "the court of conscience."[14]

The Hocking-Chafee disputes led to formation of a Subcommittee on Press-Lying, which Hocking called the Committee on Whether and How the Law Can Frown Effectively on Overt and Demonstrable Lying by the Press on Serious Public Issues without Risking Infringement upon the Divine Right to Report Things as One Pleases. In addition to Chafee and Hocking, Niebuhr and Harold Lasswell were on the subcommittee, and White was secretary. Lasswell made minimal contributions. Niebuhr, despite misgivings, was willing to go along with Chafee, in part out of a belief that falsehoods in the press can never be eliminated, for "all men are liars." But Hocking, backed by White, fought on. Chafee made a pilgrimage to Hocking's New Hampshire farm in hopes of resolving the disagreement. Afterward he reported to Robert Leigh that he and Hocking had "pretty well eliminated" their differences, "except"—a big except—"a certain fundamental divergence of outlook."[15]

Chafee and Hocking agreed that the government was regulating the operations of many businesses, yet the press maintained almost total autonomy. For Chafee, this autonomy meant that editors must accept a weighty moral responsibility, whereas Hocking saw it as a loophole to be closed. Chafee believed that "the government can do a lot in keeping the market [of ideas] a real market," but he didn't "think it ought to tell the merchant what he brings into that market"; whereas Hocking believed that the citizen's need for accurate information leaves the state no choice but to regulate the marketplace, including the goods brought in. The state regulates food safety, he said. Isn't the public entitled to "uncontaminated mental food"?[16]

A more fundamental divergence separated the two. Though Hocking had taught a seminar with Harvard Law School dean Roscoe Pound (and dedicated a book to him), he acknowledged that he was "an amateur in the law." He was a philosopher, and he approached constitutional issues from a philosophical perspective, excavating first principles and fashioning them into new theories. He valued creativity in philosophical analysis. In his view, "a theory is false if it is not interesting." Chafee was impatient with abstract theorizing. "At this day," he wrote, "there are no new principles of freedom of speech." Virtually anything can qualify as a truth in philosophy, he believed, but the test of truth in constitutional law is whether it can attract the votes of five justices. He thought Hocking's maximalist, content-regulating vision of the positive First Amendment was irrelevant, because the Supreme Court would inevitably reject it. Whereas Hocking construed a passage in the Associated Press case as a wholehearted endorsement of his theory—the Court "enwraps the whole work of the press in a public interest publicly guaranteed"—Chafee dismissed it as having little applicability beyond antitrust. When Hocking called for the state to give citizens " 'positive guidance' honestly directed toward freedom," Chafee told him it was a losing argument under First Amendment doctrine. "Insofar as you intend to call for governmental guidance of discussion," he said, "the constitutional opinions of the Supreme Court have pretty well settled the law against you." Hocking found such objections unpersuasive. "I don't care what you say *legally*," he told Chafee at one point.[17]

The two men also disagreed about the relationship between moral rights and legal rights. Hocking believed that the existence of a right to speak depends in part on the speaker's fulfillment of moral responsibilities. A speaker forfeits the moral claim by misstating facts, fueling hatred, or "commercializing the potential vulgarities of the crowd." In dealing with these "traitors to freedom," he said, the state may choose to leave the legal right intact, because the speech causes little damage or because punishing the abuses would be too difficult. But once the moral right has been forfeited, the state has discretion to act as it pleases. The security of a legal right, Chafee responded, cannot be made contingent on fulfillment of a moral duty. Legal rights must be distinguished from moral rights. "I find it a good rule never to use the word 'right' in isolation except when I mean a *legal* right," he told Hocking, adding, "I venture to think that you slide imperceptibly from moral problems into legal problems, or *vice-versa*." Privately, Chafee complained about Hocking to Robert Leigh: "Frankly, I am getting a little weary of completing his education. He seems to suffer a relapse after every conference."[18]

In discussions, Hocking sometimes resisted Chafee's efforts to pin him down. When Hocking tried to distinguish censorship from legislation, Chafee pushed for a definition. By *censorship*, did he mean the censor's review of materials or the imposition of penalties?

"I mean a method of *sifting*," replied Hocking.

Chafee tried again. Did he envision criminal prosecutions?

"No, not necessarily," said Hocking. "It is just a sifting process: 'This shall be shown; this shall be printed; this shall not be printed.'"

Chafee asked if an official would decide what could not be printed in advance—a prior restraint—or if the law would punish the speech after the fact. "That is an important difference," he said.

"It is important not to go into those details," said Hocking.

"Then I don't like the word *censorship* at all," said Chafee.

"I am not so afraid of the word *censorship*, because it has its historical meaning, which does say a sifting process," Hocking replied.

"Yes," said Chafee, "but that isn't what it means in . . . freedom of the press. It means an individual who licenses or deletes, and that sort of thing."[19]

The men contested the meaning of other concepts too, especially *community*. Every communication between speaker and listener, Hocking said, includes the community as a third party; therefore, the community must supervise the press. Chafee considered the word a dodge. In terms of developing and enforcing regulations, he said, *community* means *government*. "I can't allow myself to be carried away by Chafee's eloquence," said Hocking. He accused Chafee of twisting the concept of community into "a magnified censor in terms of a ward alderman," on the basis of an "unjustified distrust of democratic institutions." The argument continued in the margins of Hocking's book. When Hocking described the Bill of Rights as "a legal limitation of the sovereign by the sovereign," an unnamed colleague—almost surely Chafee—responded in a footnote, "I object to this mystifying and absurd phrase."[20]

At times Hocking took Chafee's objections seriously and tried to come up with alternatives. At one point he suggested privatizing the task of determining truth: a tribunal of citizens would decide whether a news organization had knowingly lied, and the government would require it to publish a correction and perhaps impose punishment. Hutchins said that the state probably wouldn't enforce the edicts of a private body. At another point, Hocking proposed judicial rulings without punishment: "There would be no fines, no suspensions, nothing but the decision—'On this point, the *Monitor* lied.' ... It would throttle nobody; it would be a balance wheel for responsibility." Chafee responded that judges would resist such a task. "They want to make decisions only when they will seriously affect somebody," he said, whereas determining the accuracy of a news article, with no possibility of punishment or damages, "is just an academic controversy." Hutchins remarked that Chafee failed to appreciate the gravity of academic controversies.[21]

Others at times also thought Hocking went too far. He insisted that rights entail responsibilities and wanted to say so in the commission's final report. Nothing is "more central to our whole problem," he said, than a pronouncement that rights are neither absolute nor inalienable. "I for one am not ready to declare the Declaration of Independence old hat," responded MacLeish, "in order to make the point that rights without responsibilities lead to Arthur Sulzberger."[22]

At another point, Hocking framed the notion in constitutional terms. As a "quixotic possibility," he suggested a constitutional amendment stating that "the enjoyment of all rights in a free community depends on the good faith of those who claim them." Beardsley Ruml mused, "It would be interesting to find as a result of our inquiry that not only is the First Amendment defective ... but that they are all defective, and that therefore a complete reorientation is necessary." Niebuhr said that a constitutional amendment "introduces a depth of problem that we are not dealing with." Imposing such a limitation as a matter of law and not just morality, he said, would "destroy the Bill of Rights." Hutchins, speaking "as a very retired lawyer," said it seemed "a casual way to propose a constitutional amendment." Perhaps the commission ought to draft "a new Bill of Rights with a Preamble." The discussion moved on.[23]

Hocking abandoned his constitutional amendment. At a later meeting, Ruml proposed a different change to the First Amendment: Congress shall make no law abridging freedom of the press, "except in those cases in which the press is engaged in deliberate lying." This too went nowhere. Hocking dropped his advocacy of censorship. But he wanted to leave an opening for imposing additional regulations on the press, and he continued to argue with Chafee over the role of the state. Whereas Chafee maintained that guaranteeing responsible journalism is largely up to the journalists themselves, Hocking insisted that modest forms of regulation are not "*ipso facto* a limitation on freedom." In Hocking's commission book, *Freedom of the Press*, he asserted that a "touch of government" was necessary for ensuring adequate performance by the press.[24]

Commission researcher Ruth Inglis found the phrase baffling. "Usually I am completely enchanted with your use of language," she told Hocking. But what, she asked, is a touch of government? "I suppose an automobile sticker is a touch of government," Hocking replied, "whereas if a man were to be hanged for telling a lie over the radio it wouldn't be a touch. It would be a blow. The scale is, I believe, 100 official reproofs equals one blow; 100 touches equals one official reproof."[25]

After the publication of Hocking's book, *New York Times* publisher Arthur Hays Sulzberger also asked about the phrase. "I wonder if you meant it as I read it," he wrote in a letter to Hocking. "I hope not." Hocking replied that he had used the phrase "somewhat maliciously to annoy the lawyers in our company." Copyright law, postal delivery of publications, and laws banning burlesque parlors were all "touches of government." The way to understand the issue, he said, was by an analogy between "clearing the public highways of the drunken drivers—to the greater freedom of all the decent drivers—and clearing the newsways of drunken scandal sheets." Sulzberger responded, "To my regret, your letter . . . confirmed my fears as to your meaning."[26]

Hocking believed the argument in his book resembled a barbed-wire fence, but several specialists in media studies and freedom of

speech praised it. Leo Rosten called it "the most profound and as-
tute examination of the principles of freedom and responsibility"
since John Stuart Mill. Writing in *Journalism Quarterly*, Curtis D.
MacDougall declared it "brilliant." Morris Ernst and Fred S. Siebert
were also admirers. The *Chicago Tribune*, by contrast, judged it "vi-
cious, irresponsible, and irrational," the work of "a true totalitarian."
Hocking framed the *Tribune* review and hung it in his study.[27]

"Touch of government" doesn't appear in *A Free and Responsible
Press*, the report of the full commission, but in other respects the
book leans toward Hocking's position. The first chapter includes a
long passage, which Hocking drafted, about the purposes of free
expression. A twenty-seven-page summary of the principles of free
speech, written by Hocking and signed by all the members, appears
as an appendix.

Chafee seems to have picked his battles. The report obliquely
threatens new regulations if the press doesn't shape up, a position
Hocking and others favored. With regard to specific recommendations, though, Chafee stood his ground. In the passage that probably mattered most to him, *A Free and Responsible Press* declares, "We
do not believe that the fundamental problems of the press will be
solved by more laws or by governmental action." When *A Free and
Responsible Press* came out, Kenneth Stewart of *PM* complained that
its "mountainous build-up" of diagnosis leads to recommendations
that are "mousy platitudes." Much of the buildup came from
Hocking. Chafee was principally responsible for the mousiness.[28]

CHAPTER NINE

Resurrecting Free Speech

A RCHIBALD MACLEISH STOOD APART. Of the thirteen American members of the Commission on Freedom of the Press, he alone hadn't earned tenure at a university, though he had spent a year running the Nieman Foundation fellowship program for journalists at Harvard. He alone worked full-time for the Roosevelt administration, first as librarian of Congress and then as assistant secretary of state for public and cultural relations, while the commission was meeting. Earlier, as head of the Office of Facts and Figures, he had been the administration's spokesman on military preparedness. He alone had worked for Henry Luce, as *Fortune*'s most prolific writer during its first nine years; Luce was probably closer to MacLeish than to anyone else on the commission, including Robert Hutchins. *Fortune*, the Office of Facts and Figures, and the Nieman Foundation had given MacLeish more firsthand experience with journalists and journalism than anyone else on the commission. Whereas most other commission members were scholars, MacLeish alone was an artist: a Pulitzer-winning poet. Every writer, he believed, "keeps up a running quarrel with his time." Impassioned, energetic, egotistical, and sometimes bullheaded, he also kept up running quarrels with colleagues on the Hutchins Commission. Despite stepping down for eight months to work at the State Department, he ended up as one of the most influential members of the group.[1]

"I was asked to serve by Bob Hutchins, although I didn't know him at the time," MacLeish said in 1966, when a college student interviewed him about the commission. "I not only didn't know him, I didn't like him. I got to love him later. . . . I was in the University Club in Chicago, sitting in the library, and he walked in and said, 'Would you like to serve on a commission on freedom of the press?' I said, 'No, of course not.' So then I did." In truth, the two had known each other for several years before Hutchins extended the invitation. MacLeish's recollection may have been warped by his assessment of the commission's final product, which he described to the student as "gobbledygook."[2]

MacLeish was born in 1892, in Glencoe, Illinois. His father had gotten rich in Chicago's dry-goods business after the Civil War. At Yale, he excelled in sports and, he later boasted, "won all the prizes" for writing verse. "I was one of those models," he said, "that young men make for themselves, plagued by the fact that I seem to be able to do more or less well things which don't commonly go together." After contemplating a career as a literature professor or a preacher, he studied at Harvard Law School (Zechariah Chafee was one of his professors). He found the law stimulating and considered himself "quite good at it." After an interruption to serve in World War I, he got his JD in 1919.[3]

Again MacLeish contemplated career options. The dean invited him to join the Harvard Law faculty, and he taught a constitutional law class several times. But he decided against academia. It was too remote, too insulated, too safe; he wanted to be in the arena. In the limelight, too. "I wish to Christ I didn't want fame so much!" he once said. While studying for the bar in 1920, MacLeish spent two months filling in for an absent editor at the *New Republic*. Working alongside Walter Lippmann, he pondered a life in journalism, a field that he believed "offers a chance for thought & study & for the attempt to make one's conclusions current in the world," though the low social status gave him pause. (His son would later note his "populist ideals and patrician prejudices.") MacLeish took the conventional path, albeit temporarily, by joining a Boston law firm. He called lawyering the "best indoor sport in the world," even though its benefit to society is "exactly and precisely zero." After three years in the law firm, MacLeish decided to devote himself to poetry. Bostonians talked for years afterward, he claimed, about "what a disaster" it was that he "gave up a career as a first-rate lawyer to become a third-rate poet." In 1923, he joined Ernest Hemingway, Ezra Pound, and other American artists in Paris. MacLeish was disillusioned by World War I, but he rejected the label commonly applied to the group. "We weren't expatriates," he maintained. "Our patria, as we knew it, had vanished." While in Paris, he published works that established him as a major poet, including "The End of the World," "You, Andrew Marvell," and the book-length poem *The Pot of Earth*.[4]

MacLeish had gotten to know Henry Luce at Yale. Luce "was an admirer of mine," he said. After college, the two kept in touch. MacLeish declined to invest in *Time*—"I knew better than that"—but agreed to work part-time as the education editor during the magazine's first year, rewriting newspaper clippings into *Time* prose. Luce and his first wife, Lila, visited MacLeish in Paris while on their honeymoon. (Recounting their travels, Luce told MacLeish that the bed in their room at Vézelay had been so small that "Lila had to sleep on the floor.") When MacLeish brought his family back to the United States in 1928, after five years, Luce offered him a full-time job writing for a business magazine that Time Inc. was developing. When MacLeish said he knew nothing about business, Luce replied that "it is easier to turn poets into business journalists than to turn bookkeepers into writers." MacLeish said he couldn't abandon poetry, so Luce proposed a flexible arrangement: he could work at *Fortune* for as long as necessary to pay his family's bills, take a leave of absence to write poetry, and return when he ran out of money. MacLeish said yes. He became the star writer at what was then a writer's magazine. Whereas *Time* homogenized articles into a single style, *Fortune* featured distinctive voices and resisted the *Time* fetish of concision. While producing one cover story after another, MacLeish continued to write poetry and drama. In 1933, he won a Pulitzer Prize; in the 1950s, he would win two more. One colleague called him "a veritable Donne and Bradstreet."[5]

At Time Inc., Luce grew closer to MacLeish. Their mutual affection against the backdrop of an employer-employee hierarchy, by one account, served as the model for the relationship between

Jed Leland and Charles Foster Kane in *Citizen Kane*. Part of their closeness stemmed from a shared faith. "With however many and long wanderings from that knowledge," Luce told MacLeish, "you and I have known and agreed that God lives." One morning in late 1934, Luce phoned MacLeish at his desk and asked to talk outside the office. They met in the empty ballroom of the Commodore Hotel. Sitting in semidarkness, Luce told MacLeish he was in love with the playwright Clare Boothe Brokaw. At dinner the night before, he had declared his intent to marry her. She had laughed. "He was afraid he'd made a fool of himself," MacLeish recounted. He told Luce what he plainly wanted to hear: leave Lila for Clare, for "love is all there is."[6]

The MacLeish-Luce friendship transcended not just the workplace hierarchy but the wide gulf separating their political views. In 1934, MacLeish said of American capitalists: "They are greedy; they are arrogant; they are gross; they lack honor; their existence insults the intelligence. It is a pleasure—almost a duty—to hate them." He came close to joining the Communist Party early in the Depression, according to his biographer Scott Donaldson. He did help organize the Party-sponsored Congress of the League of American Writers in 1935, and he wrote for the Party-allied *New Masses* and spoke at a fund-raiser for the magazine. But he rejected the ideological litmus tests that communists ("intellectual terrorists," he called them) applied to the arts.[7]

In the early years of *Fortune*, it reflected MacLeish's politics more than Luce's. MacLeish, Dwight Macdonald, and the other Old Bolsheviks on the staff, as Luce called them, had considerable leeway to express their views at first, but Luce's tolerance of ideological diversity didn't last. *Fortune*, he said, could be "either a great Communist magazine or a great Capitalist magazine." Macdonald resigned in 1936 and became a lifelong critic of what he called the "Lucepapers." ("As smoking gives us something to do with our hands when we aren't using them, *Time* gives us something to do with our minds when we aren't thinking.") MacLeish left Time Inc. in 1938 to direct the Nieman program during its maiden year. Though he declined Luce's repeated invitations to return, he did contribute phrases to "The American Century" and occasionally wrote for *Life*.[8]

Looking back, MacLeish had mixed feelings about his years at *Fortune*. Although "certainly it wasn't literature," he said, "it was the greatest box seat. . . . It took me all over the place and behind scenes." He considered Luce a superb editor but was less taken with his backbiting colleagues. In addition, Ernest Hemingway and other literary friends derided him for working for Luce, especially after *Time* sided with Franco in the Spanish Civil War. As if to defend himself, MacLeish later claimed he took the job out of financial necessity during the Depression. Actually, as the historian Robert Vanderlan points out, he started work before Black Friday. He was hardly destitute; his son, William, later remarked that the family always employed servants, "even in the worst times."⁹

In 1939, after MacLeish had run the Nieman program for a year, FDR asked him to become librarian of Congress. He turned down the offer; but Roosevelt pressed, and he gave in. He won confirmation over considerable opposition. Librarians, trying to establish their bona fides as a profession, opposed him as a poet with no evident qualifications, while conservatives opposed him as a poet with left-wing views. "The criticism most often expressed against me is the fact that I am a poet, not that I am a bad poet," MacLeish remarked. "Simply to call a man a poet is, apparently, to throw a bad egg at him."¹⁰

MacLeish used the Library of Congress as a platform to call for intervention in the European war. He considered Americans "dangerously ignorant" about fascism, which he thought "presented the greatest threat to civilization since the Barbarian invasion." In a speech in 1939, he declared that "time is running out, not like the sand in a glass, but like the blood in an opened artery." The librarian of Congress proceeded to alienate many of his former allies. In a slender book published in 1940, *The Irresponsibles*, he denounced those artists and scholars who weren't joining the fight against fascism. For calling on others to fight oppression, MacLeish was accused of oppression. Communists who had welcomed his antifascist pronouncements during the Spanish Civil War denounced his antifascist pronouncements after the Hitler-Stalin Pact of 1939. The *New Masses* accused him of trying to "sell an imperialist war . . . with slightly shopworn poetry." Many writers rebelled against what they construed as a directive from the librarian of Congress to produce antifascist propaganda. James T. Farrell said MacLeish seemed to be calling for "a kind of Moscow Trials of American culture." Dwight Macdonald accused him of "patrioteering" and likened him to Goebbels. In a gentler critique, Malcolm Cowley wrote in the *New Republic* that MacLeish harbored the misconception, common among artists and intellectuals, that artists and intellectuals can affect the course of American politics.[11]

MacLeish was concerned about the attitudes of the masses as well as those of artists. After lunching with him in May 1941, FDR adviser Harold Ickes wrote in his diary that MacLeish thought the administration needed "an effective propaganda machine." Five months later, President Roosevelt named him to head a newly created agency to publicize defense preparedness, the Office of Facts and Figures. (He also stayed on as librarian of Congress.) MacLeish pledged to follow "the strategy of truth," but the centralized information rankled administration officials, journalists, and congressional Republicans; after Pearl Harbor, morale-boosting superseded truth-telling. Within a year, OFF was subsumed in a new agency, the Office of War Information, headed by Elmer Davis of CBS News.[12]

During the war, MacLeish sent the Declaration of Independence and the Constitution to Fort Knox for safekeeping. Rather than let the Library of Congress as a whole go into suspended animation during the hostilities, MacLeish assigned different offices, old and new, to work with defense, intelligence, and other agencies. The poet with no managerial experience proved to be a savvy administrator, even an empire builder. An idealist in national politics, he was a pragmatist in office politics. In early 1942, he told J. Edgar Hoover that a wartime "wave of witch hunting" seemed likely, and "things as far apart as liberal belief and communist membership will get wrapped up together in certain minds." Under the circumstances, he said, "I thank God that we have people like you running the law enforcement agencies."[13]

MacLeish was less inclined to sweet-talk journalists. Particularly during his time at OFF, he fought bad press, including attacks on a member of his staff, Malcolm Cowley (who had criticized *The Irresponsibles* in the *New Republic*). When *Time*, in an article by Whittaker Chambers, censured Cowley for his left-wing associations, MacLeish told Luce that it was "as outrageous a piece of journalism" as he had ever seen. At Luce's direction, the next issue featured a largely positive article on the OFF staff.[14]

Complaints about unfairness were unlikely to sway other critics in the press, most notably Robert McCormick of the *Chicago Tribune* and his relatives Joseph Patterson of the *New York Daily News* and Eleanor "Cissy" Patterson of the *Washington Times-Herald*. MacLeish charged that McCormick and the Pattersons were helping Hitler with their ceaseless criticism of President Roosevelt. The "McCormick-Patterson axis," as FDR dubbed them, fought back. In early July 1942, after Roosevelt announced that MacLeish's OFF would be replaced by the Office of War Information, the *Washington Times-Herald* published an article by Cissy Patterson about MacLeish ("The Bald Bard of Balderdash") and his "array of literary floosies." She called on Americans to celebrate the "joyful whizbang" of MacLeish's downfall on Independence Day. The *Chicago Tribune* quoted Patterson's article at length.[15]

"I have achieved the ultimate in something," MacLeish wrote in a note to President Roosevelt. The *Tribune*, he said, had proclaimed that "the chief significance of this year's Fourth of July is the fact that the country has gotten rid of / Yours always, / Archie!"[16]

The president replied that McCormick and the Pattersons "deserve neither hate nor praise—only pity for their unbalanced mentalities."[17]

Along with MacLeish's career path, he differed from many colleagues on the Hutchins Commission in philosophy. He was an earnest, outspoken patriot. He called the United States "the most creative and productive nation on the earth," credited the Declaration of Independence with laying out "the most precisely articulated national purpose in recorded history," and defined the American Dream as "the liberation of humanity." In 1952, when Reinhold Niebuhr impugned the nation's founding ideals in *The Irony of American History*, MacLeish said he was "as wrong as it is possible for a wholly honest and highly intelligent man to be." MacLeish saw blemishes in American history but no fundamental contradictions, no irony. Above all, he was a Jeffersonian, a man to whom "free society" was an oxymoron, for "freedom means individual freedom." He celebrated the individualism that William Ernest Hocking considered outmoded and corrosive.[18]

At times, MacLeish joined Hocking and others in calling for punishment of falsehoods in the press. Freedom of speech, he said, means the citizens' "right ... to know not *any* words but *true* words." Mostly, though, he focused on speakers rather than listeners. The commission must stress "the right of a man to say his say" rather than "the need of the hungry sheep" for information. "Sheep always lead to shepherds," he said, "and shepherds are what we in this day don't want." He thought citizenship should be active. Press freedom to him meant an individual with a message and a right not just to speak but to be heard.[19]

He believed that this right to be heard reflected the First Amendment's original meaning, as a right belonging to all people and not just the privileged. In the 1790s, he said, hand presses were cheap, and anyone could use state-of-the-art technology to spread ideas. But the press had become big business, with newspaper companies selling for millions of dollars. When only a few people own the machinery necessary to exercise free speech, they owe a fiduciary duty to the masses. They must use their property so as to fulfill the original purpose: "publication of the widest possible variety of opinions." At the time of the Framing, government represented the main obstacle to reaching an audience, so a barrier against the state ("Congress shall make no law") sufficed to protect freedom of the press; but that was no longer the case. Freedom of the press was now a "lost right," said MacLeish, "roughly equivalent to freedom to take a rocket to the moon." The original meaning of the First Amendment must be restored.[20]

Others on the Hutchins Commission sometimes questioned MacLeish's account of history. (Later, so did several scholars, including the journalism historians Frank Luther Mott and Fred S. Siebert.) Mostly, though, they struggled to figure out the implications. What would it mean to restore the First Amendment's original meaning? Meeting at the Hotel Del Prado in Chicago in May 1946, they tried to pin him down.[21]

MacLeish said he was advocating a right for all Americans "to *use* the press."

Did he mean that the First Amendment ought to be interpreted to give citizens a legal right against private power—monopolistic publishers—as well as state power?

No, said MacLeish.

Was he advancing a philosophical argument rather than a constitutional one?

"It is in the First Amendment."

Did he mean citizens ought to be able to force newspapers to publish their views?

"No, certainly not!"

Was he saying that speakers had a right to reach an unwilling audience?

"No, that was never suggested."

If every American had a right to use a press, *what* press?

"It is the right to use the press that I can acquire."

"That I understand perfectly," said Robert Hutchins. "Now you haven't got the money to get it."

"That is all I am asking for. ... The right itself was never a right to own a press or to go to somebody else to use a press, but to use it when you got it."

"There is a step omitted in here," said Hutchins. What about people who can't afford a press?

"That is the point I want to get to," MacLeish replied. If the original meaning of the First Amendment could no longer be fulfilled—if Americans couldn't reach the public through the principal media of mass communication, as they could in the 1790s—then the commission should admit it. Its report should be "perfectly frank and explicit in stating that the original hope and expectation has been defeated by circumstances."

Hutchins remarked that MacLeish's formulation of the constitutional issue "is not particularly helpful."

"It certainly confused this Commission," MacLeish said.[22]

MacLeish was touching on the concept of media access, which Jerome A. Barron would advocate in "Access to the Press: A New First Amendment Right," published in the *Harvard Law Review* in 1967. The Communications Act of 1934 creates a limited form of media access, by requiring broadcasters to sell advertising time to candidates for federal office. Before and after the Commission on Freedom of the Press, courts and legislatures considered arguments for broader rights of access—to print as well as broadcasting, to news as well as advertising, to noncandidates as well as candidates—and mostly rejected them.[23]

Though puzzled by the policy implications of MacLeish's argument, other commission members shared his belief that publishers ought to open their pages to a wider variety of views. If participating in public discourse required an expensive piece of equipment, said Reinhold Niebuhr, and the wealthy monopolized it, "you would be breaking down the democratic process." Ultimately the members called on the press to act as a common carrier, a public utility, or a business affected with a public interest. These terms, which they used interchangeably, refer to monopolistic and near-monopolistic businesses that are legally required to provide universal service. The owner of the only ferry across a river, for instance, must carry all who can pay the fare. Telephone companies are also common carriers. Hutchins described the idea of applying the common-carrier notion to the press as the commission's "most substantial single contribution."[24]

Generally they discussed it as an aspiration and a metaphor, not as a set of regulatory standards. In a meeting in 1945, though, Hutchins proposed making it a legal requirement. As he outlined the plan, "some type of legal machinery ... would impose public utility responsibility" when a media organization's audience reached a certain size. (MacLeish was on leave, working for the State Department at the time. When he returned a few months later, he too endorsed a legal mandate. Without it, he said, the common-carrier proposal was the equivalent of "we recommend that you be a good boy.")[25]

Under this law, Zechariah Chafee asked, could *anybody* demand time on a radio station or space in a newspaper?

Yes, said Hutchins, at least "reputable persons." Laws and regulations would define "reputable."

Chafee asked if news organizations would be required to publish every letter to the editor.

Hutchins acknowledged difficult questions, but if the outcome would be desirable, "then we could apply our ingenuity to finding out how to do it."

Chafee said it would violate the Constitution. The common-carrier model might apply to the business side of the press, as with the Supreme Court ruling that the Associated Press must make its services available to anyone who pays, but content had to remain unregulated. "I don't think we can say that because the AP ought to behave like a railroad, the *Chicago Tribune* ought to behave like a railroad."

Hutchins said he raised the issue "merely to test out what the Commission meant by common carrier." But he thought the discussion spotlighted a deficiency in their analysis. After identifying worrisome problems in the news media, they had systematically rejected almost every possible regulatory solution. If they believed that media monopolies prevent important ideas from reaching the public, he said, they had three potential remedies: increase competition in the marketplace through antitrust enforcement, impose the common-carrier model in some binding fashion, or have the government foster the creation of media organizations through subsidies. They had to recommend *something*. "You can't sit around and say we can't promote competition among the giants," Hutchins said, "and then say we can't make them public utilities unless you are going to write the whole Report off."

Beardsley Ruml proposed a new legal entity, a federally chartered "instrument of communication" that would be regulated to "conform to our evolving standards." An instrument of communication could operate under the limited-liability corporate structure. Media organizations that wouldn't accept government oversight would have to operate as partnerships, with individual liability for owners. "They take terrific risks in doing that," Ruml said; "nevertheless, there are some people who like it that way." Limited liability, like broadcasters' use of the public airwaves, would be treated as a privilege accompanied by conditions.

"That sounds very good," said Hutchins.

Niebuhr said the approach would require "some big regulatory agency like the FCC in the field of newspapers." He was fine with that. "It wouldn't be dangerous from the standpoint of free speech," he maintained, "but it would be a general regulation in the field of communication to prevent monopoly of opinion"—an application of the positive First Amendment.

Chafee said this too would be unconstitutional. "I don't think we can say that we would take away a newspaper's charter if the government officials in charge didn't like the quality of its editorials."[26]

Ultimately, Ruml's proposal was dropped. Instead, the commission called on media organizations to "regard themselves as common carriers of public discussion," with a footnote stipulating that "the Commission does not intend to suggest that the agencies of communication should be subject to the legal obligations of common carriers."[27]

Even as a moral right, the common-carrier approach raised questions. As a practical matter, newspapers could not simply turn over space to anyone who requested it. But that meant editors and publishers would decide which views deserved airing and which did not; the commission was trying to get away from that. The members sought to frame a neutral rule. Whereas Hutchins had talked of media access for "reputable persons," staff director Robert Leigh proposed access for "substantial groups who seek . . . to express their ideas." That phrase set off MacLeish, who found the emphasis on groups "unacceptable from every relevant point of view." The First Amendment, he said, guarantees "the freedom of the human spirit— which is a spirit sole. Do we expect a 'group' to conceive the *Areopagitica?*" In the end, commission members dropped "reputable persons" as well as "substantial groups" and instead called on the press to open its pages to "all the important viewpoints and interests in the society."[28]

As the men struggled for ways to get diverse views into the press, they developed their own diverse views about the fundamental meaning of freedom of speech. For Hocking, freedom of speech meant protecting the community from the media corporation. For MacLeish, it meant protecting the individual speaker from the media corporation. For Chafee, it meant protecting the individual speaker from the state. As for media corporations, Chafee believed the state could regulate their business activities but not their content; the Supreme Court agreed.

Two other members of the Hutchins Commission developed views of their own, which they espoused during discussions of monopolistic tendencies in the media. Beardsley Ruml wanted to regulate content but not business activities. In addition to requiring news organizations to submit to content regulation in exchange for the benefits of incorporation, he favored criminalizing the knowing publication of falsehoods. Otherwise, the central meaning of freedom of speech, in his eyes, was the consumer's freedom to buy cheap news and entertainment. The law professor and former anti-trust enforcer John Dickinson combined Chafee's aversion to content regulation with Ruml's aversion to business regulation. For Dickinson, the central meaning of freedom of speech was protecting the media corporation from the state.

CHAPTER TEN

Is Bigness Badness?

A s THE MEMBERS OF the Commission on Freedom of the Press probed the American media industry, *Time* later said, they "were amazed by the bigness and badness." Like many other critics of the press, they believed that much of the badness stemmed from the bigness. Newspaper companies were growing, partly because consolidation was shrinking the number of newspapers. Since 1909, the number of dailies in the United States had dropped by nearly a third, from about twenty-six hundred to about seventeen hundred; most of the drop predated the Depression. In the two years before the commission was launched, more than a hundred daily papers had shut down or merged with competitors. The number of newspaper owners was declining faster than the number of newspapers, because more and more papers were owned by chains. In *The Disappearing Daily* in 1944, Oswald Garrison Villard wrote that chain ownership could lead to homogenization of editorial positions and a loss of distinctive voices. In *The First Freedom* two years later, Morris Ernst warned that "our press is fast evaporating," raising the specter of a "dictatorship of the mind."[1]

Archibald MacLeish agreed. The concentration of ownership threatened self-government, he said, and the commission must recommend energetic enforcement of antitrust law. "I would like to see ... newspaper owners taken away from radio stations, and other combinations broken down," said MacLeish. "I would like to see absentee ownership of the press made impossible. I would like to see chains substantially broken down."[2]

At the beginning, MacLeish's views were widely shared. The first full draft of the commission's report, in 1945, called for "vigorous, continuous governmental intervention under existing statutes and, if necessary, under new statutes to prevent monopoly of mass communication ownership in any community and to maintain competition in all areas." Far from violating the First Amendment, such intervention "is directly on behalf of freedom of the press under its proper meaning"—an application of the positive First Amendment. But what enhanced press freedom in 1945 abridged it a year later. Breaking up large media corporations via antitrust law "seems to us undesirable," the commission said in 1946, and could be "very dangerous to the freedom and the effectiveness of the press." Robert Hutchins considered this retreat from antitrust law the commission's "most dramatic shift."[3]

Two commission members were largely responsible: the business executive who argued that concentrated ownership presented no problem and the antitrust lawyer who argued that antitrust law provided no solution.

Hutchins called Beardsley Ruml "the founder of the social sciences in America." Born in Iowa in 1894, Ruml received a bachelor's degree from Dartmouth College and a doctorate in psychology from the University of Chicago. In addition to intelligence testing, the topic of his dissertation, he studied nostalgia, which he considered the foundation of patriotism, a bulwark of stability in social life, and, in extreme cases, a debilitating mental illness. In 1922, he became director of a $74 million foundation, the Laura Spelman Rockefeller Memorial, where he underwrote extensive research in the social sciences. In 1930, when the University of Chicago restructured several departments into a Social Science Division, Hutchins hired Ruml as the first dean.[4]

He resigned in 1934 and took another job, not at a university or a foundation but at the R. H. Macy Co., where he served as treasurer and then chairman of the board. Maude Phelps Hutchins said that "he left ideas for notions." In the new position, Ruml remarked on the differences between a campus and a corporation. "The things that you are trying to do in the University are important," he said, "but you can't do them. The things that I am trying to do here are not important, but I can do them." He took note of another distinction, too: "If things don't work out in business, it affects profits. If things don't work out in a university, it affects nothing." Alongside the Macy's job, Ruml advised the Roosevelt administration. He was a chief architect of the pay-as-you-go policy of federal tax withholding. In addition, he became a director of the Federal Reserve Bank of New York in 1937 and chair in 1941. In a three-part profile, published in 1945, the *New Yorker* reported that Ruml "is now practically stumping the country in favor of abolishing the corporate tax."[5]

Ruml was cheerful in countenance, cynical in outlook, and epicurean in tastes. *Fortune* called him a "board-room Falstaff." Like Hutchins, he hated exercise. He once said he would set foot on a tennis court only if it stood between him and the bar. At commission meetings, he drank Manhattans out of tall water glasses. "The more he drank," staff researcher Milton Stewart would recall forty years later, "the more lyrical he became."[6]

Ruml considered big business a wellspring of liberty and order. Concentration of ownership, he argued, enhances the effectiveness, independence, and responsibility of media outlets. Consumers are better off with one or two big, profitable news organizations than with lots of small, insolvent ones. "You can get better competition between giants than you can between pygmies, because they have some fat to throw around." He suggested that the commission compare the quality of twenty profitable papers and twenty unprofitable ones. Believing that successful companies are those that serve the needs of consumers, he objected to the notion of subsidizing unprofitable media. "What does size have to do with it?" he said of a proposal to reduce postal rates for small periodicals. "The reason for the postal rates is to make it possible for people to have access to publications, and the more people who want the publication, I should say, the more justified the concession." If a media product couldn't attract a big audience, in his view, it didn't deserve one. He seemed more willing to restrict the content of the media product than the business practices of the media corporation. He proposed requiring news outlets to submit to content regulation as a condition of limited-liability corporate structure, and he suggested a constitutional amendment to exclude intentional falsehoods from First Amendment protection. Zechariah Chafee shot down both ideas.[7]

Though hostile to lying journalists, Ruml endorsed a category of government lies. Fostering national ideals, he said, could require "the deliberate use of error as if it were fact in order to portray what ought to be true." In his view, "we are probably one of the most bigoted, race-conscious peoples of the world, but it is better not to stress the fact." Accuracy might have to be balanced against other social interests. He returned to this topic several times. Reinhold Niebuhr demurred. "If you follow Ruml," he said, "you are almost demanding propaganda. It seems to me we should move in the opposite direction."[8]

Ruml eventually dropped his call for propaganda to promote national ideals, but others came to agree, at least in part, with his defense of big business. They wanted the press to stand up to pressure groups. Large companies could ignore boycott threats; small ones couldn't. Nonetheless, the commission as a whole continued to believe that concentration of ownership *could* raise dangers. *A Free and Responsible Press* says that the "great concentrations of private power" in the media can have deleterious effects and can even be "a threat to democracy." Yet the report largely rejects law as a safeguard against that threat. John Dickinson was the driving force behind the commission's shift from reliance on antitrust law to renunciation.[9]

John Sharpe Dickinson was born in 1894 in eastern Maryland. He received his AB at Johns Hopkins at nineteen, followed by a PhD at Princeton and an LLB at Harvard. The broad-shouldered, pipe-smoking Dickinson taught political science at Harvard and Princeton and then, from 1929 to 1948, law at the University of Pennsylvania. In addition to many scholarly articles, he published a treatise on administrative law, a book on economic policy, and a translation from Latin of the twelfth-century philosophical work *Policraticus*.[10]

A posthumous tribute by a University of Pennsylvania colleague, George L. Haskins, seems to damn Dickinson with effusive praise: "he would talk for hours about some obscure problem in canon law";

"the brilliance of his conversation, and the range of subjects upon which he delighted to discourse, was almost overwhelming"; "students found it hard to interrupt a veritable cascade of learning." The Roosevelt aide and future Supreme Court justice Felix Frankfurter told a colleague that Dickinson rubbed people the wrong way. In descriptions of him, the word *pompous* often appears. Behind his back, some called him "the Pope." Like his eighteenth-century ancestor and namesake, a delegate to the Constitutional Convention, Dickinson underlined his signature with a flourish.[11]

In 1933, at the invitation of the presidential adviser Raymond Moley, Dickinson joined the Roosevelt administration as assistant secretary of commerce. He soon took on a variety of additional tasks. Most notably, he helped write what FDR called "the most important and far-reaching legislation ever enacted by the American Congress," the National Industrial Recovery Act. In characteristic fashion, President Roosevelt assigned the task of drafting the bill to two teams, neither of which knew of the other's existence. One draft, prepared by General Hugh S. Johnson, former head of the Army's Purchase and Supplies Division, would enhance presidential power over industry. Dickinson favored self-regulation. He wanted industries to develop and enforce codes of economic conduct, with antitrust laws suspended to allow such collaboration. FDR then ordered the two teams to hammer out a single bill, which followed Dickinson's model in important respects. Congress passed it, and the president signed it into law. Critics charged that it was little more than a Chamber of Commerce wish list, but it was in keeping with Roosevelt's initial resistance to trust-busting. In 1934 and 1935, Dickinson went on the road defending the administration against charges of economic dictatorship. The Depression tolled the end of "rugged individualism," he said, for "today we all live by taking in one another's washing." He credited Roosevelt with "unprecedented effectiveness because of his unprecedented insight." The *Washington Post* called him "a tower of strength to the New Deal."[12]

Even so, when Dickinson's name was floated as a candidate to head the Justice Department's Antitrust Division, several of the president's senior advisers lobbied against him. Before joining the administration, Dickinson had defended the Sugar Institute in an

antitrust case and had written articles in which he called the
Sherman Act unworkable. Felix Frankfurter told the president that
Dickinson couldn't be trusted to enforce antitrust law, a charge
that found its way into the *New York Times*. A *New Republic* writer
concurred: "Mr. Dickinson would have made an excellent Assistant
Attorney General under Coolidge." FDR nominated him anyway,
and the Senate confirmed him on July 1, 1935.[13]

It was a decisive time in antitrust enforcement. The Supreme
Court had struck down the National Industrial Recovery Act a
month before Dickinson took office. The industry-wide self-regulation that he favored was no longer an option in its original form.
Yet he seemed reluctant to bring antitrust cases. In 1936, his only
full year in the position, his office filed just four, the fewest of any
year of FDR's administration. Some people began to call the Antitrust Division the Justice Department's graveyard. Dickinson defended his record. He argued that the Sherman Act was difficult to
enforce. It didn't cover some anticompetitive acts, and for those it
did cover, it set high standards of proof. (The attorney general
agreed.) He also complained that he lacked resources for adequate
enforcement. He insisted that he was fully committed to the law.[14]

Dickinson held the job through the 1936 election. Despite his
Justice Department position, he was a delegate to the Democratic
convention and helped draft the party platform. (The Hatch Act,
with its restrictions on partisan activities of federal officials, came
three years later.) He publicly announced his resignation from the
Antitrust Division on Christmas Eve, news that made the front
page of the *New York Times*. The Justice Department said he was
leaving for "urgent personal reasons," but his Penn colleague
George Haskins suspected that he felt out of step with the president's ramped-up castigation of big business. Dickinson joined the
legal staff of the Pennsylvania Railroad and returned to teaching.[15]

Antitrust enforcement remained lax under Dickinson's successor, the future Supreme Court justice Robert H. Jackson, and initially under Jackson's successor, Thurman Arnold, who took over in
March 1938. Like Dickinson, both Jackson and Arnold believed
the Antitrust Division needed more resources. In part because monopolistic practices seemed to contribute to a recession in late
1937 and 1938, antitrust became a priority for the administration,

and Arnold and his allies persuaded Congress to increase the division's funding. From less than half a million dollars during Dickinson's tenure, the annual budget swelled to $1.3 million in 1940 and 1941 and then to $2.3 million in 1942. The division filed enforcement actions in unprecedented numbers: nearly ninety in 1941 and again in 1942, versus Dickinson's 1936 total of four. In addition to the case against the Associated Press, the Justice Department brought cases against auto manufacturers, Hollywood studios, oil companies, insurance companies, the American Medical Association, the carpenters' union, and manufacturers of ice-cream sticks. Having turned against the president, Raymond Moley, the White House adviser who had recruited Dickinson, wrote that Roosevelt "lurch[ed] between the philosophy of controlling bigness and the philosophy of destroying bigness, between the belief in a partnership between government and industry and the belief in trust busting." (FDR characterized Moley's book as "kiss-ass-and-tell.") Dickinson helped manage the business-government partnership phase of the New Deal; Arnold, the trust-busting phase.[16]

As Arnold led the Antitrust Division to the left, Dickinson, like Moley, moved to the right. The conservative writer George Sokolsky, later an outspoken critic of *A Free and Responsible Press*, quoted Dickinson at length in columns, and they exchanged warm letters. Whereas in 1935 Dickinson had pronounced the end of "rugged individualism," now he called on the state to eschew "Humanitarian Absolutism" and "leave individuals to their fate." He blamed the Depression on excessive regulation and likened social planning to Nazism: "both are totalitarian, in the sense that they contemplate unlimited, or practically unlimited, government control of everything, property, natural resources, all human conduct and human relations." The principal villain behind social planning was Charles Merriam, Dickinson wrote in the *Proceedings of the American Philosophical Society* in 1943, a few months before they became colleagues on the Commission on Freedom of the Press.[17]

Dickinson's "prejudices were few," according to Haskins, "but they were deep-seated." They sometimes emerged on the Hutchins Commission. In one meeting, he declared that local discussion groups sponsored by *Reader's Digest* possessed no influence, and "nobody who is of any importance belongs" to them. Hutchins replied, "That is the most aristocratic piece of baloney I ever listened to in my life." In another meeting, Dickinson rhapsodized over dictatorship, much as Columbia president Nicholas Murray Butler had done in 1931. Electoral politics favors "very mediocre people," he maintained, so government tends to act with greater intelligence in a dictatorship. When Zechariah Chafee asked if the Nazis on trial at Nuremberg were brilliant men, Dickinson acknowledged exceptions.[18]

In place of the civic republicanism of William Ernest Hocking, Hutchins, and others on the commission, Dickinson believed in the politics of pluralism, with citizens massing in pursuit of self-interest while public officials act as brokers. He considered the concept of the public interest a self-serving fiction. Government officials in the United States believe they're advancing the public interest, he told his commission colleagues; so do government officials in the Soviet Union. "The trouble," he explained, "is that people differ about what the public interest is, and it seems to me that really the valuable thing about freedom of the press is that it does give the people a right to differ about what the public interest is and to say so."[19]

Chafee, who considered Dickinson a friend, called him "the conservative liberal." The two were allies at times. "This preliminary report bothers me a good deal and I am very grateful for your help," Chafee told him in 1944. But their viewpoints diverged. Distasteful as Chafee found agitators, radicals, dissenters, and other unpopular speakers, he sought to protect them from censorship. Dickinson seemed concerned principally with the rights of corporations. He thought that the commission's study of threats to free expression ought to include the National Labor Relations Board's restrictions on employers' antiunion speech, and he wanted the report to present a favorable depiction of the profit motive.[20]

At a meeting in July 1946, at the Waldorf-Astoria in New York, Dickinson almost single-handedly dissuaded the commission from endorsing antitrust enforcement against giant media companies. At the outset, commission members had seen antitrust law as a far-reaching remedy for the problem of media concentration. While most had abandoned that perspective, they still believed antitrust could play an important role. Accordingly, the draft report under discussion took a measured approach, recommending antitrust law "as a proper, though essentially negative, means of maintaining desirable diversity in the agencies of mass communication." Hutchins said that the recommendation in essence means that antitrust law "should be enforced where it applies."[21]

Dickinson objected. Antitrust law was no solution to ownership concentration, he maintained, for "the remedy would be worse than the disease." While in the Roosevelt administration, he had considered antitrust law so weak that it was virtually useless. Now he depicted it as a tool for tyrants. Antitrust law is worded so broadly, he said, that it can be deployed against nearly anybody. Most antitrust suits result from political pressure, and if the Justice Department could order a media company to sell some of its newspapers, it would wield vast powers of censorship. He depicted Manichean alternatives: "some form of self-regulation" or "turn the thing over to the government more or less on the Russian basis."[22]

The Hutchins Commission was behind schedule. This July meeting was supposed to be its last, but one more would be necessary to complete the report. The members had already concluded that antitrust enforcement was no panacea, contrary to the original views held by most of them. Now Dickinson insisted that antitrust law was a menace to freedom. Perhaps some members felt browbeaten by his hyperbolic arguments. In addition, he was the expert. Chafee said he didn't share Dickinson's view of the law, but, he added, "he knows a great deal more about the cases than I do." He suggested that the report avoid a detailed discussion of antitrust. "Perhaps we have been a little too favorable in the text here," he said.[23]

Archibald MacLeish, who sometimes found Dickinson "tendentious," wasn't inclined to give in. "Mr. Chairman," he said, "as an innocent little boy who once went to law school . . . I am loath to say this, but I haven't the remotest idea what this discussion is about." The draft report merely recommended that the antitrust laws be enforced as written. "The fact that some of us don't like the Supreme Court is no reason why we should all become anarchists."[24]

Hutchins said he understood that Dickinson, "the learned gentleman who is on the right in one sense and on the left in the other," opposed any endorsement of antitrust actions against media companies. Correct, said Dickinson. If the commission approved of antitrust enforcement against the media under *any* circumstances, "the Department of Justice might feel that they were being invited into some new green pastures." With Dickinson and MacLeish deadlocked, Hutchins moved on to another topic.[25]

The commission gathered again, for the last time, in September 1946. This time Dickinson was absent. Charles Merriam said that parts of the current draft of their report seemed unduly hostile toward government. He hadn't spoken out against Dickinson's position at the previous meeting, he said, "because I thought probably it did not reflect at all the general opinion of the Commission."

"That was a very long discussion," said Hutchins.[26]

MacLeish said he too disliked the implication that the commission feared government, particularly in the report's discussion of antitrust law, which had been revised in accordance with Dickinson's arguments. The draft now said that antitrust law should "be sparingly used" against the press, because statutes could be enforced in partisan ways. MacLeish wanted the recommendation reframed: antitrust enforcement against media organizations "may be desirable when you get monopoly," but it should be done "cautiously for the reasons here given."[27]

"Nobody on the Commission is opposed to the use of the antitrust laws," said Hutchins, overstating the case. "The only question is whether they should be extensively or sparingly used."[28]

MacLeish complained that the harshest statements in the report targeted antitrust law rather than irresponsible journalism. "Three times in three paragraphs we say we don't think anything ought to be done." He talked of submitting a dissenting opinion but ultimately dropped the idea.[29]

As published, *A Free and Responsible Press* largely reflects Dickinson's distrust of antitrust. The laws ought to be used "to maintain competition among large units and to prevent the exclusion of any unit from facilities which ought to be open to all"—a reference to the Associated Press case, though Dickinson thought it had been wrongly decided—but not "to force the breaking-up of large units." The report goes on to call antitrust laws "extremely vague" and "very dangerous." Antitrust enforcement "might cure the ills of freedom of the press, but only at the risk of killing the freedom in the process."[30]

The commission might have reached another conclusion if it had included a different expert on antitrust. In initial planning, Hutchins proposed Thurman Arnold as a member, though the two had a strained relationship; Hutchins had once likened Arnold to a rattle-snake, and Arnold referred to Hutchins as the Cardinal. Henry Luce said he didn't think Arnold would be a good fit for the commission, and he wasn't invited. Unlike Dickinson, Arnold was an energetic an-titrust enforcer, and he believed the law ought to be applied to the press. He brought the antitrust case against the Associated Press. In 1946, after leaving the Justice Department and then serving as a fed-eral appellate judge, Arnold praised Morris Ernst's book *The First Freedom* in the *New York Herald Tribune*. Ernst had produced "the most objective and most persuasive presentation" of the evils of con-centrated media ownership so far, he wrote, and "the tide can and must be turned" to restore competition in the press.[31]

William Ernest Hocking viewed the press from a philosophical perspective, Zechariah Chafee from a jurisprudential perspective, Archibald MacLeish from a historical perspective, and Beardsley Ruml and John Dickinson from a laissez-faire business perspective. One member argued that all of these analyses were inadequate and incomplete. It was a mistake, he said, to try to fashion remedies be-fore they fully understood the problems. According to Harold Lasswell, the Commission on Freedom of the Press was bound to fail unless it relied on the methods of social science.

CHAPTER ELEVEN

Gadgeteer

A T A MEETING OF the Commission on Freedom of the Press in April 1945, George Shuster raised a question so basic that the group had never considered it. In the midst of a conversation about limited-liability corporations, he asked, "Doesn't all this discussion assume that people are actually influenced by what the newspaper prints?" Nobody answered. The conversation moved on.[1]

Some of the men believed that mass communications can profoundly influence people. Archibald MacLeish thought that propagandists were manipulating the public with "emotional symbols and sub-rational stereotypes." In the view of William Ernest Hocking, the American system of communication is "helpless against . . . partisan propaganda." Reinhold Niebuhr believed state propaganda can engender a "fascist corruption of the public mind," though he also observed that the word *propaganda* "is used as a *Schimpfwort*"—swear word—"referring to any viewpoint we object to."[2]

Commission members were familiar with propaganda, sometimes firsthand. Charles Merriam ran the Rome office of the American Committee on Public Information in 1918. After the war, he wanted to write a book on propaganda, but the University of Chicago Press said nobody would read it. In 1944, Shuster prepared and delivered propaganda speeches for the Office of War Information to broadcast to Germans. MacLeish, at the Library of Congress, oversaw a propaganda-analysis project run by Harold Lasswell. And Lasswell, the commission's foremost expert on the subject, had published *Propaganda Technique in the World War* in 1927.[3]

Lasswell agreed with Niebuhr that propaganda lies in the eye of the beholder. If you promote communism in Chicago, said Lasswell, you're a propagandist; if you promote it in Moscow, you're a teacher. He also thought Americans tended to overstate the impact of communications media, a bias that he termed "propaganda neurosis." Unshakable distrust in media and messages, he believed, can be as bad as unshakable trust. People who consider propaganda all-powerful may conclude that truth is undiscoverable, prompting them to withdraw from public affairs. Such a development, he said, could undermine citizenship and even democracy.[4]

The impact of mass communications is largely unknown, Lasswell told his commission colleagues in 1944. Conclusions are tentative, because the field of study is so new. He had invented much of it.[5]

By some estimates the most prolific political scientist ever, Harold Dwight Lasswell wrote or edited some sixty books and three hundred articles. The American Council of Learned Societies called him "master of the social sciences and a pioneer in each." He essentially founded the fields of political psychology and policy science as well as the methodology of content analysis, and he also wrote about economics, sociology, law, anthropology, and much else. His eclecticism in research extended beyond scholarship. According to his friend William Benton, he used himself as a guinea pig to study the effects of narcotics.[6]

Lasswell was born in 1902 in Donnellson, Illinois. Like Robert Hutchins and Henry Luce, he was the son of a Presbyterian minister. He enrolled at the University of Chicago at sixteen and stayed on to get his PhD under Charles Merriam, who helped get him an appointment as assistant professor. In the book based on his dissertation, *Propaganda Technique in the World War*, Lasswell characterized propaganda as "one of the most powerful instrumentalities in the modern world." (He later changed his mind.) In 1928, funded by the Social Science Research Council, he studied the interview techniques of psychoanalysts in Vienna and Berlin; one of Freud's students, Theodor Reik, took him on as an analysand. Back in the United States, Lasswell arranged special discounts for his students at the Chicago Institute for Psychoanalysis.[7]

Lasswell, like his mentor Merriam, for a time believed that the trouble with democracy was the citizenry. "Familiarity with the ruling public," he wrote, "has bred contempt." As a step toward "control[ling] the public in the interest of ... sound policy," he sought a fuller understanding of voters' personalities via lengthy questionnaires that asked about masturbation, bed wetting, dreams, fantasies, and phobias. Again like Merriam, Lasswell by the 1940s had backed away from his more antidemocratic views. "In these trying days, we must rely more than ever upon the proper functioning of public opinion for the preservation of democracy," he wrote in 1941. Now he sought ways to help the masses rather than sideline them. Instead of deploying propaganda, he wanted social scientists to train citizens to spot its chicanery. He also proposed requiring that books and articles hostile to democracy bear a warning label, which would explain the danger and identify "a suitable antidote." Such a rule wouldn't infringe on free speech, he maintained, but would be a "regulatory measure that *preserves* free speech"—an application of the positive First Amendment.[8]

Great Books devotee Robert Hutchins couldn't abide social science. "The gadgeteers and the data collectors, masquerading as scientists, have threatened to become the supreme chieftains of the scholarly world," he wrote. Worst was the "pompous triviality" of the quantitative studies that were Lasswell's specialty. In 1938, Hutchins refused to promote him to full professor at the University of Chicago, and he resigned.[9]

Thereafter Lasswell took on a wide range of projects and consultancies. In 1939, at William Benton's urging, Henry Luce paid him $300 for a memo summarizing what was wrong with *Time*. Quite a bit, Lasswell reported: with its all-knowing cynicism, the magazine cheapened human life and eroded the sense of trust that links individuals to the community. He took on such piecework to avoid the necessity of self-censorship. With multiple projects and multiple paymasters, he said, "I am more free to express ruthlessly candid judgments, free of 'collegial' restraint." He also taught at Yale Law School, first as a visiting lecturer and then as a professor.[10]

Lasswell was tall, heavy-set, and idiosyncratic. A former student, Leo Rosten, recalled him as egotistical and awkward, self-sufficient in solitude but convivial in company, reticent about personal matters but voluble about ideas, and capable of delivering "three- to five-hour monologues that remain the most extraordinary exhibitions of brilliance and non-alcoholic inebriation I have ever heard." Rosten once asked the father of the fox-hedgehog model, Isaiah Berlin, how he would categorize Lasswell. Berlin replied, "Queer duck," and did not elaborate. Lasswell seemed to view humanity from afar, according to Rosten, with a sort of quizzical fondness, though not *all* humanity. Sloppy and shallow thinkers elicited his sarcasm. Another former student speculated that Lasswell may have had himself in mind when he quoted Albert Einstein: "My passionate interest in social justice and social responsibility has always stood in curious contrast to a marked lack of desire for direct association with men and women."[11]

Lasswell was notorious for jargon-clotted writing. Reviewing his *World Politics and Personal Insecurity* in the *American Political Science Review* in 1935, a critic wrote that "it is hard to see how our universities can help our laboring, lumbering democracy by telling people what they know in language they will not understand." Lasswell joked about his prose, calling one of his books an "experiment in clarity" and, in the preface to another book, thanking a colleague for a "courageous though losing battle on behalf of readability."[12]

After Lasswell left the University of Chicago, he moved to Washington, DC. The truck bringing his belongings crashed and burned in Michigan, killing one man and severely injuring another. Authorities at first suspected "a communistic element" behind the accident, according to the *Chicago Tribune*, when they found charred pamphlets such as "The Bolshevik Revolution" and "Fundamentals of Communism" around the truck—Lasswell's propaganda research.[13]

Despite the misfortune, the new location proved propitious. In 1940, Lasswell became chief of the Experimental Division for the

Study of War Time Communications, housed in the Library of Congress and largely funded by the Rockefeller Foundation. The project, Lasswell wrote, aimed "to perfect tools of research on mass communication" and "to recruit and train personnel for service in the agencies of propaganda, information, and intelligence." He created a center for analyzing media alleged to be pro-Axis, domestic as well as foreign. Content analysis turned out to be much in demand across the federal government, and Lasswell's many clients included the State Department, the Office of Facts and Figures (and its successor, the Office of War Information), the FCC's Foreign Broadcast Intelligence Service, the Psychological Warfare Branch of the Army, the Justice Department's Special War Policies Unit, and the bureau of the U.S. Post Office that barred seditious materials from the mails. He worked with two others later associated with the Hutchins Commission: Librarian of Congress Archibald MacLeish, who also headed the Office of Facts and Figures, and Robert Leigh, who headed the Foreign Broadcast office at the FCC. When Lasswell's services were in peak demand, he had a staff of more than fifty and, according to Leigh, operated in "an atmosphere of great secrecy."[14]

Lasswell's content analysis helped send people to jail, based on the theory that those who sound like Nazis are, perforce, Nazis, much as Senator Joseph McCarthy would later assert that those who sound like communists are, perforce, communists. As an expert witness in 1942, Lasswell testified that 1,195 passages in William Dudley Pelley's *Galilean* magazine matched Axis propaganda themes. Pelley was convicted of sedition and sentenced to fifteen years in prison. The U.S. Court of Appeals for the Seventh Circuit upheld the reliance on Lasswell's guilt-by-rhetorical-association analysis. In another case, Lasswell testified that a news agency, Transocean, was distorting information in a pro-Nazi direction; he used the *New York Times* as his neutral baseline. In a subsequent case, he compared allegedly seditious magazines to the *Saturday Evening Post* and *Reader's Digest.*[15]

As part of the administration's efforts to silence Robert McCormick, Lasswell and his staff applied the same methodology to the *Chicago Tribune.* The *Tribune*'s anti-Roosevelt themes, they found, overlapped with the anti-America themes of the Axis. Both contended that communists ran the U.S. government, that FDR was corrupt, and that the administration was bungling the war effort. A Justice Department attorney recommended indicting the *Tribune* for sedition. Intent, said the attorney, didn't matter: "Whether this is deliberately contrived by seditious elements or is the honest view of patriotic but blind Americans is of minor importance; the result is the same." The attorney general declined to prosecute.[16]

Although Lasswell testified in criminal trials, he preferred to work backstage. "As you know," he told Benton in 1942, "I am a perpetual adviser, a man of words and not of acts."[17]

Hutchins, despite his disdain for Lasswell's content studies, recruited him for the Commission on Freedom of the Press—at forty-one, he became the youngest member—and paid him $650 a month to handle administrative duties until staff director Leigh joined full-time. Before the second meeting, Lasswell distributed a forty-five-page list of fifty-four numbered topics for discussion, "obviously tentative and incomplete," including newspaper-owned radio stations, group libel, anonymous speech, personal privacy, crisis communication, pressure groups, securities regulation, juries, civil service, soap operas, and dances. One recipient was nonplussed. The list "covers almost the whole of American life," Zechariah Chafee told Lasswell. He added, "If you will pardon me for saying so, I think that you are inclined to make a broader swing in your projects than is quite practicable." He said he hoped their final report would avoid Lasswell's technical jargon, too, lest it "bewilder and repel readers."[18]

As with Lasswell's list of topics, he wanted the commission's report to set forth a wide variety of potential remedies, even if some were "a little eccentric or crackpot in their character." Maybe, he suggested, the government could require monopoly newspapers to publish material "centrally edited by a government commission," subsidize start-up newspapers on condition that they make space available to community organizations, shut down newspapers if their editorial pages were one-sided, require journalists to be licensed, or publish its own newspaper on the model of the Tennessee Valley Authority. Even if the commission didn't recommend such "hellfire" options, he said, they might be presented as "devices that society might regretfully adopt under certain circumstances." Other members generally resisted Lasswell's policy notions. "I have some qualms about the Lasswell proposal," Hutchins said of requiring monopoly papers to publish government-edited material. "First, it seems a little mechanical, and second, I am sure it is unconstitutional." Hutchins also rejected Lasswell's idea of setting forth a broad array of possible actions. He wanted to issue a set of recommendations ready for implementation, not a list of experiments worth trying.[19]

In meetings and memos, Lasswell stressed that the commission needed to be informed, systematic, and precise. When Niebuhr spoke of the "vulgarity of the media," Lasswell asked if "vulgar" was a technical term. Niebuhr said he would include "vapid" as well as "vulgar." Lasswell replied that it was important to "define terms in such a way that purely aesthetic considerations would be ruled out." He also thought it essential to undertake original research. No one would try to analyze the economy without data; the same should be true of analyzing the mass media. He told colleagues that they mustn't base their conclusions solely on "a variety of personal anecdotes, partially authentic instances, a few well-studied cases, and folklore." They were admonishing journalists not to publish falsehoods and half-truths; they must apply the same standards to their own work. For a bird's-eye view of mass communication in the United States, he recommended sampling news from different periods, as disseminated by different media, addressing different audiences, in communities of different sizes. They should devote half of their budget to research. The guiding question, he wrote, ought to be, "Who says what in what channel with what effect on whom?"[20]

The staff agreed. At the FCC, Robert Leigh had relied on Lasswell's content studies, and he assumed that the commission would do the same. So did the commission's two researchers at the time, Ruth Inglis and Milton Stewart, both of whom had published quantitative studies of media content.[21]

Hutchins, however, believed the commission's mission was not to assemble data but to develop a philosophical analysis. He told Inglis, "I do not believe that research can give us the facts," a statement she found so remarkable that she quoted it to friends. After others kept pushing, especially Leigh, Hutchins grudgingly approved one quantitative project: a book-length content study of news coverage, to be written by Stewart with an introduction by Lasswell. It was more than Hutchins wanted but far less than Lasswell and the staff believed they needed. "My part of the work is interesting to me and I have enjoyed it," Inglis told a friend, "but the Commission as a whole has been somewhat of a disappointment. Their lack of interest in research is appalling." Later, she charged that the commission "preferred to meander in vague philosophical generalities rather than do the dirty hard work of digging for facts."[22]

In January 1946, after two years in operation, the commission spent an evening with two experts on media effects: Inglis's mentor Paul F. Lazarsfeld, of the Bureau of Applied Social Research at Columbia, and Erich Fromm, a professor at Bennington College and the author of the 1941 book *Escape from Freedom*. As was frequently the case, Robert Hutchins was absent.[23]

Over dinner at the Carlyle Hotel in New York, Robert Leigh opened the discussion by asking the guests to summarize "the impact, effect and significance of symbols as used by mass communication." "It is hard to know where to begin," replied Fromm.[24]

Lazarsfeld raised a couple of issues. People, he said, "expose themselves only to those things which reinforce their opinions. . . . The Democrats listen only to Democrats and the Republicans listen only to Republicans." Additional complications arise from the economic structure of the mass media. To maximize profits, media organizations try to maximize the audience, but the information citizens need for self-government may not attract the biggest audience. He wondered how commission members were approaching this pivotal issue. Were they exploring ways of decoupling news from the commercial marketplace? Or were they merely asking what marginal improvements might be feasible within a commercial system? Nobody answered.[25]

MacLeish asked whether information had to be dramatized in order to influence the citizenry. Picking up the theme, John Dickinson wondered whether, with the rise of mass literacy, many citizens would ignore issues in public affairs unless they were dramatized. The commission members may have hoped to hear that citizens can learn without drama; instead they were told that citizens, at least the unmotivated ones, can't learn even with it. "A fellow who doesn't give a damn about public affairs," Lazarsfeld said, "smells the educational racket in a dramatized discourse." To get people interested, "you must give it to them in personalized form; you must give it to them closely attached to their experience of every day; you must give it to them in extremely simple form; and you must always . . . link it up with pressures from outside the media." Media effects are dwarfed by the effects of unmediated, in-person contacts. Perhaps only 20 percent of the audience pays attention to news about public affairs, Lazarsfeld said; but they "really absorb it," and they in turn provide "the foundation for the 80 percent who will not absorb it."[26]

In the course of the evening, Lazarsfeld and Fromm said the media weren't omnipotent manipulators of opinion and corruptors of taste, and by the same token, ideal media, media that matched the commission's highest aspirations, wouldn't do much to clarify opinion or raise taste. Both experts also questioned whether the press could be significantly improved within an audience-maximizing, for-profit system. As the discussion neared its end, Lasswell complimented the "clear addition to the analysis which has been presented modestly and succinctly by [the] distinguished witnesses." Some of the other commission members, though, were dismissive. Charles Merriam said that Lazarsfeld and Fromm had told him nothing new. Every successful speaker tries to connect with the audience. "Those are old textbooks." Whereas Merriam found the lessons obvious, William Ernest Hocking considered them wrongheaded. If people care only about matters that directly affect them, how can the jury system work? "I just wish to record my belief," he said, "that the peculiarity of the human animal is that he can be interested in things that don't concern him." After a few desultory exchanges, the meeting broke up.[27]

Earlier, in a letter to MacLeish, Leigh had made a shrewd observation. It would be interesting, he said, to see whether "the Commission itself will be able to absorb and evaluate the insights of these specialists on a rational rather than on a sub-rational level." The answer turned out to be no. Most commission members continued to believe that the mass media have powerful effects. In their own minds, this belief may have enhanced the value of their communal undertaking. The more powerful the media, the more vital the work of the Commission on Freedom of the Press. Accordingly, their final report says that media represent "instruments of incredible range and power," capable of "molding the minds of men." The evening's discussion seemed to underscore one of Lazarsfeld's points: when information clashes with deep-rooted preconceptions, the audience tends to reject it.[28]

Though Lasswell mostly kept his propensity for sarcasm in check, it occasionally revealed itself, once on the question of research. Six months after the dinner with Lazarsfeld and Fromm, commission members discussed how the law might punish people who spread falsehoods in the media.

Beardsley Ruml outlined possible levels of culpability. Whereas one speaker may knowingly lie, another may spread falsehoods out of negligence. "The information was available," Ruml said, "if he had only taken the trouble to find it out. I would call it lying in the second degree."

Lasswell, believing that the Commission on Freedom of the Press was operating without the necessary data, proposed a different term for what Ruml called second-degree lying.

"That," said Lasswell, "is what I call a Commission report."[29]

Time Inc. editor in chief Henry Luce wanted a restatement of freedom of the press, so he underwrote the greatest collaboration of public intellectuals in the twentieth century, the Commission on Freedom of the Press. (© Yousuf Karsh)

Life sent a photographer to a meeting of the Commission on Freedom of the Press in July 1946, at the Waldorf-Astoria Hotel in New York City: *from left*, social-scientist-turned-business executive Beardsley Ruml, political scientist Charles E. Merriam, Robert D. Leigh (director of the research staff), economist John M. Clark, University of Chicago chancellor Robert Maynard Hutchins (chair), Ruth A. Inglis (staff researcher), Hunter College president George N. Shuster, philosopher William Ernest Hocking, Llewellyn White (staff researcher), historian Arthur Schlesinger Sr., First Amendment scholar Zechariah Chafee Jr., filmmaker John Grierson (foreign adviser), and poet and playwright Archibald MacLeish. (Cornell Capa / The LIFE Picture Collection / Getty Images)

After Robert Maynard Hutchins became president of the University of
Chicago in 1929, age thirty, he eliminated the championship football
program, fashioned a new curriculum around the Great Books, inveighed
against vocational education in general and schools of journalism in
particular, and considered running for president. (Special Collections
Research Center, University of Chicago Library)

Maude Phelps Hutchins, an avant-garde artist and writer, kept her distance from the university community. (Special Collections Research Center, University of Chicago Library)

With funding—ultimately $200,000—from Luce, Hutchins (shown here with University of Chicago students), organized the Commission on Freedom of the Press at the end of 1943. (Special Collections Research Center, University of Chicago Library)

Librarian of Congress Archibald MacLeish, a Pulitzer-winning poet and playwright (here with Franklin and Eleanor Roosevelt), maintained that the First Amendment had become a dead letter, because everyday citizens no longer could be heard over the din of the mass media. (Harris & Ewing, courtesy of the Franklin D. Roosevelt Library)

According to the philosopher William Ernest Hocking, too many Americans lacked the fundamental underpinning of intellectual morality, a "willingness to listen to the other side." (1943; Lilo Kaskell, photographer; UAV 605 Box 6, Harvard University Archives)

Harvard law professor Zechariah Chafee Jr. acknowledged serious problems with the American press, but he maintained that regulation would only worsen the situation. (Harvard Law School Library, Historical & Special Collections)

The theologian Reinhold Niebuhr believed that American democracy was facing its gravest crisis ever, with citizens fragmenting into hostile factions and partisan media outlets acting as enablers. (Portrait by Bachrach Photography; University Archives, Rare Book & Manuscript Library, Columbia University Libraries)

In the 1930s, the University of Chicago political scientist Charles E. Merriam argued that social scientists and other experts ought to replace "jungle governors"—politicians—in the development of public policy. (Special Collections Research Center, University of Chicago Library)

During the war, the propaganda expert Harold D. Lasswell dissected news coverage to ascertain which media might be advancing the interests of the Axis. (Special Collections Research Center, University of Chicago Library)

Beardsley Ruml left a deanship at the University of Chicago to become an executive of Macy's department stores. He believed that the government should use domestic propaganda to "preserve the illusion of democracy." (Courtesy of the Rockefeller Archive Center)

As director of the staff, Robert D. Leigh overspent the budget, feuded with one of the researchers, and tried to claim credit for the commission's accomplishments. (Special Collections Research Center, University of Chicago Library)

The adman-turned-philanthropist William Benton toned down passages in *A Free and Responsible Press* before publication. (Harris & Ewing Collection, Library of Congress)

After *A Free and Responsible Press* received harsh reviews, researcher Llewellyn White said that those who were associated with the commission had become, in the eyes of the public, "assassins of the press." (FPG / Archive Photos / Getty Images)

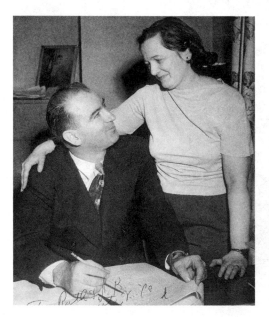

A few years after working for the commission, researcher Ruth A. Inglis, the only woman associated with the project, befriended Senator Joseph McCarthy (shown here), added names to the Hollywood blacklist, and urged the House Un-American Activities to investigate Robert Hutchins. (Courtesy of Martin Matthews)

The columnist Walter Lippmann called *A Free and Responsible Press* a model of press criticism, "brave, and often brilliant." (Harris & Ewing Collection, Library of Congress)

Robert Rutherford McCormick, publisher of the *Chicago Tribune*, said that *A Free and Responsible Press* was the work of "pinko professors" plotting to eviscerate the First Amendment, "paid for by $200,000 from Henry Luce and two cents from Robert Hutchins." (Col. R. R. McCormick Research Center)

CHAPTER TWELVE

Beguiling the Dragon

"I AM VERY MUCH distressed by the whole progress of this Commission's work," said Robert Hutchins in 1946, "because I began with such a simple answer to all these questions." The Commission on Freedom of the Press had identified many problems but few solutions. The members rejected anything approaching the far-reaching industrial planning that Charles Merriam had advocated in the 1930s. Though with several dissenters, most notably Archibald MacLeish, they largely rejected lesser methods of enforcing responsibility through law, too. Rather than "St. George killing the dragon," said Reinhold Niebuhr, "we are trying to beguile the dragon from some of his more obvious forms of depredation."[1]

Commission members considered two broad categories of beguilement. The first consisted of ways to encourage the creation of media outlets structured to produce better journalism—nonprofit, educational, or governmental. The second category consisted of ways to prod the owners and managers of the existing for-profit media to do better. The prodding might come from within the industry, broadly defined, through self-regulation, professionalism, mutual criticism, training, or the introduction of academic models into the newsroom; or from the outside, through pressure groups, universities, the onetime guidance of the commission, or the ongoing guidance of a press council.

Commission members believed that business considerations unduly influenced news organizations, partly because of advertising, but they rejected the theory that advertisers control news coverage. More insidious, they believed, was the press's habit of kowtowing to its audience in pursuit of profit. The members discussed the creation of media outlets operating on endowments, though they decided against recommending it in their report. (Niebuhr suggested endowed movie theaters, too.) They also talked about nonprofit media outlets run by foundations, libraries, religious organizations, and, especially, universities, which might cater to audiences whose tastes were ignored by mainstream outlets. Some members were enthusiastic, but not Hutchins. "To whom is this [recommendation] addressed?" he asked. "If this is addressed to me as chief executive of the University of Chicago, I say the hell with it." A few years earlier, he said, he had met with CBS president William Paley to propose that the network broadcast educational programs produced by the university. Paley declined, according to Hutchins, "because it might be good and, if it was good, then he couldn't get rid of it" if an advertiser wanted the time slot. "If we could have guaranteed a bad program, he might have taken it. . . . At that point I wrote off commercial broadcasting as an educational medium." As published, *A Free and Responsible Press* declares that nonprofits, including educational institutions, libraries, and religious organizations, ought to run more media outlets, but they "should not be expected to do the whole job." Commercial media must also support "activities of high literary, artistic, or intellectual quality."[2]

As another possible alternative to for-profit media, the commission considered options for government-funded information services. Two were relatively straightforward, and the commission recommended both. First, if private media fell short, the government ought to provide news about the United States to foreign audiences. The international flow of information is the topic of a commission-sponsored book, *Peoples Speaking to Peoples*, by Llewellyn White and Robert D. Leigh. Second, again if private media fell short, the government ought to inform citizens directly about its policies. Merriam said, "It is necessary to get away from the idea that any government document is pure propaganda."[3]

Several commission members thought the government might go beyond publicizing its own activities and operate full-fledged media outlets serving American audiences. Government-owned or -managed media had been tried a few times in the United States, including the *Municipal News*, a newspaper operated by a city commission in Los Angeles from 1912 to 1913, and WNYC Radio, launched by New York City in 1924. At the outset of World War II, the Roosevelt administration briefly considered taking control of NBC's Blue Network. "The state may itself enter the field of news supply," William Ernest Hocking wrote, "not to compete with or to displace, but to supplement the yield of private agencies." Niebuhr brought up the government-funded British Broadcasting Corporation. "We ought at least to show that this kind of a setup has got some very definite advantages over our completely competitive and highly commercialized proposition," he said, though he acknowledged a "justified fear of government broadcasting in the domestic scene." Foreign adviser John Grierson also endorsed the concept. He started writing a book on the topic for the commission, called *The Voice of the State*, but never completed it. Even Zechariah Chafee was open to the idea of government-run media outlets, but he doubted they would make much difference. "The evils of bigness," he wrote, "will persist in a big government newspaper, unless indeed it is so unenterprising and dull as to be unread."[4]

Another possibility was a program of subsidizing some media outlets, such as start-ups or those serving niche audiences, either directly with government funding or indirectly with reduced postal rates or taxes. That idea had prominent supporters, including Morris Ernst. On the commission, George Shuster, the former managing editor of *Commonweal*, favored subsidies for small magazines. Beardsley Ruml and John Dickinson generally opposed them as unwarranted interference with the free market. Chafee also disapproved. "Subsidies are like spectacles," he said. "Once you get to depend on them, you cannot live without them." Dependency would make subsidized media organizations vulnerable to manipulation, he maintained, and "control of the press by party in power is the greatest of all dangers to its freedom."[5]

A Free and Responsible Press says the government does not endanger press freedom by using media facilities "to state its own case, to supplement private sources of information, and to propose standards for private emulation." The notion of proposing standards seems to refer to government-run domestic media; the report says that "the Commission has given little consideration" to it, but the WNYC example suggests one approach if private media prove inadequate. The report also calls for "facilitating in every way short of subsidy the creation of new units in the industry," though despite Chafee's objections, it does approve of indirect subsidies for media start-ups through reduced tax or postal rates.[6]

Whatever role nonprofit and government-run media might play, commission members recognized that the vast majority of Americans would get their information from for-profit corporations. Hutchins pushed the others to admit that high quality and high profits might not go together. He wanted to say that if all media organizations tried to meet the commission's standards of performance, some might go bankrupt, but "the industry as a whole can succeed." Others agreed. "Are we ... trying to kid ourselves with the idea that no real financial sacrifice would be involved?" wrote John M. Clark. "I'd be willing to face this possibility." If corporate capitalism stood in the way of high-quality media, perhaps they should take a hard look at capitalism. Harold Lasswell said, "Let us frankly pose the problem: To what extent can we get a free press and retain private ownership?" Paul Lazarsfeld and Erich Fromm, dining with the commission in 1946, also talked of the deleterious effects of the press's for-profit underpinnings.[7]

The tension between viewing audience members as consumers— mere "buying machines," in Grierson's phrase—and viewing them as citizens was a topic worth exploring. Instead, the commission brushed it aside. *A Free and Responsible Press* notes the contention that "the variety, quantity, and quality of information and discussion which we expect from the press cannot be purveyed at a profit." The report inflates the argument to straw-man proportions—"if the press tries to rise higher than the interests and tastes of the mass audience ... it will be driven into bankruptcy, and its existence as a private business will be at an end"—and, unsurprisingly, rejects it: "We have weighed the evidence carefully and do not accept this theory. As the example of many ventures in the communications industry shows, good practice in the interest of public enlightenment is good business as well." Will the companies make as much money as before? *A Free and Responsible Press* never addresses the question directly, but it suggests that the answer is no. In the discussion of antitrust law, the report says that media organizations should be allowed to collaborate to raise standards, "even though they result in higher costs."[8]

Throughout, commission members talked of the need for the press to behave more responsibly, though they struggled to find an enforcement mechanism. When Merriam spoke of *accountability*, MacLeish said the word has "magic"; it might be "the greatest contribution thus far made to the solution to our problem." But, he added, it raised important questions. "To whom is this accountability owed? Before what body can the owners and controllers of the press be called to account?"[9]

Industry self-regulation seemed unpromising. The American Society of Newspaper Editors had a strong ethics code, but nobody had ever been punished for violating it. The concerns of the American Newspaper Publishers Association were limited to business practices and profits. In other media, only Hollywood had meaningful self-regulation, the Hays Code, which the commission believed led to insipid movies. "We don't like the results," said MacLeish, "but as a matter of self-regulation, it is a honey."[10]

In place of formal mechanisms of judgment and punishment, Beardsley Ruml brought up informal mechanisms of reputation and prestige, the judgment of one's peers, which, in his view, could influence the decisions of business leaders. "At a certain point," he said, "you are sufficiently free to make an alternate choice to the profit motive in order to maintain the respect of the people from whom you want respect." MacLeish said he hoped they could come up with something more rigorous. Accountability to one's fellow publishers, he said, "washes out into pretty thin water." Researcher Llewellyn White, a longtime journalist, believed Ruml was right: publishers' yearning for approval from peers could be a powerful lever of change. He thought the other commission members reflexively dismissed Ruml's observations as "alcoholic exhibitionism."[11]

The members had more hope for a different system of peer judgment, professionalization, which Chafee defined as "self-regulation which works well by our standards." Since the turn of the century, reformers had promoted professionalization as a means of leavening the pursuit of profits with a sense of public responsibility. One of the markers of a profession, the future Supreme Court justice Louis Brandeis said in 1912, was that "the amount of financial return is not the accepted measure of success." Professionalism also lay behind Merriam's idea of scientific politics, though the goal there was to sever performance from partisanship rather than from profit.[12]

The professionalism model doesn't precisely fit journalism. Professionals generally provide services one-on-one rather than to a large audience. In addition, inept and corrupt doctors and lawyers can be ejected from their professions, but not journalists. Further, newspaper articles pass through many hands, and, says *A Free and Responsible Press*, "the employer, not the writer, takes the responsibility." Yet commission members believed that even without the formal structures of a profession, the rhetoric of professionalism could be helpful, by exhorting journalists to adhere to high standards despite the pressures of the marketplace. The report dismisses the idea that "the test of public service is financial success." The problems of restructuring journalism as a profession are "perhaps insurmountable," it says, but "there are some things which a truly professional man will not do for money."[13]

Another element of professionalization is education, a topic on which Hutchins held implacable views. He had long criticized vocational education in general and journalism education in particular. In a draft of the report, he called journalism schools "a low form of academic life." It was, he claimed, the only place he expressed his own judgment rather than the commission's. Colleagues objected, so he softened it.[14]

In the final meeting, journalism education sparked the sharpest argument of the commission's two-and-a-half-year tenure, sharper even than the debates over antitrust law. George Shuster was president of Hunter College, a women's school (later coed) that offered journalism courses, and he defended them. A class in news writing, he said, can substitute for the usual required class in English composition.

"What a choice!" said Hutchins. "They both ought to be abolished."

If they took such a stance in their report, Shuster replied, "we may justly be criticized for being a bit snobbish and high-brow." Around 120 Hunter graduates had worked for New York newspapers in recent years, and all but two had taken journalism classes. "That does seem to indicate you have got to give the undergraduate some kind of training."

"I don't see that that indicates anything," said Hutchins. A professional school is justified only for professions with unique intellectual content, and journalism doesn't qualify. More than six hundred colleges and universities were offering courses in radio announcing and other "half-baked stuff," he said, "a very dangerous trend" that "will further disrupt the already disrupted educational institutions of the country."

Shuster reiterated his support for at least a few technical and skills classes in journalism.

"I have no objection to your proposal," said Hutchins, "except that it will ruin the education of the young people who have to experience it at Hunter College. The extent to which you insist that a girl going into journalism should take journalism courses at Hunter, to that extent you limit her educational opportunities."

Shuster said mildly, "Well, I don't think that is necessarily so."

Hutchins replied, "I will bet you $100,000 of Mr. Rockefeller's money that it is so." (John D. Rockefeller was the University of Chicago's founding benefactor.)

MacLeish suggested it was time to move on to other topics. "Ruml and I, non-teachers, think enough attention has been paid to this matter." If the educators wanted to continue the debate, he said, they should do so in footnotes to the report.

Shuster, seemingly cowed, withdrew his objection.[15]

A Free and Responsible Press expresses the Hutchins view of journalism schools. "With few exceptions they fall short of professional standards," it says. The schools teach "the tricks and machinery of the trade," whereas the practice of responsible journalism requires "the broadest and most liberal education" to train students "in the exercise of judgment on public affairs." In addition, true professional schools act as "independent centers of criticism," unlike journalism schools. The report calls on universities to launch "academic-professional centers of advanced study, research, and publication in the field of communications," including graduate education. It also recommends that universities consider nontraditional models of educating journalists, such as the Nieman fellowships at Harvard, the program once headed by MacLeish.[16]

When discussing ways to encourage better performance from the press, some commission members cited models from academia. A staff document proposed a right for journalists to have their words published unchanged, though editors could respond in print. Hutchins suggested guaranteeing newsroom employees substantial independence after a probationary period. A near-final draft of the report says, "We do not suggest that reporters should acquire the life tenure which the higher grades of university faculty enjoy; we should suppose that three-year contracts would be sufficient." In the typewritten draft of the report sent to Henry Luce, the sentence about tenure for reporters is crossed out. Luce wrote in the margin, "thank God this out."[17]

Some of those who were associated with the commission also believed that journalists ought to pay more attention to professors. At the commission's first meeting, foreign adviser Hu Shih faulted journalists for their "slavery to the public demand." Why, he asked, did Rudolph Valentino's death in 1926 receive *far* more attention in the press than the death, one day earlier, of Harvard president Charles W. Eliot? They also lamented Hollywood's stereotyping of college professors. Several members wanted journalists to invite academics to provide expert analysis of the news of the day. Niebuhr thought the press not only should publish the opinions of academics but should pay them, at least modestly: "Jack Benny gets thousands upon thousands, but the experts are expected to do this thing free." Ultimately, though, they opted not to say anything in the report about restructuring journalism along the lines of academia or expanding news coverage of professors. Merriam cautioned against what he described as "glorification of our own profession."[18]

MacLeish wanted to slam journalists for failing to cover libel suits, government investigations of news organizations' improper business practices, and "rumors, reports and charges of scandal and malpractice in the press." In his view, "press criticism of the press is forbidden."[19]

One of the most prominent and prolific press critics of the day, George Seldes, repeatedly tried to catch the commission's attention. He offered to share "what is probably the most complete file of evidence of the corruption of the American press that exists." Although his name appeared on an early list of potential witnesses, the commission ended up ignoring him. Seldes's evidence "does not hold up," Robert Leigh said, and "we just cannot do business with him." After the report appeared, Seldes told an audience that he had offered to provide so much proof of corruption that the commission could have produced "a 100-million word report." Commission member John Clark, also at the event, replied, "I think that's what frightened us."[20]

Some members of the commission were reluctant to emphasize self-criticism within the press. John Dickinson considered it "perfectly natural and normal" for people in a field to avoid criticizing one another. To several others, it seemed too trivial a point to qualify as a recommendation. But MacLeish remained adamant. As head of the Office of Facts and Figures, he had called on other newspapers to criticize the *Chicago Tribune*, to little effect. Now he said that the discussion of mutual criticism in the draft report is "one of the few places where you really drive the knife in." The others acquiesced. *A Free and Responsible Press* recommends that "members of the press engage in vigorous mutual criticism" by pointing out "the mistakes and errors, the frauds and crimes," and the "gross departures from truthfulness" of other news organizations, in part as a substitute for a formal mechanism for disciplining wrongdoers.[21]

Commission members believed the press would respond to external pressure, for better or worse. They classed most pressure groups under "worse." Hutchins and others viewed them as greater threats to the press than government censorship. As on many topics, researcher Ruth Inglis disagreed. She viewed pressure groups as a legitimate form of democratic participation. "Those citizens who take an active part in social life," she wrote, "align themselves with others of their kind and together try to do something about what concerns them, and presto! you have a pressure group." She acknowledged that the groups might at times force their views on others, but her solution was to empower more groups with varying viewpoints. In her commission book, *Freedom of the Movies*, she praised the effectiveness of the Legion of Decency's threats to boycott films it deemed immoral, and she suggested that liberal groups learn from its example. Though she was free to express her own views in *Freedom of the Movies*, she didn't persuade the commission.[22]

A Free and Responsible Press presents a largely negative depiction of pressure groups. Although they "often correct unconscious bias or mistakes and bring into view neglected areas of discussion," they "are quite as likely to have bad influence as good" by "impairing the free interchange of news and ideas." The report adds, "we are not in favor of a revolt"—that is, a boycott demanding better service from the press—because "we cannot tell what direction a revolt might take; it might lead to government control or to the emasculation of the First Amendment." The report does repeat one recommendation, from staff researcher Llewellyn White's book on radio, that calls for "organizations of listeners in the communities" to push for higher-quality broadcasting. How such organizations differ from pressure groups is not explained.[23]

Commission members believed that external pressure could be brought to bear for positive reasons, such as the pressure they themselves aimed to bring with their report. But they worried that *A Free and Responsible Press* wouldn't be enough. Increasingly, they were drawn to the idea of a well-funded nonprofit organization that would report annually on the press's performance. By September 1945, this press council had become the commission's "single remedy for all ills," said Hutchins. (The commission didn't call it a press council, but Hutchins later used the term.) Fundamentally, the organization appealed to the men as a way to achieve regulation without involving the state. One document refers to it as "non-governmental but essentially public." The press council also promised to extend the reach of the commission itself. In an interview, Hutchins later said that journalists would have to pay attention to an ongoing press council and its annual reports, whereas they could dismiss the one-shot report of the commission by saying that "everybody on it is a liar, a thief, or a professor."[24]

Though commission members spoke of the organization as "a body of citizens," they envisaged it led by elites much like themselves: "public-spirited citizens of known repute," including civic leaders, lawyers, history professors, university presidents, and "other expertly-trained academicians." At times they linked the Commission on Freedom of the Press to the proposed organization by referring to it as the "continuing commission." They expected media companies to fund the press council's annual budget of $300,000 to $500,000, just as Time Inc. had funded their own work, with a ten-year trial run followed by an assessment of its record.[25]

A Free and Responsible Press assigns the press council eleven overlapping tasks, including developing ideals of performance (MacLeish wanted it to determine "the range of opinions and points of view . . . which a truly diversified and representative press ought to present"), promoting media projects that appeal to niche audiences, assessing coverage of minority groups, investigating "press lying" (Ruml proposed awarding prizes for the biggest lies), monitoring government actions involving the media, encouraging university research on communications, and publicizing its work. Hutchins wondered if they were assigning more duties than private philanthropy could afford; "only the taxpayer could support it."[26]

Some commission members raised questions about the impact of the press council. Newspapers might refuse to publish its findings. It might pull its punches for fear of libel suits. Efforts to debunk misinformation might merely spread it. Niebuhr wondered how the council would differ from the nineteenth-century censors of Boston's Watch and Ward Society. Ruml said it might calcify into "a bunch of old men . . . puttering around the Century Association." Partisans might launch their own organizations, and, said Merriam, "in a most confusing way they would all be finding each other guilty of lying." The commission wanted competition among news media but monopoly for its press council.[27]

The issue of the press council, like antitrust law, also brought to light some deeper fissures. Ruth Inglis objected to its proposed structure. Chafee opposed the notion of nongovernmental regulation of speech in general. Niebuhr thought that they were overemphasizing the press council and, for that matter, all of their recommendations.

Inglis contended that the citizens' agency, as the men sometimes called it, left no room for citizens. "Let the public be represented and speak for itself," she told Leigh in a memo in 1945. She understood the sluggishness of the masses, she said, but an organization of everyday citizens would be "more sound and democratic than assuming that a board of wise governors knows what is good for the public." The argument paralleled her defense of pressure groups. Leigh "violently disagreed" with her, Inglis told a friend. "I say it is, then, a misnomer to call it a citizens' agency." She was already dismayed over the commission's failure to conduct substantial research. Now the tussle with Leigh seemed to exasperate her. "They know what's best," she said of the commission. "It is a sort of omniscient paternalism based on the assumption that they have no personal biases or prejudices and that they know what the public should want."[28]

Chafee downplayed the importance of the press council in discussions, and he seemed to distance himself from it in his own commission book. "We shall not solve the problem of quality by vesting coercive powers in private groups rather than in government officials," he wrote in *Government and Mass Communications*. "The tyranny of irresponsible organizations may be as deleterious to the life of the spirit as the tyranny of the state, and perhaps more so. . . . The solution of the problem of quality does not lie in changing the source of coercion but in getting away from the whole idea of coercion." (Hutchins and others would come to agree with Chafee a few years later, with the rise of the anticommunist blacklists in film and TV.)[29]

Niebuhr questioned the efficacy of the press council. Publishers are like everyone else, he believed, in being inherently selfish, and they aren't likely to heed moral admonitions to sacrifice profits; "power must be challenged by power." A onetime Socialist Party candidate for the New York State Senate, Niebuhr was probably the commission's left-most member. In a meeting, he remarked that everyone in the room might reject pure Marxism, but "this doesn't mean that some of us wouldn't want to socialize property" if necessary. Yet more sharply than others on the commission, and more sharply than *A Free and Responsible Press,* he also articulated the dangers of reliance on the state. American government mustn't be discussed in the abstract, he said; it's always the government of a particular party. The party in power will someday yield it, and "it is a sound practice in a democracy not to establish an engine of government which we are unwilling to put into the hands of our enemies." If the state could evaluate the content of newspapers in setting postage rates, a Republican administration might raise rates on Democratic papers, and vice versa. His argument was nuanced. Not all slopes are slippery: "Norman Thomas said during the war all the time, 'If you restrict the civil liberties during war time to any degree you will land in Fascism.' We didn't land in Fascism." He didn't rule out action by the state, either. He favored the surgical use of antitrust law and was open to other possible roles for the state, including the BBC model.[30]

Even so, Niebuhr was outspoken about the flaws in every proposed solution, a note he struck throughout the commission's two and a half years of meetings. For him, acknowledging the inadequacy of all options didn't represent defeatism or failure to reach a conclusion; it represented a powerful conclusion in itself. He believed the commission could succeed by showing that all solutions fail. The problems of the press weren't unique in this regard; "democracy," he once wrote, "is a method of finding proximate solutions for insoluble problems." If Niebuhr had written *A Free and Responsible Press,* it might have explained, in depth, what makes the problems insoluble. But Hutchins wanted to avoid so strong a word and to bury so stark a conclusion.[31]

In April 1945, Hutchins reviewed and summarized the "vast mass of documents" that the commission had produced up to that point. He could identify only four recommendations that had attracted general support. "I am sure you will feel that the recommendations are meager," he said. "So do I." But the men assured one another that it didn't matter. Even if they hadn't solved the problems, they had clarified them. Merriam thought their major contribution was the diagnosis, though they would need to formulate their conclusions "very carefully in order to avoid the charge, in effect, of futility." Hutchins believed that an outline of philosophical principles by William Ernest Hocking, to be published as an appendix to the report, would be their most significant statement.[32]

Even if the commission members could get by without comprehensive policy solutions, though, they needed to agree on the structure, analysis, and tone of the final report. Months passed with key decisions still up in the air. The Commission on Freedom of the Press, Hutchins later wrote, was proceeding "at a leisurely pace." It was also running out of money. Much of the fault lay with the chairman.[33]

CHAPTER THIRTEEN

Consider Yourself Pedestaled

ROBERT HUTCHINS WAS CHRONICALLY overcommitted. In the mid-1940s, he headed the Committee to Frame a World Constitution, the Great Books Foundation, the executive committee and the board of editors of Encyclopædia Britannica, the executive committee of Encyclopædia Britannica Films, and the board of visitors of Great Books–centric St. John's College in Maryland, plus the Commission on Freedom of the Press. He was editor in chief of the Great Books of the Western World. He served on many other nonprofit and governmental boards, councils, commissions, and committees, as well as the occasional for-profit board. (Though often in debt, Hutchins didn't generally take on projects for money; he turned over most of his outside earnings to the university, including the Time Inc. payments for the commission.) With Mortimer Adler, he also taught a weekly Great Books seminar to undergraduates—"it is not very good for the students," he said, "but it is very good for me." The duo led adult Great Books discussions too. In addition, Hutchins spent two hours each morning writing speeches and articles, which he called "the only fun I have." On top of all else, he was trying to chart a post-Chicago career and struggling with a tumultuous marriage.[1]

Throughout Hutchins's life, he was nearly always behind in his work. "As far as I can see," he once said, "there's no possibility of ever catching up."[2]

"You had better be nice to me," Hutchins told a friend, "or I'll drop one of my atomic bombs on you." It was August 7, 1945, the day after an American A-bomb, developed in part at the University of Chicago, had killed some seventy thousand people in Hiroshima. He soon abandoned his flip tone and became somber and re-proachful. On a radio roundtable, he charged that the United States had forfeited its "moral prestige" by using the bomb. Having worked on a superweapon to stop the Nazis, the nation should have forsworn its use when Germany surrendered, because Japan's defeat was inevitable. As for the future, Hutchins called for sharing the secret of the bomb with Stalin right away in order to dispel any fears of a preemptive attack. Long term, humanity's sole hope for survival was world government. Dwight Macdonald called him "the eminent anti-militarist whose university brought into being, while his back was turned, the atomic bomb."[3]

With the world confronting a new crisis, Hutchins once again summoned his fellow thinkers to devise a solution. The Committee to Frame a World Constitution initially included Commission on Freedom of the Press members Reinhold Niebuhr, William Ernest Hocking, Beardsley Ruml, and Robert Redfield, though only Red-field stayed to the end. Like the commission, the constitution com-mittee comprised mostly professors. Hutchins thought politicians didn't have "the vision, the knowledge, or the detachment which the crisis demands," so the job fell to "that much maligned race, the intellectuals." The constitution committee, like the commis-sion, assembled for multiday closed-door meetings over a couple of years' time in New York and Chicago, with transcribed delibera-tions and more than a hundred numbered documents for internal use. Hutchins headed both groups.[4]

In March 1948, the Committee to Frame a World Constitution released its draft constitution. (*A Free and Responsible Press* had been published a year earlier.) *Common Cause*, the committee's magazine, prefaced it with quotations from the Bhagavad Gita, Muhammad Rumi, Simón Bolívar, and Fyodor Dostoevsky, plus a dedication to

Mahatma Gandhi, who, the magazine said, would have been a shoo-in for world president if not for his assassination a few weeks earlier. But despite the gestures toward globalism, the constitution's signers were seven Americans, three Europeans who were naturalized American citizens, and one Canadian.[5]

The constitution divided the Federal Republic of the World into nine electoral regions: Europa, Atlantis, Eurasia, Afrasia, Africa, India, Asia Major, Austrasia, and Columbia. (The United States would be in Atlantis; the United Kingdom could choose between Europa and Atlantis.) It provided for a world president (Protector of the Peace) with a single six-year term, a unicameral legislature, and a supreme court, plus a Chamber of Guardians to oversee the armed forces, a Tribune of the People to represent minorities, and a Syndical Senate to represent labor unions and other occupational groups. The constitution imposed duties on citizens, including "do unto others as he would like others to do unto him." It also guaranteed positive liberties, including a right to "rewards and security according to merit and needs" and a right to education in state-funded schools. Those who drafted the document said they merely wanted to stimulate discussion; they were framing *a* world constitution, not *the* world constitution. Even so, in moments of grandiosity, they likened their *Common Cause* explications of the draft constitution to the Federalist Papers, and they brainstormed about such trappings of sovereignty as an anthem ("Ode to Joy") and a flag (perhaps a rainbow, though one member considered it garish).[6]

The possibility of a global state was taken seriously in the late 1940s. Those who supported some variant included Pope Pius XII, Albert Einstein, Wendell Willkie (whose 1943 book *One World* was a best seller), Supreme Court Justice William O. Douglas, former justice Owen Roberts, Walter Lippmann, E. B. White, nearly 150 members of Congress, and several scientists from the Manhattan Project. The Chicago committee, according to the legal scholar Robert L. Tsai, produced the most fully thought-out, best-known draft constitution. The concept of world government also attracted opposition. After briefly serving on the committee, Reinhold Niebuhr became an outspoken critic. In his view, a precondition for global democracy was global community, and that was a pipe dream. Face facts, wrote Niebuhr: "We are living in a very unsafe world; and it will be unsafe for a long time."[7]

By the early 1950s, interest in a global state had waned. *Common Cause* stopped publishing in 1951. In 1953, Niebuhr called the notion of world government "harmless but also irrelevant." With years of Hutchins's labor being dismissed as folly, he said he had been set up as the fall guy: the Committee to Frame a World Constitution was really the Committee to Frame Robert Hutchins.[8]

According to Hutchins, splitting the atom augured wonders as well as horrors. Atomic power would bring virtually costless energy, cures for most diseases, extraordinary new metals, "communication devices which will eliminate time and space," and even flowers in never-before-seen hues. The forty-hour workweek would be a thing of the past, with leisure almost limitless. Humanity's greatest challenge would be filling all its free time. If people sought escape through comic books and movies, he warned, the result would be a "peace more horrible than war," for leisure without intellectual stimulation is inherently degrading. Instead, they must dedicate their free time to the pursuit of wisdom. He urged Americans to stop thinking of education as a childhood disease like measles—"having had it once you need not, in fact you cannot, have it again."[9]

For adults as for undergraduates, Hutchins believed that the Great Books lay at the heart of a proper education. He and Mortimer Adler taught Great Books seminars to University of Chicago students starting in 1930. In 1943, they began offering a class to trustees, business people, and others, in exchange for a $150 donation to the university. (One participant, the trustee Walter Paepcke, went on to found the Aspen Institute, with seminars modeled on Great Books discussion groups.) As word of the adult classes spread, others wanted to take part, so Adler launched a University of Chicago training program for discussion leaders. In 1947, the training program was getting too big for a university sideline, so Hutchins shifted it to the newly formed Great Books Foundation. By the end of the decade, the Great Books adult seminars had become "a nationwide middlebrow vogue," said *Time*, with an estimated fifty thousand people taking part.[10]

Early in the fad, as Alex Beam chronicles in *A Great Idea at the Time*, Hutchins's friend William Benton, a member of the first Hutchins-Adler adult seminar, decided to publish the Great Books through Encyclopædia Britannica. (Through a deal he had brokered a few years earlier, Benton and the University of Chicago jointly owned Britannica.) Hutchins at first resisted—the books would become living-room décor, he said, purchased not for self-improvement but for shelf-improvement—but he soon acquiesced and agreed to serve as editor. To help select the canon, he and Adler assembled an advisory board, including John Erskine, who had founded the ur-seminar on Great Books at Columbia in the 1920s, called Classics of Western Civilization; two leaders of St. John's College, president Stringfellow Barr and dean Scott Buchanan; and the philosopher Alexander Meiklejohn. (Archibald MacLeish declined an invitation to join the committee.) After two years of deliberations, the committee selected 443 works by 74 authors. Each author, according to Hutchins, represented an important voice in civilization's Great Conversation. Britannica published the works in a fifty-four-volume set in 1952.[11]

The fad may have appealed to middlebrows, but the Britannica texts were sternly highbrow, neither watered down nor tarted up. On the principle that readers must experience classic works directly, with no intermediaries, the editors eschewed prefaces, footnotes, glossaries, and other tools for clarifying and contextualizing. Nearly all of the works were unabridged. The text was small and mostly in double columns. In a preface and an introductory essay, Hutchins sacralized the reading experience without trying to sugarcoat it. Citing Aristotle for the proposition that learning can be painful, he said, "no one will deny that many arid stretches are contained in the works of the great writers," but "it would be presumptuous for us to do the reader's skipping for him." He promised that the Great Books "are genuinely intelligible," though "perhaps late and with difficulty." Any reader who reached the end of the volumes should start over, he said, because a liberal education ought to be "interminable."[12]

In other respects too, as Dwight Macdonald pointed out in a barbed *New Yorker* review, the Britannica editions didn't give readers much of a foothold. Editors relied mainly on existing translations, some of them clunky, rather than commissioning new ones. Six volumes reprinted scientific treatises that represented leaps of understanding when written but that had been superseded by other works. Macdonald questioned the value of mastering Hippocrates's admonition to "avoid wetting all sorts of ulcers except with wine, unless the ulcer be situated in a joint." A team of scriveners (including twenty-eight-year-old Saul Bellow) had traced 102 Great Ideas running through the 443 Great Books to prepare a two-volume index, which Adler dubbed the "Syntopicon." Macdonald judged it virtually useless, partly because it didn't distinguish incidental mentions from major themes. Although Macdonald's review is often read as a takedown of the Great Books concept, that wasn't his intent. He objected to Adler's "sales talk" in trying to popularize high culture, he said elsewhere, but not to the study of the Great Books: "I think it at the worst harmless, and at best a very fine idea, to encourage laymen to read the classics, and so am sympathetic to 'the Great Books idea.' "[13]

A set of the Britannica Great Books in 1952 cost $249.50, about as much as a refrigerator. Although some of the works were out of print, most were available elsewhere, usually in cheaper editions. Since 1941, Walter J. Black had run the Classics Club, with works selected by Pearl Buck and other literary eminences. On the model of the Book of the Month Club (founded in 1926), the Classics Club offered free books to get people to sign up and shipped later selections to them with invoices. Black's hardbound volumes, many of which included explanatory introductions, cost $2 or $3 plus shipping, whereas each Britannica volume cost nearly $5. Penguin Classics also brought out paperbacks of several titles from the Great Books list in the early 1950s. Its *Canterbury Tales* cost $1.25, *Don Quixote* (a new translation) $1, and *The Odyssey* (also a new translation) $0.25.[14]

A fuller batch of the canonic readings came from a man who has been airbrushed out of Great Books history, the conservative publisher Henry Regnery. (He also worked with Hutchins on the University of Chicago's cultural journal, *Measure*.) In 1949, the Great Books Foundation partnered with Regnery to publish the seventy-two books covered in the first four years of a Great Books seminar. His firm turned out pocket-sized paperbacks in boxed sets, $9.60 for eighteen titles. "Have you put off reading the Great Books," asked a Regnery ad, "because you couldn't afford them?" The Great Books Foundation abrogated the contract without warning in 1951, accusing Regnery of having tarnished the brand. Foundation president Charles F. Strubbe Jr. refused to be specific, but the provocation was probably *God and Man at Yale*, a Regnery best seller, in which William F. Buckley Jr. accused American universities of undermining students' faith in both Christianity and free enterprise. With the Britannica Great Books about to be published, in addition, the foundation may have wanted to stop sponsoring low-budget alternatives. Henry Regnery, having invested heavily in the project, proposed taking his company's name off and continuing the partnership, but the foundation insisted on a complete severance. In a letter to Hutchins, Regnery remarked that certain voices seemed to be unwelcome in civilization's Great Conversation.[15]

Other dissonances also arose in the merchandising of the Great Books. After an anemic start, sales of the Britannica set increased thanks to an aggressive marketing campaign whose message flatly contradicted its chief editor. A Great Books education, wrote Hutchins, teaches that there's much more to life than money, so it "may interfere with getting rich." Britannica, by contrast, promised that the books would "help you achieve success in business" by supplying "the counsel and brilliant fluency of the world's greatest minds when you prepare business reports."[16]

University of Chicago trustees periodically complained about Hutchins's many side projects, but he was losing interest in the school. He felt the war had turned it into "a military establishment." About half of the faculty and staff were engaged in government work, and classrooms were full of soldiers studying military optics, meteorology, and map reading—vocational education for warriors. Running the university had become a job for a manager, he thought, not a leader. He couldn't build on his legacy. In bouts of despair, he wondered if he would leave much of a legacy at all. "It is an appalling record," he told Thornton Wilder after two decades at the university. "It makes your flesh creep." In public, he said, "I greatly fear that my administration will be remembered solely because it was the one in which intercollegiate football was abolished."[17]

The trustees had other complaints as well. Except for the war years, the university ran a million-dollar budget deficit, which Hutchins called a sign of determination and confidence. Some trustees disagreed. Some were also concerned about undergraduate enrollment, which had been declining even before the war. The nature of the students seemed to be changing, too. The university under Hutchins, according to his successor, Lawrence A. Kimpton, gained a reputation for catering to the type of undergraduate who "wears glasses, does not dance, deplores sports, and . . . is confident that he would have been happier had he lived in the age of Pericles." High schoolers who didn't fit the mold stopped applying.[18]

Hutchins wanted to leave. "I can think of nothing but resignation," he told a colleague in 1944. He tried to shed some duties in 1945 by shifting from president to the newly created position of chancellor, and then he arranged to take a sabbatical in 1946 and 1947 to work full-time at Britannica. Friends tried to find him a suitable job. William Benton recommended him for UNESCO director general, Mortimer Adler urged him to take on the presidency of St. John's College, and Henry Luce invited him to join Time Inc. None of the possibilities appealed to him. He told Wilder, "I am too full of inertia to seek anything." For all his certitude about the proper path for the nations of the world, he couldn't chart a path for himself.[19]

Maude Phelps Hutchins's career, meanwhile, was thriving. She had more than twenty solo shows of her paintings, sketches, and sculpture, and one of her *Diagrammatics* drawings became a mural at the 1934 Century of Progress Exhibition in Chicago. She was gaining attention as a writer, too, with verse in the *New Yorker* and *Poetry* as well as fiction and short plays in literary magazines. (Later, after her divorce, she would publish eight novels and two collections of short fiction, including a 1950 novel, *A Diary of Love*, that was so sexually explicit that the Chicago police tried to ban it and a British magistrate ordered it burned.)[20]

Professional success didn't bring peace of mind. Maude suffered from anxiety and exhaustion, and her years in Chicago were interrupted by long stints in a local hospital and rest cures in Arizona. Her condition worsened in the 1940s. When immobilized by depression, she rarely left the house, and she once spent four weeks in bed. Their three daughters—the last was born in 1942—were often overseen by nannies.[21]

"How long ago had she begun to be disquieted?" Maude wrote in her 1946 story "Morning Till Night," a third-person interior monologue of a woman whose mind caroms from topic to topic: the fragility of artist, the idiocy of most people, men's fear of losing control to women, mothers' duty to love unlovable children, the hopefulness of making plans and the disappointment of executing them, and the "hateful little beast" of terror that attacks without warning and then vanishes. "Was she mad?" she wonders. Madness is confining, she thinks, but so is sanity. Her stampeding thoughts in fact may turn out to be a blessing. "She had all the material she could possibly use put away in her head," wrote Maude, "so that if she did not have actual contact with reality again for a long time, she would be busy."[22]

For the role of first lady of the University of Chicago, Maude may have been ill equipped by nature and nurture at the outset and by temperament and circumstance thereafter. Her father, Warren Ratcliffe McVeigh, was a prideful, pugnacious reporter for the *New York Sun*. In 1895, he exchanged insults with an actor named Paul T. Wilkes (a distant cousin of John Wilkes Booth), culminating in a duel. McVeigh was shot in the hand and Wilkes in the arm; both survived. McVeigh married Maude Louise Phelps in 1896, and they had two daughters. At the beginning of 1900, McVeigh's wife fell ill, reportedly with scarlet fever, and died a week later. McVeigh became so distraught that he stopped eating and sleeping. Two weeks later, according to the *New York World*, he "died of a broken heart." The younger daughter, Maude Phelps McVeigh, had just turned one year old.[23]

Maude was raised by grandparents on her mother's side and a great-aunt on her father's side. They dissuaded her from pursuing an education ("ladies do not go to college"). Later, in a short story, Maude wrote of a little girl's relief upon learning that her parents were dead, because she could love them unreservedly without the inconvenience of being raised by them. Much of the household conversation during her childhood centered on the families' blue-blood ancestry, the servants who tried to rise above their station, the relatives who married below theirs, and the distinctions between "gentlefolk" and commoners. "I have a wicked temper," she said of her young self, "and I hate people, quite a few almost constantly." When in the throes of rage, she would slam her bedroom door so hard that plaster fell in her hair and then hurl something to the floor. During one tantrum, she shattered her framed pictures of her parents. Her grandfather (maternal) told her that she was "cross-grained and horrid," just like her father.[24]

Elements of Maude's childhood character—imperiousness, volatility, misanthropy—remained with her in adulthood. She refused to try to charm people who bored her, and almost everyone bored her. She didn't merely resist criticism of her work; she assailed it. When the writer and editor Clifton Fadiman said that without a plot, a novel she had written was unpublishable, she replied that a plot would wreck it, so she would have to give him a zero on his critique. In 1942, she protested minor editing of her poem so vehemently that the *New Yorker* revoked its acceptance; for once, she backed down.[25]

Sexism no doubt magnified some of Maude's conflicts in the 1930s and '40s. A male *Chicago Tribune* writer in 1942 called her "indefatigable," "dominating," "quite formidable," "frightening in her boundless energy," and, tellingly, "ambitious." Although some people thought she wanted to outshine her husband, she asked *Who's Who* to condense her entry in 1945 because she was embarrassed to discover it was longer than his. Indeed, she and Robert often worked together. She drafted some of his letters, stringing together his ready-made phrases about liberal-arts education. They were also partners in the movement to keep the United States out of the European war before Pearl Harbor. Collaborating with (but not joining) the America First Committee, they befriended the isolationist leader Charles Lindbergh. Maude, rather than seeking greater renown than her husband, may have yearned simply to be treated as a serious professional rather than as a dilettante ("Society Girl Wins Art Prize") or a spouse ("University President's Wife Makes Name as Artist, Poet"). Reviewing a 1942 exhibition of her paintings and sculptures, *Time* called her "a gifted amateur,"

prompting her to send a telegram of protest to Henry Luce: "I
HAVE PAID AN INCOME TAX ON MY WORK SINCE 1924 WHICH MAKES ME
GIFTED BUT NOT AN AMATEUR."²⁶

Maude especially balked at the expectations of the University of
Chicago community. The Hutchinses rarely entertained at home,
and they declined the vast majority of invitations. Parties, she wrote,
make intelligent people want to cry; only fools enjoy them. She
considered University of Chicago professors unattractive, unintelli-
gent, lazy, cowardly, unethical, disloyal, and selfish, and the students
were so hidebound that "they are their own ancestors." She felt that
the university didn't leave much of a mark on its graduates. Asked
how a Chicago education might affect a young woman, she replied
that college "is a small part of her life and should not be overesti-
mated."²⁷

Robert tried to cushion her. He pressured friends and colleagues, including William Benton and Mortimer Adler, to buy her
art. In 1939, when the *Maroon* tittered over her recruitment of students as nude models, he told the editors to lay off: they could
mock him—he got paid for it—but, he said, "my wife doesn't." In
1946, he contemplated leaving the university to work for Encyclopædia Britannica in New York, because, he told his father, the
move might help Maude. *Something* had to change; home life had
become "a permanent emergency," he said, with Maude erupting in
rages that could "blow the roof off." At times she directed him not
to leave the house or, when he did leave, insisted that he return by
five p.m. He tried to comply. When he persuaded her to accom-
pany him to events, he sometimes regretted it. After one awkward
evening, he told Marshall Field III, the editor of the *Chicago Sun*, "I
apologize once more for the eccentric behavior of my wife."²⁸

Maude's writings suggest that rightly or not, she felt neglected.
A university president must be married, she wrote in a short story,
but he is forbidden to spend much time with his wife. In another
story, she described a man so brilliant that he could ignore his wife
in eight languages. She suspected that Robert, in drafting the
global constitution, was angling to become the first world president. "Consider yourself pedestaled," she wrote in a poem. After an
exhibition featured her sketch of her husband's folded hands, titled
"Fragments of a Philosopher," she sent out a poem in which the

narrator keeps, as a trophy, the still-warm severed hands of someone she loathes. Later, she wrote a short story in which an artist
ends her twenty-five-year marriage to an inattentive, taciturn
husband—like Robert Hutchins, a boyish-looking intellectual who
smokes a pipe—by fatally shooting him.[29]

Thornton Wilder witnessed some of the outbursts. "Maude's
going crazy," he told Gertrude Stein in 1940, "and in such a way that
one is torn between pitying her for a desperately sick mind and hating her for a vulgar pretentious tiresome goose." Robert repeatedly
implored Wilder to come to Chicago. "I need you very badly," he
wrote in 1946. "The situation with which you—and only you—are
familiar has grown steadily worse. . . . I can't travel any more, & can
seldom even get out in the evening." Wilder visited several times, and
Robert was forever grateful. "Those days would have been intolerable
without you," he told Wilder years later.[30]

Though only Wilder knew the details, the protracted decay of
the Hutchins marriage was common knowledge at the university.
With Robert seeming "feminine and masochistic in his sufferance,"
remarked one student, the divorce took years to consummate. Some
people wondered if on some level, martyrdom gratified him. His
friend and biographer Milton Mayer thought he loved to suffer.[31]

At last, Robert Hutchins became resolute. In March 1947, he
moved out of the house. (Two weeks later, he presided over the official release of *A Free and Responsible Press* in New York City.) In a
letter to Maude, he said the marriage was finished. She was aston-
ished, she told an acquaintance; he left without warning, and his
only explanation was some arguments that she acknowledged were
her fault. He stayed with friends and in hotels, and he wouldn't
take her calls or acknowledge her letters. When she did manage to
reach him by phone in a hotel, he listened for a while and then
hung up. She asked a mutual acquaintance, the publisher James
Laughlin, to forward a letter to Robert because she couldn't find
him. She also asked their former ally in isolationism Charles Lindbergh if he would try to mediate. She told both Laughlin and
Lindbergh that she was terrified.[32]

If Lindbergh interceded, he was unsuccessful. "He left me,"
Maude testified in court in July 1948. "I gave him no reason." Robert didn't attend the divorce hearing; according to some accounts,

he and Maude never saw each other again. She and two of their daughters moved to Connecticut (the third was already out of the house). The following year, Robert married his former Encyclopædia Britannica secretary, Vesta Orlick. To a reporter in 1956, eight years after the divorce, he declined to talk about his first marriage, saying, "I just want to forget it."[33]

The distractions took a toll. Robert Hutchins missed five of the seventeen meetings of the Commission on Freedom of the Press, more than any member except Archibald MacLeish, who resigned to take a State Department job at the end of 1944 and returned in fall 1945. Hutchins couldn't attend the first meeting, in New York in late 1943, because of family illness, according to the minutes. "My wife's condition has been so discouraging that I did not dare to go," he told the movie czar Will H. Hays in 1945, after missing a commission discussion with him. At one point, he told Robert Leigh, "You will be surprised that I expect to be at the meeting on the 16th." Zechariah Chafee took on the position of vice chair and ran several meetings. Hutchins would have missed even more sessions, but he held many of them in Chicago even though most commission members lived on the East Coast.[34]

The members at times spoke of their lack of progress. "I feel we might fall short of our possibilities," Charles Merriam told one commission colleague; to another, he said, "I wonder whether we are really on the right track." Chafee distributed a memo titled "Where Do We Go from Here?" William Ernest Hocking said they were "in a mess," though he expected it to pass. Harold Lasswell expected "the sense of the guillotine" to reinvigorate their work. But the problems ran deeper.[35]

The initial deadline for the draft report was September 1945. In November, Henry Luce told Hutchins, "I am looking forward to reading most any day now your Commission's report on Freedom of the Press." He would have to wait another year.[36]

CHAPTER FOURTEEN

All Great Problems Are Insoluble

THREE YEARS AFTER A *Free and Responsible Press* was published, researcher Llewellyn White typed up a sour reflection on his experience. The commission had crafted its understanding of journalism from "shadows, legends and professors' books," he told Max Ascoli, his boss at the *Reporter* magazine. A better approach would have been to convene small groups of conscientious journalists and, he said, have "*them* tell *us* what ails them," thus developing "a sympathetic bill of particulars virtually drafted by the best elements in the press themselves." White said that "the Harvard trio"—William Ernest Hocking, Zechariah Chafee, and Arthur Schlesinger—had supported his alternative approach, in "rump bull-sessions in one or another's hotel room," but they had "deferred too long a time to Hutchins [and] in the end hesitated to join an open revolt against him (though the Harvard-Chicago spiritual schism was always in the air)." He closed his memo on a note of futility: "Looking back on it, though, I doubt if any such result would have been possible, given the personalities involved. Luce's money was a handicap. Hutchins' chairmanship was a disaster. Hutchins' selection of a milquetoast nonentity [Robert Leigh] as director was probably in the nature of an anticlimax. Perhaps our one useful legacy was a demonstration of how NOT to conduct a citizen inquiry into the press."[1]

Whether led by Hutchins or someone else, commission conversations often meandered. "Our discussion on this subject, like most of our discussions, is a trifle circular," Hutchins said in one meeting. To a friend, he wrote, "The only conclusion the Commission has reached to date is that it cannot figure out what to do about the freedom of the press."[2]

At times, commission members couldn't even seem to agree on their overarching mission. After eight meetings and more than a year, George Shuster said, "our *purpose* has never been defined with adequate care." Archibald MacLeish thought they should emphasize First Amendment law. Charles Merriam said their analysis ought to be "cultural-philosophical-ethical-cooperative-democratic." Harold Lasswell, Hocking, and Leigh wanted to concentrate on policy. Hutchins at the outset said they were working to solve policy problems; at the end, he said their task was philosophical. Henry Luce provided no help. At various times, he said he expected an abstract analysis of philosophy and morality, practical guidance for editors, "a disquisition on worldwide freedom of the press," a statement that would inspire the public to support press freedom, and an investigation of the media's cultural impact.[3]

Another disagreement concerned whether to study movies and other forms of entertainment. Some members said entertainment merits attention because of its social and political effects, because it draws people's attention away from news, and because, in Hocking's words, "there is nothing more important for the long-time build-up of a community than the way it amuses itself." MacLeish, though, argued for ignoring cinema, "a piffling product" subject to "a piffling censorship." If they studied movies, he said, why not theatrical performances and window displays in department stores? Others wondered if they would need to include picture postcards, burlesque shows, public schools, and phonograph records. "We are a Commission on the Freedom of the Press," Hutchins said, "and not a Commission on How You Can Get Information to Anybody on Any Subject Through Any Medium." The members ultimately focused on mass media, particularly news of public affairs, with secondary attention to entertainment other than music. A supplementary volume, by Ruth Inglis, examined film censorship. But even at the commission's final meeting, MacLeish continued to argue that they were wasting their time discussing entertainment.[4]

Beyond the scope of the study, some of the commission's views were incompatible. The point is not that members disagreed, though they did, but that some of their consensus positions could not be reconciled with other consensus positions. "We are against absentee ownership, we are for the expression of conviction," Hutchins said. "Yet, I suppose we feel that the worst newspaper situations in this country are those where the owners are most active and most deeply convinced." He cited William Randolph Hearst, Robert R. McCormick, and Joseph Medill Patterson. "It would be fine if either they would not express their convictions, or if they were absentees."[5]

Many other inconsistencies arose. Commission members wanted the press to publish only truthful material while offering an open forum for diverse voices, but some of the diverse voices might propagate falsehoods. They wanted the press to reduce social divisions by providing balanced representations of minorities, but they also wanted editors to resist the demands of self-interested groups trying to influence coverage, including, in Merriam's words, "extremely touchy minorities." They wanted fact separated from opinion, but they also wanted "the truth about the fact," which, Reinhold Niebuhr maintained, is a matter of opinion. They lamented the ineffectiveness of journalistic ethics codes, but they also lamented the effectiveness of the Hays Code over movies. They wanted owners to keep their hands off newspaper content, but when told that an owner had instructed a columnist to attack Eleanor Roosevelt no more than three times a week, John Dickinson called it "a modest request." They applauded editors who stood their ground in the face of a boycott by Father Charles Coughlin's followers, but they also supported editors who, when Jewish advertisers threatened a boycott, agreed to devote more coverage to Nazi atrocities. Broadly, they wanted the press to be both "free from the menace of external compulsions from whatever source" and "accountable to society"—"two different perspectives," said Niebuhr, "which have never really been worked out."[6]

The commission staff had its own problems. Eric Hodgins of Time Inc. called Robert Leigh "an estimable gentleman on whose imagination and humor I would hate to rely if I were the only other inhabitant of a desert island." Elsewhere he said of Leigh, "no Aristotle, he."[7]

Like Hutchins, Leigh had lost interest in his job in higher-education administration, as founding president of Bennington College. Faculty and staff complained about his inattention, and at the request of the chair of the board of trustees, he resigned in 1941. The following year, he became director of the Foreign Broadcast Intelligence Service at the FCC. He left the FCC in 1944, when Hutchins hired him to direct the staff of the Commission on Freedom of the Press.[8]

Although Leigh's specialty in political science was administrative organization, at the commission he proved unable to handle a three-person staff. "I hope and pray we are going to get through this job without undiplomatic developments," MacLeish told Hutchins in early 1946, after spending time in the commission offices. The researchers "disagree among themselves on some of the basic facts," he said, and "my attempts to get them to reconcile their differences have turned up an underlying unhappiness."[9]

Llewellyn White was the most disruptive figure. A longtime journalist, he joined the commission as a researcher in December 1944 and rose to assistant director in October 1945. Though prolific, he antagonized colleagues, lashed out in response to criticism, and at times adopted a tone that Merriam characterized as "supercilious" and "execrable." When Leigh took issue with White's draft of the commission-sponsored book on radio, White accused him of plotting to get his name on it. Later, White told the FBI that another commission researcher, Milton Stewart, was immature, unstable, neurotic, egotistical, a self-described former Trotskyite, and a security risk. The third researcher, Ruth Inglis, considered White "a louse."[10]

In addition to Leigh's shortcomings as a manager, he bridled against Hutchins's authority, particularly over the question of research. Like Lasswell, Leigh wanted the commission to study media content and effects. Unlike Lasswell, he wouldn't take no for an answer. At the outset, he envisioned a $500,000 research program, including content analysis of newspapers, magazines, radio, and movies. The commission as a whole had a budget of $120,000, soon raised to $200,000. After talking with Hutchins, Leigh came back with a $60,000 research proposal, which he discussed with Luce and Hodgins at Time Inc. Hutchins said no. Leigh brought up the idea in commission meetings in September 1944 and February 1945. Both times, Hutchins was absent. Several members said that the research sounded useful.[11]

Hutchins finally agreed to a single study. Milton Stewart would analyze coverage of the 1945 gathering in San Francisco that produced the United Nations Charter. The findings would be published as a book, *The American Press and the San Francisco Conference*, with an introduction by Lasswell. Hutchins and Leigh allocated $10,000 for the project. Assembling and coding the news articles for content analysis ran over budget, reaching $13,465. Leigh insisted that the cost would have been much greater if not for his "strong-arm methods." "The only thing that hurts me is the San Francisco Study," Hutchins told Leigh in early 1946. "I will bet you $10,000 that it does not affect the conclusions in the report at all."[12]

The study didn't affect the conclusions, because Stewart never finished it. The initial deadline was spring 1946, but he said that difficulties in hiring trained coders had pushed him back a few months. He left the commission payroll around the end of 1945. Thereafter he consulted for a management firm, worked on a congressional investigation, and joined the staff of President Truman's Committee on Civil Rights—all, apparently, in 1946—while insisting that he was writing the book in his spare time. Leigh told Hutchins in February 1946 that "poor Milton Stewart has become very guilty about the matter." In March, Stewart reported that the book was progressing. In July, he promised to finish by October 1. After that deadline passed, Lasswell began a letter to Stewart, "Dear Author." In February 1947, Leigh said Stewart promised to finish the manuscript by March 1. The University of Chicago Press finally canceled the book in 1948. After working with Stewart, Morris Ernst described him as brilliant but incapable of finishing a job.[13]

As *Time* would put it thirty years later, as Robert Hutchins's California think tank was foundering, he "firmly believes in sparing no expense in the pursuit of knowledge." At the outset, Henry Luce agreed to a two-year study at $60,000 per year. A few months later, Hutchins told Hodgins that $120,000 would not be enough, but, he said, "I have not felt like spending much time trying to figure out" the final cost. Luce agreed to raise the grant to $100,000 a year. If Hutchins had proposed $200,000 at the start, Luce later said, "I would have told him it was too much." When Time Inc. raised the cap midway through the first year, according to Hodgins, Hutchins argued that the $30,000 spent to that point should be deemed "spilled milk" and not count against the $200,000, "a rather brash attempt" that the company rejected. A few months into the project, when Time Inc. asked for a budget, Hutchins said he thought he was free to spend the money as he pleased. To Hodgins, Luce wrote that Hutchins must be made to understand that Time Inc. would require a full accounting of expenditures.[14]

Leigh received a full-time salary of $15,000, the equivalent of about $215,000 today. (Hutchins turned his commission salary over to the University of Chicago.) Members were paid $300 per meeting, about $4,300 in today's dollars. "I am sorry to miss the opportunity of association with you in this noble enterprise," Raymond Fosdick of the Rockefeller Foundation said when he declined Hutchins's invitation to join the commission, "and I am sorry to miss $300 a meeting!"[15]

Increasingly it became apparent that $200,000 would not be enough. In October 1945, Leigh projected a deficit of $2,500, which Hutchins said he could cover through a university foundation. In February 1946, Leigh's projected deficit broke $10,000, too much for the university fund. Over lunch, Hutchins asked Luce for another $25,000. Luce said he would think it over. Two weeks later, he said no. Although he had initially wanted Time Inc. to be the only donor, now he said that Hutchins should feel free to look elsewhere. Through Encyclopædia Britannica, William Benton provided $15,000 to complete the work. Soon, though, the commission scraped bottom again. While Leigh taught summer school at the University of Chicago, staff checks were delayed. Office bills went unpaid. Ruth Inglis bought postage. Leigh told Hutchins they needed $5,000. Finally, Hutchins raided a University of Chicago fund for $4,000, which proved to be enough. Leigh calculated that the commission's final balance would be between $4 and $10.[16]

"The Commission," Hutchins told Luce, "has been worth $200,000—to the members."[17]

At the end of 1944, Archibald MacLeish resigned from the commission. The administration had nominated him to be assistant secretary of state for public and cultural relations, and he thought that the new position "simply won't mix with the Commission's work." At the State Department, MacLeish worked to build public support for the United Nations. He resigned after eight months, following the death of President Roosevelt, and returned to the commission.[18]

"Now I have some hope for our Commission," Hutchins said. He had a job for MacLeish. The legacy of the commission's inquiry would rest on *A Letter to the Press*, one of the working titles for the report. "To me it is quite clear that if this Commission is to justify itself," Hutchins said, "its Report must be a landmark in the history of the subject." Because the commission's recommendations were unexceptional, the report's renown would depend on its "tone, style and literary quality." He asked the Pulitzer-winning poet to draft it. MacLeish agreed. "I think this Report is the most important thing that anybody has to think about right now," he said. "I will put in all of the time I possibly can until the Commission winds up."[19]

Robert Leigh had been working on the report since joining the staff a year earlier. In fact, he started even before the group had formulated research questions. "This may seem like putting the cart before the horse," he said, "but it avoids having the mountain bring forth a mouse." His prose tended toward the leaden: "if in all the five media, there could be such a provision of highly qualitative units available to all, it would be a most promising means of raising standards by increasing diversity with the means of developing audience discrimination, training junior professionals, and altering the sense of prestige and success in the mass media generally so as to include recognition of high quality as well as profitable quantity." Some of his points were trifling, too. In one draft, he called on the media to reject ads for palm readers. He included a chart showing that children liked "Dick Tracy" whereas the elderly preferred "Bringing Up Father."[20]

MacLeish began writing the report in October 1945, at a salary of $900 a month, and completed a draft in January 1946. He opened with a slam at his former boss, Henry Luce: in sponsoring the study, Time Inc. cared only about "freedom of the press from interference by government," but the press was already freer in this regard than ever before. MacLeish went on to vilify conservative publishers and praise the Roosevelt administration. He also contrasted the American press and the Soviet press. American journalists construe freedom of the press as a duty to be irresponsible, he wrote, whereas Soviet journalists view it as a duty to be "responsible to the people—or at least to a government which claims to be the people."²¹

"I am delighted with the style and dash of the draft report," Hutchins told MacLeish. "If I have a general criticism, it is that the draft is too dashing and gives a partisan impression."²²

When the commission assembled at the end of January, at the Carlyle Hotel in New York, others took issue with MacLeish's draft. They deemed it too negative, too quick to impute bad motives, too incendiary, and as Hutchins had said, too partisan. Niebuhr suggested a shift in register from "moral indignation to moral imperative." Some of the men thought MacLeish was setting too high a standard for the press. They shouldn't "demand the impossible," Hutchins said. "The problem is awfully complex," said John Dickinson.²³

MacLeish replied that they mustn't get lost in complexity. "Unless your analysis is simple enough to make a recommendation," he said, "we are going to be one of the funniest groups of people who have met for three years. We have to come out with *some* answer."

Niebuhr wasn't sure. "Maybe this is wrong," he said, "but I think that actually we have an insoluble problem. If you have an insoluble problem for which you can only find proximate solutions, you are not going to give very tremendous solutions which will shock the whole world. But if you have an insoluble problem of great complexities, and you illumine the complexities, you may be able to make quite a great contribution."

"Are we willing to come out with a statement that this is an insoluble problem?" MacLeish asked. "Because if we are, this report is going to be helped a great deal."

"All great problems are insoluble," Niebuhr replied.

"The word 'insoluble' is a little strong," said Hutchins.

MacLeish called for a vote on whether the problem was insoluble.

Hutchins tried to placate everyone. He said he would be happy with "a thorough, penetrating, vigorous analysis of an extremely difficult problem" that "pointed the way to future possible solutions," even if it didn't have all the answers.[24]

On February 15, MacLeish sent Hutchins his second draft, "which I hope and pray will meet the criticisms of the Commission." Zechariah Chafee said he was willing to sign the revision. The report's recommendations against government action largely reflected his views, and he seemed willing to compromise on all else. But others continued to find fault. Leigh, perhaps miffed that authorship had been taken from him, was especially caustic. He said the draft oversimplified the problems, overstated the role of the citizen, distorted the meaning of the First Amendment, and omitted important issues. He considered it worse than MacLeish's original. The mild-mannered Leigh's response surprised MacLeish, who told Hutchins, "The miracle of the loaves into the fishes was nothing at all compared to the miracle of milk toast into red meat which a typewriter works in Leigh's spirit."[25]

MacLeish had to miss the next meeting, from March 31 to April 2 at the Shoreland Hotel in Chicago. In his absence, the commission decided to junk his draft and work from a series of lectures that Leigh had given in Seattle, which included toned-down passages from MacLeish. Hutchins wired MacLeish that the commission planned "to retain large sections" of his draft alongside additional material by Leigh. "I hope you will give him all help you can. The Commission is very grateful to you."[26]

In the 1930s, when MacLeish was *Fortune*'s star writer, an editor said that "Arch is very easy to handle editorially provided you don't change as much as a comma in his copy without consulting him." When MacLeish saw Leigh's rewrite, he was irate.[27]

At the May 1946 meeting, the fifteenth since the commission had begun, MacLeish read a prepared statement. He said he had produced his first draft of the report, listened to "several days of free-for-all criticism," and produced a second draft, only to see "the whole thing shoveled down the drain." The experience forced him to question what the commission stood for. Now, he said, Leigh's rewrite "adds considerably to the darkness of my state of mind." Leigh had bungled the report's structure, weakened its arguments, and drained all energy from its prose. The sharpest criticisms of the press had vanished, too. "Why don't we state the facts?" MacLeish said. "These are facts. Believe me, if we with our financial backing weasel on this kind of thing—"

"I think that what we have stated here are the facts," Leigh interrupted.

Hutchins tried to split the difference. The commission had deemed MacLeish's draft "slightly on the acidulated side," but the Leigh version suffered from "a certain denaturing."

MacLeish said his work struck the proper tone, and he would publish a portion of it as a dissenting statement.

Leigh set to work on a revision. "I am purely a servant of the Commission," he said, "attempting to express its somewhat divergent desires."[28]

Two months later, in July 1946, the men gathered at the Waldorf-Astoria Hotel in New York for their last planned meeting. (Hutchins managed to attend despite his wife's condition.) They dissected Leigh's revision, the seventh draft of the report. The new draft, like the previous one, irritated MacLeish. "There are a lot of observations which are certainly mild enough to turn away no mind," he said. "But they are all quite obvious. They have all been said thousands of times. . . . They don't indicate why a large number of busy men should have spent two years thinking about it."[29]

While MacLeish wanted a more emphatic indictment of publishers, other commission members suggested a variety of revisions. Their scattershot arguments revealed the group's fragmentation. Beardsley Ruml wanted a more favorable depiction of big business. John Dickinson wanted a less favorable depiction of big government. Harold Lasswell wanted more attention to social science. William Ernest Hocking wanted a more positive explanation of the Soviet conception of press freedom. Reinhold Niebuhr wanted a declaration that "there are no simple solutions." As the criticisms mounted, said Ruth Inglis, "I was embarrassed for Leigh."[30]

Leigh defended his work. "Probably it is not helpful to remind the Commission of what it decided last time to do," he said. Privately, he likened the experience to being a "circus bareback rider straddling three horses." He asked how the men proposed to rearrange the material, "assuming that the draft should be clarified and sharpened by someone who could do that job." Clearly, *he* didn't want the job.[31]

After a lengthy discussion, Hutchins asked if everyone was agreed on how the report ought to be restructured.

"We are until we see it," said Charles Merriam.[32]

At one point, Chafee asked if the chairman would rewrite the opening chapter.

"Well, I think it is a serious question whether he should," Chairman Hutchins replied, sounding as though he didn't want the job either. He said he could condense the first chapter, but as for substance, "I am not at all clear as to what the Commission would like to have." Finally Hutchins agreed to rewrite the entire report before another meeting, *definitely* the last one, in September.[33]

CHAPTER FIFTEEN

Jefferson's Epitaph

IN JULY 1946, DURING what was supposed to be a vacation on Fishers Island, off the Connecticut coast, Robert Hutchins rewrote the report of the Commission on Freedom of the Press. In place of Archibald MacLeish's fulminating and Robert Leigh's plodding, Hutchins presented an indictment in crisp, stern, Olympian tones. From the start, he had opposed "piety in every form" in the report. Now he excised passages he considered naïve. He also slashed away sections on obscenity, sedition, and other topics unrelated to mainstream media. With what he called a "passion for brevity," the same passion that drove Henry Luce and Briton Hadden to found *Time*, he cut much more as well. When he finished, the manuscript was half its previous length. Hutchins's writing was exactly what his chairmanship had not been: focused and disciplined.[1]

Some commission members thought he had gone too far. Zechariah Chafee wondered if the manuscript had been "trimmed . . . so much to the bones that it lacks the allure of fleshly curves and roseate skin." MacLeish, while praising the "masterful" condensation overall, thought one chapter had been cut to the point that it "reads like a skeleton." More important, MacLeish remained disgruntled over the substance. After saying he was "reluctant to criticize," he unleashed five pages of criticism. "It still has too much water in the milk or milk in the whiskey or whatever," he wrote. "We can be objective and lawyerlike and scholarly and whatever else we wish to be without pulling our punches." He reiterated that he planned to file a dissenting opinion with more pointed denunciations of press performance.[2]

Despite the report's call for diverse voices in the media, Hutchins wanted the commission to speak with a single voice, so he mediated some disagreements and buried others. In the draft report, he called for radio to receive the same First Amendment protection as newspapers and books and for the FCC to retain its authority to review program content during license renewals. Researcher Llewellyn White termed the recommendation "meaningless double-talk." If the government evaluates media content, then something less than print-level First Amendment rights apply (as is the case now). But the wording satisfied commission members on different sides of the issues. On lesser matters, too, Hutchins tried to please everyone. They had argued over which term was more appropriate, *accountability* or *responsibility*. Hutchins used both. "The key word of the report," he said at their final meeting, "is responsibility or accountability." The men had also disagreed over whether the present moment represented a singular crisis in free speech or just another stage. "This is a stage," Hutchins said, "and yet it is a peculiar crisis." He revised the first chapter and sent it only to MacLeish, who judged it "a lovely piece of editing and synthesis and organization and everything else it ought to be," except that "it says nothing which requires contradiction by anybody including Frank Gannett, Arthur Sulzberger and Colonel Bertie": "Some of our colleagues will consider that a virtue. I, alas, do not." He added, "The Commission is convinced and I remain unconvinced. Which is why I have been remitted to the necessity of dissent."[3]

Most other potential dissenters had agreed to compromise. Chafee had been prepared to sign MacLeish's second draft. George Shuster once had planned to dissent if the discussion of pressure groups emphasized Catholic organizations like the Legion of Decency; now he said his objections were unimportant. John M. Clark said he would prefer to add a couple of quibbles in footnotes, but he wouldn't insist, "especially if footnotes don't seem to be the order of the day." Charles Merriam had talked of dissenting over film censorship, which he supported, whereas the commission's majority favored extending the First Amendment to movies. Hutchins finessed the recommendation, just as he had done with the FCC one. Extending freedom of speech to films, he wrote, "would not abolish state boards of review; it would require them to operate within the First Amendment." Merriam agreed to sign. He told his friend Harold Ickes, "I did not agree with all the details of this Report, but I went along with its general trend."[4]

A month before the commission's final meeting, *Variety* published an article suggesting that relations among its members were fraying. "At least two or three members of the commission may file minority reports," *Variety* said, and it quoted the insinuations of an unnamed commission insider concerning the supplemental volumes by staff researchers, which would include Llewellyn White on the radio industry and Ruth Inglis on Hollywood. "It has suddenly been discovered that there isn't enough money to probe the press, the magazine field or the book field," the source said. "As a result, there will be frank and open discussion of the radio and film industries. But, by some strange circumstance, the fields to which Luce is closest will be discussed only in the general report." The commission had started looking into the print press, according to the article, and spent about $12,000 on research conducted by two midwestern professors, but "the stuff is in the files." It's true that Ralph Casey and Ralph Nafziger, both then at the University of Minnesota, had conducted research for the commission. It's also true that Robert Leigh had tentatively planned to have them write brief reports to be published by the commission—*Newspaper Self-Regulation*, by Casey, and *Newspapers, Radio, Motion Pictures: Organization and Experiences in Some Foreign Countries*, by Nafziger—but the idea had been dropped long before. The identity of the source is unknown; however, *Variety* had previously interviewed the documentary filmmaker John Grierson, the foreign adviser who extolled sensationalism.[5]

The commission assembled at the Shoreland Hotel in Chicago on September 15, 1946, for a final three-day meeting. Four members—Harold Lasswell, Reinhold Niebuhr, John Dickinson, and John Clark—were absent, as was John Grierson. Those attend-

ing seemed eager to put the project behind them. Chafee characterized it as "an unusually successful meeting as well as a grand
time."[6]

William Ernest Hocking thought they had done a "magnifi-
cent" job, ranking with Aristotle's *Politics* and Milton's *Areopagitica*.
Substantial parts of the draft report reflected his thinking. An appendix featured a twenty-seven-page summary of his commission
book, *Freedom of the Press: A Framework of Principle*. In addition, a
section of his philosophical analysis appeared in the opening chapter. Several members objected to what they considered a surfeit of
Hocking, especially in the first chapter. Chafee said the effort to
meld Hutchins's concrete urgency with Hocking's abstract philosophy was "like expounding *The Critique of Pure Reason* while intro-
ducing oneself to a young lady at a dance."[7]

Hutchins defended the chapter. Given the makeup of the commission, he said, readers would expect a philosophical analysis. In
passing, he mentioned another consideration. "Our benefactor is
under the impression that the whole Commission is busily doing
what Hocking has done," by "producing a monumental philosophical treatise." For that reason, he said, "I think the report will be regarded by our benefactor as deficient." But he quickly added, "Not
that that should determine us." The Hocking material stayed, and
no more was said about Henry Luce's expectations.

Archibald MacLeish at first complained about the draft's "pu-
sillanimity." He wanted the report to denounce concentrated ownership in the media industries and endorse antitrust law as a
remedy. He again promoted his notion of press freedom as the
right to use the press, "the right of a man to publish." His argument continued to baffle others. "I don't get it still; I'm sorry," replied Hutchins. "This has bothered me for two years." As the hours
passed, MacLeish softened. He praised Hutchins's edits, punched
up the opening paragraphs, and stopped talking about publishing a
dissent. Still, he remained skeptical that admonitions without the
force of law would be enough to effect meaningful change.

Chafee brought up the antitrust case against the Associated
Press. In an article published before the first court ruling, he had
urged the AP to change its rules voluntarily and thereby moot the
case. The AP had paid no heed.

"I failed miserably," Chafee said.

"We will too," replied MacLeish.[8]

One discussion at the final meeting concerned the press council or, as they sometimes called it, the "continuing commission": whether it was weighty enough to be their principal recommendation and whether they ought to try to launch it before disbanding.

"If I were working for Colonel McCormick and were given this General Report to review," said Hutchins, "I would entitle it 'Mr. Luce's $200,000 mouse.' . . . You have worked together for two and a half years, spent all this money, got all these great figures together, what is the upshot? The upshot is that we ought to have a Commission to keep on doing this thing every year."

Beardsley Ruml suggested that they solicit a public response in the report. If readers wrote letters asking them to establish the organization, they would proceed; "if the thing falls on barren soil, to the devil with it."

"There is a slight element of the 'phony' in there somewhere," said Hutchins. "It is going to look as though we are sitting around waiting for proper applause so that we can get together and have some more expensive meetings and eat expensive meals. . . . The sensibilities in the situation require us to be extremely backward in coming forward."

Chafee, who was cool to the recommendation anyway, agreed. "If enough people want it, it will be done," he said. "I am not worried." The discussion moved on.[9]

The men negotiated substance, style, and minutiae—overuse of the word *dilemma*, the meaning of *obviate*, whether to add subheads. Finally Hutchins said, "I hate to mention it but the time is running out."

MacLeish asked for two minutes to make a statement. He set aside his disagreements and paid tribute to the chairman. "I would like to express for myself what I know everybody else would like to say to you, Hutchins," he said. "I think that whatever else comes out of the work of the Commission or its Report, the thing has been a human triumph for you. I think every one of us ends with a feeling of confidence and respect and admiration and affection. It has been a most difficult thing to do; I can't imagine a more difficult group of people to try to move together, and a more difficult subject. As one who has a few grinding wheels over his face, I feel it very strongly. I would like to say I think you have done a superb job and I am very proud and very, very happy to have had anything to do with it."

The men applauded.

"If I had the choice which Thomas Jefferson had . . . of picking the epitaph on a tombstone," Hutchins responded, "I would pick the fact that I have had the pleasure and honor of associating with you gentlemen for these two and a half years. It has been a great experience and a great privilege."[10]

That evening, the men dined at Hutchins's house, and, according to Robert Leigh, "everybody engaged in self-congratulation."[11]

After the September 15 meeting, Hutchins revised the draft. On October 18, he sent the others a new manuscript, with the title *A Free and Accountable Press: A General Report on Mass Communication—Newspapers, Radio, Motion Pictures, Magazines, and Books*. (It was among the first works to use *mass communication*, though MacLeish considered the term "awfully clumsy.") At the beginning of November, Leigh sent commission members thirty-nine revised pages "to take account" of their "most recent suggestions."[12]

Many of these final changes, some of them significant, seem to have come not from any commission member but from a funder: William Benton, who had contributed $15,000 through Encyclopædia Britannica. Benton in 1929 had cofounded Benton & Bowles, among the first ad agencies to take radio seriously. After leaving advertising in 1936, he worked with Hutchins at the University of Chicago and then served in the State Department, where he helped create the Voice of America. Benton's Benton & Bowles payout and his later investments made him a wealthy man. He owned the Muzak Corporation—the source, he said, of the only music on Earth designed not to be heard—and a controlling interest in Britannica, which was about to publish the Great Books.[13]

Benton, then the assistant secretary of state for public affairs, "sat up all one night in Washington rewriting" the report, he said later. "I made hundreds and hundreds of changes. . . . Thank God I did. If I hadn't, the criticisms would have been far more severe."

He excised some recommendations, such as a call to enhance the independence of journalists by putting them on three-year employment contracts. He deleted an assertion that better journalism might "reduce somewhat the huge profits" of media organizations, but this "would be a small price to pay for the continued freedom of the press." He cut a passage describing advertising as "irrelevant to the formation of a rational judgment." Even the title changed: *A Free and Accountable Press*, as Leigh had called it, became *A Free and Responsible Press*. Hutchins evidently didn't tell the others about Benton's role.[14]

MacLeish protested some of the new changes, writing in a telegram to Hutchins, "The matter cut out is in all cases true and relevant." Given the report's criticism of the news media for caving in to pressure groups, it would be "intolerable and most embarrassing" for the commission to pull its punches. He insisted that Hutchins restore three passages from earlier drafts. "I am unyielding."[15]

Hutchins restored some of the material but in a form so heavily edited as to be almost unrecognizable. One of Benton's excisions said that the pursuit of scoops "often seems childish, and sometimes cruel"; Hutchins diluted it to say that the pursuit "seems often to lead to unfortunate excesses." The original, before Benton's edits, said that the premature announcement of the German surrender, when the Associated Press broke an embargo, "led to doubts about the value and legitimacy of a game that could be played with such irresponsibility and heartlessness." Hutchins's rewrite said that the incident "unsettled people's confidence ... and marred the generally good war record of the press in safeguarding important announcements." MacLeish also insisted on restoration of the demand for media organizations to use some of their "huge profits" for public service. This demand, Hutchins simply ignored. MacLeish was en route to Paris, having been appointed chair of the American delegation to UNESCO by Assistant Secretary of State Benton.[16]

A different demand came from John Dickinson, the enforcer-turned-opponent of antitrust laws. In a letter to Hutchins, he complained that the University of Chicago's jacket copy for *A Free and Responsible Press* indulged in the same sensationalism that the report criticized. Hutchins invited him to rewrite it. Dickinson eliminated a reference to "gigantic business units" and toned down other criticisms of media corporations.[17]

Hutchins's foreword to *A Free and Responsible Press* deals with two potential objections. The first is the report's dearth of names, dates, and details. The members "heard testimony" from 58 people, wrote Hutchins, and the staff conducted more than 225 additional interviews, though "the Commission did not conduct elaborate 'research.'" (A. J. Liebling later remarked that Hutchins seemed to regard *research* as a neologism.) The report includes "only so much factual description of the press as is necessary to understand its conclusions"; six separately published studies would provide more thorough treatments. Five of the six promised books ultimately appeared, two by members (Zechariah Chafee on First Amendment law and William Ernest Hocking on the philosophy of press freedom) plus three by staff (Llewellyn White on radio, White and Robert Leigh on international communication, and Ruth Inglis on movies). Milton Stewart never finished his book on news coverage of the conference that led to the United Nations Charter. Second, Hutchins acknowledged the thinness of the recommendations. They are "not startling," he wrote. "The most surprising thing about them is that nothing more surprising could be proposed." The recommendations are "all that can properly be done," and "it is of the utmost importance, then, that these things should actually be done."[18]

The report itself sets the groundwork with three general observations about freedom of expression. First, it is a uniquely vital freedom, the bedrock of a free society, the chief protector of all other freedoms. Second, it is a uniquely imperiled freedom, because of the "inveterate and probably ineradicable" desire to silence opinions that differ from one's own. Third, it is a uniquely dangerous freedom, because words can incite passions, spread vulgarity, and fuel cynicism. "If we are to live progressively we must live dangerously."[19]

The news media always play an essential role in nurturing "the mind of democracy," the report says, but "the present world crisis" has raised the stakes. The citizen's need for information is greater than ever before. The press, particularly the print press, is more powerful than ever before. It can "endanger the peace of the world," or it can help safeguard it by building a global community of mutual understanding. (Hutchins ignored Ruth Inglis's objection: "Understanding may lead to hatred as well as brotherly love.") The media are falling short—so short, in fact, that "it becomes an imperative question whether the performance of the press can any longer be left to the unregulated initiative of the few who manage it."[20]

In the course of the report's analysis, it talks of freedom and duty, moral rights and legal rights, freedom *from* and freedom *for,* private censors and public censors, speaker rights and listener rights, responsibility and accountability, all of which boils down to this: the press must provide a platform for diverse opinions as well as "uncontaminated mental food" in the form of balanced and accurate news. In arguing for diverse opinions, the report adopts Archibald MacLeish's account of history. When the First Amendment was written, "anybody with anything to say had comparatively little difficulty in getting it published." Now, though, "the right of free public expression has . . . lost its earlier reality," because "the owners and managers of the press" can censor ideas as effectively as the government. To restore true freedom of expression, "the great agencies of mass communication should regard themselves as common carriers of public discussion." With regard to coverage of public affairs, the report enumerates factors that twist the news, including sensationalism, intentional falsehoods, reinforcement of group stereotypes, the blurring of fact and opinion, the blurring of news and advertising, "keyhole gossip, rumor, character assassination," and especially "the evil effects" of concentrated ownership.[21]

From the beginning, commission members had talked of listing the press's principal duties. In early 1944, Harold Lasswell set forth thirteen "performance standards." Leigh proposed additional criteria, including a ban on ads for lotteries. After several revisions, the last Leigh draft set forth five requirements. Hutchins considered the list "naïve, eye wash, Pollyannish, . . . pietistic and impractical," but because other commission members liked it, he sharpened the phrasing and left it in: "Today our society needs, first, a truthful, comprehensive, and intelligent account of the day's events in a context which gives them meaning; second, a forum for the exchange of comment and criticism; third, a means of projecting the opinions and attitudes of the groups in the society to one another; fourth, a method of presenting and clarifying the goals and values of the society; and, fifth, a way of reaching every member of the society by the currents of information, thought, and feeling which the press supplies."[22]

What could be done to improve the press? With other institutions, the report says, "government as the representative of the people as a whole" can seek change through regulation. But the system of free expression is different. Because "public opinion is a factor in official livelihood," those who are in power may be tempted to manipulate the debate. Accordingly, the law must always be a last resort. Owners, managers, editors, and reporters must do better on their own, out of recognition that they are "performing a public service of a professional kind." If they fail to improve, the press will sooner or later lose its freedom, because "no democracy ... will indefinitely tolerate concentrations of private power irresponsible and strong enough to thwart the aspirations of the people." Curtailment of press freedom would be calamitous: we would "lose our chief safeguard against totalitarianism—and at the same time take a long step toward it." But curtailment is inevitable unless the press improves its performance. The First Amendment will provide no shield; "the amendment will be amended."[23]

The passive voice reflects the commission's fuzziness on what might happen. At one point, Hutchins asked who would deprive an irresponsible press of its freedom, and how: "*What* is *who* going to do about it?" Some members suggested that an angry public might rise up and repeal the First Amendment. Others thought the danger was an indifferent public. "When people have come to regard a publication as trash," wrote Zechariah Chafee, "they do not care much if it is kept from them." Reinhold Niebuhr and several others favored a different argument: an irresponsible press doesn't threaten freedom of the press in isolation; rather, it threatens a free society, including freedom of the press.[24]

Near the end, the report delicately addresses the issue of an undemanding audience. Whereas it earlier frets that the public may rebel against journalistic irresponsibility, now it frets that the public hasn't even noticed. "We have the impression that the American people do not realize what has happened to them. ... They have not yet understood how far the performance of the press falls short of the requirements of a free society in the world today. The principal object of our report is to make these points clear."[25]

The closing chapter reiterates the warning that the press faces a choice between accountability from within and regulation from without. It then presents five recommendations for government, five for the press, and three for the public, though other recommendations are sprinkled throughout. For government, the report says, "we do not believe that the fundamental problems of the press will be solved by more laws," though reconsideration might be necessary in the event of new abuses. Instead, it urges extending full First Amendment protection to radio and motion pictures; using antitrust laws cautiously to promote competition but not "to force the breaking-up of large units" or to bar compacts intended to raise standards; enacting laws that provide for retractions or replies as an alternative to libel lawsuits; repealing laws against advocating revolutionary change absent a clear and present danger (a Chafee recommendation that, after Hutchins's extensive cuts, was unrelated to anything else in the report); and publicizing government policies domestically and internationally through the media, including, if necessary, government-owned media. The recommendations for the press include accepting "the responsibilities of common carriers of information and discussion"; financing media undertakings of "high literary, artistic, or intellectual quality," even without quick profits; engaging in "vigorous mutual criticism"; raising the competence (including the salaries) of the staff; and, for radio, taking program control away from sponsors.[26]

Finally, the report addresses the public. The success of boycotts "indicates what a revolt of the American people . . . might accomplish," but, it adds, "we are not in favor of a revolt," which "might lead to government control or to the emasculation of the First Amendment." Instead, it recommends that universities and other nonprofit institutions use the mass media to supplement the for-profit press, that universities create centers of scholarly study in mass communications and offer broad liberal educations to journalism students, and—its final recommendation—that "a new and independent agency" be created "to appraise and report annually upon the performance of the press." The report devotes two pages to the press council. The three numbered recommendations listed under "Public" actually address universities and nonprofits; the only actual recommendation for the public is the unnumbered counsel against boycotts.[27]

Hutchins sent the draft of *A Free and Responsible Press* to several friends and colleagues. Mortimer Adler was rapturous. The report is "so very good, so reasonable, so cogent, so clear," he said, that it "out-areos the pagitica." Laird Bell, chair of the board of trustees of the University of Chicago, thought the commission was too hasty in rejecting new regulations. "Do you adequately threaten them with sanctions if they don't regulate themselves?" he asked. Sims Carter, a former Justice Department aide working for Hutchins, was dismissive. As the report begins, he wrote, the commission is "on the horns of a dilemma," trying to "make the press accountable without impairing its freedom." In the end, "the dilemma wins."[28]

Walter Lippmann heard about the report from William Benton. "Is there any chance I could have a look at it?" he asked Hutchins. "I have great hopes of it." Hutchins sent it to him and solicited his comments but cautioned, "I do not need to tell you that this is SECRET!" After reading it, Lippmann told Hutchins that the report was "exceptionally able" as well as "brilliantly written." He thought some of the recommendations merited more emphatic treatment, and he suggested adding a discussion of the press's invasions of personal privacy. "I shall do what I can with your criticisms," Hutchins replied by telegram, "though I must admit that I am so sick of the subject that I hate to look at the report again."[29]

Hutchins heard from one of the researchers, too. Ruth Inglis, perhaps presumptuously, told him how he could have avoided "the weakness" of the report. He should have consulted with commission members individually or in small groups, drafted the report, listened to the others' criticisms, revised the draft, and published it under his own name. "A group can no more write a good 'General Report' than it can paint a good picture," she wrote. "It must be the work of one mind, one competent mind dedicated to truth." At the end of her note, she seemed to feel obliged to buck Hutchins up. "Don't be discouraged for long," she said. "A lot of people believe in you. I need to believe in you, for good objective reasons and irrational ones. You are smart and true and you greatly resemble my father."[30]

In response, Hutchins cordially disagreed. "In the first place," he wrote, "I think that the Commission did some thinking as a group. . . . In the second place, I have a little better opinion of the report than you have. . . . In the third place, the impact of the statement by one man, even as great and good a man as me, does not seem to be comparable to the effect of a statement by fifteen men of the caliber of the members of the Commission." Of the remark at the end of her letter, he said, "I am very sorry about your father."[31]

One more early reader remained to be heard from: the one who came up with the original idea for the Commission on Freedom of the Press, collaborated with Hutchins to select its members, provided the bulk of its funding, and got excluded from its meetings.

CHAPTER SIXTEEN

Gentleman's "C"

I T'S UNCLEAR HOW MUCH Henry Luce knew about the deliberations of the Commission on Freedom of the Press; but he knew something, and he didn't like it. In July 1946, four months after he had declined to give Robert Hutchins another $25,000, Luce visited William Ernest Hocking at his farm in New Hampshire. Afterward, Hocking sent Luce a draft of his appendix to *A Free and Responsible Press.* His accompanying letter sounded concerned: "A fragment of the debate will be helpful in understanding what emerges; and it seems to me to the interest of all concerned that, in *your* mind at least, there should be the three-dimensional picture—process plus result."[1]

At the commission's final meeting in September, Hutchins remarked that Luce might find the report disappointing because it wasn't "a monumental philosophical treatise." It was the first time he had suggested they were offtrack. During that meeting, Hutchins received a telegram from Luce, asking to meet in New York.[2]

Almost three years after the project's launch, Luce read the draft report of the Commission on Freedom of the Press. The Time Inc. archives contain the typewritten manuscript with his handwritten commentary in the margins. He wrote "excellent" alongside the epigraph, a quotation from John Adams supplied by Arthur Schlesinger: "If there is ever to be an amelioration of the condition of mankind, philosophers, theologians, legislators, politicians and moralists will find that the regulation of the press is the most difficult, dangerous and important problem they have to resolve. Mankind cannot now be governed without it, nor at present with it."[3]

After that, Luce's comments were mostly negative. He thought the commission blamed the press for all the flaws of American politics while failing to credit its positive contributions. He rejected Archibald MacLeish's contention that Americans could easily spread their views in the late eighteenth century. He believed that the report overstated the perils of concentrated ownership. He complained about undefined terms: what constitutes an "adequate" press or a press "available" to all? The charges of errors in the press irked him, too. He circled a reference to Time-Life Inc. and scrawled beneath it, "Gross factual inaccuracy!" The company was Time Inc.[4]

At some points, Luce seemed incensed. In response to the report's assertion that "there are no simple solutions," he wrote, "A real understanding of a problem often yields a brilliantly simple solution!" When the report said "we see" that news of public affairs accounts for only a small part of the media product, Luce wrote "we see" that professors spend only a small part of their time talking to students. A reference to "concentrations of private power ... strong enough to thwart the aspirations of the people" prompted the remark, "It may thwart *you*, but you are not the people." Other marginalia include "Shabby superficial paragraph," "childish," "God!" "Jesus!" and "Nuts!" Across the top of one page, he scrawled, "after 2nd reading I think whole thing so naïve & unsophisticated I say the Hell with it." Of Hocking's appendix, signed by all the members, Luce wrote, "Is this the best philosophy can do?"[5]

Luce circulated the draft report to members of his senior staff. Their reviews, too, were harsh. Editors and executives called the report "irritating," "over-adjectived," and "platitudinous," with "neither the fire and conviction of the crusader ... nor the detached and timeless penetration of the true philosopher." Eric Hodgins, the liaison between Time Inc. and the commission, said he was "appalled" by "how bad and how shallow" it was. Hutchins, he said, "always talks a better game than he plays."[6]

Luce evidently gave Hutchins a preliminary critique right away. In a letter to commission members on October 18, Hutchins reported that Luce "thinks there are not enough pats on the back" to the media industries. Two commission members agreed; others evidently didn't respond. Hutchins added a paragraph saying that the best American media outlets "have achieved a standard of excellence unsurpassed anywhere in the world." In a note to Zechariah Chafee, he said, "Luce is trying to decide whether to publish our report in his magazines or suppress it."[7]

On October 29, Hutchins sent a revision to Roy E. Larsen at Time Inc. In a cover note, he said, "I am sorry I ever met Harry Luce." Soon he would have reason to feel even sorrier.[8]

"I am disappointed," Luce told Hutchins in a two-page letter dated November 29, 1946, "having perhaps expected too much." He said he liked the last chapter's recommendations, but he found the account of the press's performance "elementary, naïve, superficial, uncritical and obsolete." He added, "As to the general philosophical treatment of the problem, I give your distinguished Commission a gentleman's 'C' and no more. In this area, which I regard as the most important of all, I believe that each member of the Commission could have done a better job by himself than has been done for or by the whole Commission."[9]

At the outset, Time Inc. had pledged to respect the commission's independence. Luce had acquiesced when told to stop attending meetings. Now, though, he pressed Hutchins to rework the report. Some of the major deficiencies could be remedied with "comparatively little more effort," he wrote, so "I earnestly request that you call a special meeting of the Commission in which I may present my full opinion of the Report, together with a plea that the job is worth doing better." He was speaking, he said, "as a friend of the Commission. You may deny me the right to speak in this capacity. In that case I will ask you to define the capacity in which I am entitled to be heard." If Hutchins would not reconvene the commission, then, Luce said, "I will take the Report as is and give it all the publicity in magazine form which I think it deserves."[10]

Over lunch a few days later, on December 5, Reinhold Niebuhr and Luce had a long talk. According to Niebuhr, Luce thought the report should lay greater stress on its conclusion that "since there is no legal way of enforcing the responsibility of the press without destroying its freedom, there must be a tremendous burden upon the conscience of those who control the press." Luce apparently complained about the prose as well. Niebuhr thought that an informal conversation between him and a small group of members might suffice, rather than a full commission meeting. Hocking agreed. "Harry doesn't at all realize with what strain the formulation of the Report was done," he told Hutchins. He also thought they had been "needlessly strict" in excluding Luce from deliberations, and "this blow-off may have a slight emotional basis which a small informal and unofficial conference might wholly relieve." Hocking drafted a letter to Luce but evidently didn't send it. Luce, he wrote, ought to understand that it had taken "considerable effort" to reconcile "a right and a left wing in the Commission," including a "brother with strong Morris Ernst leanings [who] is also a great Sir Galahad"—Archibald MacLeish. As for the prose, Hocking said that "poor Bob Hutchins was on the griddle all summer, after two draftsmen had failed to satisfy the Commission, and was working like a Navvy against time. Under those conditions, Pegasus makes no flights!"[11]

In a phone call with Luce on December 9, Hutchins proposed a disingenuous compromise. Luce would explain his criticisms privately, and Hutchins would convey "any meritorious suggestions" to the commission "without indicating their source." Hutchins said he would not convene a meeting for Luce to tell commission members how to rewrite the report. Luce replied that there was nothing improper in his efforts to weigh in, because "he was not an ordinary donor" and "he had had some share in the paternity of the idea." Hutchins said they could have organized a collaborative project between Luce and the commission at the start, but they hadn't. "On the contrary, all parties had insisted on the complete independence of the Commission from Time Inc. from the outset," Hutchins said, recounting the call to Niebuhr. "We would not play it both ways. He agreed." *A Free and Responsible Press* would appear as a book from the University of Chicago Press, Hutchins told Luce. If Luce didn't want to publish the report in one of his magazines, he added, that was fine; other magazines had expressed interest.[12]

Luce and Hutchins scheduled a meeting. Luce said he would detail his criticisms beforehand in writing. On December 15, 1946, he sent Hutchins what he called a "stream-of-consciousness" summary of "what's biting me."[13]

Luce's twenty-two-page critique, titled "General Commentary," is in the Commission on Freedom of the Press files in the Time Inc. company archives. Hutchins seems to have kept it out of the official records of the commission. It hasn't been found among his personal papers at the University of Chicago or in the collections of commission documents at the University of Chicago, Columbia, Brown, or the University of Washington. He did send a copy of the criticisms to William Benton, who had secretly edited the draft report, with a note saying, "I am showing them to nobody else."[14]

In the critique, Luce first mused on what had gone wrong. "Perhaps," he wrote, "the whole idea was a bad one—or not well enough thought-out, or organized on too small a scale." Maybe the *Time* model of group journalism didn't apply, and "a good philosophical production must be, ultimately, individual." Although several commission members had called the project intellectually exhilarating, he found the report "a rather tasteless dish with little suggestion of the intellectual ferment that went on among the cooks in the kitchen."[15]

Luce rattled off a series of points. He reiterated that the report oversimplified the workings of the news media. Oversimplification was a complaint frequently leveled at *Time*, a response that he tried to preempt: "TIME may often be grossly in error but it is rarely . . . so elementary!" He complained that the commission used *press* to encompass newspapers, magazines, movies, radio, and books; why not Tin Pan Alley, universities, and comic books? He charged that the report's offhand references to "our kind of society" implied universal ideals and visions. "If the Commissioners really think that the differences between the *New Republic* and the *New York Times* are relatively trivial—hardly more than Tweedledee and Tweedledum—that would be a dramatic observation: it should be explicitly made!" He rejected the commission's contention that valuable ideas were going unheard. "Wouldn't it be truer," he wrote, "to say that in our day even anybody with *nothing* to say has no difficulty in getting it published?" And he faulted the commission for neglecting culture, where he thought the press's influence was greater than in public affairs and its shortcomings more obvious.[16]

Luce's major criticism went deeper. He found the report "disappointing in the essential respect in which it was hoped that it would be excellent": philosophy. In sponsoring the study, he said, "I was not concerned ... about getting more freedom for my publications, nor about warding off any particular threats to their freedom. ... I *was* interested in a contemporary clarification of the *foundations* of my particular freedom as an editor in a general context of freedom." He also wanted a sophisticated examination of the tension between freedom and order, a topic Reinhold Niebuhr had brought up at the first meeting. "How do you restrain freedom in the interests of more freedom?" Luce asked. The commission didn't answer that question. Instead, it focused on "prudent expediencies," by arguing that "unless I and my fellows discharge our obligations more fully, our freedom may be taken away—somehow. Now this may be a very salutary warning but, as philosophy, it is scarcely inspiring."[17]

Luce went on to address the issue of accountability. "With what seems to me the most appalling lack of even high-school logic," he wrote, "the Draft Report fails to state: Who is accountable? And to whom? And for what?" The question of "to whom" loomed largest. "In order to establish the moral responsibility of the press, you must first disclose a doctrine of the moral responsibility of individual man." For Luce, Christianity supplied the answer; but the commission left it unanswered:

> It is certainly not clear whether the Commission believes in responsibility to God or only to Society. And I suppose the Commission is divided on this point and did not wish to admit such a scandal of disagreement among wise men.
>
> But, gentlemen, we look to you for the Truth as you see it. We will not accept from you any common currency of ambiguity.
>
> *If* you can all agree on a doctrine of moral responsibility to something called Society—without having to press the question of God to a conclusion—you are entitled to do so. ... But then state your doctrine clearly. Why am I responsible to Society? And who is Society? And where is it?

If such a doctrine proved insupportable, then the commission must adopt the alternative—explicitly. "The Commission," wrote Luce, "must not be afraid to announce the greatest and most exciting discovery and rediscovery man ever makes: man is responsible to his Creator."[18]

The question of responsibility *to whom* had arisen at commission meetings. The members generally believed the press's ultimate responsibility could not be to owners, advertisers, interest groups, or even to readers, if that meant giving them whatever they wanted. The press had to be responsible to a vision of the public interest, which meant addressing audience members as citizens rather than consumers. In one meeting, Hocking said the parties to any communication are speaker, listener, and a third party, the community. "And if you want to come to metaphysics," he added, "the third party is God." This was a "private judgment," he said, and probably inappropriate for a commission document. But it seemed to be what Luce had in mind.[19]

Luce traveled to Chicago and met with Hutchins on December 17. After listening to Luce's objections, Hutchins all but ignored them, making only cosmetic changes to the report. In response to Luce's overarching question—To whom does a publisher owe responsibility?—Hutchins added a few sentences to the end of the fifth chapter, including the assertion that a journalist's "responsibility is to his conscience and the common good." He made other changes to his foreword. "I decided to put it all in the Foreword," he told Luce on December 26, "not because I couldn't get—or even assume—Commission approval, but because I couldn't get the stuff into the report in any artistic way. What I need is art lessons."[20]

William Benton, the former adman, found Luce's comments on the report fascinating. They showed, he told Hutchins, that the publisher viewed the report as highly important. Benton wondered whether Hutchins had done enough in response to Luce's commentary. "You aren't as impressed with a client as I am," he said. "Further, we must both concede that Harry Luce is no ordinary client, as his comments amply demonstrate."[21]

Hutchins made no further revisions. *A Free and Responsible Press* was on its way to publication.

CHAPTER SEVENTEEN

The Luce That Laid the
Golden Egg

"I SHALL GET TO work to see what I can do to get your name in the *Tribune*," Robert Hutchins told Henry Luce in early February 1947. It wasn't hard. Time Inc. sent *Chicago Tribune* publisher Robert R. McCormick an embargoed advance copy of *A Free and Responsible Press* later that month. "You will find the opinion of our book reviewer in our book section when it is published," McCormick replied. "As to myself, I have not time to read the outpourings of a gang of crackpots."[1]

McCormick soon found the time. On March 4, nearly four weeks before the report's official release, he broke the embargo. In a speech to the International Brotherhood of Paper Makers, published in full in the *Tribune*, he warned of an effort to subvert freedom of the press on the part of Robert Hutchins, "always seeking, and seeking futilely, a position of leadership in any movement"; Henry Luce, "editor of today's 'Town Topics,' who paid the others, striving to disassociate himself in the public mind from Walter Winchell"; and a "group of pinko professors living off the money other men have made." During the year that followed, Colonel McCormick repeatedly denounced the "so-called report" written by "evil and ignorant men" and "paid for by $200,000 from Henry Luce and two cents from Robert Hutchins."[2]

"Our Report must be better than I thought if it has stirred the General to such depths," Charles Merriam told Hutchins.[3]

Despite Luce's disenchantment, Time Inc. orchestrated a splashy release for *A Free and Responsible Press*. A month before its publication, the company's public-relations coordinator moved to Chicago to oversee publicity. The report, minus William Ernest Hocking's appendix, would appear in *Fortune*. Advance copies went out to forty-six hundred publishers (including McCormick), editors, journalism professors, broadcasters, and others, accompanied by galleys of a *Fortune* editorial. "We have devoted a great deal of time studying the Report, and have undertaken in this critique to suggest to our readers some interpretations which we believe important," managing editor Ralph D. Paine Jr. wrote in a cover note.[4]

The initial draft of the *Fortune* editorial called the report "deeply disappointing, an opportunity missed," with prose that is "often opaque" and "sometimes seems devious." When Hutchins read it, he complained to William Benton that Luce was behaving "just like Colonel McCormick: get sore at any criticism, no matter how mild, and then misrepresent your critic from hell to breakfast." In hopes of modifying the magazine's judgment, Hocking, Zechariah Chafee, and Arthur Schlesinger met in Cambridge with a delegation from *Fortune*. "I think we enlightened the boys quite a bit," Chafee said afterward. The *Fortune* editors softened the editorial, though one said that the professors' explanations left him more confused than ever.[5]

The commission's overspending meant that several plans got shelved. At the outset, Hutchins and Time Inc.'s Eric Hodgins had planned to convene a Journalistic Board of Review to read and comment on the report before publication. It never happened. The commission at one point planned hearings in two dozen cities, with journalists and news consumers talking about the press and its problems. As the money dwindled, the multicity hearings, featuring citizens discussing the press, got whittled down to a single hearing in New York, with journalists and commission members discussing the report. Even that never happened. Perhaps the Journalistic Board of Review and the hearings would have improved the report; they surely would have improved its reception.[6]

Before the release of *A Free and Responsible Press*, Hutchins went to Washington, DC, presented a copy to President Truman, and met with twenty-eight columnists and journalists for an off-the-record conversation. The official release came at a news conference in New York, attended by most commission members. Staff members Robert Leigh, Llewellyn White, and Ruth Inglis came too, but not Milton Stewart, who never completed his book. Also absent was Henry Luce.[7]

In an opening statement at the news conference, Hutchins seemed to walk back the criticism in the report. "The emphasis on the irresponsibility of some units of the industry is not to be taken as suggesting that the American press as a whole is irresponsible or that all units are failing to discharge their responsibility," he said. "The Commission recognizes the great accomplishments of the American press as a whole and the leadership of some units in particular." He also made a point of saying the report "is aimed directly at the owners and managers," not reporters. When asked about the *Fortune* critique, he replied, "Since it is largely devoted to the obscurity of my literary style I will reply that I don't understand the editorial." As for substance, he declared, "It is inconceivable to me that Henry Luce would disagree with the general conclusions of the report."[8]

Given that *A Free and Responsible Press* castigated the press for sloppy reporting, it had to be airtight in its factual assertions. It wasn't. A footnote inaccurately said that the Gannett Newspapers chain was limited to upstate New York. Critics pounced on the minor error. A Rutgers journalism professor said he would expect better reporting from any freshman. (Time Inc. had saved the commission from a second error, the one that Luce had labeled a "gross factual inaccuracy" on his copy of the manuscript. Ralph Paine told the University of Chicago Press that the company was not Time-Life Inc. but Time Inc., and it got corrected.) "Mr. Hutchins naturally feels quite badly about the inaccuracies in the Commission's final report," Time Inc.'s Bernie Auer told colleagues. "And this is the main reason why he is so terribly disappointed in Leigh, as Leigh was the one who furnished the facts and was responsible for the research."[9]

Leigh, meanwhile, angled for as much credit as he could get. His draft of the foreword to the report acknowledged "the director and staff" on a par with commission members. Hutchins deleted it. Leigh told the University of Chicago Press that it would be "highly improper and unfair" to identify Hutchins as the book's editor; the book names Leigh instead. Though he said he was "greatly embarrassed" to make the request, he asked to be added to the acknowledgments in Zechariah Chafee's book. Chafee agreed.[10]

In an article declaring that "for the time and the money, and the caliber of the men, it was a disappointing report," *Time* said that Archibald MacLeish wrote the first draft of *A Free and Responsible Press* and Hutchins and Leigh collaborated on the final one. (Actually, Leigh wrote two drafts, followed by two by MacLeish, three by Leigh, and three by Hutchins.) Hutchins complained that the *Time* story was completely false, "a perfect example of the type of irresponsible journalism which the Commission was attacking." He may have feared Pulitzer-winner MacLeish's response to the insinuation that his prose had been unsatisfactory. *Time* staff tracked down the source of the information on authorship: Robert Leigh. A researcher at the magazine remarked on "Leigh's insistence that he get credit for his share of the writing." When *Time* checked back after Hutchins's outburst, Leigh said that he had misspoken and that MacLeish hadn't written any drafts at all. "Leigh, not TIME, seems to be to blame for all the confusion," a Time Inc. staff member told colleagues. "He is by nature, I understand, somewhat discoordinated." In a letter about the authorship fracas, Luce chided Hutchins: "It is desirable that the press should not lie. It is also desirable that the press should not be lied *to*."[11]

In *Fortune*'s editorial, it commended several elements of *A Free and Responsible Press*, including retraction as an alternative to libel, the common-carrier model, and the press council. But it said the report exaggerated the threat of monopoly, rhapsodized about a Golden Age of American journalism that never existed, and unjustly criticized press performance. The editors also judged the report "exasperatingly cryptic." At times, it "seems to say precisely the opposite of what, on balance, it appears the Commissioners meant." In a letter to Luce, MacLeish said, "Teaching one's grandmother to suck eggs has nothing on the effort of a FORTUNE editor to teach Bob Hutchins how to write clear English."[12]

Other responses to *A Free and Responsible Press* varied widely. The report received praise in some circles, ranging from gushing ("one of the most important books in many years"—*New Republic*) to tepid ("a pretty good job"—*Los Angeles Times*). Several reviewers found it humdrum. Kenneth Stewart of *PM*, writing in *Saturday Review*, said the report's bottom line seemed unhelpful: "the press can be better if it will be better." In a short, unsigned review, the *New Yorker* called it "an interesting document, but without much wallop." The *New York Times Book Review* said that the commission "bit off more than it could chew." ("I'm afraid that is true," said commission member John Clark.)[13]

A few young journalists found the report inspiring. Harry S. Ashmore of the *Arkansas Gazette* applauded it; later he went to work for Hutchins and then wrote a biography of him. Partly out of admiration for the Hutchins Commission, Harold Evans of the *Manchester Evening News*, future editor of the *Sunday Times*, decided to study at the University of Chicago on a Harkness Fellowship in the mid-1950s, though Hutchins was no longer there. "Some of us in the trenches were stirred," recalled Norman E. Isaacs of the *St. Louis Star-Times*, later a prominent editor, publisher, and educator. "We were, however, an all-but-silenced minority."[14]

Press critics gave the report mixed reviews. In the *Nation*, A. J. Liebling of the *New Yorker* said, "I was inclined to wonder uncharitably as I read the book what they had spent the $200,000 on; it contains some sound, unoriginal reflections, but nothing worth over one grand even at *Ladies Home Journal* rates." George Seldes called *A Free and Responsible Press* "the most important report on the press in our history," though he lamented that it didn't back up its assertions with the evidence he had offered to provide. In a letter to Robert Leigh, Morris Ernst called the report "exciting reading and a real important contribution," but he issued a harsher judgment in a review published in several newspapers: "I'm bitter about this report. Bitter because I liked the members; some I consider friends and each one is on the side of the angels: i.e. a free marketplace of thought." But their report made "liberty seem vague, freedom seem doubtful, and democracy seem less than an answer to communism." I. F. Stone dismissed *A Free and Responsible Press* as "a lot of high-class crap."[15]

Much of the journalism fraternity seemed to respond with a mix of panic and fury. Some of the harshest commentators believed, or claimed to believe, that *A Free and Responsible Press* called for draconian regulation of the news media. The *Wall Street Journal* construed *responsibility* as a code word for *censorship*. According to Kent Cooper, executive director of the Associated Press, the commission seemed to endorse "the Russian Soviet conception of press control." In *Editor & Publisher*, Frank Thayer, a lawyer who taught journalism at the University of Wisconsin, charged the commission with adopting "the theories of the Star Chamber." Members of the American Society of Newspaper Editors debated, at times with rancor, whether to denounce the commission or ignore it; the latter faction prevailed.[16]

Under the headline " 'A Free Press' (Hitler Style) Sought for U.S.," the *Chicago Tribune* inveighed against *A Free and Responsible Press* as "a major effort in the campaign of a determined group of totalitarian thinkers ... who want to discredit the free press of America or put it under a measure of government control sufficient to stop effective criticism of New Deal socialism, the one-world doctrine, and internationalism." Reviewer Frank Hughes said the report embodies the spirit of "the late Adolf Hitler and the late Joseph Goebbels." Convinced that the commission was part of a conspiracy to destroy a free press, Colonel McCormick paid Hughes to write a book-length exposé. The 642-page red-baiting diatribe, *Prejudice and the Press: A Restatement of the Principle of Freedom of the Press with Specific Reference to the Hutchins-Luce Commission*, appeared in 1950, three years after *A Free and Responsible Press*.[17]

As for specific complaints, some journalists resented the commission for lumping them in with radio and movies, a point Luce had raised as well. "How the billboard escaped is not explained," wrote Frank Tripp of Gannett Newspapers. He called for a report on the state of the American university, with *university* defined to include "dancing classes, hair-dressing courses, riding academies and the Brooklyn Dodgers."[18]

Virtually without exception, the denunciations stressed that *A Free and Responsible Press* was the work not just of nonjournalists (though this too occasioned comment) but of professors. Some of the book's fans seemed defensive on this point. "Though the report comes from a group of academicians," said *Printer's Ink*, "it is worthy of serious consideration." According to some critics, the analysis was theoretical and impractical—therefore academic—because the commission failed to do any research. Columnist George Sokolsky wrote that "the professors were too busy with general pontification to make a direct study of the matter in hand"; they should have stuck with the usual topics of professorial interest such as "Icelandic Sagas and the use of the diphthong in Indo-Iranian languages." The authors were accused of naïveté, too. Of the report's call for coverage of music education in schools, *Editor & Publisher* said, "EXTRA! BEETHOVEN CRASHES FIRST GRADE!" Others charged that the authors were elitists bent on establishing a dictatorship of the professoriate. Wilbur Forrest, president of the American Society of Newspaper Editors, said that nonprofit news outlets, one of the commission's recommendations, could be expected to "tell the reader what someone thinks he ought to know, whether the reader likes it or not," suggesting that advertisers were the only thing standing between the newspaper reader and a Great Books lecture. Like *Fortune*, many critics judged the report poorly written, and some blamed academia. *Editor & Publisher* called it an incomprehensible "philosophical treatise" and said that "what the Free Press Commission needed was a good reporter like Walter Winchell." Winchell quoted the line in his column, adding, "Oh, daahleeng! You may kiss my hand." Finally, some critics charged that the recommendations were motivated by self-interest. Sokolsky observed that if journalists were better educated, it would mean more jobs for professors. Of the commission's call for a press council supported by outside funding, Kenneth Stewart said, "Why destroy the Luce that laid the golden egg?"[19]

Of the report's recommendations, the press council appealed to many commentators, even some of the critics. Forrest said he would support it if it included journalists. *Editor & Publisher* endorsed the idea, saying that the organization "might even help to straighten out the professors' thinking." MacLeish's call for "vigorous mutual criticism" among journalists proved less popular. Such criticism "must always be suspected of a self-interested motive," said the *New York Times Book Review*. Walter Lippmann thought that "mutual criticism, like marital criticism, if it is publicly made, is too hard for mortal men to take." (He didn't mention that he had read and commented on the report before publication.) External criticism, though, was a different matter. Lippmann thought the commission's greatest legacy would be its endorsement of press criticism and the example it provided—a "brave, and often brilliant, attempt to show how those who cherish freedom can equip themselves intellectually and morally to criticize a free press." A. J. Liebling agreed that "a chief service of the volume is that it makes criticism of the press respectable."[20]

In the public eye, those who were associated with the Hutchins Commission, said researcher Llewellyn White, had become "assassins of the press." Hutchins, though, said the reaction wasn't as harsh as he had expected. "It is odd that the Press in general has reacted as well to our report as it has," he told Zechariah Chafee; "our severest critic is our Benefactor!" Time Inc. meticulously reviewed reaction to the report. Media coverage was heavy, but *Time* and *Fortune* received hardly any letters on the topic; and the book sold poorly. A Time Inc. staff member said that "the public seems apathetic."[21]

After publication of *A Free and Responsible Press*, Henry Luce scrawled a short note to two of his executives, apologizing for the $200,000 the corporation had spent on the Commission on Freedom of the Press. "Now that it's about all over," he wrote, "let me say I'm sorry I got you into such a bad thing." He added, with a reference to the corporate tax rate at the time, "But I really don't think it did Time Inc. much harm—and the dollars were mostly 30¢ dollars."[22]

Nonetheless, Luce thanked commission members for their work. The Time Inc. archives contain a draft of his letter. "Nothing in a long time has brought me such great good cheer," he wrote, "for your Report is a marvelously striking demonstration of how utterly dependent we are on the mercy of God. . . . My only serious criticism . . . is that you did not think it expedient so to violate the contemporary taboos regarding the Almighty as to publicly and humbly confess this ultimate reliance." Luce decided to omit these sentiments from the final letter, which simply thanked the men for their "service to The Press and to the cause of Freedom." ("Mr. Luce has not included me among the number of people to whom he sent his letter, indicating that he appreciated their services," Robert Leigh complained to Charles Merriam. "I don't think he appreciates mine.")[23]

"You are the ideal benefactor," Hutchins replied. "In addition to the regrets which I have already expressed orally, I have only to add that I am sorry that very difficult personal problems in the past three years have prevented me from giving the Commission the kind of leadership it ought to have had and the kind which you were entitled to expect from me." He had moved out of the house and left his wife three weeks earlier.[24]

Elsewhere, Hutchins adopted a jocular tone about *A Free and Responsible Press*. He told a Time Inc. executive that the project might be remembered as the Luce Commission rather than the Hutchins Commission, adding, "I certainly will do everything to encourage it."[25]

The journalism historians Margaret A. Blanchard and Victor Pickard both write that *A Free and Responsible Press* set forth a perspective whose time had come. At first, actually, it looked like a perspective whose time had come and gone. In fact, the book's timing could hardly have been worse. The Cold War "changed almost everything about American intellectual life," writes Louis Menand.[26]

Those who were involved with the Hutchins Commission noted the shift. Instead of elation over the end of the war, Mac-Leish wrote in early 1946, Americans "feel only apprehension." In July, the commission foreign adviser John Grierson remarked that "only a year after victory, the long downward spiral seems to be beginning over again," just as it did after the First World War. On November 5, the day Hutchins thanked Walter Lippmann for his prepublication comments on the report, Republicans won control of both the House of Representatives and the Senate. Garry Wills dates the beginning of the McCarthy era to 1947, the year *A Free and Responsible Press* appeared, when President Truman signed an executive order to screen the federal civil service for loyalty, the Justice Department compiled its first list of subversive organizations, the members of the Hollywood Ten were cited for contempt of Congress, and three former FBI agents launched the blacklist newsletter *Counterattack*. Hutchins had applauded the Brains Trust in 1933; in 1947, with loyalty investigations, hyperpartisanship, and tirades against public employees, he said he no longer could recommend that University of Chicago professors or graduates work in government.[27]

In the 1940s, commission members identified with the masses. Explaining the commission to a radio audience, George Shuster said that "the American public actually sat in criticism over its newspapers." A few years later, when much of the American public supported Senator Joseph McCarthy (whose rallies featured the song "Nobody Loves McCarthy but the People"), the masses seemed alien to intellectuals. And vice versa: to many Americans in the early Cold War years, intellectuals were not simply muddle-headed denizens of the Ivory Tower but traitors providing aid and comfort to the enemy. Brains Distrust had set in.[28]

Hutchins agreed to meet with Frank Hughes of the *Chicago Tribune*, who was working on his *Tribune*-financed book about the Commission on Freedom of the Press, *Prejudice and the Press*. In Hutchins's office, Hughes began listing commission members' affiliations with allegedly communist-tainted organizations. "Oh, so that's it, is it?" Hutchins shouted. In Hughes's account, "He insisted that any evidence of pro-Communist affiliations on the part of members . . . was 'ridiculous' and 'absurd.' It was explained to him with some difficulty, because both the Chancellor and the interviewer were trying to talk at once, that nobody was suggesting the 'commissioners' were Communists. The use of their names in Communist front organizations, which are documented in government records, certainly indicated, however, a predominately sympathetic approach . . . toward this brand of totalitarianism. Mr. Hutchins denied this, categorically."[29]

At the end of 1947, one of the former commission researchers came to the attention of the FBI director. After learning of his criticism of the bureau-blessed radio show *This Is Your FBI*, J. Edgar Hoover asked an aide, "Just who is Llewellyn White?" Agents prepared a memo on White and the Hutchins Commission. After reading it, Hoover wrote at the bottom, "It is significant to note the background & slant of not only White but also some of the members of the Commission under which he operated." The FBI was already compiling files on suspicious activities and affiliations of several of those associated with the commission, including Hutchins, Reinhold Niebuhr, Archibald MacLeish, and Harold Lasswell, as well as staff director Robert Leigh and White's fellow researcher Milton Stewart. "No investigation has been conducted concerning this organization [i.e., the commission] by the Bureau," one FBI agent wrote.[30]

The other researcher, Ruth Inglis, had supported FDR, but her views began to change while she worked for the commission. As an additional recommendation for the final chapter of *A Free and Responsible Press*, she proposed calling on magazines to disclose the political affiliations of their writers, particularly "membership in Communist fronts." Her suggestion was ignored. When a commission member asked her about George Seldes's newsletter, *In Fact*, she responded, "I find it revealing that the sheet is printed by the New Union Press (union label No. 412) which is a business enterprise of the Communist Party." The information probably came from the man she was dating, J. B. Matthews, the former research director of the Dies Committee (predecessor of the House Un-American Activities Committee) and a prominent writer, lecturer, consultant, and expert witness in anticommunist circles. Inglis and Matthews married in 1949, and she left her post–Hutchins Commission job as a sociology professor at the University of Washington and moved to New York. There, she helped ghostwrite a book for Senator McCarthy, held a party for Ayn Rand, befriended William F. Buckley Jr., dug for dirt to discredit Edward R. Murrow after his McCarthy takedown, and added names to the Hollywood blacklist. Her onetime mentor Paul Lazarsfeld called her a fascist. In a speech in 1957, ten years after telling Hutchins that he reminded her of her father, she called for the House Un-American Activities Committee to investigate the anti-red-baiting Fund for the Republic and its "arrogant" president, Robert Hutchins.[31]

Times had changed. In 1947, the sales manager of University of Chicago Press said of *A Free and Responsible Press*, "Future generations may well consider this one of the most important documents on human freedom produced in our time." Less than a decade later, it seemed like a relic of a bygone era. In 1956, the University of Chicago Press decided against reissuing it. "Much of the general report consists of declarations of principles with a moral flavor," one editor wrote, "and though the sermon part may not be outdated, I imagine the listeners have tired of it in this particular form." Accordingly, *A Free and Responsible Press* was "best left unresurrected."[32]

But rebirth was already under way, in an unlikely place.

CHAPTER EIGHTEEN

From Target to Canon

IN 1944, ROBERT LEIGH hired Ralph D. Casey, head of the School of Journalism at the University of Minnesota, as a research consultant. "I quite blithely defy the Commission prejudice against schools of journalism (which I heartily share) in thinking of Casey for this job," Leigh told Robert Hutchins. "He is really an exception to the rule." A journalist-turned-scholar with a doctorate from the University of Wisconsin, Casey had published articles in the *Annals of Political and Social Science*, collaborated with Harold Lasswell on a bibliography of scholarship on propaganda, and worked as a consultant to Archibald MacLeish's Office of Facts and Figures. Under contract to the Hutchins Commission, he prepared a memo on newspaper self-regulation (he was paid $225) and attended several meetings. The commission's list of planned reports at one point included *Newspaper Self-Regulation*, by Casey, but it got scrapped, perhaps for budgetary reasons.[1]

Over lunch at the Shoreland Hotel in Chicago in 1945, Casey told commission members about trends in journalism education. According to notes taken by Leigh, he said that the better schools were stressing scholarly research, a development that he predicted would bolster their standing in academia. He acknowledged that many schools were "of very inferior grade as to teaching personnel," but he maintained that they were improving. Students were required to take only three or four skills classes; the bulk of coursework, he said, was in the liberal arts. Hutchins, unsurprisingly, suggested eliminating the skills classes altogether. Casey said they were necessary. "He confirmed our worst fears," Hutchins said afterward. Casey, for his part, told an acquaintance that during his twenty minutes with the commission, he had endured fifteen minutes of insults.[2]

When Casey read *A Free and Responsible Press* in 1947, he was floored. The report says that "tricks and machinery of the trade" dominate the journalism-school curriculum, to the neglect of the liberal arts—the opposite of what he had told the group. In a letter to Leigh, he demanded to know where the commission had gotten its information. "Who conducted the studies?" he asked. "We have a right to know." Other journalism educators also complained. J. Edward Gerald of the University of Minnesota charged that the commission used the "hit-and-run tactics" of tabloids. Grant M. Hyde, head of the journalism school at the University of Wisconsin, said Hutchins "would show a more scholarly spirit" if he would gather facts before opining.[3]

At the end of 1947, Hutchins answered the question about where the commission had gotten its information. Addressing a conference of journalism professors, he promoted *A Free and Responsible Press* and its recommendation for a press council. In passing, he took note of the charge that the commission had disparaged journalism schools out of ignorance. Not so, said Hutchins. The commission "had a special study made of education in journalism by the dean of one of the best schools." He provided no further details. The "special study" was Leigh's page and a half of notes on Casey's twenty-minute presentation, which Hutchins ignored when writing the report.[4]

Hutchins never embraced journalism education, but with time, journalism educators embraced the Hutchins Commission. It started 140 miles from Chicago.

Fred S. Siebert, a First Amendment expert who directed the University of Illinois School of Journalism, sometimes aided Robert McCormick's lawyers. In 1928, he provided research for the Supreme Court briefs in *Near v. Minnesota*; in gratitude, the Colonel arranged a $1,000 grant to support his research. In 1946, Siebert testified in favor of McCormick's unsuccessful effort to reverse the AP antitrust decision in Congress. A year later, when a *Tribune* lawyer asked Siebert what he thought of the newly published *Free and Responsible Press*, Siebert replied that "something ought to be done about some of the major assumptions of the Luce committee," including the Golden Age characterization of founding-era newspapers, which "is, of course, historically false."[5]

Thereafter, first in a speech in 1953 and then in a book chapter published in 1954, Siebert sketched four "distinguishable theories of the function and purpose of the mass media": authoritarian, libertarian, communist, and what he termed "Social Responsibility (Hutchins Commission) Theory." (William Ernest Hocking's appendix to the report talks of "social responsibility.") Siebert didn't endorse social-responsibility theory, but notwithstanding his letter to the *Tribune* lawyer, he didn't disparage it either.[6]

The social-responsibility theory of the press developed alongside corporate social responsibility, a concept that Hutchins Commission members John M. Clark and Beardsley Ruml had discussed in print. In 1953, around the time Siebert first outlined his four models, the Williams College economist Howard R. Bowen published what became the classic work on corporate social responsibility, *Social Responsibilities of the Businessman*. Echoing the Commission on Freedom of the Press, Bowen wrote that business leaders must "follow those lines of action which are desirable in terms of the objectives and values of our society," even if it means subordinating the pursuit of profit. Freedom, he wrote, depends on responsibility: "If those who exercise freedom are unwilling . . . to relate their private decisions and actions to the attainment of valued social objectives, that freedom is in jeopardy."[7]

Siebert used his four theories in a class he taught on government and the press, and his University of Illinois colleague Wilbur Schramm summarized them in a book, *Responsibility in Mass Communication*, which featured an introduction by Reinhold Niebuhr. (Niebuhr characterized social responsibility as "only a slight variation of the libertarian theory.") The National Council of Churches funded Schramm's book, and some grant money remained. While Schramm completed his own manuscript, he offered the surplus to Siebert for a quick book on the four theories. Siebert said he didn't

have time to write a whole book, but he could set forth two of the
theories if Schramm and another Illinois colleague, Theodore Peterson, would write about the other two. Schramm agreed. So did
Peterson, a new member of the faculty who had finished his doctorate under Siebert and Schramm a year earlier. Peterson hoped
to be assigned the chapter on libertarian theory, but Siebert took it.
"As junior author," Peterson later recounted, "I was stuck with social responsibility."[8]

As Siebert had done in his original taxonomy, Peterson credited
the Hutchins Commission with laying out the most detailed explanation of the social-responsibility model. But he diverged from the
commission on a few points. His chapter points out, as *A Free and
Responsible Press* does not, that social-responsibility theory rests on an
unflattering view of the citizen as "not so much irrational as lethar-
gic" and vulnerable to manipulation by demagogues, advertisers, and
propagandists. Accordingly, the press must find ways to draw the audience's attention. It also must safeguard the public by acting as a
watchdog against corruption and abuse of power in government, a
function omitted from *A Free and Responsible Press*.[9]

Although Peterson later said he tried to explicate and not to
advocate, the chapter depicts a model tailored to the times. "Pure
libertarian theory is obsolescent, as the press as a whole has in fact
recognized," the chapter concludes. "Taking its place is an emerging theory which puts increasing emphasis on the responsibilities
of the press. . . . Individuals who still speak of freedom of the press
as a purely personal right are a diminishing breed, lonely and
anachronistic."[10]

The University of Illinois Press published *Four Theories of the
Press* in 1956. It soon began appearing on syllabi, and Peterson's
chapter introduced journalism students to the Hutchins Commission's ideas. With time, professors went beyond the exegesis and
assigned the original writ. Students in many journalism schools
were studying *A Free and Responsible Press*, William E. Ames of the
University of Washington told Henry Luce in 1966, because it was
the only systematic evaluation of the American press. By then the
anticommunist frenzy of the 1950s had faded, and the Hutchins
Commission's idealistic internationalism no longer seemed subversive. In addition, by featuring a chapter on the Soviet conception

of the news media, *Four Theories of the Press* sharpened the line between collectivist communism and the Hutchins Commission's collectivist communitarianism. Before long, most textbooks on media ethics quoted the commission's five goals for journalism.[11]

Scholars paid more attention to the Commission on Freedom of the Press starting in the mid-1960s. At the 1967 conference of the Association for Education in Journalism in Boulder, Colorado, the AEJ marked the report's twentieth anniversary with the best-attended panel of the year, featuring a Hutchins associate from the Center for the Study of Democratic Institutions, the Pulitzer Prize–winning journalist Harry S. Ashmore, as well as Ben H. Bagdikian of the *Washington Post*, another Pulitzer winner. Both men called on AEJ to sponsor the press council recommended by the Hutchins Commission. *Columbia Journalism Review* that year published an article by James Boylan, "The Hutchins Report: A Twenty-Year View," along with an annotated and updated version of the commission's recommendations. At Hutchins's think tank, the in-house *Center Magazine* published its own twenty-year retrospective on *A Free and Responsible Press*.[12]

A body of academic literature grew. Hilda M. Bryant seems to have been the first to study the commission's unpublished documents, for a master's thesis at the University of Washington in 1969; she likened Hutchins, MacLeish, Niebuhr, et al. to Washington, Franklin, Madison, et al. Margaret A. Blanchard published a monograph in 1977, followed by major works by Jerilyn S. McIntyre in the 1970s and 1980s, Roger Simpson and Jane S. McConnell in the 1990s, Brett Gary in the early 2000s, and Victor Pickard in the 2010s, as well as my own monograph and articles starting in the 1990s, plus nearly a dozen theses and dissertations. In 1993, the Poynter Institute in St. Petersburg, Florida, convened what it billed as a three-day "Fan Club meeting" devoted to the Hutchins Commission; the invitation compared commission fans to Trekkies. The University of Illinois at Urbana-Champaign, home of *Four Theories of the Press*, in 1997 convened a symposium for the fiftieth anniversary of the Hutchins report, with proceedings published in *Communication Law and Policy*.[13]

Many scholars rank *A Free and Responsible Press* as a seminal work. The report, Everette E. Dennis and Melvin L. DeFleur write, is "regarded as one of the most important documents in the history of American media." To C. Edwin Baker, it's "the most influential modern American account of the goals of journalistic performance." James Curran considers it "perhaps the most cogent and elegant report on media policy ever published in the English language." If not timeless, as some call it, much of it has aged well. Curran deems one section "especially applicable" to the post-9/11 war on terror. Thomas Patterson applies the commission's criteria to news coverage of the 2016 presidential campaign; Jack Snyder, to political discussions on Reddit; Jessica Roberts, to the "Humans of New York" social-media feed. Wiebke Lamer argues that the report is as relevant today as it was in 1947, "arguably even more so considering the disinformation dangers of the digital age."[14]

Although some contemporary critics faulted *A Free and Responsible Press* for its paucity of examples, its most specific sections are the most dated ones, such as the assertion that "Edward Noble used money from the sale of Lifesavers to buy the Blue network," as well as the chapter on emerging media technologies, which devotes equal attention to the "facsimile newspaper," with print delivered over airwaves, and to television. ("There is something about communications technology that causes some very clever people to leave their wits behind them," writes Curran.) Criticism of journalism, like journalism itself, tends to be evanescent. By looking beyond the controversies of the moment, the commission succeeded in producing a short book that's still read, quoted, and remembered.[15]

Although many of the indictments and recommendations were familiar when *A Free and Responsible Press* was published, it examines nuances overlooked by contemporaries. It's one of the first works to discuss pressure groups and their effects on media content, positive as well as negative. In Hocking's appendix to the report and in his own book, he sketched a boundary between permissible and impermissible nongovernmental pressures on expression. The report notes not just the evils of concentrated ownership but also the virtues of bigness, including the strength to withstand outside pressure. It largely dismisses a concern that had preoccupied many earlier press critics, advertisers' influence over news coverage; a more pernicious influence comes from the fact that publishers consort chiefly with fellow members of the prosperous classes. The book's list of five requirements for an adequate press, which Hutchins wanted to jettison, has proved to be a lasting contribution despite its omission of the watch-dog function. The report's chief recommendation, the press council, supplies one answer to Lee C. Bollinger's question: "The press may be a check on the government, but what is the check on the press?"[16]

The report's greatest weakness is that its self-assuredness at times outstrips its clarity. On certain points, scholars can't agree on what it says. It's libertarian to some and authoritarian to others; it invites regulation and repudiates regulation; it challenges the established order and buttresses that order; it depicts the masses as virtuosos and numskulls; it wants the press to approach the state as muckraker and cheerleader. The commission's "most important finding was that the press should remain self-regulated," writes Victor Pickard. "The Commission said it saw no hope in self-regulation," observes an earlier commentator, Robert Hutchins. Pickard has the better of this one.[17]

To be sure, scholars argue over the meaning of other works, including Walter Lippmann's *Public Opinion*. In *A Free and Responsible Press*, though, ambiguity was the price of unanimity, a price Hutchins was willing to pay. After seventeen meetings, two and a half years, and a great deal of talk, important disputes remained unresolved and probably unresolvable. Archibald MacLeish embraced individualism; Reinhold Niebuhr and William Ernest Hocking decried it. Some members favored additional regulatory steps—not always the same ones—while Zechariah Chafee opposed them. In general, MacLeish focused on speakers without audiences, Hocking on citizens without information, and Chafee on regulators without scruples. It turned out that great minds—at least these particular great minds—didn't think alike. Although Hutchins tried to camouflage the disputes, some readers spotted them. Herbert Solow of *Fortune* wrote that *A Free and Responsible Press* "represents nobody's viewpoint, but tries to leave a door open at either end so that Chafee, who is 100% for the first amendment, can come in and shake hands with Hocking, who is much more inclined toward Article 125 of the Soviet Constitution."[18]

A decade after the commission last met, Hutchins, as president of the Fund for the Republic, recruited Niebuhr, Henry Luce, and several other public intellectuals for a program called Basic Issues, structured along the lines of the commission. In papers and discussions, the thinkers tested American institutions against ideals of free-dom and justice. As Hutchins had done with the commission, he pushed for consensus. Luce considered it a mistake. Disagreements, he said, ought to be probed, not swatted away. In his view, Hutchins harbored a misconception shared by many intellectuals: the belief that a thorough discussion invariably produces consensus.[19]

Hutchins was a prophet at conceptualizing but a gadfly at imple-menting. Most of his legacies, lightly tethered, drifted away in subsequent decades. The University of Chicago undid most of his changes. Though the Great Books curriculum lives on at St. John's College, Encyclopædia Britannica no longer sells the thirty-thousand-plus-page sets for home libraries. (Of course, Britannica no longer sells printed encyclopedias, either.) Hutchins's world constitu-tion died; so did his Santa Barbara think tank. The Hutchins niche in American society, celebrity educator, vanished as well. "A remarkable man, Robert Hutchins, perhaps a great one," Nicholas von Hoffman wrote in the *Washington Post* after his death in 1977. "Unhappily, he won't be missed, he won't even be remembered." Yet Hutchins's memory lives on in the corner of academia that he detested above all others, journalism schools.[20]

But Hutchins's view of journalism education as trade school, outdated in the 1940s, is much more so now. From the 1940s through the end of the century, schools of journalism grew increas-ingly academic. Professors with doctorates accounted for 14 percent of faculty in 1940, versus 55 percent in 2013. Today, the average journalism professor is a scholar who has spent more time in the classroom than in the newsroom. The emphasis on doctoral degrees has produced more doctoral programs, which in turn have produced more research. To be sure, much of this research is the quantitative, "gadgeteer" work that Hutchins despised. "The impression I have is that most of the communications research doesn't require any thought at all," he told a student interviewer in 1966. "You just count things as they pass by." He dismissed the media scholar (and coau-thor of *Four Theories of the Press*) Wilbur Schramm as "a computer type," somewhat unjustly; quantitative researcher Schramm was also a former director of the Iowa Writers' Workshop, and he recom-mended that would-be journalists study the Great Books.[21]

Hutchins talked in the 1940s of replacing journalism schools with institutes of communication study. He accepted data gathering as a necessary component of research, but he hoped to segregate the function in nonteaching institutes so that classroom instructors could focus on principles rather than facts. He never moved forward with that notion, but others did. The University of Minnesota's journalism school already had a research division, created in 1944 by Ralph Casey and Ralph O. Nafziger, both of whom worked on contract for the Hutchins Commission. Schramm founded the Institute of Communications Research at the University of Illinois in 1947; he went on to run the Institute for Communication Research at Stanford, followed by the Communication Institute of the East-West Center in Honolulu. Answering the Hutchins Commission's call for "academic-professional centers of advanced study, research, and publication in the field of communications," the Gannett Center for Media Studies operated from 1985 to 1998, headquartered at Columbia University for most of that time. During those years, as the Gannett Center's founding executive director, Everette E. Dennis, points out, many additional foundations and universities began paying attention to the media. Other university-affiliated research centers have arisen since, including the Shorenstein Center on Media, Politics and Public Policy at Harvard.[22]

A Free and Responsible Press faults journalism schools for failing to "act as independent centers of criticism" of the media. Despite the overall disenchantment with the report among journalism professors at the time, some conceded the validity of this critique. One said that "schools are afraid to speak out in criticism for fear of alienating the goodwill of the newspapers." Such qualms faded over time. In 1959, Theodore Peterson, author of the social-responsibility chapter in *Four Theories of the Press*, said that journalism education didn't belong in the university unless it instilled in students a critical attitude toward the news media. In 1970, the Association for Education in Journalism called for the creation of a Journalism Center that would determine, among other things, what sort of information democratic citizens need that the media aren't currently providing. In 1974, media criticism was the theme of the annual AEJ conference.[23]

The Hutchins Commission itself has been subjected to quantitative study, including a survey asking journalism professors and journalists if they agreed with propositions set out in *A Free and Responsible Press*. In the study, which appeared in *Journalism Quarterly* in 1981, the professors were much likelier than the journalists to say that sensationalism skews the news, that concentration of ownership threatens the free flow of information, that journalism schools ought to criticize the media industry, and that an independent organization should be created to monitor the press. Other studies have found journalism professors to be more critical of the press than journalists are. The professors' criticisms don't precisely track those of the Hutchins Commission. In a study published in 1988, many academics faulted the press for being insufficiently adversarial toward the government, whereas some Hutchins Commission members found the press of the 1940s excessively adversarial. Nonetheless, the professors' critical stance toward the press today represents a shift from earlier patterns. It's probably no coincidence that, during the years that *A Free and Responsible Press* has gained acceptance in schools of journalism, faculty journalists who identified with the press have been replaced by faculty scholars more inclined to identify with the Hutchins Commission.[24]

Some leading commentators in journalism schools find the commission's critique too tame. In *America's Battle for Media Democracy*, Victor Pickard argues that American policy makers of the 1940s contemplated restructuring the media, but the Hutchins Commission instead gave its blessing to the doctrine of "corporate libertarianism," which—here he echoes William Ernest Hocking—"conflates corporate privilege with First Amendment freedoms and is girded by a logic that advances individualistic negative liberties at the expense of the collective positive liberties that are central to a social democratic vision." Pickard suggests that for all the report's chastisement of irresponsibility, *A Free and Responsible Press* left the corporate media stronger than ever. Whereas many prominent academic critics in 1947 thought the Commission on Freedom of the Press went too far, many of its academic critics today think it didn't go far enough.[25]

Although Hutchins Commission ideas have entered the curriculum of journalism schools, nobody has been able to create the national press council it recommended. At times in commission meetings,

Hutchins questioned whether the men were overselling the organization and overburdening it with tasks. Nonetheless, off and on for three decades, from publication of *A Free and Responsible Press* in 1947 until his death in 1977, he tried to get the press council launched. He was aided, cajoled, blandished, and hectored by his friend William Benton.[26]

Benton was one of the staunchest champions of what he called "our" commission. He publicly gave it $15,000, through Encyclopædia Britannica, and he secretly edited the manuscript of *A Free and Responsible Press* before it went to Luce. In 1948, for a *Saturday Review* feature, he said he was currently reading *A Free and Responsible Press* "for the third time," along with *Moby Dick* and *History of the Decline and Fall of the Roman Empire*. In 1949, Connecticut's Governor Chester Bowles, Benton's former ad-agency partner, appointed him to complete a term in the U.S. Senate. Benton introduced a bill to create a presidential advisory committee on broadcasting, a variant of the press council, though official rather than private and focused on radio and TV rather than print. The idea, he later said, "derived wholly and absolutely from the Hutchins Commission." The bill never came up for a vote, and Benton lost his seat in 1952.[27]

In 1964, four writers from *Television Age*, on strike to protest interference with their copy, asked Hutchins to reassemble the Commission on Freedom of the Press for the purpose of implementing its press council recommendation. The writers sent copies of the letter to the surviving members of the commission. William Ernest Hocking, age ninety, said he was eager to serve. Harry Ashmore, who worked for Hutchins at the Center for the Study of Democratic Institutions, came up with a plan for one or two meetings, which would feature some of the original commission members plus six or seven new appointees such as the former FCC chair Newton N. Minow, the ad maker Ray Rubicam, the former MGM executive Dore Schary, the former CBS News correspondent Edward R. Murrow, and the journalism professor and former Hutchins Commission researcher Ralph Casey. Benton agreed to supply half of the $75,000 budget.[28]

Hutchins reached out to the principal funder of the Commission on Freedom of the Press. "Bill writes that he will put up half of the required amount if Harry Luce will put up the other half," said Hutchins. "Will you?"[29]

Luce replied, "I am sorry to say that I do not respond enthusiastically to your suggestion of reviving the Commission."[30]

Before and after the failed attempt to reunite the commission, Benton and Hutchins, with Ashmore's aid, tried to start a press council on their own. They wanted prestigious public figures for its board, such as Minow, Adlai Stevenson, Walter Lippmann, *Newsday* publisher Alicia Patterson, and the former CBS correspondent William Shirer, as well as former Hutchins Commission members Reinhold Niebuhr, Archibald MacLeish, Harold Lasswell, and George Shuster. For staff director, Benton favored Murrow, who seemed interested at first but ultimately declined. Eric Sevareid of CBS expressed interest, but Murrow told Benton he was an inept administrator. Hutchins at one point proposed Hugh Downs, the only man he knew who had read all fifty-four volumes of the Great Books from start to finish, but then decided "he's not bright enough." Luce told Benton that he would be willing to make a modest monetary contribution as long as the board consisted solely of industry professionals. In Benton's account, Luce believed that "people like Hocking were not wise choices" for the original commission.[31]

The biggest sticking point turned out to be a university base for the organization. Although Benton was willing to put up half a million dollars, Harvard, Yale, Princeton, and the University of Chicago all declined. "A commission of the sort proposed—that would sit in judgment over the press, radio, and television—is an inappropriate activity for a university, or at least it seems to me inappropriate for Harvard," wrote Harvard president Nathan M. Pusey. Although Hutchins didn't want the press council housed in a school of journalism, Benton engaged in lengthy negotiations with Edward W. Barrett, dean of the Columbia School of Journalism. Barrett pressured Benton to forget the press council and underwrite the new *Columbia Journalism Review* instead. When Benton insisted on a press council, Barrett replied along the lines of Pusey: "There is much feeling at Columbia that it would appear rather presumptuous for this University—or any university—to stand up and announce to the world that it was setting up a commission to review the performance of radio, television, press and all of the news media." The wave of university and foundation interest in the media was still more than a decade away. Universities, said Ashmore, seemed reluctant to do anything that might antagonize "the man with the megaphone."[32]

One university was ready to welcome the press council. Former Hutchins Commission member George Shuster extended an invitation on behalf of the University of Notre Dame. After retiring as president of Hunter College, Shuster had become assistant to Notre Dame president Theodore Hesburgh. "A good many people around here like you and hold you in esteem," Shuster told Hutchins. Hesburgh was enthusiastic about the press council, and the school offered $100,000 a year from a Ford Foundation grant to match donations from Benton and others. Hutchins and Ashmore favored Notre Dame, but Benton had misgivings about affiliating the press council with a religious school. Notre Dame spent its Ford funds on other projects. The Hutchins-Benton-Ashmore efforts petered out.[33]

A journalism-monitoring organization did get under way in 1973, the Twentieth Century Fund's National News Council. The commission had a long list of tasks for its proposed press council, including issuing annual reports on the state of the media, whereas the National News Council mainly adjudicated individual disputes, such as charges of inaccurate or unfair coverage. Hutchins nonetheless thought the News Council had potential, and its first chairman, Roger Traynor, the former chief justice of the California supreme court, spoke at his Center for the Study of Democratic Institutions. Benton gave the News Council $10,000. But the council, cold-shouldered by the *New York Times*—publisher Arthur O. Sulzberger said that "the real threat to a free press comes from those seeking to intimidate it"—and unable to attract a major funder on an ongoing basis, shut down in 1984.[34]

Another effort to reform the press, conceptual rather than institutional, also had its roots in the Hutchins Commission. It originated in an appropriate place: the Robert Maynard Hutchins Center for the Study of Democratic Institutions, at the University of California, Santa Barbara. In 1979, UCSB absorbed the center and named it after Hutchins, who had died in 1977. In 1986, the Hutchins Center convened a symposium on the media and public discourse, funded by one of the center's Hollywood supporters, Paul Newman. James W.

Carey, dean of the University of Illinois College of Communications, lamented in his presentation that contemporary journalism "justifies itself in the public's name but . . . the public plays no role except as an audience." Citizens had abandoned the public square, he said, when the nineteenth-century model of journalism as conversation gave way to journalism as one-way flow of information. He sketched a communitarian "democratic journalism" that would reconnect citizens to civic life. Carey's talk laid the groundwork for what came to be called public journalism or civic journalism, an influential movement during the last decade of the twentieth century. Although public journalism didn't fully align with the approach of the Commission on Freedom of the Press, Carey and other scholars said that the movement embodied the commission's democratic spirit and its estimation of the centrality of the press.[35]

Beyond public journalism, the commission's impact on the newsroom is much debated. The report did cheer some discontented reporters at the time. The press changed after 1947, too, often in ways that the commission recommended. Through op-ed columns and other features, many papers made it possible for outsiders to reach a big audience. Owners also grew less flagrant in promoting their own interests. Sensationalism faded. Newsroom ethics codes became more common. Nonprofit and university-affiliated media proliferated, especially broadcast and online media. Journalists, further, became better educated. Examining the educational backgrounds of national journalists in 2016, researchers found that 30 percent of *Wall Street Journal* staff writers and 39 percent of *New York Times* staff writers were Ivy League graduates. Yet it is difficult to ascribe these changes to the Commission on Freedom of the Press.[36]

A Free and Responsible Press did make a prominent appearance in First Amendment jurisprudence, with the Supreme Court quoting and implicitly following it. The 1974 case *Miami Herald Publishing Co. v. Tornillo* concerned a Florida right-of-reply law. If a newspaper criticized a candidate during a particular period, the law required it to publish the candidate's response, free of charge. Earlier, in a 1969 case, *Red Lion Broadcasting v. Federal Communications Commission,* the Supreme Court had ruled that FCC regulation of broadcast content doesn't violate the First Amendment, because the broadcaster's right of free speech is secondary to the public's right to learn about "social, political, esthetic, moral, and other ideas"—William Ernest Hocking's strong version of the positive First Amendment. If the justices took the same approach in *Tornillo*, the Florida law would probably be upheld.[37]

Jerome A. Barron, a constitutional scholar and the leading advocate of media access, defended the statute in the Supreme Court. He told the justices that the press had become big business, unaccountable to outsiders, with the power to censor ideas that editors and publishers disfavored. Archibald MacLeish had made the same arguments on the Hutchins Commission. No longer, said Barron, could individuals effectively convey their views to their fellow citizens. MacLeish had said the same thing. Barron maintained that the law "does not detract from expression one iota"; on the contrary, it advances the values of the First Amendment. Hocking had likewise argued that restrictions on some speakers can promote First Amendment principles. To strike down the law under the First Amendment, Barron said, would subordinate the American public's right of free expression to "the property rights of those who own communication facilities." MacLeish, Hocking, Reinhold Niebuhr, and others on the commission had likewise insisted that property rights don't give media owners carte blanche to do as they please; they must be accountable to society.[38]

The Supreme Court issued its opinion two months later. Writing for a unanimous Court, Chief Justice Warren Burger referred to "the report of the Commission on Freedom of the Press, chaired by Robert M. Hutchins, in which it was stated, as long ago as 1947, that '[t]he right of free public expression has . . . lost its earlier reality.' " Publishing was inexpensive when the First Amendment was ratified, and it was relatively easy to bypass hostile newspaper editors and disseminate information directly, the Court said, citing *A Free and Responsible Press*. But technological and economic developments had made "entry into the marketplace of ideas served by the print media almost impossible" and thereby "place[d] in a few hands the power to inform the American people and shape public opinion." In a footnote, the Court quoted a MacLeish remark that appears in Hocking's book: "Freedom of the press is a right belonging, like all rights in a democracy, to all the people." The Supreme

Court's *Tornillo* analysis, Samantha Barbas writes, "channeled the Hutchins Commission."[39]

Ultimately, the justices did just what the commission had done: they accepted MacLeish's account of history and many of his arguments while declining to try to restore the original balance. Instead, they struck down the Florida law as a violation of the Constitution. The positive First Amendment, it seems, generally permits content regulation only if the speaker is using the public airwaves. The Court said that "a responsible press is an undoubtedly desirable goal, but press responsibility is not mandated by the Constitution and like many other virtues it cannot be legislated"—much as the Hutchins Commission had concluded, over MacLeish's and Hocking's objections.[40]

Barron later summarized the holding in *Tornillo*. "Massive concentrated media power was a reality and a problem," he wrote. "But apparently, under the First Amendment, nothing could be done about it." Concerning action by the state, the Commission on Freedom of the Press had reached the very same conclusion.[41]

CHAPTER NINETEEN

Democracy on the Skids

MOLDED BY THE DEPRESSION, written during and just after World War II, and released at the beginning of the Cold War, *A Free and Responsible Press* lives on. Just as it transcends its times, it surmounts its dubious method of preparation: philosophy by committee; an investigation of American journalism that excluded journalists as a matter of principle and journalism professors as a matter of prejudice. The report is a much better work than Henry Luce would admit, his disapproval magnified by chagrin over his exclusion from meetings and then by irritation over Robert Hutchins's refusal to reconvene the group for one more rewrite.

Although thirteen men signed it, *A Free and Responsible Press* is above all the handiwork of Hutchins, who reengaged with the seemingly doomed project at the last minute. The book tells reporters that they must resist pressures to conform, just as he had told University of Chicago graduates, and that there's more to life than money, a message at the heart of his vision of liberal education. He believed that voters must understand equality, justice, and other eternal principles, as well as candidates, issues, and other up-to-the-minute facts. Principles come from the Great Books and facts from the Great Newspapers, or even the Pretty Good Newspapers. Together, they form the curriculum for the only kind of vocational education he could support: training for the vocation of democratic citizenship. "You are educators," he told the American Society of Newspaper Editors, "whether you like it or not."[1]

Much of the commission's work still resonates. The members worried that the restless searchlight of news coverage, as Walter Lippmann put it, jerks to a stop on what's unimportant and darts past what's important. They called on the press to view the audience as citizens rather than, in the foreign adviser John Grierson's phrase, as "buying machines." William Ernest Hocking suggested that the "decisive, staccato presentation" of the news was aggravating "the difficulties of an emotionally shallowing age." He also diagnosed, as "the disease of our time," a culture in which "publicity has become a substitute for merit." And he asked a compelling question: "The cure for distorted information may be more information, but what is the cure for too much information?"[2]

The commission prefigured the work of scholars as well. Archibald MacLeish argued for a right of media access more than twenty years before the *Harvard Law Review* published Jerome A. Barron's "Access to the Press: A New First Amendment Right." *A Free and Responsible Press* talks of dual approaches to freedom, positive and negative; a decade later, Isaiah Berlin developed the same distinction in *Two Concepts of Liberty*. Scholars generally cite Alexander Meiklejohn for the theory of the positive First Amendment and for the model of democratic discourse as a meeting in need of a moderator, but Hocking had already explored both ideas in print. Hocking's broad analysis of rights and responsibilities anticipates the communitarian political philosophy that Amitai Etzioni and others developed starting in the 1980s.

Commission members also pondered the social and political implications of media technology. Sounding like Marshall McLuhan, Zechariah Chafee observed, "men seek personal Devils to explain whatever is wrong, but we of the Commission know that the linotype and the radio tube are as much responsible for our anxiety as Hearst." In a technologically advanced society, said Reinhold Niebuhr, "traditional and organic forms of cohesion" give way to "synthetic, mechanistic and artificial forms." Further, according to Niebuhr, technology can magnify economic inequality, which can spark social unrest. When it came to the particulars of emerging technologies, though, the members were less incisive. "The thing that is puzzling me," John Dickinson said in a meeting, "is why a man should be interested in seeing a man's mouth working as he makes a speech over the radio." They debated whether two technologies represented a revolutionary change or just another phase: the facsimile newspaper, with data delivered over the airwaves and printed in the subscriber's home, and television.[3]

Half a century later came a revolution beyond dispute. The internet aids the cause of democracy in some ways that would hearten members of the Hutchins Commission. MacLeish predicted that technology someday would enable "the traveling salesman motoring across the Arizona desert" to spend downtime watching the United Nations. UN sessions may not attract the viewership MacLeish hoped, but they're now accessible. Vast quantities of factual information are more widely available and cheaper than ever before. Niche cultural offerings are more prevalent too. Commission members at times envisaged news as an ongoing conversation between media and audience. The internet makes it possible. It also serves, in the commission's words, as "a forum for the exchange of comment and criticism," including bounteous media criticism. Entry costs to the media of the 1940s were immense, as the commission said. No longer. Not everyone can attract a big audience, but the avenues for doing so are more numerous than ever.[4]

Yet the blessings turn out to be mixed. Concentration of media ownership alarmed commission members. Some internet entities now are far larger than the biggest media companies of the 1940s. The public's reliance on them is far greater, too, globally as well as in the United States. Timothy Garton Ash calls these companies nonnation superpowers. In addition, according to some studies, Americans are devoting less time to news and more time to other forms of media. Those who share the view that Gertrude Stein once expressed to Robert Hutchins—"government is the least interesting thing in human life"—have lots of alternatives. Despite the unprecedented abundance of information about public affairs, researchers are finding civic knowledge in decline.[5]

The internet's impact on the news industry has been devastating. Formerly, readers and advertisers who didn't care about coverage of (for instance) the state legislature nonetheless helped underwrite it.

The internet disassembled the product, and as a report from Columbia's Tow Center for Digital Journalism points out, subscribers and advertisers alike responded by fleeing from newspapers. Between 2006 and 2018, according to the Pew Research Center, U.S. daily newspaper circulation and newsroom employment both fell by nearly half, and revenue from advertising fell by 70 percent. Hundreds of papers closed or merged. Though not the sole factor behind the carnage, the internet was an important one. "The first duty of the press," Henry Luce once said, "is to survive"—but even Time Inc. died, swallowed in 2018 by the Meredith Corporation, which put *Time* and *Fortune* up for sale. A Commission on Freedom of the Press today wouldn't call on media companies to devote some of their "huge profits" to highbrow offerings, as a draft of *A Free and Responsible Press* did before William Benton's edits. Hocking's "touch of government" today would be a hand with a checkbook.[6]

Many scholars and activists are calling on the state to fund news coverage, perhaps through a BBC-like entity that is much larger than present-day public broadcasting. According to advocates, news is a public good, like education; the commercial marketplace doesn't create adequate incentives for the sort of coverage that citizens need; paternalism is justified in this realm; and, writes Victor Pickard, "nothing less than democracy is at stake." Opponents of subsidies point to countries where state-funded press organs (including the BBC) have cozied up to the party in power or at least muted their criticisms. Proponents respond that we trust the government to set postage rates for periodicals and to award broadcast licenses, despite the risk of favoritism toward some media outlets, and to operate public schools and libraries, despite the risk of favoritism toward some ideas. All of these arguments arose in meetings of the Hutchins Commission.[7]

Hocking proposed a test for assessing the propriety of a state-funded news outlet. The government can supplement the efforts of private media organizations, he said, but it must not "compete with or ... displace" them. Large-scale supplementation without competition seems difficult to achieve now. When newspapers were first going online, according to Richard J. Tofel of ProPublica, many editors rejected paywalls as self-defeating. They believed that readers, rather than buying subscriptions, would switch to sources without paywalls, such as the Associated Press stories on Yahoo News. Tofel considers this a major miscalculation. He thinks newspapers ought to have erected paywalls and tried to get the AP to stop giving away its coverage. An American BBC, with free content, would provide another means of keeping up with the news without paying for it, which could further enfeeble the private press.[8]

A Free and Responsible Press largely argues that an inadequate press (lazy, reckless, partisan, greedy) was shortchanging an adequate electorate (alert, rational, open-minded, public-spirited). Outside the report, however, commission members painted a much less favorable picture of the masses. They believed that behind the façade of Good War unity, the American citizenry was fractured and fractious, hotheaded and hateful. The press hadn't created the problems, but it was exacerbating them. Democracy, Niebuhr said at a meeting in 1944, "seems to be on the skids."[9]

Citizens were breaking off from the broader community and forming what commission members called "social islands" based on ideology, race, nationality, or economic interests. The situation was complicated. Arthur Schlesinger said there was never any "golden age of unity." Some forces in society draw people together; others pull them apart. Their relative strength is always shifting, and any balance is fragile and temporary. Even so, the forces of disintegration seemed to be growing. Fascism could not have taken hold in Europe, Niebuhr said, if not for the "decaying [of] democratic society."[10]

Social fragmentation, according to commission members, can warp the political debate in several ways. First, it can erode citizens' commitment to deliberation in pursuit of the common good. With difficulty, individuals can set aside self-interest and reason together, but when they splinter into antagonistic groups, this becomes nearly impossible. People who strongly identify with a faction will seek to advance its interests, regardless of the impact on others. Second, fragmentation can undermine common knowledge. Different Americans, said John M. Clark, were inhabiting "different worlds of fact and judgment." When people reject information that conflicts with their preconceptions—when, as Chafee put it, they "eat only what agrees with them"—community-wide discourse falters. Finally, politicians may stir up intergroup hostility as a way of gaining attention and support. One result can be policy-making gridlock. When leaders "thrive on conflict," said Clark, "reasonable solutions are often vulnerable and handicapped precisely because they are reasonable."[11]

Commission members believed that the press in the 1940s was, on balance, making a bad situation worse. A politically neutral press can help keep partisan passions in check, said George Shuster, but a one-sided press can inflame the citizenry and "pull the house apart." A media outlet and its audience can become a closed system, said Hocking, with people reading only those publications that "bellow out their own opinions." Such outlets may stoke the audience's rage—a potentially lucrative business model, according to Hocking, because "a man who hates will pay to have his hate increased." The demonization of opponents in turn may create fertile ground for conspiracy theories, inviting what the foreign adviser Jacques Maritain called the "systematic poisoning of public opinion." As media and audiences grow increasingly polarized, fewer voices can be heard across the gulf. *Reader's Digest* conservatives, said researcher Llewellyn White, couldn't speak the same language as *PM* liberals.[12]

On the left as well as the right, some groups not only vilified opponents but also sought to silence them, through coercion directed against employers, sponsors, or platforms. The American Legion, according to researcher Milton Stewart, was trying to suppress putatively unpatriotic views by threatening boycotts against newspapers, pressuring school boards to fire teachers, and urging event sponsors to disinvite speakers. Such efforts can intimidate people into silence, a nonstate chilling effect.[13]

Propagandists in sheep's clothing, as John Grierson called them, were worsening the discord: organizations with shadowy identities, sponsorship, and agendas. Extremist groups pretended to be mainstream, corporate-backed ones pretended to be grassroots, biased ones pretended to be neutral, trolling provocateurs pretended to be helpmates, and, on a bigger scale, media outlets controlled by foreign governments pretended to be independent truth tellers. Such deceit could hobble a system of self-government. It's impossible for citizens to deliberate fruitfully, said Harold Lasswell, if they can't tell who's speaking.[14]

In combination, these factors—the tribalism, the partisan media, the conspiracy theories, the suppression of unpopular speakers, and the unsourced misinformation and disinformation—were imperiling American democracy. Although the specter of authoritarianism in the United States had receded by the time the commission met, the men believed that societal and media fragmentation might revive it, particularly if there were another depression. Citizens who feel they've lost control over their destinies could gravitate toward the easy answers of fascism. Clark feared that the nation was "in danger of falling into chaos, inviting dictatorship." Niebuhr believed that in an age of increasing globalization, automation, and inequality, the white working class, with an insecure foothold and uncertain economic prospects, might rally behind a demagogue who blamed their troubles on people of different nationalities, races, or religions.[15]

Or fascism might arise indirectly. When people are hypervigilant against being duped, said Hocking, they perceive "propaganda both where it is and where it is not." It's dangerous to accept propaganda as fact; it's equally dangerous to reject fact as propaganda. Bewildered Americans, he said, might decide that "truth is not to be had," reflexively distrust all news media, and withdraw into "mud-pie lethargy"— spectators in a post-truth world. Lasswell argued that citizens in a democracy must believe both that they can comprehend political events and that they can influence them. If citizens lose confidence in their information or their efficacy, the United States might follow the model of some European countries, where, according to Maritain, people stood by impassively and watched their institutions collapse. "The death of democracy is not likely to be an assassination from ambush," Hutchins would write a few years later. "It will be a slow extinction from apathy, indifference, and undernourishment."[16]

What could be done? To keep the American people from being hoodwinked, Hocking proposed bringing fraud prosecutions against speakers who misrepresent their identity or purpose. Lasswell wanted to prohibit some forms of anonymous speech, though Robert Redfield said the notion smacked of Stalinism. Lasswell also advocated education for media literacy, which would include lessons on the necessity of consulting multiple news outlets. The goal, as researcher White put it, would be to make the citizen "as critical of his mass media as he is of his restaurants, comedians, preachers, fishing tackle and football matches." In addition, commission members discussed prohibiting the spread of conspiracy theories like *The Protocols of the Elders of Zion*, though Chafee argued against it. None of these proposals made it into *A Free and Responsible Press*.[17]

Although commission members talked at length of the shortcomings of citizens, they ended up focusing their report almost solely on those of the media. Henry Luce had brought them together to evaluate the press, not the people. Anyhow, the press was an industry whose managers might—*might*—respond to chastisement, whereas there was no reason to think the masses could be shamed or bullied into good citizenship. So the commission contended that reinvigorating the democratic system was a job for journalists. A more responsible press would help produce more responsible citizens, which would restore some measure of social unity, at least in the long run. In the short run, said Redfield, "We have to ask the press to be better than its public."[18]

If the press didn't improve, according to *A Free and Responsible Press*, "the partially insulated groups in society will continue to be insulated," and their "unchallenged assumptions . . . will continue to harden into prejudice." But if the press did get better, mutual understanding would rebound, because when "people are exposed to the inner truth of the life of a particular group, they will gradually build up respect for and understanding of it." It was no panacea—familiarity, said Ruth Inglis, sometimes breeds contempt rather than respect—but it seemed better than surrendering to the status quo.[19]

John Dickinson, the railroad lawyer and defender of corporate power, was the only commission member who might be considered a conservative Republican. He was untroubled by the size of media companies. He championed survival-of-the-fittest individualism. He rejected the notion of a common good or a public interest; such terms, he maintained, simply "conceal the competition of interests." On these and other points, he disagreed with commission colleagues. But he shared their concerns about the fragmentation of society and their hope that the press could help mend it. "I don't think there is any more urgent need," he said, "than to have some agency of communication cut across those divisive lines and bring these people into some degree of community by presenting them with common information and common images."[20]

Spreading common information and common images would require common media. "The freedom of the press is not served by
every group in the community having its own press," said Hocking. "It
is served only when mass media reach the entire community." Fostering mutual understanding might entail a nationwide *New York Times*,
in its comprehensiveness and its professionalism, or, said Hocking, it
might entail a *Times*-quality newspaper in every major city. A nationwide *Time*, broadcasting the unchallenged assumptions of Henry
Luce, wasn't enough. Cultural offerings ought to be diverse, according
to the commission, but public-affairs news ought to be homogenized.[21]

To succeed, this *Times*-like (not *Time*-like) press would have to
break through the information bubbles and serve as "a forum for the
exchange of comment and criticism"—a common carrier. But with
the possible exception of Archibald MacLeish, commission members
didn't want anything approaching a true common carrier, open to
all. They talked of access for "reputable persons," "substantial
groups," and "important viewpoints," but not for those with "nothing to say." Hutchins thought the *Des Moines Register and Tribune*,
with some two dozen ideologically diverse columnists, provided a
model for "the ideal large newspaper of the future." Reputable, substantial, important, something to say: editors who adopted the commission's common-carrier recommendation still would have to
decide which voices to amplify and which to reject. Rather than an
unfiltered pipeline, a free-for-all, commission members wanted a
civil debate moderated by public-spirited editors. Their solution to
the problem of intolerant gatekeepers was eliminating the intolerance, not eliminating the gatekeepers.[22]

In the years after publication of *A Free and Responsible Press*, the
American media moved in the direction favored by the commission. In the cultural realm, television brought about "a soft conformity," wrote Niebuhr in 1957. By then, the villains of commission
meetings were gone—William Randolph Hearst died in 1951,
Robert R. McCormick in 1955—and big newspapers across the
country were embracing norms of objectivity and professionalism.
By century's end, most major cities had newspapers that sounded
something like the *New York Times*, and soft conformity came to
dominate news coverage as well as culture.[23]

But by the early twenty-first century, even as the soft conformity spread (including a global *New York Times*), a hard nonconformity had arisen alongside, with new voices spreading divergent messages via partisan content providers—cable news, talk radio, and political news and commentary websites—as well as social-media platforms. The partisan content providers at times purvey skewed accounts of events in an authoritative news voice (today, as in the 1940s, the major conservative outlets reach much-larger audiences than the major liberal ones do), while social media at times purvey skewed accounts of events in the voice of fellow citizens. In some ways, the resulting media landscape raises difficulties that commission members identified in the 1940s. There are new ways to avoid political information that challenges one's preconceptions; new ways to silence opponents through organized campaigns targeting employers, sponsors, or social-media platforms; new ways for provocateurs, including foreign ones, to hide their identity and sponsorship as they spread half-truths and lies; and new ways to propagate hoaxes and conspiracy theories.

As in the 1940s, the situation is complicated. Elements of the media system promote disunity and falsehood in some respects but unity and truth in others, according to Yochai Benkler, Robert Faris, and Hal Roberts, writing in the 2018 book *Network Propaganda*. Political leaders and activists, driven by partisan passions of varying strengths, interacting with news organizations with varying commitments to objectivity, disseminate messages in varying ways. "Technology is not destiny," the authors write. Many factors have driven the American media system away from what they call "the institutional heart of the post–World War II professional ethos": *A Free and Responsible Press*.[24]

A modern-day counterpart of the Hutchins Commission illuminates the continuities and the changes. In 2017, the Knight Foundation and the Aspen Institute launched the Knight Commission on Trust, Media and Democracy. The Knight Commission was bigger than the Hutchins Commission (twenty-seven members, versus the Hutchins group's thirteen American members and four foreign advisers) and more diverse, with women, African Americans, journalists, and conservatives. But it resembled the Hutchins Commission in other respects. It employed a small staff for research and administration, used outside experts for additional research, adopted official-sounding jargon (*commission, witnesses, testimony*), and produced a final report with lively prose, a manageable length, the unanimous backing of members on major points, and a tone of urgency if not desperation.[25]

Published in 2019, the Knight report, *Crisis in Democracy: Renewing Trust in America*, is full of terminology that was unknown in the 1940s—*augmented reality, bots, deepfakes, memetic warfare*—yet much of its analysis parallels *A Free and Responsible Press*. Citizens, the Knight report says, are divided and distrustful. What they once shared—a vision of the common good, a national narrative, a set of agreed-upon facts—has shriveled. Instead, many people inhabit ideological silos, aided by social media and partisan news outlets. They're uninformed about some important topics and misinformed about others. To help reverse the trends, the Knight Commission calls for depicting the full diversity of American society, separating fact and opinion, separating news and advertising, identifying sources of information, exploring nonprofit models, and exposing people to different points of view. It looks to academia to help devise solutions. It raises the possibility of government funding. It recommends that other entities continue its work. It says that media companies owe a fiduciary duty to users. It tells corporate managers that they must do better, or else the government may step in and regulate them. And it argues, repeatedly, that freedom of speech must be tempered with responsibility. All of this guidance also appears in the works of the Commission on Freedom of the Press.

But the guidance at times points in different directions. For the Hutchins Commission, a major remedy for bad speech was more speech. It wanted the *Chicago Tribune* to publish ideas other than McCormick's and *Time* to publish ideas other than Luce's, even if McCormick and Luce considered the ideas wrong. By contrast, one of the Knight Commission's principal remedies for bad speech is less speech. Social-media companies must stop publishing some ideas that their managers believe to be wrong. The common-carrier model was part of the solution in 1947. Now it's part of the problem.

Even so, the two reports' lodestar is the same. Both *A Free and Responsible Press* and *Crisis in Democracy* adopt the view that the media do more than inform a community; they also help form the community. Both emphasize the necessity of common facts and a shared commitment to the public interest. And both address what Niebuhr identified as the paramount challenge of the age: finding ways to "maintain the old ideal of a free society against the hazards created by the new conditions."[26]

Some historians maintain that Henry Luce had an ulterior motive in underwriting the Commission on Freedom of the Press: he wanted a blue-ribbon report that would absolve big media of their sins and forestall government regulation. Not so. Luce was inquisitive as well as acquisitive. He esteemed intellectuals even when they disesteemed him. He believed in new answers to age-old questions, and, a Medici of ideas, he thought he could bring them to light. It was in character for him to decide that "this whole business of 'the Freedom of the Press' needed an airing" and to hire a committee of thinkers to do it. It was also in character for him to plan to attend the meetings. As patron, he wanted to watch the symphony being composed and contribute a few notes, not just show up for the premiere. Had he been part of the commission's deliberations, as Robert Hutchins wanted, his evaluation of *A Free and Responsible Press* might have been more positive, for reasons intellectual— having followed along as the men discovered, explored, and rejected different philosophical approaches and policy options—as well as emotional.[27]

Enough people have admired the work of the Commission on Freedom of the Press that there are occasional calls for a sequel. But the commission can't be replicated. Not only do Luce-like patrons of great thinkers no longer exist, but the great thinkers themselves may be dying out, as Russell Jacoby has written. The generalists of the 1940s have turned into specialists, academic intellectuals rather than public intellectuals, hedgehogs rather than foxes. A Hutchins Commission, implausible in the 1940s, is inconceivable today. It was the first of its kind and the last.[28]

Yet the questions that commission members confronted live on. How can the press balance access and accuracy? How can it serve both its public and its shareholders? How can the state avoid partisan manipulation when it regulates the press or when it subsidizes it? Broadly, how can citizens get the information they need to self-govern, especially when they don't really want it? The Commission on Freedom of the Press didn't answer these questions, but it helped bring them into focus. Its deliberations and conclusions may enable us to see a bit farther into the distance, beyond the restless searchlights of today.

Notes

Abbreviations

CFP:	Commission on Freedom of the Press
CFP Brown:	Commission on Freedom of the Press Documents and Reports, John Hay Library, Brown University
CFP Columbia:	Commission on Freedom of the Press Records, Rare Book and Manuscript Library, Columbia University
CFP UW:	Commission on Freedom of the Press Records, University of Washington Libraries Special Collections
FRP:	Commission on Freedom of the Press, *A Free and Responsible Press* (Chicago: University of Chicago Press, 1947)
HRL:	Henry R. Luce
RMH:	Robert Maynard Hutchins
RMH Chicago:	Robert Maynard Hutchins Papers, Special Collections Research Center, University of Chicago
RMH Oral History:	Robert M. Hutchins and Associates Oral History Interviews, Special Collections Research Center, University of Chicago
RMH UCSB:	Robert Maynard Hutchins Collection, Special Collections, University of California, Santa Barbara
WEH:	William Ernest Hocking

Archival Collections

William Ames Papers, University of Washington Libraries Special Collections
Thurman Arnold Papers, American Heritage Center, University of Wyoming
Max Ascoli Collection, Howard Gotlieb Archival Research Center, Boston University

Harry S. Ashmore Collection (Mss 155), Department of Special Research Collections, UCSB Library, University of California, Santa Barbara

William Benton Papers, Special Collections Research Center, University of Chicago

Francis Biddle Papers, Franklin D. Roosevelt Presidential Library

Willard G. Bleyer Papers, Record Group 7, College of Letters and Science, University of Wisconsin–Madison

William F. Buckley Jr. Papers, Manuscripts and Archives, Yale University Library

Center for the Study of Democratic Institutions Collection (Mss 18), Department of Special Research Collections, UCSB Library, University of California, Santa Barbara

Central Files, Rare Book and Manuscript Library, Columbia University

Zechariah Chafee Jr. Papers, Historical and Special Collections, Harvard Law School

John Maurice Clark Papers, Rare Book and Manuscript Library, Columbia University

Commission on Freedom of the Press Documents and Reports, John Hay Library, Brown University

Commission on Freedom of the Press Records, Rare Book and Manuscript Library, Columbia University

Commission on Freedom of the Press Records, Special Collections Research Center, University of Chicago

Commission on Freedom of the Press Records, University of Washington Libraries Special Collections

Hugh Baker Cox Papers, American Heritage Center, University of Wyoming

Homer S. Cummings Papers, Special Collections Department, University of Virginia

Felix Frankfurter Papers, Historical and Special Collections, Harvard Law School

Fund for the Republic Inc. Records, Department of Special Collections, Princeton University

Maxwell Geismar Papers, Howard Gotlieb Archival Research Center, Boston University

Richard Henry Goldstone Papers, Yale Collection of American Literature, Beinecke Rare Book and Manuscript Library

Learned Hand Papers, Historical and Special Collections, Harvard Law School

William Ernest Hocking Papers, Houghton Library, Harvard University

Don Hollenbeck Broadcast Papers, Archives and Special Collections, University of Nebraska, Lincoln

Frank Hughes Papers, Col. Robert R. McCormick Research Center, Cantigny Foundation, Wheaton, IL

Maude Phelps Hutchins Papers, Howard Gotlieb Archival Research Center, Boston University

Robert Maynard Hutchins Collection (Mss 154), Department of Special Research Collections, UCSB Library, University of California, Santa Barbara

Robert Maynard Hutchins Papers, Special Collections Research Center, University of Chicago (collection subsequently reorganized and boxes renumbered)

Robert M. Hutchins and Associates Oral History Interviews, Special Collections Research Center, University of Chicago

Hutchins Administration Records, Office of the President, Special Collections Research Center, University of Chicago

Ruth Inglis Papers, personal collection

Harold Dwight Lasswell Papers (MS 1043), Manuscripts and Archives, Yale University Library

Charles Augustus Lindbergh Papers (MS 325), Manuscripts and Archives, Yale University Library

Walter Lippmann Papers (MS 326), Manuscripts and Archives, Yale University Library

Henry R. Luce Papers, New-York Historical Society Museum and Library

George A. Lundberg Papers, University of Washington Libraries Special Collections

Dwight Macdonald Papers (MS 730), Manuscripts and Archives, Yale University Library

Archibald MacLeish Papers, Manuscript Division, Library of Congress

J. B. Matthews Papers, Rubenstein Library, Duke University

Lowell Mellett Papers, Franklin D. Roosevelt Presidential Library

Charles E. Merriam Papers, Special Collections Research Center, University of Chicago

Edward R. Murrow Papers, Digital Collections and Archives, Tufts University

National News Council Records, Social Welfare History Archives, University of Minnesota

New Directions Publishing Corp. Records, Houghton Library, Harvard University

Reinhold Niebuhr Papers, Manuscript Library of Congress

Theodore B. Peterson Papers, University of Illinois Archives, University of Illinois at Urbana-Champaign

Roscoe Pound Papers, Historical and Special Collections, Harvard Law School

Robert Redfield Papers, Special Collections Research Center, University of Chicago

Henry Regnery Papers, Hoover Institution, Stanford University

Franklin D. Roosevelt, President's Personal Files, Franklin D. Roosevelt Presidential Library

George Sokolsky Papers, Hoover Institution, Stanford University

Gertrude Stein and Alice B. Toklas Papers, American Literature Collection, Beinecke Rare Book and Manuscript Library, Yale University

Arthur Hays Sulzberger Papers and New York Times Co. Records, New York Public Library

W. A. Swanberg Papers, Rare Book and Manuscript Library, Columbia University (spelling corrected in quotations from Swanberg's typed interview notes)

Time Inc. Archives, New-York Historical Society Museum and Library

Rexford G. Tugwell Papers, Franklin D. Roosevelt Presidential Library

University of Chicago Press Records, Special Collections Research Center, University of Chicago

Thornton Wilder Papers, Yale Collection of American Literature, Beinecke Rare Book and Manuscript Library

Numbered Documents of the Commission on Freedom of the Press

The Commission on Freedom of the Press distributed around 150 official documents to members and staff, including transcripts of meetings, drafts of the report and other books, notes of interviews, and memoranda on substance and procedure. The commission numbered the documents. Brown University, the University of Chicago, Columbia University, and the University of Washington have more or less complete sets. The personal papers of several commission members include copies of some too. Because these numbered commission documents are available in multiple places, I don't cite archival sources for them here.

Doc. 1, WEH, "Definition and Scope of the General Problems before the Group," Jan. 1944

Doc. 3, Harold D. Lasswell, "Memorandum on Problems and Procedures," Feb. 2, 1944

Doc. 4, "Synopsis, Commission Meeting of Feb. 2, 1944," n.d.

Doc. 4A, "Conference on Freedom of the Press, University Club, New York," Dec. 15, 1943

Doc. 9, "Statement of the Executive Committee on a Free Society," Mar. 7, 1944

Doc. 10, Harold D. Lasswell, "Statement on Research Possibilities," n.d.

Doc. 14, "Synopsis of Commission Meeting of March 21, 1944," Mar. 21, 1944

Doc. 16, "Statement of Importance of the Commission's Work," Apr. 26, 1944

Doc. 16A, WEH, "Statement of the Importance of the Commission's Work," Apr. 26, 1944

Doc. 17, "Synopsis of Commission Meeting, May 8–9, 1944," May 9, 1944

Doc. 17A, "Chafee's Note on Discussion of the Commission Meeting, May 8 and 9," June 2, 1944

Doc. 19, Jacques Maritain, "Statement Regarding General Principles of Freedom and Democracy," Sept. 7, 1944

Doc. 20A, "Parts I, II, and III of First Draft of the Report," Sept. 13, 1944

Doc. 21, "Summary of Discussion and Action, Commission Meeting Sept. 18–19, 1944," n.d.

Doc. 25, "List of Possible Witnesses and Consultants," Nov. 15, 1944

Doc. 26, "Minutes and Summary of Discussion of the Meeting of the Commission, Nov. 20–21 [1944]," Jan. 17, 1945

Doc. 27, "In the Matter of the U.S. v. the AP," Dec. 29, 1944, 3 (reprinting articles from 1943 by Zechariah Chafee Jr. and Fred S. Siebert on the AP case)

Doc. 31, "Minutes and Summary of Discussion, Meeting Jan. 22–23, 1945," Feb. 10, 1945

Doc. 34, "Draft Report (First Revision)," Feb. 17, 1945

Doc. 36, "Summary of Discussion of the Draft Report," Feb. 26–27, 1945

Doc. 37, "Outline and Memoranda from Commission Members Dealing with Major Areas of Discussion," Feb. 26–27, 1945

Doc. 37A, "Shuster Memorandum," Mar. 29, 1945

Doc. 37L, John Grierson, "Outline and Memoranda re Major Areas of Discussion," Apr. 10, 1945

Doc. 41, Robert D. Leigh and Llewellyn White, "Proposed Standards for Mass Communications Agencies in a Free Society (A First Attempt)," Apr. 10, 1945

Doc. 42, WEH, "Tentative Proposals for a Chapter on Principles," Apr. 11, 1945

Doc. 47, "Witnesses for Questions," Apr. 16, 1945

Doc. 48, "Minutes and Summary of Discussion, Meeting April 16–17, 1945," May 25, 1945

Doc. 49, Reinhold Niebuhr, "General Propositions Deduced from the Investigation of the Freedom of the Press Commission," May 11, 1945

Doc. 52, WEH, "Memorandum and Unfinished Business Regarding Frame of Reference," May 19, 1945

Doc. 55, "Meetings, June 5–6, 1945," June 8, 1945

Doc. 66, "Summary of Discussion of the Meeting, June 5–6," July 11, 1945

Doc. 70, Harold D. Lasswell, "Standards for Mass Communication," Aug. 24, 1945

Doc. 75, "Minutes, Meeting of the Commission, Chicago, Sept. 16–19," Oct. 26, 1945

Doc. 76, WEH, "Report of the Sub-Committee on Untruth and Unfairness in the Press," Oct. 26, 1945

Doc. 79, "Memo for Commission on Continuing Citizens' Agency," Dec. 6, 1945

Doc. 79A, "Memo for Commission: Summary of Commission Discussion and Documents," Dec. 6, 1945

Doc. 83, Archibald MacLeish, "General Report Draft, Chapters I, II, III," Jan. 21, 1946

Doc. 85, WEH, "The Framework of Principle," Jan. 21, 1945

Doc. 87, "Review of Material in Commission Documents," Jan. 29, 1946

Doc. 89, "General Report (MacLeish—Revised Draft)," Feb. 26, 1946

Doc. 90, "Summary of Discussion and Action: Meetings, Jan. 27–29, 1946," Mar. 16, 1946

Doc. 90A, "Summary of Discussion—January Commission Meetings," Mar. 22, 1946

Doc. 91, "Comments and Suggestions by Members of the Commission and Staff on Doc. 89," n.d.

Doc. 91B, John Dickinson, "Comments on MacLeish Draft of General Report," Feb. 26, 1946

Doc. 91C, Beardsley Ruml, "Comments on MacLeish Draft of General Report," Mar. 28, 1946

Doc. 91F, "Comments of Harold D. Lasswell," n.d.

Doc. 94, "Minutes of Chicago Commission Meeting, March 31–April 2," Apr. 9, 1946

Doc. 94A, "Summary of Discussion, Meeting, Mar. 31–Apr. 2, 1946," Apr. 25, 1946

Doc. 97, "General Report (5th Revision)—Leigh," May 4, 1946

Doc. 98I, "Proposed Commission Statement for the Chafee Report," n.d.

Doc. 99, "Commission Meeting, Del Prado Hotel, May 6–8, 1946," May 24, 1946

Doc. 101A, "Comments on Doc. 101, *Freedom for the Movies*, by Ruth A. Inglis," n.d.

Doc. 104, Robert D. Leigh, ed., "Draft of the General Report: Sixth Revision," June 26, 1946

Doc. 106, John Grierson, "The Voice of the State: The Interchange of Public Information between Government and People," July 1946

Doc. 107, Milton D. Stewart, "Report to the Commission," July 6, 1946

Doc. 108, "Minutes of Meeting (N.Y.), July 7–9, 1946," July 1946

Doc. 108A, "Summary of Discussion, Meetings July 7–9, 1946," July 31, 1946

Doc. 108B, "Summary of Discussion (III), July 7–9, 1946, Meeting," Aug. 21, 1946

Doc. 108C-D, "Summary of Discussion (III) and (IV), July 7–9, 1946 meeting," Aug. 21, 1946

Doc. 109, RMH, "Draft of the General Report: Seventh Revision," Aug. 1, 1946

Doc. 111, RMH, "Draft of the General Report: Eighth Revision," Aug. 26, 1946

Doc. 111A, "Comments on Hutchins Draft by Niebuhr," Sept. 4, 1946

Doc. 111C, George Shuster, "Comments on Hutchins Draft No. 111," Sept. 4, 1946

Doc. 111E, "Classification of Comments on Hutchins Draft," Sept. 12, 1946

Doc. 111F, Ruth Inglis, "Comments on the General Report—8th Revision," Sept. 4, 1946

Doc. 111-1, Zechariah Chafee Jr., Archibald MacLeish, and Robert D. Leigh, "Comments on General Report (7th Revision)," Aug. 26, 1946

Doc. 112, "Comments by Clark and MacLeish on Hocking's Doc. 100F," Aug. 27, 1946

Doc. 119, "Summary of Discussion, Meeting Sept. 15–17, 1946," n.d.

Doc. 120, "General Report: Final (9th) Revision," Oct. 15, 1946

Doc. 120A, "Revised Pages for Doc. 120," Oct. 1946

Introduction

1. *CBS Views the Press*, Dec. 4, 1948, 6, Hollenbeck Broadcast Papers, box 5; "Worst Kind of Troublemaker," *Time*, Nov. 21, 1949; HRL, "Indispensable Men," speech delivered at University of Chicago, April 19, 1933, 12, HRL Papers, box 47.

2. Harold D. Lasswell, *Democracy through Public Opinion* (Menasha, WI: George Banta, 1941), 105.

3. *FRP*, 80.

4. "Free Means Free," *Wall Street Journal*, Apr. 7, 1947; Frank Thayer, "Right to Own Press Can't Be Denied Legally," *Editor & Publisher*, Aug. 16, 1947, 54; "Controlled Press Opposed by Cooper," *New York Times*, Aug. 2, 1947; Frank Hughes, " 'A Free Press' (Hitler Style) Sought for U.S.," *Chicago Tribune*, Mar. 27, 1947, 38; Stephen Bates, "Is This the Best Philosophy Can Do? Henry R. Luce and *A Free and Responsible Press*," *Journalism and Mass Communication Quarterly* 95, no. 3 (2018): 820; Bernie Auer to Bernard Barnes, Mar. 22, 1947 (one of two memos with that date), Time Inc. Archives.

5. Memo on Commission on Freedom of the Press books, Mar. 15, 1956, University of Chicago Press Records, box 118; Everette E. Dennis and Melvin L. DeFleur, *Understanding Media in the Digital Age: Connections for Communication, Society, and Culture* (New York: Allyn and Bacon, 2010), 387; James Curran, "What Democracy Requires of the Media," in *The Press*, ed. Geneva Overholser and Kathleen Hall Jamieson (New York: Oxford University Press, 2005), 135; Wiebke Lamer, *Press Freedom as an International Human Right* (New York: Palgrave Macmillan, 2018), 29; *Miami Herald Publishing Co. v. Tornillo*, 418 U.S. 241 (1974).

6. WEH, *Freedom of the Press: A Framework of Principle* (Chicago: University of Chicago Press), viii; Doc. 99, 196; Doc. 26, 13.

7. WEH, *Freedom of the Press*, ix.

8. Doc. 99, 17.

9. Doc. 119, 23; Jerilyn S. McIntyre, "Repositioning a Landmark: The Hutchins Commission and Freedom of the Press," *Critical Studies in Mass Communication* 4 (1987): 152.

10. "Radio, Film Reports Absorb All of Luce's 200G; Mag, Press Probes Off?," *Variety*, Aug. 14, 1946, 21; Doc. 119, 193.

11. Louis Menand, *The Metaphysical Club* (New York: Farrar, Straus and Giroux, 2001), xii; Harold D. Lasswell, *Psychopathology and Politics* (Chicago: University of Chicago Press, 1930), 1.

12. Memo, n.d., att'd to Frank Hughes to Don Maxwell, Apr. 28, 1947, Hughes Papers, box 27; Stephen Bates, "Prejudice and the Press Critics: Colonel Robert McCormick's Assault on the Hutchins Commission," *American Journalism* 36, no. 4 (2019): 430; Harold D. Lasswell, "The Developing Science of Democracy," in *The Future of Government in the United States: Essays in Honor of Charles E. Merriam*, ed. Leonard D. White (Chicago: University of Chicago Press, 1942), 34.

13. Doc. 70, 4–5; Doc. 16, 21.

14. Llewellyn White, "Seven Keys to Addlepate," *Harper's*, Oct. 1945, 337; Doc. 16A, 2; Reinhold Niebuhr, *The Children of Light and the Children of Darkness: A Vindication of Democracy and a Critique of Its Traditional Defense* (New York: Scribner, 1944), 146; WEH to RMH, July 24, 1946 (typo corrected), RMH Chicago, box 8.

Chapter One. Skunk at the Garden Party

1. Milton Mayer, interview with RMH, Oct. 3, 1973, 1, Ashmore Collection, box 13; RMH to HRL, Feb. 12, 1945, Time Inc. Archives; Stephen Bates, "Is This the Best Philosophy Can Do? Henry R. Luce and *A Free and Responsible Press*," *Journalism & Mass Communication Quarterly* 95, no. 3 (2018): 815.

2. RMH, foreword to *FRP*, v; HRL, "General Commentary I," Dec. 15 (?), 1946, 1–3, Time Inc. Archives; Frank Hughes, *Prejudice and the Press* (New York: Devin-Adair, 1950), 19–21; HRL to WEH, Dec. 1, 1943, 1, Time Inc. Archives; HRL, "Address to the Commissars," April 30, 1937, in *The Ideas of Henry Luce*, ed. John K. Jessup (New York: Atheneum, 1969), 42.

3. Eric Sevareid, *Conversations with Eric Sevareid* (Washington, DC: Public Affairs Press, 1976), 127; RMH to HRL, Oct. 24, 1929, RMH Chicago, box 157; Martha Wallace to James Grier Miller, Sept. 10, 1982, Center for the Study of Democratic Institutions Collection, box 466.

4. HRL, "General Commentary I," 2.

5. William Benton to W. A. Swanberg, Aug. 26, 1969, 2, Swanberg Papers, box 1; Frank K. Kelly, "Trees Grew in Brooklyn," *Center Magazine*, Nov. 1968, 16–19; "Midway Man," *Time*, June 24, 1935; Tom Pettey, " 'Bob' Hutchins, U. of C. Prexy, Is Regular Guy," *Chicago Tribune*, Apr. 27, 1929, 3.

6. Joseph Epstein, "The Sad Story of the Boy Wonder," *Commentary*, Mar. 1990, 89; Edward Shils, "Robert Maynard Hutchins," in *Remembering the University of Chicago: Teachers, Scientists, and Scholars*, ed. Shils (Chicago: University of Chicago Press, 1991), 186; interviews with RMH, Jan. 6 and 8, 1975, 13, RMH Oral History, box 1; J. P. McEvoy, "Young Man Looking Backwards," *American Mercury*, Dec. 1938, 482; RMH to Laurence E. Morehouse, July 28, 1952, RMH UCSB, box 2.

7. Thurman Arnold, *Fair Fights and Foul: A Dissenting Lawyer's Life* (New York: Harcourt, Brace and World, 1965), 16, 59; interview with Harry S. Ashmore, Aug. 5, 1974, 5, RMH Oral History, box 1; RMH to HRL, Nov. 28, 1949, RMH Chicago, box 157; William Benton to RMH, Apr. 23, 1959, Benton Papers, box 167.

8. William H. McNeill, *Hutchins' University: A Memoir of the University of Chicago, 1929–1950* (Chicago: University of Chicago Press, 1991), 27, 97; Shils, "Robert Maynard Hutchins," 193; "Worst Kind of Troublemaker," *Time*, Nov. 21, 1949; RMH, *No Friendly Voice* (Chicago: University of Chicago Press, 1936), 87; Milton S. Mayer, "Rapidly Aging Young Man," *Forum and Century*, Nov. 1933, 308.

9. RMH, "Memorial Tribute to the Honorable William Benton" (June 11, 1973), *University of Chicago Record*, Sept. 11, 1973, 233; John W. Boyer, *The University of Chicago: A History* (Chicago: University of Chicago Press, 2015), 252–261; Anne H. Stevens, "The Philosophy of General Education and Its Contradictions: The Influence of Hutchins," *Journal of General Education* 50, no. 3 (2001): 169–170.

10. "Worst Kind of Troublemaker"; Mortimer J. Adler, *Philosopher at Large: An Intellectual Autobiography* (New York: Macmillan, 1977), 138; McEvoy, "Young Man Looking Backwards," 484; John Dewey, "President Hutchins' Proposals to Remake Higher Education," *Social Frontier* 3, no. 22 (Jan. 1937): 104; Alan Ryan, *John Dewey and the High Tide of American Liberalism* (New York: Norton, 1995), 278–281; RMH, *The Higher Learning in America* (New Haven, CT: Yale University Press, 1936), 19; RMH, "Education for Freedom," *Harper's*, Oct. 1941, 526; RMH, "Threat to American Education," *Collier's*, Dec. 30, 1944, 20–21.

11. Katharine Graham, *Personal History* (New York: Knopf, 1997), 82; Agnes E. Meyer, "Hutchins' Flight from Reality," *Washington Post*, Feb. 7, 1937, B7; John Dewey to Agnes E. Meyer, Feb. 8, 1937, in InteLex Past Masters database, http://www.nlx.com/home.

12. RMH, "Dark Hours in Our History," convocation address, University of Chicago, June 10, 1941, *Vital Speeches*, July 1, 1941, 570; George B. de Huszar, "The Classics and International Understanding," in *Learning and World Peace: Eighth Symposium*, ed. Lyman Bryson, Louis Finkelstein, and R. M. MacIver (New York: Conference on Science, Philosophy and Religion in Their Relation to the Democratic Way of Life, 1948), 482; Henry Regnery, *Memoirs of a Dissident Publisher* (New York: Harcourt

Brace Jovanovich, 1979), 56–57; Harry S. Ashmore, *Unseasonable Truths: The Life of Robert Maynard Hutchins* (Boston: Little, Brown, 1989), 271–272; *Measure* tables of contents, 2, no. 1 (Dec. 1950), 2, no. 2 (Spring 1951), 2, no. 3 (Summer 1951); Edward Shils, *Portraits: A Gallery of Intellectuals* (Chicago: University of Chicago Press, 1997), 130.

13. Dwight Macdonald, *The Ford Foundation: The Men and the Millions* (1955; repr., New Brunswick, NJ: Transaction, 1989), 152; "Midway Man"; RMH to HRL, Aug. 1949, 1, Time Inc. Archives; Ashmore, *Unseasonable Truths*, xvi; Milton Mayer, *Robert Maynard Hutchins: A Memoir* (Berkeley: University of California Press, 1993), 2; Meg Greenfield, "The Great American Morality Play," *Reporter*, June 8, 1961, 13.

14. RMH, *Higher Learning in America*, 56; RMH, "Education for Freedom," 522; RMH, *The Learning Society* (New York: Praeger, 1968), 30; RMH, "What Education Cannot Do," *Inland Bulletin*, Mar. 10, 1938, 133.

15. Laura Bergquist, "Kay Meyer Goes to College," *Ms.*, Oct. 1974, 53; "The Columnists," *Center Magazine*, Sept.-Oct. 1977, 42; George Steiner, "An Examined Life," *New Yorker*, Oct. 23, 1989, 142; Zachary Leader, *The Life of Saul Bellow: To Fame and Fortune, 1915–1964* (New York: Knopf, 2015), 254; Irving Kristol, "Memoirs of a Trotskyist (1977)," in *The New York Intellectuals Reader*, ed. Neil Jumonville (New York: Routledge, 2007), 45; McNeill, *Hutchins' University*, 158.

16. McEvoy, "Young Man Looking Backwards," 483; RMH, *No Friendly Voice*, 1, 4.

17. Mayer, *Robert Maynard Hutchins*, 147–166, 389–391 (quote on 148).

18. RMH, "Toward a Durable Society," *Fortune*, June 1943, 159–160, 194–207; McNeill, *Hutchins' University*, 94; "Midway Man"; "Worst Kind of Troublemaker"; RMH to HRL, Mar. 1, 1939, Time Inc. Archives; HRL to RMH, Apr. 10, 1942, RMH Chicago, box 157; "Publisher's Letter," *Time*, Jan. 16, 1956, 15. The publisher's note appeared after Hutchins left the university; *Time* continued its coverage.

19. RMH, speech to American Society of Newspaper Editors, in *Problems of Journalism: Proceedings of the 1930 Convention*, by American Society of Newspaper Editors (Columbia, MO: American Society of Newspaper Editors, 1930), 133–134; RMH, "U.S. Radio 'Disgrace,' Hutchins Tells British; 'Degrades' People's Taste," *Variety*, May 10, 1950, 22.

20. William Hesse, interview with RMH, Mar. 8, 1966, 24–25, Ames Papers; "Text of Hutchins Speech before Society of Newspaper Editors," *New York Times*, Apr. 22, 1955, 16.

21. RMH, speech to American Society of Newspaper Editors, 130–131; RMH, "Freedom Requires Responsibility," speech to National Conference of Editorial Writers, Nov. 19, 1948, *Vital Speeches*, Jan. 1, 1949, 175; McEvoy, "Young Man Looking Backwards," 482; RMH to Gilbert Seldes, Nov. 15, 1963, RMH UCSB, box 2; RMH notes on *Time* article, Nov. 28, 1949, RMH Chicago, box 157; "Midway Man"; Ashmore, *Un-*

seasonable Truths, 111; "Education Post in Cabinet Urged," *New York Times*, Oct. 31, 1933, 4; Donald Slesinger, "Dr. Hutchins Looks beyond the Campus," *New York Times*, Dec. 9, 1934, 9, 18; Milton Mayer, "The Red Room," *Massachusetts Review* 16 (1975): 522.

22. "Hutchins Speech Starts a Boom," *New York Times*, June 28, 1932, 16; Mayer, *Robert Maynard Hutchins*, 211; "Sinclair Lewis Picks Hutchins for President," *Washington Post*, Feb. 25, 1938, X19; "Midway Man"; Mayer, "Rapidly Aging Young Man," 312–313.

23. Harold L. Ickes, *The Secret Diary of Harold L. Ickes: The First Thousand Days, 1933–1936* (New York: Simon and Schuster, 1953), 198, 201, 209–211, 219–220; Ickes, *The Secret Diary of Harold L. Ickes: The Inside Struggle, 1936–1939* (New York: Simon and Schuster, 1954), 182, 298, 588–589; Ickes, *The Secret Diary of Harold L. Ickes: The Lowering Clouds, 1939–1941* (New York: Simon and Schuster, 1954), 256; Mary Ann Dzuback, *Robert M. Hutchins: Portrait of an Educator* (Chicago: University of Chicago Press, 1991), 210; McNeill, *Hutchins' University*, 99; [RMH], day-by-day account of discussions with Roosevelt administration officials over NRA position, Sept. 26–Dec. 12, 1934, Tugwell Papers; interview with Rexford G. Tugwell, Jan. 8, 1975, 1, RMH Oral History, box 2; interview with RMH, Jan. 6, 1975, 7, RMH Oral History, box 1; Sidney Hyman, *The Lives of William Benton* (Chicago: University of Chicago Press, 1969), 231 (capitalization altered).

24. RMH, "America and the War," *Journal of Negro Education* 10, no. 3 (July 1941): 441; RMH, "The Proposition Is Peace," *Vital Speeches*, Apr. 15, 1941, 391; Mayer, *Robert Maynard Hutchins*, 256; Richard Norton Smith, *The Colonel: The Life and Legend of Robert R. McCormick, 1880–1955* (Boston: Houghton Mifflin, 1997), 403; George Tagge, "Hutchins Tells What We Lose If We Go to War," *Chicago Tribune*, Mar. 31, 1941, 1, 5; Ickes, *Secret Diary: Lowering Clouds*, 472.

25. Ashmore, *Unseasonable Truths*, 34–35, 44.

26. Thornton Wilder to Mabel Dodge Luhan, Oct. 7, 1934, in *The Selected Letters of Thornton Wilder*, ed. Robin G. Wilder and Jackson R. Bryer (New York: HarperCollins, 2008), 284, 285; [Maude Phelps Hutchins], "What Makes People Rude?," n.d., M. Hutchins Papers, box 23; M. Hutchins to R. H. Goldstone, Oct. 25, 1971, 1–2, Goldstone Papers, box 3; Richard H. Goldstone, *Thornton Wilder: An Intimate Portrait* (New York: Saturday Review Press, 1975), 64–65; M. Hutchins to Mark Van Doren, Dec. 30, 1942, 3, Geismar Papers, box 217. See also Terry Castle, introduction to *Victorine*, by M. Hutchins (1959; repr., New York: New York Review Books, 2008), vii–xxxi.

27. Lloyd Wendt, "The Midway's Versatile First Lady," *Chicago Tribune*, June 21, 1942, H2; Maude Phelps Hutchins and Mortimer Jerome Adler, *Diagrammatics* (New York: Random House, 1932); Adler, *Philosopher at Large*, 157–159.

28. M.P.M.H., introduction to Hutchins and Adler, *Diagrammatics;* C. J. Bulliet, "Mrs. Hutchins, Rebel," *Art Digest* 21 (1947): 22; Wendt, "Midway's Versatile First Lady"; Adler, *Philosopher at Large,* 159; Ashmore, *Unseasonable Truths,* 173–174; David C. Levine, "Diagrammatics Still a Puzzle after Hutchins-Adler Lecture," *Daily Maroon,* Apr. 19, 1933, 1.

29. "Merry Christmas," *Time,* June 6, 1938, 23; Maude Phelps Hutchins to I. Van Meter, July 7, 1938, 2, Time Inc. Archives.

30. Carol Atwater, "What Price Sanity," *Daily Maroon,* Sept. 18, 1944; Liesl Olson, *Chicago Renaissance: Literature and Art in the Midwest Metropolis* (New Haven, CT: Yale University Press, 2017), 122–123, 198–207, 320n41; Roy Morris Jr., *Gertrude Stein Has Arrived: The Homecoming of a Literary Legend* (Baltimore: Johns Hopkins University Press, 2019), 128; Geoffrey Johnson, "Portrait of a Lady," *Chicago Magazine,* Oct. 2008, 90–95, 113–119; Castle, introduction to *Victorine,* xii; "Renaissance Society Hangs New Works of Maude Phelps Hutchins," *Chicago Tribune,* Feb. 20, 1937, 17. Several writers speculate that Maude Hutchins was romantically involved with Bobsy Goodspeed rather than Barney, based on Janet Malcolm's account of a letter from Bernard Faÿ to Gertrude Stein. Malcolm, *Two Lives: Gertrude and Alice* (New Haven, CT: Yale University Press, 2007), 102. The actual letter (Malcolm slightly misquotes it) and an earlier one from Faÿ make clear that Barney Goodspeed was the one allegedly having the affair. Bernard Faÿ to Gertrude Stein, June 30, 1934, Stein and Toklas Papers, box 106; Faÿ to Stein, June 11, 1934, Stein and Toklas Papers, box 106. On Faÿ, see Barbara Will, *Unlikely Collaboration: Gertrude Stein, Bernard Faÿ, and the Vichy Dilemma* (New York: Columbia University Press, 2011).

31. RMH to Thornton Wilder, Nov. 10, 1971, Wilder Papers, box 43; RMH to Harold L. Ickes, Jan. 9, 1951, RMH Chicago, box 142; Harold D. Lasswell to William Benton, Jan. 28, 1948, 2, Benton Papers, box 102; Dwight Macdonald, "Foundation (III): The Philanthropoids," *New Yorker,* Dec. 10, 1955, 81–82; RMH to William Benton, Dec. 2, 1963, RMH UCSB, box 2.

32. Dzuback, *Robert M. Hutchins,* 275; interview with RMH, Nov. 24, 1958, 3, RMH Oral History, box 1; Mortimer J. Adler, *A Second Look in the Rearview Mirror: Further Autobiographical Reflections of a Philosopher at Large* (New York: Macmillan, 1992), 42; RMH to Leo Rosten, June 15, 1959, RMH Chicago, box 195.

33. Alex Beam, *A Great Idea at the Time: The Rise, Fall, and Curious Afterlife of the Great Books* (New York: PublicAffairs, 2008), 1, 103–114; "Hutchins, Family Flee; Fire Destroys Mansion," *Chicago Tribune,* Sept. 25, 1964, 1; Ashmore, *Unseasonable Truths,* 465–466, 503–522; Mayer, *Robert Maynard Hutchins,* 491–502; Frank K. Kelly, *Court of Reason: Robert Hutchins and the Fund for the Republic* (New York: Free Press, 1981), 490–496, 501–506, 508–519, 522–638; RMH to William Benton, Sept. 23, 1960, Benton Papers, box 167.

34. Ashmore, *Unseasonable Truths*, 479–481; Mayer, *Robert Maynard Hutchins*, 496, 504; RMH to Thornton Wilder, Aug. 29, 1974, Wilder Papers, box 43.

35. RMH to Thornton Wilder, n.d., Wilder Papers, box 43; RMH to Wilder, Sept. 23, 1966, 1, Wilder Papers, box 43; RMH to Wilder, Apr. 27, 1973, 1, Wilder Papers, box 43; RMH to Wilder, May 16, 1973, 2, Wilder Papers, box 43; Kelly, "Trees Grew in Brooklyn," 21; Kelly, *Court of Reason*, 644; RMH to Wilder, Mar. 24, 1975, 2, Wilder Papers, box 43; RMH to Wilder, Apr. 23, 1975, 2, Wilder Papers, box 43.

36. W. H. Ferry, "Robert Hutchins's Platonic Grove," *Nation*, Jan. 30, 1988, 120; interview with RMH, Jan. 12–13, 1977, 25, RMH Oral History, box 1; RMH to Wilder, Sept. 23, 1966, 1.

37. Sid Landfield, "The Sid Landfield View: Interview—Part Two," *Quincy (IL) Herald Whig*, Apr. 5, 1967; RMH to HRL, May 7, 1936, Time Inc. Archives.

Chapter Two. Unlucky Crusader

1. Alan Brinkley, *The Publisher: Henry Luce and His American Century* (New York: Knopf, 2010), 13, 54, 88, 99; Robert T. Elson, *Time Inc.: The Intimate History of a Publishing Enterprise, 1923–1941* (New York: Atheneum, 1968), 4, 7, 43–45, 66; "His Warm Remembrances of How It All Began," *Life*, Mar. 10, 1967, 38; Isaiah Wilner, *The Man Time Forgot: A Tale of Genius, Betrayal, and the Creation of "Time" Magazine* (New York: Harper Collins, 2006), 76–99; W. A. Swanberg, interview with Duncan Norton-Taylor, Feb. 18, 1970, 2, Swanberg Papers, box 18; Wilfrid Sheed, *Clare Boothe Luce* (New York: Dutton, 1982), 91.

2. Ralph G. Martin, *Henry and Clare: An Intimate Portrait of the Luces* (New York: Putnam, 1991), 91; Wilner, *Man Time Forgot*, 126–143; Norberto Angeletti and Alberto Oliva, *Time: The Illustrated History of the World's Most Influential Magazine* (New York: Rizzoli, 2010), 32–41; James L. Baughman, *Henry R. Luce and the Rise of the American News Media*, rev. ed. (Baltimore: Johns Hopkins University Press, 2001), 43–45; Elson, *Time Inc.*, 83–88; Mary McCarthy, "The Menace to Free Journalism in America," *Listener*, May 14, 1953, 791; "Anabasis," *Time*, July 2, 1923, 3; Wolcott Gibbs, "Time … Fortune … Life … Luce," *New Yorker*, Nov. 28, 1936, https://www.newyorker.com/magazine/1936/11/28/time-fortune-life-luce; W. A. Swanberg, interview with William Benton, Aug. 18, 1969, 1, Swanberg Papers, box 18.

3. Elson, *Time Inc.*, 33; HRL to WEH, Mar. 21, 1952, 1, Time Inc. Archives; David Halberstam, *The Powers That Be* (New York: Knopf, 1979), 48; Stephen Bates, "Public Intellectuals on *Time*'s Covers," *Journalism History* 37, no. 1 (Spring 2011): 41; Wilner, *Man Time Forgot*, 226–232; Robert Vanderlan, *Intellectuals Incorporated: Politics, Art, and Ideas Inside Henry Luce's Media Empire* (Philadelphia: University of Pennsylvania Press, 2010),

93–97, 199–205; John Kobler, "The First Tycoon and the Power of His Press," *Saturday Evening Post*, Jan. 16, 1965, 32; Baughman, *Henry R. Luce*, 165; Dwight Macdonald, "Masscult and Midcult (I)," *Partisan Review* 27, no. 2 (Spring 1960): 213.

4. Thomas Kunkel, *Genius in Disguise: Harold Ross of the "New Yorker"* (New York: Random House, 1995), 89, 93, 100–101, 202–204, 288–294; Brendan Gill, *Here at the "New Yorker"* (New York: Random House, 1975), 9, 201; Brinkley, *Publisher*, 198–201, 416.

5. John K. Jessup, introduction to *The Ideas of Henry Luce*, ed. Jessup (New York: Atheneum, 1969), 27; *St. Louis Post-Dispatch Symposium on Freedom of the Press: Expressions by 120 Representative Americans* (St. Louis: St. Louis Post-Dispatch, 1938), 4, 45–46; Carl W. Ackerman to Lowell Mellett, Aug. 1, 1938, Mellett Papers, box 15; Arthur Hays Sulzberger to Nicholas Murray Butler, Aug. 4, 1938, Central Files, box 251; Arthur Hays Sulzberger to Carl W. Ackerman, Aug. 15, 1938, Central Files, box 360; Susan E. Tifft and Alex S. Jones, *The Trust: The Private and Powerful Family behind the "New York Times"* (Boston: Little, Brown, 1999), 217; "Mess," *Time*, Dec. 13, 1937, 24; James Boylan, *Pulitzer's School: Columbia University's School of Journalism, 1903–2003* (New York: Columbia University Press, 2003), 88.

6. HRL, "Address to the Commissars," April 30, 1937, in Jessup, *Ideas of Henry Luce*, 36–43; Thomas Griffith, *How True: A Skeptic's Guide to Believing the News* (Boston: Little, Brown, 1974), 98; Allen C. Carlson, "Luce, *Life* and 'The American Way,' " *This World* 13 (Winter 1986): 71; Hedley Donovan, *Right Places, Right Times: Forty Years in Journalism, Not Counting My Paper Route* (New York: Holt, 1989), 212.

7. Thomas Griffith, *Harry and Teddy: The Turbulent Friendship of Press Lord Henry R. Luce and His Favorite Reporter, Theodore H. White* (New York: Random House, 1995), 304; Theodore H. White, *In Search of History: A Personal Adventure* (New York: Harper and Row, 1978), 207; Jessup, introduction to *Ideas of Henry Luce*, 9; Brinkley, *Publisher*, 438; Bates, "Public Intellectuals on *Time's* Covers," 41; T. S. Matthews, "Tall, Balding, Dead Henry R. Luce," *Esquire*, Sept. 1967, 132; Robert E. Herzstein, *Henry R. Luce: A Political Portrait of the Man Who Created the American Century* (New York: Scribner, 1994), 112; Halberstam, *Powers That Be*, 467; Martin, *Henry and Clare*, 169, 274, 348, 376.

8. Brinkley, *Publisher*, 78, 117, 191–195, 410–412, 432–434; Martin, *Henry and Clare*, 335–346, 353–355, 364–375; W. A. Swanberg, notes of interview with Lady Jean [*sic*] Campbell, Sept. 16, 1972, 1, Swanberg Papers, box 2.

9. W. A. Swanberg, notes of interview with Senator William Benton, Aug. 18, 1969, 4, Swanberg Papers, box 18; Stephen Bates, "Is This the Best Philosophy Can Do? Henry R. Luce and *A Free and Responsible Press*," *Journalism & Mass Communication Quarterly* 95, no. 3 (2018): 815; Herz-

stein, *Henry R. Luce*, 83, 226; HRL, "The American Century," *Life*, Feb. 17, 1941, 65; Brinkley, *Publisher*, 283.

10. Brinkley, *Publisher*, 240–241, 352–353; Halberstam, *Powers That Be*, 93; Sheed, *Clare Boothe Luce*, 79; Francis Pickens Miller, *Man from the Valley: Memoirs of a 20th-Century Virginian* (Chapel Hill: University of North Carolina Press, 1971), 95; Swanberg, notes of interview with Campbell, 1; Martin, *Henry and Clare*, 329.

11. William Benton to RMH, May 19, 1959, 1, 4, Benton Papers, box 167; Benton to RMH, Jan. 11, 1965, Benton Papers, box 168; Benton to Paul Hoffman, Dec. 28, 1962, 1, Benton Papers, box 177.

12. Archibald MacLeish to HRL, ca. July 20, 1938, in *Letters of Archibald Mac-Leish, 1907 to 1982*, ed. R. H. Winnick (Boston: Houghton Mifflin, 1983), 293 (punctuation corrected); MacLeish to HRL, ca. Sept. 8, 1938, in *Letters of Archibald MacLeish*, 297; MacLeish to HRL, Sept. 8, 1943, in *Letters of Archibald MacLeish*, 316–317; Scott Donaldson, *Archibald MacLeish: An American Life* (Boston: Houghton Mifflin, 1992), 252, 280–281, 451; W. A. Swanberg, interview with MacLeish, July 26, 1968, 1, 3, Swanberg Papers, box 18; Bates, "Is This the Best Philosophy Can Do?," 817; HRL to MacLeish, Aug. 18, 1949, 1, Time Inc. Archives.

13. Brinkley, *Publisher*, 416–419, 438–439; *Life*, Dec. 26, 1955; John K. Jessup, "Henry R. Luce, 1898–1967: The Values That Shaped His Work," *Life*, Mar. 10, 1967, 31; RMH to Thornton Wilder, Dec. 29, 1955, Wilder Papers, box 108.

14. RMH to William Benton, Mar. 22, 1968, RMH UCSB, box 2.

15. HRL, "General Commentary I," Dec. 15 (?), 1946, 2, Time Inc. Archives; jacket copy, *FRP*, University of Chicago Press Records, box 287; Bates, "Is This the Best Philosophy Can Do?," 816.

16. Notes of conversation between HRL and RMH, n.d., 1, RMH Chicago, box 7; Mary Ann Dzuback, *Robert M. Hutchins: Portrait of an Educator* (Chicago: University of Chicago Press, 1991), 94–100, 175–178.

17. Notes of conversation between HRL and RMH, 1.

18. RMH to Roy Larsen, Oct. 29, 1946, RMH Chicago, box 8; Bates, "Is This the Best Philosophy Can Do?," 820.

Chapter Three. Disillusionment in Democracy

1. Victor Pickard, *America's Battle for Media Democracy: The Triumph of Corporate Libertarianism and the Future of Media Reform* (New York: Cambridge University Press, 2015), 135–136; Sam Lebovic, *Free Speech and Unfree News: The Paradox of Press Freedom in America* (Cambridge, MA: Harvard University Press, 2016), 138; Arthur M. Schlesinger Jr., *The Vital Center: The Politics of Freedom* (1949; repr., New Brunswick, NJ: Transaction, 1998), x; Everett M. Rogers and Steven H. Chaffee, "Communication and

Journalism from 'Daddy' Bleyer to Wilbur Schramm: A Palimpsest," *Journalism Monographs* 148 (1994): 12–14; Willard Grosvenor Bleyer, "Freedom of the Press and the New Deal," *Journalism Quarterly* 11, no. 1 (1934): 33, 35. Bleyer originally delivered the paper at the American Association of the Schools and Departments of Journalism, Chicago, Dec. 27, 1933. Bleyer Papers, box 3.

2. Rowland A. Egger, "The Collapse of Democracy," *American Mercury*, Apr. 1930, 462; Henry Hazlitt, "Without Benefit of Congress," *Scribner's*, July 1932, 13; "Dr. Butler Deplores Calibre of Leaders," *New York Times*, Sept. 24, 1931, 1; Alonzo L. Hamby, *For the Survival of Democracy: Franklin Roosevelt and the World Crisis of the 1930s* (New York: Free Press, 2004), 3–4; Harold J. Laski, *Democracy in Crisis* (London: George Allen and Unwin, 1933), 16; Stephen H. Norwood, "Complicity and Conflict: Columbia University's Response to Fascism, 1933–1937," *Modern Judaism* 27, no. 3 (2007): 264.

3. José Ortega y Gasset, *The Revolt of the Masses* (New York: Norton, 1932), 17, 70; James L. Baughman, *Henry R. Luce and the Rise of the American News Media* (Baltimore: Johns Hopkins University Press, 1987), 111–112; John K. Jessup, introduction to *The Ideas of Henry Luce*, ed. Jessup (New York: Atheneum, 1969), 13; interview with RMH, May 24, 1976, 11, RMH Oral History, box 1; Richard W. Steele, "Fear of the Mob and Faith in Government in Free Speech Discourse, 1919–1941," *American Journal of Legal History* 38 (1994): 55–83; Robert S. Lynd and Helen Merrell Lynd, *Middletown in Transition: A Study in Cultural Conflicts* (New York: Harcourt, Brace, 1937), 492–510.

4. Richard Wightman Fox, *Reinhold Niebuhr: A Biography* (1985; repr., Ithaca, NY: Cornell University Press, 1996), 135–136; Alden Whitman, "Reinhold Niebuhr Is Dead; Protestant Theologian, 78," *New York Times*, June 2, 1971, 1, 45.

5. Larry Rasmussen, "Author's Note," in *Reinhold Niebuhr: Theologian of Public Life*, ed. Rasmussen (London: Collins, 1989), ix; Hans J. Morgenthau, "The Influence of Reinhold Niebuhr in American Political Life and Thought," in *Reinhold Niebuhr: A Prophetic Voice in Our Time*, ed. Harold R. Landon (Greenwich, CT: Seabury, 1962), 109; Andrew J. Bacevich, introduction to *The Irony of American History*, by Reinhold Niebuhr (1952; repr., Chicago: University of Chicago Press, 2008), ix; Daniel F. Rice, *Reinhold Niebuhr and John Dewey: An American Odyssey* (Albany: State University of New York Press, 1993), 217; Whitman, "Reinhold Niebuhr Is Dead," 45.

6. Neil Jumonville, *Critical Crossings: The New York Intellectuals in Postwar America* (Berkeley: University of California Press, 1991), 102, 125; Reinhold Niebuhr, "Ideologies: Mental Corruption Is No 'Capitalist' Monopoly, Special Interests Pervert Thinking on the Left," *New Leader*, Aug. 16, 1941, 4B; [Niebuhr], "Reason and Interest in Politics," *Christianity and Society*, Winter 1944, 9; Niebuhr, "The Unhappy Intellectuals," *Atlantic*

Monthly, June 1929, 793–794; Niebuhr, "After Capitalism—What?," *World Tomorrow*, Mar. 1, 1933, 204.

7. Reinhold Niebuhr, "A Faith for History's Greatest Crisis," *Fortune*, July 1942, 122; [Niebuhr], "The Blindness of Liberalism," *Radical Religion* 1, no. 4 (Autumn 1936): 4–5; Niebuhr, "The Response of Reinhold Niebuhr," in Landon, *Reinhold Niebuhr*, 121; Niebuhr, *Moral Man and Immoral Society: A Study in Ethics and Politics* (New York: Scribner, 1936), xv–xvii, 21; Niebuhr, *Leaves from the Notebook of a Tamed Cynic* (1929; repr., Cleveland, OH: Meridian, 1957), 158; Niebuhr, "Modern Utopians," *Scribner's*, Sept. 1936, 142.

8. Niebuhr, *Irony of American History*, 63; Reinhold Niebuhr, *Beyond Tragedy: Essays on the Christian Interpretation of History* (New York: Scribner, 1937), 28; Niebuhr, *The Children of Light and the Children of Darkness: A Vindication of Democracy and a Critique of Its Traditional Defence* (New York: Scribner, 1944), xi; Fox, *Reinhold Niebuhr*, 138, 170.

9. Reinhold Niebuhr, "The Revival of Feudalism," *Harper's*, Mar. 1935, 483; Niebuhr, "Pawns for Fascism," *American Scholar*, June 1937, 149–152; Niebuhr, *The Nature and Destiny of Man*, vol. 1, *Human Nature* (London: Nisbet, 1941), 226; Niebuhr, "After Capitalism," 204.

10. Fox, *Reinhold Niebuhr*, 149, 218; Arthur Schlesinger Jr., "Reinhold Niebuhr's Role in American Political Thought and Life," in *Reinhold Niebuhr: His Religious, Social, and Political Thought*, ed. Charles W. Kegley and Robert W. Bretall (New York: Macmillan, 1956), 142–143.

11. Thomas Griffith, *How True: A Skeptic's Guide to Believing the News* (Boston: Little, Brown, 1974), 94; HRL to Ralph D. Paine Jr., May 11, 1942, 1, Time Inc. Archives; Reinhold Niebuhr, "Our Country and Our Culture," *Partisan Review* 19, no. 3 (May–June 1952): 302; Niebuhr, "Awkward Imperialists," *Atlantic Monthly*, May 1930, 674; Niebuhr, *Discerning the Signs of the Times: Sermons for Today and Tomorrow* (New York: Scribner, 1946), 11, 78; [HRL], "Discerning the Signs of the Times," June (?) 1946, 2, Time Inc. Archives; Niebuhr to HRL, Dec. 11, 1944, Time Inc. Archives; Niebuhr, "The Fight for Germany," *Life*, Oct. 21, 1946, 65–72; Niebuhr, "For Peace, We Must Risk War," *Life*, Sept. 20, 1948, 38–39; *Time*, Mar. 8, 1948, cover; Jessup, introduction to *Ideas of Henry Luce*, 15–16; Whitman, "Reinhold Niebuhr Is Dead"; Stephen Bates, "Is This the Best Philosophy Can Do? Henry R. Luce and *A Free and Responsible Press*," *Journalism & Mass Communication Quarterly* 95, no. 3 (2018): 817.

12. Doc. 99, 22–23, 195; Doc. 4, 1; Doc. 16, 21; Doc. 75, 101.

13. Charles E. Merriam, "The Assumptions of Democracy," *Political Science Quarterly* 53, no. 3 (Sept. 1938): 329.

14. Barry D. Karl, *Charles E. Merriam and the Study of Politics* (Chicago: University of Chicago, 1974), x, 2, 44, 50, 75–81, 89–95, 202–205, 234–235; Albert Somit and Joseph Tanenhaus, *The Development of American Political Science: From Burgess to Behavioralism* (Boston: Allyn and Bacon, 1967),

43–45, 83–85; Charles E. Merriam, "The Education of Charles E. Merriam," in *The Future of Government in the United States: Essays in Honor of Charles E. Merriam*, ed. Leonard D. White (Chicago: University of Chicago Press, 1942), 3–6; Merriam, "Progress in Political Research," *American Political Science Review* 20, no. 1 (Feb. 1926): 4; George Z. F. Bereday, introduction to *The Making of Citizens*, by Merriam (1931; repr., New York: Teachers College Press, 1966), 2, 4; Louis Brownlow, *A Passion for Politics: The Autobiography of Louis Brownlow—First Half* (Chicago: University of Chicago Press, 1955), 584.

15. Charles E. Merriam, "Political Research," *American Political Science Review* 16 (1922): 320; Merriam, *New Aspects of Politics*, 2d ed. (1925; repr., Chicago: University of Chicago Press, 1931), xiii; Somit and Tanenhaus, *Development of Political Science*, 87–88, 110–113; Merriam, "Human Nature and Science in City Government," *Journal of Social Forces* 1 (1922–23): 462; Raymond Seidelman with Edward J. Harpham, *Disenchanted Realists: Political Science and the American Crisis, 1884–1984* (Albany: State University of New York Press, 1985), 130–131; Karl, *Charles E. Merriam*, 132, 248.

16. Merriam, *New Aspects of Politics*, viii, xi, 20–22, 155, 247; "Merriam Pictures Toil-Free Nation," *New York Times*, June 28, 1935, 21; Karl, *Charles E. Merriam*, 178; Merriam, "Assumptions of Democracy," 342; Merriam, review of *Public Opinion*, by Walter Lippmann, *International Journal of Ethics* 33, no. 2 (1923): 210; Merriam, "The Possibilities of Planning," *American Journal of Sociology* 49, no. 5 (Mar. 1944): 404–405; Merriam, "Recent Tendencies," 27; Paul Mark Fackler, "The Hutchins Commissioners and the Crisis in Democratic Theory, 1930–1947" (PhD diss., University of Illinois at Urbana-Champaign, 1982), 221.

17. President's Research Committee on Social Trends, *Recent Social Trends in the United States*, vol. 1 (New York: McGraw-Hill, 1933), v–vi, xi; William A. Tobin, "The Making of *Recent Social Trends in the United States*, 1929–1933," *Theory and Society* 24, no. 4 (Aug. 1995): 543–544; Michael J. Lacey and Mary O. Furner, "Social Investigation, Social Knowledge, and the State: An Introduction," in *The State and Social Investigation in Britain and the United States*, ed. Lacey and Furner (Washington, DC: Woodrow Wilson Center Press, 1993), 42–49; Karl, *Charles E. Merriam*, 209–225.

18. President's Research Committee, *Recent Social Trends*, xxiii, lxix, lxxiv, xciv–xcv.

19. Richard Hofstadter, *The Age of Reform: From Bryan to FDR* (New York: Vintage, 1955), 257, 261; Michael Schudson, "What Public Journalism Knows about Journalism but Doesn't Know about 'Public,' " in *The Idea of Public Journalism*, ed. Theodore L. Glasser (New York: Guilford, 1999), 123–124; Walter J. Shepard, "Democracy in Transition," *American Political Science Review* 29, no. 1 (Feb. 1935): 19.

20. Charles Edward Merriam, *Political Power: Its Composition and Incidence* (New York: McGraw-Hill, 1934), 191–192; Karl, *Charles E. Merriam*, 235–259, 270–282; National Planning Board, *Final Report, 1933–1934*

(Washington, DC: Government Printing Office, 1934), 52; National Resources Planning Board, *National Resources Development Report for 1942* (Washington, DC: Government Printing Office, 1942), 3–4; National Resources Planning Board, *National Resources Development Report for 1943: Part I. Post-war Plan and Program* (Washington, DC: Government Printing Office, 1943), 3; Merriam, "The National Resources Planning Board: A Chapter in American Planning Experience," *American Political Science Review* 38, no. 6 (Dec. 1944): 1075–1088.

21. Richard Polenberg, *Reorganizing Roosevelt's Government: The Controversy over Executive Reorganization, 1936–1939* (Cambridge, MA: Harvard University Press, 1966), 12–27, 35–41, 51, 191–195; Hamby, *For the Survival of Democracy*, 342–344.

22. Polenberg, *Reorganizing Roosevelt's Government*, 20–21; Hans J. Morgenthau, "Truth and Power," *New Republic*, Nov. 26, 1966, 9.

23. Marquis Childs, "The Hiss Case and the American Intellectual," *Reporter*, Sept. 26, 1950, 25; Aaron Lecklider, *Inventing the Egghead: The Battle over Brainpower in American Culture* (Philadelphia: University of Pennsylvania Press, 2013), 116–125; Karl, *Charles E. Merriam*, 231; H. L. Mencken, "The New Deal Mentality," *American Mercury*, May 1936, 4.

24. Seymour Martin Lipset, "The Fuss about Eggheads," *Encounter*, Apr. 1957, 17; Stephen Bates, "Public Intellectuals on *Time*'s Covers," *Journalism History* 37, no. 1 (Spring 2011): 41; David Goodman, *Radio's Civic Ambition: American Broadcasting and Democracy in the 1930s* (New York: Oxford University Press, 2011), 194–198.

25. Charles E. Merriam, *The New Democracy and the New Despotism* (New York: McGraw-Hill, 1939), 7; Merriam, "Education of Charles Merriam," 19–20; Patrick J. Deneen, *Democratic Faith* (Princeton, NJ: Princeton University Press, 2005), 41–44; "Merriam Predicts Aid for US in Reich," *New York Times*, Aug. 29, 1943, 22; Reinhold Niebuhr, "Dr. Merriam Sums Up," *Nation*, Oct. 13, 1945, 379; Niebuhr, "Force and Reason in Politics," *Nation*, Feb. 10, 1940, 217; Niebuhr, *Moral Man and Immoral Society*, xiv–xv, 214; Niebuhr, "Intellectual Autobiography," in Kegley and Bretall, *Reinhold Niebuhr*, 13. On the relationship between the philosophical outlooks of Niebuhr and Merriam, see Karl, *Charles E. Merriam*, 294–296.

26. Fox, *Reinhold Niebuhr*, x, 270; Milton Mayer, "The Red Room," *Massachusetts Review* 16, no. 3 (Summer 1975): 534; Charles E. Merriam to Reinhold Niebuhr, Mar. 27, 1944, Merriam Papers, box 66; Niebuhr to Merriam, Mar. 29, 1944, Merriam Papers, box 66.

Chapter Four. Synthetic Dead Cats

1. Charles Dickens, *Martin Chuzzlewit*, vol. 6 in *The Works of Charles Dickens* (London: Chapman and Hall, 1901), 220; Will Irwin, *The American Newspaper* (Ames: Iowa State University Press, 1969) (reprinting 1911 articles), 7;

Upton Sinclair, *The Brass Check: A Study of American Journalism* (Pasadena, CA: self-published, n.d. [1919]); Walter Lippmann, *Liberty and the News* (New York: Harcourt, Brace and Howe, 1920); Lippmann, *Public Opinion* (New York: Harcourt, Brace, 1922); Oswald Garrison Villard, *Some Newspapers and Newspaper-Men* (New York: Knopf, 1923); Silas Bent, *Ballyhoo: The Voice of the Press* (New York: Boni and Liveright, 1927); H. L. Mencken, "Learning How to Blush," *American Mercury*, July 1925, 379. On the history of press criticism in the United States, see Marion Tuttle Marzolf, *Civilizing Voices: American Press Criticism, 1880–1950* (New York: Longman, 1991); Arthur S. Hayes, *Press Critics Are the Fifth Estate: Media Watchdogs in America* (Westport, CT: Praeger, 2008); Lee Brown, *The Reluctant Reformation: On Criticizing the Press in America* (New York: David McKay, 1974); Tom Goldstein, ed., *Killing the Messenger: 100 Years of Media Criticism* (New York: Columbia University Press, 1989); Sam Lebovic, "When the 'Mainstream Media' Was Conservative: Media Criticism in the Age of Reform," in *Media Nation: The Political History of News in Modern America*, ed. Bruce J. Schulman and Julian E. Zelizer (Philadelphia: University of Pennsylvania Press, 2017), 63–76; Robert W. McChesney and Ben Scott, eds., *Our Unfree Press: 100 Years of Radical Media Criticism* (New York: New Press, 2004); Theodore Peterson, Jay W. Jensen, and William L. Rivers, *The Mass Media and Modern Society* (New York: Holt, Rinehart and Winston, 1965), 226–246.

2. Leo C. Rosten, *The Washington Correspondents* (New York: Harcourt, Brace, 1937); Herbert Brucker, *The Changing American Newspaper* (New York: Columbia University Press, 1937), 11; Curtis D. MacDougall, *Interpretative Reporting* (New York: Macmillan, 1938); Sidney Kobre, *Backgrounding the News: The Newspaper and the Social Sciences* (Baltimore: Twentieth Century, 1939); Oswald Garrison Villard, *The Disappearing Daily: Chapters in American Newspaper Evolution* (New York: Knopf, 1944); Morris L. Ernst, *The First Freedom* (New York: Macmillan, 1946); Harold L. Ickes, *America's House of Lords: An Inquiry into the Freedom of the Press* (New York: Harcourt, Brace, 1939); Ickes, ed., *Freedom of the Press Today: A Clinical Examination by 28 Specialists* (New York: Vanguard, 1941); George Seldes, *Lords of the Press* (New York: Julian Messner, 1938); Seldes, *The Facts Are: A Guide to Falsehood and Propaganda in the Press and Radio* (New York: In Fact, 1942); *Newsmen's Holiday: Nieman Essays—First Series* (Cambridge, MA: Harvard University Press, 1942); Leon Svirsky, ed., *Your Newspaper: Blueprint for a Better Press, by Nine Nieman Fellows* (New York: Macmillan, 1947); Victor Pickard, *America's Battle for Media Democracy: The Triumph of Corporate Libertarianism and the Future of Media Reform* (New York: Cambridge University Press, 2015), 124–135. On Seldes and his newsletter, see Pamela A. Brown, "George Seldes and the Winter Soldier Brigade: The Press Criticism of *In Fact*, 1940–1950," *American Journalism* 6 (1989): 85–102.

3. Carl Macauley, "War and the Press," *New Masses*, Jan. 17, 1939, 9; Roy Hoopes, *Ralph Ingersoll: A Biography* (New York: Atheneum, 1985), 407;

Virginius Dabney, "Press and Morale," *Saturday Review of Literature*, July 4, 1942, 5–6, 24–26; Margaret Marshall, "Columnists on Parade: II. Westbrook Pegler," *Nation*, Mar. 5, 1938, 273–276; Raymond Sokolov, *Wayward Reporter: The Life of A. J. Liebling* (New York: Harper and Row, 1980), 177; Louis M. Lyons, introduction to *Reporting the News: Selections from "Nieman Reports,"* ed. Lyons (Cambridge, MA: Harvard University Press, 1965), 1–2; "Is the American Press Really Free?," *Town Meeting* 12, no. 25 (Oct. 17, 1946); Don Hollenbeck, "CBS Views the Press," *Atlantic Monthly*, Sept. 1948, 49–51; *CBS Views the Press*, Dec. 4, 1948, Hollenbeck Broadcast Papers, box 5; Marzolf, *Civilizing Voices*, 177–181.

4. "The Fortune Quarterly Survey: III," *Fortune*, Jan. 1936, 144; Eric Hodgins to HRL, Nov. 20, 1943, part 2, 5, Time Inc. Archives; "The Press and the People—A Survey," *Fortune*, Aug. 1939, 70–72; Villard, *Disappearing Daily*, 8–9; Hazel Erskine, "The Polls: Opinion of the News Media," *Public Opinion Quarterly* 34, no. 4 (Winter 1970): 641–642; "Liberty of the Press," in *Public Opinion, 1935–1946*, ed. Hadley Cantril (Princeton, NJ: Princeton University Press, 1951), 417; "Press Is Warned of Dictatorship through Radio," *Tuscaloosa News*, Apr. 27, 1938, 1; Marzolf, *Civilizing Voices*, 133, 182; Silas Bent, *Newspaper Crusaders: A Neglected Story* (New York: Whittlesey House, 1939), 7 (quoting *Editor & Publisher*); Wilbur Forrest, "Anti-Press Literature," *Editor & Publisher*, June 8, 1946, 34.

5. Graham J. White, *FDR and the Press* (Chicago: University of Chicago Press, 1979), 1–2, 31, 65, 89–91; "80-Year History of Chicago Tribune Unbroken Record of Falsehood by This Outstanding Enemy of the People," *In Fact* 4, no. 7 (Nov. 24, 1941): 1; Harold L. Ickes, *The Secret Diary of Harold L. Ickes*, vol. 1, *The First Thousand Days, 1933–1936* (New York: Simon and Schuster, 1953), 212.

6. Fred W. Friendly, *Minnesota Rag: The Dramatic Story of the Landmark Supreme Court Case That Gave New Meaning to Freedom of the Press* (1981; repr., New York: Vintage, 1982), 66; Richard Norton Smith, *The Colonel: The Life and Legend of Robert R. McCormick, 1880–1955* (Boston: Houghton Mifflin, 1997), 40, 56, 67, 288, 395; Robert R. McCormick to Arthur H. Sulzberger, Aug. 16, 1946, Sulzberger Papers and New York Times Co. Records, box 132; "Outlines Plot to Destroy U.S. Press Freedom," *Chicago Tribune*, Mar. 5, 1947, 4; Studs Terkel, *Hard Times: An Oral History of the Great Depression* (New York: Pantheon, 1970), 9–10; McCormick to William Benton, Dec. 31, 1945, Benton Papers, box 76; McCormick to Benton, May 18, 1945, Benton Papers, box 76; McCormick to RMH, Nov. 20, 1946, Benton Papers, box 76.

7. Smith, *Colonel*, 52, 255, 257, 328, 331, 345, 354, 412n, 424, 458; "Book Exposes Hutchins-Luce Press Attack," *Chicago Tribune*, June 11, 1950, 6; Robert R. McCormick to Arthur H. Sulzberger, Aug. 1, 1950, 2, Sulzberger Papers and New York Times Co. Records, box 132; Stephen Bates, "Prejudice and the Press Critics: Colonel Robert McCormick's Assault on

the Hutchins Commission," *American Journalism* 36, no. 4 (2019): 423; William Fulton, "N.Y. Magazines Called Hotbeds of Alien Isms," *Chicago Tribune*, Feb. 26, 1951, B9.

8. Rosten, *Washington Correspondents*, 195–196, 356; H. L. Smith, "The Press Can Do No Wrong," *Forum*, Feb. 1939, 83.

9. Robert R. McCormick, *What Is a Newspaper? A Talk before the Chicago Church Federation at the Hotel Morrison, October 27, 1924* (Chicago: Chicago Tribune, 1924), 31; Smith, *Colonel*, 279–285; Eric B. Easton, "The Colonel's Finest Campaign: Robert R. McCormick and *Near v. Minnesota*," *Federal Communications Law Journal* 60, no. 2 (2008): 183–228; Philip Kinsley, *Liberty and the Press: A History of the "Chicago Tribune's" Fight to Preserve a Free Press for the American People* (Chicago: Chicago Tribune, 1944), 2, 49–50; Friendly, *Minnesota Rag*, 66; *Near v. Minnesota*, 283 U.S. 697 (1931); Edwin Emery, *History of the American Newspaper Publishers Association* (Minneapolis: University of Minnesota Press, 1950), 138, 218–246; Sam Lebovic, *Free Speech and Unfree News: The Paradox of Press Freedom in America* (Cambridge, MA: Harvard University Press, 2016), 64–87; Arthur H. Sulzberger to Elisha Hanson, Nov. 8, 1938, Sulzberger Papers and New York Times Co. Records, box 94; Bates, "Prejudice and the Press Critics," 425; *Associated Press v. National Labor Relations Board*, 301 U.S. 103, 132 (1937).

10. Robert R. McCormick, *The Freedom of the Press: A History and an Argument Compiled from Speeches on This Subject Delivered over a Period of Fifteen Years* (New York: Appleton-Century, 1936), 53–69; Margaret A. Blanchard, "Freedom of the Press and the Newspaper Code: June 1933–February 1934," *Journalism Quarterly* 54 (Spring 1977): 40–49; White, *FDR and the Press*, 51–52; Lebovic, *Free Speech and Unfree News*, 66–72; "Text of Gen. Johnson's Address before Illinois Business Men," *New York Times*, Nov. 7, 1933, 2.

11. Sally Denton, *The Plots against the President: FDR, a Nation in Crisis, and the Rise of the American Right* (New York: Bloomsbury, 2012), 158; Villard, *Disappearing Daily*, 30; John Cowles, "The American Newspapers," in *America Now: An Inquiry into Civilization in the United States*, ed. Harold E. Stearns (New York: Literary Guild, 1938), 365; Alan Brinkley, *The Publisher: Henry Luce and His American Century* (New York: Knopf, 2010), 279; White, *FDR and the Press*, 31; Betty Houchin Winfield, *FDR and the News Media* (Urbana: University of Illinois Press, 1990), 67–68; Barry D. Karl, *Charles E. Merriam and the Study of Politics* (Chicago: University of Chicago, 1974), 80, 226, 233; Ickes, *America's House of Lords*; Ickes, *Freedom of the Press Today*; "Address by Secretary Ickes before National Lawyers Guild," *New York Times*, Feb. 11, 1939.

12. Smith, *Colonel*, xvii, 331n, 406, 420, 427–428; Winfield, *FDR and the News Media*, 179; Robert R. McCormick to RMH, May 3, 1945, RMH Chicago, box 162.

13. Smith, *Colonel*, 406, 414 426–441; Harold L. Ickes, *The Secret Diary of Harold L. Ickes*, vol. 3, *The Lowering Clouds, 1939–1941* (New York: Simon

and Schuster, 1954), 659–660; Michael S. Sweeney and Patrick S. Washburn, " 'Aint [*sic*] Justice Wonderful,': The *Chicago Tribune's* Battle of Midway Story and the Government's Attempt at an Espionage Act Indictment in 1942," *Journalism and Communication Monographs* 16, no. 1 (2014): 7–97; Winfield, *FDR and the News Media*, 178–180.

14. Margaret A. Blanchard, "The Associated Press Antitrust Suit: A Philosophical Clash over Ownership of First Amendment Rights," *Business History Review* 61, no. 1 (Spring 1987): 43–85; Stephen Bates, "Regulating Gatekeepers of Information: The Associated Press as Common Carrier," *UB Journal of Media Law and Ethics* 3, nos. 1–2 (Winter–Spring 2012): 62–109; Smith, *Colonel,* xx-xxi, 410, 414, 420, 424–427; Thurman Arnold to Frank C. Waldrop, June 13, 1963, in *Voltaire and the Cowboy: The Letters of Thurman Arnold,* ed. Gene M. Gressley (Boulder: Colorado Associated University Press, 1977), 450–452; White, *FDR and the Press,* 65; Pickard, *America's Battle for Media Democracy,* 135–141; *Associated Press v. United States,* 326 U.S. 1 (1945).

15. Rosten, *Washington Correspondents,* 259–260; [Hugh Baker Cox] to Thurman Arnold, Aug. 3, 1938, Cox Papers, box 2; [Irene Till], "Memorandum on Newspapers," n.d., 1, 24, 25, Cox Papers, box 2; "Antitrust Division: Summary of Major Investigations Contemplated or Under Way," Mar. 20, 1939, Arnold Papers, box 103; *In Fact,* Nov. 18, 1940; Stephen Early to J. Edgar Hoover, Nov. 25, 1940, FBI file on George Seldes (obtained under Freedom of Information Act); Joon-Mann Kang, "Franklin D. Roosevelt and James L. Fly: The Politics of Broadcast Regulation, 1941–1944," *Journal of American Culture* 10, no. 2 (Summer 1987): 23–33; Daniel W. Toohey, "Newspaper Ownership of Broadcast Facilities," *Federal Communications Bar Journal* 20 (1966): 48–50; Pickard, *America's Battle for Media Democracy,* 45–51; Emery, *History of the American Newspaper Publishers Association,* 208–210; Winfield, *FDR and the News Media,* 110. I learned of the Till memo from Pickard, *America's Battle for Media Democracy,* 136; Pickard cites Dan Schiller as his source.

16. Linda C. Gugin and James E. St. Clair, *Sherman Minton: New Deal Senator, Cold War Justice* (Indianapolis: Indiana Historical Society, 1997), 91–102; "Minton Criticizes Press," *New York Times,* Aug. 14, 1938, 7; "Senator Hits Publishers for Combining Demand for Free Press with a Blow at President's Use of Air to State Views," *Washington Post,* Apr. 29, 1938, 1.

17. Kinsley, *Liberty and the Press,* 65.

Chapter Five. Highest Intellect Ever

1. Hadley Cantril, ed., *Public Opinion: 1935–1946* (Princeton, NJ: Princeton University Press, 1951), 417–418. For other poll results, see Cantril, 244–245, 416–418; Hazel Erskine, "The Polls: Opinion of the News Media," *Public Opinion Quarterly* 34, no. 4 (Winter 1970–1971): 631–634.

2. HRL to WEH, Dec. 1, 1943, 1–2, Time Inc. Archives; Doc. 4A, 1.

3. RMH to Learned Hand, Nov. 26, 1943, Hand Papers, box 74; Hand to RMH, Nov. 30, 1943, Hand Papers, box 74; Hand to Reinhold Niebuhr, Jan. 4, 1943 [1944], 2, Lasswell Papers, box 26; Niebuhr to Harold D. Lasswell, Jan. 5, 1943 [1944], Lasswell Papers, box 26; Doc. 4A, 1; *United States v. Associated Press*, 52 F. Supp. 362 (S.D.N.Y. 1943). Other than Judge Hand, it appears that just one person declined to join the commission: Raymond B. Fosdick, president of the Rockefeller Foundation. Raymond B. Fosdick to RMH, Feb. 8, 1944, RMH Chicago, box 7.

4. *FRP*, ii; William H. McNeill, *Hutchins' University: A Memoir of the University of Chicago, 1929–1950* (Chicago: University of Chicago Press, 1991), 39; C. Addison Hickman, *J. M. Clark* (New York: Columbia University Press, 1975), 2. See generally Jane S. McConnell, "Choosing a Team for Democracy: Henry R. Luce and the Commission on Freedom of the Press," *American Journalism* 14, no. 2 (Spring 1997): 148–163; Frederick Blevens, "Gentility and Quiet Aggression: A Cultural History of the Commission on Freedom of the Press" (PhD diss., University of Missouri, Columbia, 1995); Paul Mark Fackler, "The Hutchins Commissioners and the Crisis in Democratic Theory, 1930–1947" (PhD diss., University of Illinois at Urbana-Champaign, 1982).

5. Arthur M. Schlesinger, *In Retrospect: The History of a Historian* (New York: Harcourt, Brace and World, 1963), 93; WEH, "America's World Purpose," *Life*, Apr. 17, 1944, 102–112.

6. RMH to HRL, Nov. 4, 1943, Time Inc. Archives; Thomas E. Blantz, *George N. Shuster: On the Side of Truth* (Notre Dame, IN: University of Notre Dame Press, 1993), 62.

7. In late 1944, MacLeish left the Library of Congress to become assistant secretary of state for public and cultural relations.

8. RMH to John Grierson, Feb. 9, 1944, RMH Chicago, box 7.

9. Richard Aldous, *Schlesinger: The Imperial Historian* (New York: Norton, 2017), 7, 15–16; "Princeton Rumors Vary," *New York Times*, May 23, 1933, 7; Doc. 31, 3; Richard Wightman Fox, *Reinhold Niebuhr: A Biography* (1985; repr., Ithaca, NY: Cornell University Press, 1996), 239; WEH, "Answer to a Threat" (letter to the editor), *New York Times*, Oct. 25, 1920; "How I Shall Vote," *Forum*, Nov. 1932, 261; Alva Johnston, "Profiles: The National Idea Man—I," *New Yorker*, Feb. 10, 1945, 31; Mary Ann Dzuback, *Robert M. Hutchins: Portrait of an Educator* (Chicago: University of Chicago Press, 1991), 263–266; W. H. Ferry, "Robert Hutchins's Platonic Grove," *Nation*, Jan. 30, 1988, 120; Charles Leslie, "The Hedgehog and the Fox in Robert Redfield's Work and Career," in *American Anthropology: The Early Years*, ed. John V. Murra (St. Paul, MN: West, 1976), 161.

10. Stephen Bates, "Media Censures: The Hutchins Commission on the Press, the New York Intellectuals on Mass Culture," *International Journal of Communication* 12 (2018): 4786–4788; Brett Gary, "The Search for a Competent Public: The Hutchins Commission and Post–World War II

Democratic Possibilities," in *Democracy and Excellence: Concord or Conflict?*, ed. Joseph Romance and Neal Riemer (Westport, CT: Praeger, 2005), 83; Hickman, *J. M. Clark*, 3; Ellen Herman, *The Romance of American Psychology: Political Culture in the Age of Experts* (Berkeley: University of California Press, 1995), 26; Schlesinger, *In Retrospect*, 142–143; Blantz, *George N. Shuster*, 154; Fox, *Reinhold Niebuhr*, 197, 230. Chafee later served on the United Nations Subcommission on Freedom of Information and of the Press. Donald L. Smith, *Zechariah Chafee Jr.: Defender of Liberty and Law* (Cambridge, MA: Harvard University Press, 1986), 223–241.

11. RMH to Raymond B. Fosdick, Nov. 26, 1943, RMH Chicago, box 7; RMH to HRL, Oct. 29, 1943, Time Inc. Archives; typewritten notes of conversation between HRL and RMH, n.d., 1, RMH Chicago, box 7; Doc. 4A, 5; RMH, "The American Press," *Spectator*, Apr. 25, 1947, 455; RMH statement, news release, Mar. 27, 1947, 2, Time Inc. Archives; Frank Hughes, *Prejudice and the Press: A Restatement of the Principle of Freedom of the Press with Specific Reference to the Hutchins-Luce Commission* (New York: Devin-Adair, 1950), 34; Eric Hodgins to RMH, June 28, 1944, RMH Chicago, box 7.

12. HRL to C. D. Jackson, Sept. 10, 1945, Time Inc. Archives; *CBS Views the Press*, Dec. 4, 1948, 6, Hollenbeck Broadcast Papers, box 5.

13. Arthur Schlesinger Jr., "*Time* and the Intellectuals," *New Republic*, July 16, 1956, 17; Richard S. Kirkendall, "Franklin D. Roosevelt and the Service Intellectual," *Mississippi Valley Historical Review* 49, no. 3 (Dec. 1962): 456–471.

14. Doc. 4A; Doc. 4; Eric Hodgins to RMH, Nov. 30, 1943, RMH Chicago, box 7.

15. Doc. 4, 5. The minutes of the two initial meetings paraphrased speakers. Most later meetings were transcribed.

16. Doc. 4A, 3; Doc. 4, 5.

17. Doc. 4, 1; [HRL], "General Commentary I," Dec. 15 (?), 1946, 3, Time Inc. Archives.

18. Doc. 9, 1.

19. Office of Press Relations, University of Chicago, news release, Feb. 26, 1944, 1–2, RMH Chicago, box 7; Philip Schuyler, "Government News Gag Press Freedom Problem," *Editor & Publisher*, Apr. 8, 1944, 7.

20. "Editors Welcome Time-Life Inquiry into Press Freedom," *Editor & Publisher*, Apr. 15, 1944, 9, 60.

21. RMH to Frank Waldrop, Oct. 8, 1963, 1, RMH UCSB, box 2; Stephen Bates, "Prejudice and the Press Critics: Colonel Robert McCormick's Assault on the Hutchins Commission," *American Journalism* 36, no. 4 (2019): 428.

22. Harold D. Lasswell to Reinhold Niebuhr and Beardsley Ruml, Jan. 26, 1944, Lasswell Papers, box 26; RMH to Robert D. Leigh, Feb. 22, 1944, RMH Chicago, box 7.

23. Ruth Inglis to Elizabeth L. Titus, Aug. 29, 1946, and att'd "Statement of Training and Experience," CFP UW, box 1; Leo C. Rosten, *Hollywood: The*

Movie Colony, the Movie Makers (New York: Harcourt, Brace, 1941), viii–ix; "How to Study the Radio, Movies, and Press: Tentative Table of Contents," CFP UW, box 1; *Congressional Record*, July 18, 1978, 21258; "Milton Stewart Dies; Small-Business Expert," *Washington Post*, Nov. 7, 2004, C8; Robert D. Leigh to John M. Clark, Aug. 24, 1944, 1, Clark Papers, box 33; Milton Stewart, "FM: Radio Wave of the Future," *Common Sense*, Oct. 1945, 31–32; Loyalty of Government Employees, investigation of Milton David Stewart, Oct. 3, 1951, and att'd Personal History, FBI file on Milton David Stewart (obtained under Freedom of Information Act); Loyalty of Government Employees, investigation of Milton David Stewart, Oct. 8, 1951, and att'd Results of Investigation, FBI file on Stewart; Leigh to RMH, Dec. 12, 1944, and att'd Llewellyn White CV, RMH Chicago, box 7.

24. E.g., Robert D. Leigh to Ruth Inglis, July 29, 1944, 1–2, CFP UW, box 1.

25. Robert T. Elson, *The World of Time Inc.: The Intimate History of a Publishing Enterprise, 1941–1960* (New York: Atheneum, 1973), 7–8; Eric Hodgins to John K. Jessup, Dec. 1968, 3–4, Time Inc. Archives; Stephen Bates, "Is This the Best Philosophy Can Do? Henry R. Luce and *A Free and Responsible Press*," *Journalism & Mass Communication Quarterly* 95, no. 3 (2018): 820. See generally Eric Hodgins, *Trolley to the Moon: An Autobiography* (New York: Simon and Schuster, 1973).

26. Doc. 4A, 1; Doc. 4, 3; Doc. 14, 1; Doc. 17, 1; RMH to Waldrop, Oct. 8, 1963, 2; Bates, "Is This the Best Philosophy Can Do?," 818; transcript of "The Hutchins Commission Revisited," panel sponsored by Division of Mass Communications and Society, Association for Education in Journalism, University of Colorado, Boulder, Aug. 30, 1967, 5, Center for the Study of Democratic Institutions Collection, box 89; RMH to Leigh, Feb. 22, 1944; Harold D. Lasswell to RMH, Feb. 24, 1944, Lasswell Papers, box 26; RMH to Lasswell, Feb. 29, 1944, Lasswell Papers, box 26; McConnell, "Choosing a Team for Democracy," 158–159.

27. Hodgins to Jessup, Dec. 1968, 4 (emphasis in original); Eric Hodgins to HRL, Sept. 12, 1944, Time Inc. Archives; Bates, "Is This the Best Philosophy Can Do?," 818.

28. Hodgins to Jessup, Dec. 1968, 4; WEH to Reinhold Niebuhr, Dec. 17, 1946, Niebuhr Papers, box 3.

29. RMH, foreword to *FRP*, vi; Zechariah Chafee Jr., "Memorandum on Papers of the Commission on Freedom of the Press Deposited in the Library of Brown University," Oct. 1947, 1, 3–4, RMH Chicago, box 8 (spelling corrected).

Chapter Six. Restless Searchlights

1. Alexander Woollcott, "The Little Man with the Big Voice," *Hearst's International-Cosmopolitan* 94, no. 5 (May 1933): 142; Robert Vanderlan, *Intellectuals Incorporated: Politics, Art, and Ideas inside Henry Luce's Media Empire* (Philadelphia: University of Pennsylvania Press, 2010), 75.

2. RMH to HRL, Oct. 29, 1943, Time Inc. Archives; *Time*, Mar. 13, 1931; *Time*, Sept. 27, 1937; HRL to Walter Lippmann, Sept. 7, 1937, Lippmann Papers; William Benton to RMH, Nov. 8, 1937, 1–2, Hutchins Administration Records, box 133; Lippmann to RMH, Nov. 8, 1937, 1, Hutchins Administration Records, box 133; Ronald Steel, *Walter Lippmann and the American Century* (Boston: Little, Brown, 1980), 363–364.

3. "Elucidator," *Time*, Sept. 27, 1937; Steel, *Walter Lippmann*, 3, 9–22, 30, 59–62, 201, 274–276, 280; Margaret Marshall, "Columnists on Parade: VI. Walter Lippmann," *Nation*, Apr. 23, 1938, 464, 467. See generally Heinz Eulau, "Mover and Shaker: Walter Lippmann as a Young Man," *Antioch Review* 11, no. 3 (Autumn 1951): 291–312.

4. Walter Lippmann to Archibald MacLeish, May 26, 1949, Lippmann Papers, folder 1421; Lippmann, *Drift and Mastery: An Attempt to Diagnose the Current Unrest* (New York: Mitchell Kennerley, 1914), 189; Eulau, "Mover and Shaker," 301, 306.

5. Walter Lippmann, *Liberty and the News* (New York: Harcourt, Brace and Howe, 1920), 5, 10–11, 14–16, 47, 74–84; Lippmann and Charles Merz, "A Test of the News: An Examination of the News Reports of the *New York Times* on Aspects of the Russian Revolution of Special Importance to Americans, March 1917–March 1920," *New Republic*, Aug. 4, 1920, supp.; Bruce Bliven, *Five Million Words Later: An Autobiography* (New York: John Day, 1970), 172.

6. Walter Lippmann to Charles E. Merriam, Jan. 24, 1921, 1, Merriam Papers, box 34; James W. Carey, "The Press and the Public Discourse," *Center Magazine*, Mar.-Apr. 1987, 6; Lippmann, *Public Opinion* (New York: Harcourt, Brace, 1922), 362, 364, 379–397, 400; Steel, *Walter Lippmann*, 180–184. See generally Sue Curry Jansen, "Forgotten History: Another Road Not Taken—The Charles Merriam-Walter Lippmann Correspondence," *Communication Theory* 20 (2010): 127–146.

7. Lippmann, *Public Opinion*, 411, 418; Steel, *Walter Lippmann*, 184; Charles E. Merriam, review of *Public Opinion*, by Lippmann, *International Journal of Ethics* 33, no. 2 (Jan. 1923): 211–212; H. L. Mencken, "Demagoguery as Art and Science," *Smart Set*, June 1922, 138. See generally David Greenberg, "Lippmann vs. Mencken: Debating Democracy," *Raritan* 32, no. 2 (Fall 2012): 117–140.

8. Walter Lippmann, *The Method of Freedom* (New York: Macmillan, 1934), 76–79; Lippmann, *A Preface to Morals* (London: George Allen and Unwin, 1929); 319; Lippmann, "The Scholar in a Troubled World," *Atlantic Monthly*, Aug. 1932, 151.

9. Doc. 25, A3, B2; Doc. 99, 46, 48; Doc. 90, 135; Doc. 91, 25–26.

10. Doc. 90A, 181; Brett Gary, "The Search for a Competent Public: The Hutchins Commission and Post–World War II Democratic Possibilities," in *Democracy and Excellence: Concord or Conflict?*, ed. Joseph Romance and Neal Riemer (Westport, CT: Praeger, 2005), 75–90.

11. *FRP*, 2–5, 17, 20, 28–29, 52, 99, 105–106; Doc. 34, pt. 1, 11; Doc. 90, 109.
12. *FRP*, 54–56, 68; Doc. 20A, C4–C5.
13. *FRP*, 56; WEH, *Freedom of the Press: A Framework of Principle* (Chicago: University of Chicago Press, 1947), 43, 204–205; Doc. 90, 41–42; Doc. 52, 15–16; Doc. 1, 9.
14. Doc. 89, 24; Doc. 90, 150, 152; Gunnar Myrdal, *An American Dilemma: The Negro Problem and Modern Democracy* (New York: Harper and Row, 1944), 48; *FRP*, 26; Doc. 48, 114; Arthur Hays Sulzberger, speech to American Society of Newspaper Editors, Washington, DC, Apr. 17, 1947, 6, Sulzberger Papers and New York Times Co. Records, box 95.
15. WEH, *Freedom of the Press*, 166; *FRP*, 22; Doc. 90, 136; Doc. 83, 37.
16. James Beveridge, *John Grierson: Film Master* (New York: Macmillan, 1998), 27–29; Jack C. Ellis, *John Grierson: Life, Contributions, Influence* (Carbondale: Southern Illinois University Press, 2000), 1, 18–22; Ian Aitken, *Film and Reform: John Grierson and the Documentary Film Movement* (New York: Routledge, 1990), 48–58; "Briton Addresses Paramount Theatre Managers School," *Exhibitors Herald*, Sept. 26, 1925, 32; Doc. 37L, 30.
17. Aitken, *Film and Reform*, 48–49, 53, 65–68, 149; Ellis, *John Grierson*, 28.
18. Doc. 37L, 30; Doc. 91, 14–15.
19. Doc. 89, 58, 90; Doc. 90, 125; Doc. 91, 15; David Goodman, *Radio's Civic Ambition: American Broadcasting and Democracy in the 1930s* (New York: Oxford University Press, 2011), 307; Stephen Bates, "Public Intellectuals as Press Critics," *Society* 46 (2009): 127.
20. Doc. 99, 142.
21. Herbert Marshall McLuhan, "Dagwood's America," *Columbia* 2 (Jan. 1944): 3, 23; McLuhan, "*Time, Life*, and *Fortune*," *View* 7, no. 3 (Spring 1947): 33–37; Dwight Macdonald, "A Theory of 'Popular Culture,'" *Politics*, Feb. 1944, 20–23; Macdonald, "Memo to Mr. Luce," *Politics*, Oct. 1945, 309–311.
22. Andrej Pinter, "*Thought News*: A Quest for Democratic Communication Technology," *Public* 10, no. 2 (2003): 93–104; Willinda Savage, "John Dewey and 'Thought News' at the University of Michigan," *Michigan Alumnus Quarterly Review* 56, no. 18 (Spring 1950): 204–209; Daniel J. Czitrom, *Media and the American Mind: From Morse to McLuhan* (Chapel Hill: University of North Carolina Press, 1982), 104–108; Robert B. Westbrook, *John Dewey and American Democracy* (Ithaca, NY: Cornell University Press, 1991), 51–58; "Notes," *Nation*, Mar. 24, 1892, 229; Michael Denning, *The Cultural Front: The Laboring of American Culture in the Twentieth Century* (New York: Verso, 1996), 297, 367–370; John W. Casson, "Living Newspaper: Theatre and Therapy," *Drama Review* 44, no. 2 (Summer 2000): 107–122. Public journalism is discussed in chapter 18.
23. C. Edwin Baker, *Media, Markets, and Democracy* (New York: Cambridge University Press, 2002), 155–159; Victor Pickard, *America's Battle for Media Democracy: The Triumph of Corporate Libertarianism and the Future of*

Media Reform (New York: Cambridge University Press, 2015), 195; *FRP,* 5; Doc. 3, 14 (emphasis omitted).

24. Doc. 9, 2; Doc. 49, 1; Doc. 66, 54; Doc. 111E, 13; Doc. 111-1, 19.

25. Alan Brinkley, *The End of Reform: New Deal Liberalism in Recession and War* (New York: Knopf, 1995), 6; Richard H. Pells, *Radical Visions and American Dreams: Culture and Social Thought in the Depression Years* (New York: Harper and Row, 1973), 310; Matthew Jones, "Freedom from Want," in *The Four Freedoms: Franklin D. Roosevelt and the Evolution of an American Idea,* ed. Jeffrey A. Engel (New York: Oxford University Press, 2016), 125–163.

26. Jones, "Freedom from Want," 139; Theodore Rosenof, "Freedom, Planning, and Totalitarianism: The Reception of F. A. Hayek's *Road to Serfdom,*" *Canadian Review of American Studies* 5, no. 2 (Fall 1974): 149–165; Croswell Bowen, "How Big Business Raised the Battle Cry of 'Serfdom,'" *PM,* Oct. 14, 1945; Barry D. Karl, *Charles E. Merriam and the Study of Politics* (Chicago: University of Chicago Press, 1974), 289–292; Reinhold Niebuhr, "The Collectivist Bogy," *Nation,* Oct. 21, 1944, 480; Charles E. Merriam, review of *Freedom under Planning,* by Barbara Wootton, and *Road to Reaction,* by Herman Finer, *American Political Science Review* 40, no. 1 (Feb. 1946): 135.

27. "1,300 Here Honor Freda Kirchwey," *New York Times,* Feb. 28, 1944, 11; Archibald MacLeish, "This Cause Is Our Cause," *Representative American Speeches* 17, no. 4 (1943–1944): 244–246; Jones, "Freedom from Want," 136.

Chapter Seven. The Glorious, Mischievous First Amendment

1. WEH to HRL, Dec. 4, 1943, Time Inc. Archives; Charles E. Merriam to Harold D. Lasswell, Apr. 26, 1944, Merriam Papers, box 65 (spelling corrected).

2. Leroy S. Rouner, "The Making of a Philosopher: Ernest Hocking's Early Years," in *Philosophy, Religion, and the Coming World Civilization: Essays in Honor of William Ernest Hocking,* ed. Rouner (The Hague: Martinus Nijhoff, 1966), 9–11; "Curriculum Vitae," in Rouner, *Philosophy, Religion, and the Coming World Civilization,* xiii–xiv; WEH, "Some Second Principles," in *Contemporary American Philosophy: Personal Statements,* ed. George P. Adams and William Pepperell Montague, vol. 1 (New York: Russell and Russell, 1962), 385–386.

3. WEH, *The Meaning of Immortality in Human Experience* (New York: Harper and Bros., 1957), 213–214 (emphasis in original); Rouner, "Making of a Philosopher," 12–13.

4. WEH, "Some Second Principles," 387–393; Rouner, "Making of a Philosopher," 13–15; "Curriculum Vitae," xiii; John Kaag, *American Philosophy: A Love Story* (New York: Farrar, Straus, 2016), 16–17; Douglas R. Anderson, "W. E. Hocking and the Liberal Spirit," in *A William Ernest*

Hocking Reader, ed. John Lachs and D. Micah Hester (Nashville: Vanderbilt University Press, 2004), 305; Agnes Hocking and WEH, "Creating a School," *Atlantic*, Dec. 1955, 63–66; May Sarton, " 'I Knew a Phoenix in My Youth,' " *New Yorker*, Apr. 3, 1954, 29–33.

5. "The People's Philosopher," *Time*, June 24, 1966; Bruce Kuklick, *The Rise of American Philosophy: Cambridge, Massachusetts, 1860–1930* (New Haven, CT: Yale University Press, 1977), 495; Rouner, "Making of a Philosopher," 15; Richard Boyle O'Reilly Hocking, "William Ernest Hocking, 1873–1966," *Proceedings and Addresses of the American Philosophical Association* 40 (1966–1967): 118; Richard C. Gilman, *The Bibliography of William Ernest Hocking, from 1898 to 1951* (Waterville, ME: Colby College, 1951); John Lachs and D. Micah Hester, introduction to Lachs and Hester, *William Ernest Hocking Reader*, xi–xiii; "Selected Bibliography of William Ernest Hocking," in Lachs and Hester, *William Ernest Hocking Reader*, 383–386; WEH, *Freedom of the Press: A Framework of Principle* (Chicago: University of Chicago Press, 1947), 68, 207. See generally Leroy S. Rouner, *Within Human Experience: The Philosophy of William Ernest Hocking* (Cambridge, MA: Harvard University Press, 1969).

6. WEH to Corliss Lamont, May 17, 1963, WEH Papers, folder 3462; Marcia Graham Synnott, *The Half-Opened Door: Discrimination and Admissions at Harvard, Yale, and Princeton, 1900–1970* (Westport, CT: Greenwood, 1979), 62–66, 68–69, 210; WEH to John F. Kennedy, June 1, 1963, 1, WEH Papers, folder 3326; Rouner, *Within Human Experience*, 197–198.

7. Whittaker Chambers to WEH, Dec. 12, 1941, WEH Papers, folder 5977; WEH, "What Man Can Make of Man," *Fortune*, Feb. 1942, 90–93, 136–147.

8. HRL to WEH, June 4, 1942, Time Inc. Archives; WEH to HRL, June 7, 1942, Time Inc. Archives; WEH to HRL, June 10, 1942, Time Inc. Archives; Robert Vanderlan, *Intellectuals Incorporated: Politics, Art, and Ideas inside Henry Luce's Media Empire* (Philadelphia: University of Pennsylvania Press, 2010), 200; Alan Brinkley, *The Publisher: Henry Luce and His American Century* (New York: Knopf, 2010), 381; HRL to WEH, Dec. 16, 1958, Time Inc. Archives; HRL to WEH, June 14, 1963, WEH Papers, folder 3762; HRL to WEH, Apr. 8, 1946, WEH Papers, folder 3762; WEH to I. Van Meter, Oct. 20, 1936, WEH Papers, folder 5977; WEH to Andrew Heiskell, Oct. 28, 1942, WEH Papers, folder 3664; Stephen Bates, "Is This the Best Philosophy Can Do? Henry R. Luce and *A Free and Responsible Press*," *Journalism & Mass Communication Quarterly* 95, no. 3 (2018): 817.

9. Vanderlan, *Intellectuals Incorporated*, 199–206; Brinkley, *Publisher*, 333–335, 379–381; Robert T. Elson, *The World of Time Inc.: The Intimate History of a Publishing Enterprise, 1941–1960* (New York: Atheneum, 1973), 206–207; Dwight Macdonald, "Memo to Mr. Luce," *Politics*, Oct. 1945, 309–311; HRL to WEH, Mar. 21, 1952, Time Inc. Archives. A few years later, the University of Chicago published a quarterly called *Measure*, no relation.

10. Sarton, "'I Knew a Phoenix,'" 30; Anne Lindbergh to WEH, May 26, 1962, WEH Papers, folder 3674; Lindbergh to WEH, May 17, 1955, 1, WEH Papers, folder 3674; Clare Boothe Luce to WEH, Jan. 20, 1960, 1–2, 5–6 (spelling corrected), WEH Papers, folder 3760; C. Luce to WEH, Mar. 17, 1949, WEH Papers, folder 3760; Lindbergh to WEH, Jan. 2, 1956, 13, WEH Papers, folder 3674; WEH to Lindbergh, May 31, 1962, WEH Papers, folder 3764; WEH to C. Luce, Jan. 30, 1957, 1, WEH Papers, folder 3760; WEH to C. Luce, May 29, 1957, WEH Papers, folder 3760; Brinkley, *Publisher,* 429. On the Luces and LSD, see Stephen Siff, "Henry Luce's Strange Trip: Coverage of LSD in *Time* and *Life,* 1954–1968," *Journalism History* 34, no. 3 (Fall 2008): 126–134.

11. Kaag, *American Philosophy,* 208, 210–218.

12. Frederick Blevens, "Gentility and Quiet Aggression: A Cultural History of the Commission on Freedom of the Press" (PhD diss., University of Missouri, Columbia, 1995), 170; "One Religion for All," *Time,* Sept. 2, 1940; "The Healer," *Time,* Aug. 17, 1953; "Philosopher of Hope," *Time,* Nov. 11, 1957; "People's Philosopher"; G. A. Borgese to RMH, Oct. 20, 1945, 2 (quoting Niebuhr; spelling corrected); Rouner, "Making of a Philosopher," 9, 14 (emphasis omitted; capitalization altered); "Death and Resurrection in the Life of Nations," *University of Chicago Round Table,* Apr. 1, 1945, 2, 5–6.

13. Kuklick, *Rise of American Philosophy,* 483; Erwin D. Canham, "University of Chicago Press—Manuscript Report," Sept. 23, 1946, 2, University of Chicago Press Records, box 240; WEH, *Freedom of the Press,* 49; WEH to George Sokolsky, June 29, 1947, Sokolsky Papers, box 61; *FRP,* 136.

14. WEH to George N. Shuster, Apr. 12, 1958, WEH Papers, folder 5514.

15. WEH, *Freedom of the Press,* 11, 65, 75, 189; Doc. 42, 7–8; WEH, "History and the Absolute," in Rouner, *Philosophy, Religion, and the Coming World Civilization,* 452; WEH, "The Future of Liberalism," *Journal of Philosophy* 32, no. 9 (Apr. 1935): 233–234; WEH, "A Philosophy of Life for the American Farmer," in *Farmers in a Changing World,* by U.S. Department of Agriculture (Washington, DC: Government Printing Office, 1940), 1069; WEH, *Human Nature and Its Remaking* (New Haven, CT: Yale University Press, 1918), 206–208; RMH, "Comments on Document 100," n.d., 4, RMH Chicago, box 8; WEH, *The Lasting Elements of Individualism* (New Haven, CT: Yale University Press, 1937), 113, 127; *FRP,* 8. On Hocking's view of the state, see Donald M. Gillmor, "Who Was W. E. Hocking?," *Communications Law and Policy* 3 (1998): 235–239; plus two essays in Lachs and Hester, *William Ernest Hocking Reader:* John J. Stuhr, "The Defects of Liberalism: Lasting Elements of W.E. Hocking's Philosophy," 330–333; John E. Smith, "W. E. Hocking's Insights about the Individual and the State," 335–348.

16. WEH, *Freedom of the Press,* 53–54, 60n4, 89–90n3, 93–95, 106, 117–119, 130–131, 148–149, 164n4, 185, 187, 204–205; Doc. 42, 21; Doc. 85, 16–17; Doc. 16A, 1–2; Doc. 52, 2, 9–10; WEH to RMH, July 24, 1946,

RMH Chicago, box 8; WEH, "Future of Liberalism," 235, 239, 245; WEH, "Philosophy of Life," 1069.

17. Alexander Meiklejohn, *Free Speech and Its Relation to Self-Government* (New York: Harper, 1948); Meiklejohn, "The First Amendment Is an Absolute," *Supreme Court Review* (1961): 253–266; Susan Dell Gonders Golike, "A Grounded Theory Comparative Analysis of the Hutchins Plan Philosophy of Education and the Hutchins Commission Philosophy of the Press" (EdD diss., Oklahoma State University, 1995), 283. On the overlaps between Hocking and Meiklejohn, see Gerald J. Baldasty and Roger A. Simpson, "The Deceptive 'Right to Know': How Pessimism Rewrote the First Amendment," *Washington Law Review* 56 (1981): 368–373.

18. WEH, *Freedom of the Press*, 54–56, 158–160; Doc. 85, 6; Isaiah Berlin, *Two Concepts of Liberty* (Oxford: Oxford University Press, 1958); [WEH], "Seminary [*sic*] in Philosophy of Law and State, 1924–1925," n.d. (spelling corrected), att'd to WEH to Roscoe Pound, Jan. 13, 1925, Pound Papers, folder 1766-077-0312. Another commission member had also alluded to the distinction between positive and negative freedom of the press. Harold D. Lasswell, "The Achievement Standards of a Democratic Press," in *Freedom of the Press Today: A Clinical Examination by 28 Specialists*, ed. Harold L. Ickes (New York: Vanguard, 1941), 171.

19. WEH, *Freedom of the Press*, 74, 109; *FRP*, 18, 128–129; "Statement by the Commission," in *Government and Mass Communications*, by Zechariah Chafee Jr. (Chicago: University of Chicago Press, 1947), viii; RMH, "The Free Mind," *University of Chicago Magazine*, Nov. 1938, 15. The intertwined topics of freedom *for* and the positive First Amendment play large roles in the literature on the Hutchins Commission. E.g., Clifford G. Christians and P. Mark Fackler, "The Genesis of Social Responsibility Theory: William Ernest Hocking and Positive Freedom," in *The Handbook of Media and Mass Communication Theory*, ed. Robert S. Fortner and Fackler (New York: Wiley, 2014), 333–356; Brett Gary, "The Search for a Competent Public: The Hutchins Commission and Post–World War II Democratic Possibilities," in *Democracy and Excellence: Concord or Conflict?*, ed. Joseph Romance and Neal Riemer (Westport, CT: Praeger, 2005), 85–90; Jay W. Jensen, "Freedom of the Press: A Concept in Search of a Philosophy," in *Social Responsibility of the Newspress*, by Marquette University College of Journalism (Milwaukee: Marquette University Press, 1962), 79–83; Sam Lebovic, *Free Speech and Unfree News: The Paradox of Press Freedom in America* (Cambridge, MA: Harvard University Press, 2016), 141–145; William E. Berry, Sandra Braman, Clifford Christians, Thomas G. Guback, Steven J. Helle, Louis W. Liebovich, John C. Nerone, and Kim B. Rotzoll, *Last Rights: Revisiting "Four Theories of the Press,"* ed. Nerone (Urbana: University of Illinois Press, 1995), 83–87, 90–100; Victor Pickard, *America's Battle for Media Democracy: The Triumph of Corporate Libertarianism and the Future of Media*

Reform (New York: Cambridge University Press, 2015), 3–4, 149, 153–154, 173, 190–197.

20. Jonathan Alter, *The Defining Moment: FDR's Hundred Days and the Triumph of Hope* (New York: Simon and Schuster, 2006), 130; Paul L. Murphy, *The Constitution in Crisis Times, 1918–1969* (New York: Harper and Row, 1972), 173–174; National Resources Planning Board, *National Resources Development Report for 1942* (Washington, DC: Government Printing Office, 1942), 3–4; Matthew Jones, "Freedom from Want," in *The Four Freedoms: Franklin D. Roosevelt and the Evolution of an American Idea*, ed. Jeffrey A. Engel (New York: Oxford University Press, 2015), 137–138; Charles E. Merriam, "The National Resources Planning Board: A Chapter in American Planning Experience," *American Political Science Review* 38, no. 6 (Dec. 1944): 1083–1084; Paul Mark Fackler, "The Hutchins Commissioners and the Crisis in Democratic Theory, 1930–1947" (PhD diss., University of Illinois at Urbana-Champaign, 1982), 13–14.

21. Meiklejohn, *Free Speech*, 19–20; *Associated Press v. United States*, 326 U.S. 1, 20 (1945) (footnote omitted); WEH, *Freedom of the Press*, 171. On the AP case, see Margaret A. Blanchard, "The Associated Press Antitrust Suit: A Philosophical Clash over Ownership of First Amendment Rights," *Business History Review* 61, no. 1 (Spring 1987): 43–85; Stephen Bates, "Regulating Gatekeepers of Information: The Associated Press as Common Carrier," *UB Journal of Media Law and Ethics* 3, nos. 1–2 (Winter–Spring 2012): 80–90.

22. WEH, *Freedom of the Press*, 15, 18, 92–96, 129–133, 156, 165, 183–186; Doc. 16A, 2; Doc. 52, 11; Doc. 75, 51; Meiklejohn, *Free Speech*, 24–28.

23. [RMH], list of six numbered propositions, n.d., 2, att'd to RMH to Robert D. Leigh, Apr. 11, 1945, RMH Chicago, box 7; Milton D. Stewart, "Twentieth Century Pressure Group Techniques in the United States," July 1944, Communications Collection, Columbia University Libraries, New York, NY; Doc. 3, 10–11; Doc. 89, 75–76; Doc. 94A, 69, 71–73; *FRP*, 96.

24. WEH, *Freedom of the Press*, 99–102 (emphasis omitted), 135–141, 195; *FRP*, 113–115. Hocking wrote the appendix to the commission's report; all members signed it.

25. *Brown v. Louisiana*, 383 U.S. 131, 133 n.1 (1966) (plurality opinion); Cheryl A. Leanza, "Heckler's Veto Case Law as a Resource for Democratic Discourse," *Hofstra Law Review* 35 (2007): 1305–1320; Owen M. Fiss, "Free Speech and Social Structure," *Iowa Law Review* 71 (1986): 1416–1418.

26. WEH, *Freedom of the Press*, 166–174, 200; *FRP*, 17–18.

27. Doc. 42, 17; Doc. 85, 4; Doc. 108B, 78.

28. WEH, *Freedom of the Press*, 146; Doc. 42, 18 (emphasis omitted); Doc. 66, 53–54.

29. Zechariah Chafee Jr. to WEH, Feb. 3, 1928, 2, WEH Papers, folder 1052; Chafee, *Government and Mass Communications*, 28.

Chapter Eight. The Right to Be Let Alone

1. Zechariah Chafee Jr., *Thirty-Five Years with Freedom of Speech* (New York: Roger N. Baldwin Civil Liberties Foundation, 1952), 1–2.

2. Zechariah Chafee Jr., "Autobiographical Sketch," n.d., 1, 3–5, att'd to Chafee to Erwin N. Griswold, May 1, 1952, Chafee Papers, folder 1776-005-28; Donald L. Smith, *Zechariah Chafee Jr.: Defender of Liberty and Law* (Cambridge, MA: Harvard University Press, 1986), 71, 75; Jerold S. Auerbach, "The Patrician as Libertarian: Zechariah Chafee Jr. and Freedom of Speech," *New England Quarterly* 42, no. 4 (Dec. 1969): 513, 521.

3. Smith, *Zechariah Chafee*, 16; Zechariah Chafee Jr., "Freedom of Speech in War Time," *Harvard Law Review* 32 (1919): 960; *Schenck v. United States*, 249 U.S. 47, 52 (1919); Auerbach, "Patrician as Libertarian," 524–525; Mark DeWolfe Howe, "Zechariah Chafee Jr.," *Proceedings of the Massachusetts Historical Society*, 3d ser., 71 (Oct. 1953–May 1957): 430.

4. Zechariah Chafee Jr., *Government and Mass Communications* (Chicago: University of Chicago Press, 1947), 6, 26–28; Chafee, *The Blessings of Liberty* (Philadelphia: Lippincott, 1956), 114; Chafee, "Freedom of Speech in War Time," 958; Chafee, review of *Free Speech and Its Relation to Self-Government*, by Alexander Meiklejohn (1948), *Harvard Law Review* 62 (1949): 896–900.

5. Chafee, "Freedom of Speech in War Time," 957; Doc. 119, 44; Zechariah Chafee Jr. to WEH, May 13, 1948, 1; Smith, *Zechariah Chafee*, 120; Chafee, *Free Speech in the United States* (Cambridge, MA: Harvard University Press, 1941), 241, 561; Chafee, *Blessings of Liberty*, 113; Chafee, "The Conscription of Public Opinion," in *The Next War: Three Addresses Delivered at a Symposium at Harvard University, November 18, 1924*, by Norris F. Hall, Chafee, and Manley O. Hudson (Cambridge, MA: Harvard Alumni Bulletin Press, 1925), 63–64; Jonathan Prude, "Portrait of a Civil Libertarian: The Faith and Fear of Zechariah Chafee Jr.," *Journal of American History* 60, no. 3 (Dec. 1973): 637–638.

6. Chafee, *Thirty-Five Years*, 4; Chafee, "Freedom of Speech in War Time," 957; Chafee, "Liberty and Law," in *Freedom in the Modern World*, ed. Horace M. Kallen (New York: Coward-McCann, 1928), 95–96, 104; Chafee, *Government and Mass Communications*, 110–114, 636–643, 689–694; Doc. 21, 24; Doc. 27, 3 (reprinting articles from 1943 by Chafee and Fred S. Siebert on the AP case); Smith, *Zechariah Chafee*, 264. On Chafee as balancer, see Smith, *Zechariah Chafee*, 86–89; Alexander Meiklejohn, "The First Amendment Is an Absolute," *Supreme Court Review* (1961): 253n26; Steven J. Heyman, "Righting the Balance: An Inquiry into the Foundations and Limits of Freedom of Expression," *Boston University Law Review* 78 (1998): 1310–1312.

7. Zechariah Chafee Jr., "Lecture VI: New Conceptions of the Relationship between the Government and the Press," n.d. [1947], 2–3, 5, 6, 9, 11, 13,

17–18, Chafee Papers, box 99; Chafee, *Government and Mass Communications*, 28; Chafee, *Blessings of Liberty*, 108.

8. Smith, *Zechariah Chafee*, 188–193; Chafee, *Government and Mass Communications*, 17.

9. John Wertheimer, "*Freedom of Speech:* Zechariah Chafee and Free-Speech History," *Reviews in American History* 22, no. 2 (June 1994): 370; Leonard W. Levy, *Legacy of Suppression: Freedom of Speech and Press in Early American History* (Cambridge, MA: Harvard University Press, 1960); Levy, *Emergence of a Free Press* (New York: Oxford University Press, 1985) (revised and expanded version of *Legacy of Suppression*), vii–x; Smith, *Zechariah Chafee*, 20.

10. David M. Rabban, *Free Speech in Its Forgotten Years* (New York: Cambridge University Press, 1997), 17, 318, 329; Mark A. Graber, *Transforming Free Speech: The Ambiguous Legacy of Civil Libertarianism* (Berkeley: University of California Press, 1991), 127; Wertheimer, "*Freedom of Speech*," 374–375.

11. Chafee, *Government and Mass Communications*, xiii, 675–676; Doc. 49, 2–3; "List of Press Commission Papers Deposited by Z. Chafee Jr.," n.d., 32, CFP Brown, box 1.

12. "Address by Secretary Ickes before National Lawyers Guild," *New York Times*, Feb. 11, 1939; Linda C. Gugin and James E. St. Clair, *Sherman Minton: New Deal Senator, Cold War Justice* (Indianapolis: Indiana Historical Society, 1997), 98–101; J. B. S. Hardman, "The Newspaper Industry and Freedom of the Press," in *Freedom of the Press Today: A Clinical Examination by 28 Specialists*, ed. Harold L. Ickes (New York: Vanguard, 1941), 121–133; Chafee, *Government and Mass Communications*, 696.

13. WEH, *Freedom of the Press: A Framework of Principle* (Chicago: University of Chicago Press, 1947), 110; Doc. 75, 43–44; Doc. 108C-D, 257.

14. WEH, "Sub-Committee on the Remedies for Press-Lying: Sketch of a Possible Report," Sept. 4, 1945, 6, CFP Columbia, box 9; Doc. 42, 11; WEH to Zechariah Chafee Jr. et al., Aug. 1, 1945, 2, CFP Brown, box 1; Doc. 66, 56–57; Doc. 108C-D, 258; WEH, *Freedom of the Press*, 187–188; Doc. 94A, 76.

15. WEH to Zechariah Chafee Jr., July 23, 1945, CFP Brown, box 1; Doc. 55, 2; Doc. 108B, 66; Reinhold Niebuhr to Llewellyn White, n.d., CFP Columbia, box 9; WEH to Chafee et al., Aug. 1, 1945, 1; Chafee to Robert D. Leigh, Nov. 27, 1946, 1, CFP Columbia, box 2.

16. Chafee, *Government and Mass Communications*, 11; Chafee, "The Press under Pressure," *Nieman Reports*, Apr. 1948, 19; Doc. 48, 149; Chafee, "An Outsider Looks at the Press," *Nieman Reports*, Jan. 1953, 5; Doc. 85, 4; WEH, *Freedom of the Press*, 225.

17. WEH, *Present Status of the Philosophy of Law and of Rights* (New Haven, CT: Yale University Press, 1926), v, viii; Doc. 75, 122; WEH, *The Meaning of God in Human Experience: A Philosophic Study of Religion* (New Haven, CT: Yale University Press, 1912), xiii; Chafee, "Liberty and Law,"

82; Chafee, review of *Free Speech*, 895, 898; WEH, *Freedom of the Press*, 171, 159–160n12; Doc. 42, 20, 21; Chafee to WEH, May 25, 1945, 2, CFP Brown, box 1; Doc. 48, 145 (emphasis added).

18. WEH, *Freedom of the Press*, 76, 109–113, 124, 197, 207; Doc. 42, 11; *FRP*, 131; "List of Press Commission Papers Deposited by Z. Chafee Jr." 32; Chafee to WEH, May 25, 1945, 1; Chafee to Robert D. Leigh, May 8, 1945, 2, CFP Brown, box 1; Smith, *Zechariah Chafee*, 110.

19. Doc. 108B, 94–95 (emphasis added; internal quotation marks omitted).

20. WEH, *Freedom of the Press*, 65, 162n2; Doc. 48, 146, 148; Doc. 66, 49.

21. WEH, "Sub-Committee on the Remedies for Press-Lying," 5–6; Doc. 75, 51–52, 58; WEH to Chafee et al., Aug. 1, 1945, 3 (italicization added); Chafee, "Comment on Report of Sub-Committee on Remedies for Press-Lying," Sept. 10, 1945, 1–2, CFP Brown, box 1.

22. WEH, *Freedom of the Press*, 110; Doc. 75, 63; Doc. 112, 3.

23. Doc. 75, 63–64, 122; Doc. 76, 5; Doc. 108B, 89.

24. Doc. 108C-D, 262 (Hutchins's paraphrase of Ruml's proposal); Doc. 90, 23; WEH, *Freedom of the Press*, 186.

25. Ruth Inglis to WEH, July 23, 1946, CFP UW, box 1; WEH to Inglis, July 25, 1946, CFP UW, box 1.

26. Arthur Hays Sulzberger to WEH, Aug. 13, 1947, Sulzberger Papers and New York Times Co. Records, box 172; WEH to Sulzberger, Aug. 22, 1947, Sulzberger Papers and New York Times Co. Records, box 172 (typo corrected); Sulzberger to WEH, Aug. 27, 1947, Sulzberger Papers and New York Times Co. Records, box 172. Actually, Hocking had used "touch of government" earlier. WEH, *The Lasting Elements of Individualism* (New Haven, CT: Yale University Press, 1937), 164.

27. Leo Rosten to Robert D. Leigh, June 23, 1947 (emphasis omitted), CFP Columbia, box 10; Curtis D. MacDougall, review of *Freedom of the Press*, by WEH, *Journalism Quarterly* 24, no. 3 (Sept. 1947): 268; Morris L. Ernst to Elizabeth L. Titus, Oct. 3, 1946, University of Chicago Press Records, box 240; F. S. Siebert to Leigh, July 8, 1947, CFP Columbia, box 10; Frank Hughes, "Control Press to 'Free' It, Prof. Urges," *Chicago Tribune*, Aug. 17, 1947, C3; WEH to Charles Lindbergh, Mar. 4, 1954, WEH Papers, folder 3675.

28. *FRP*, 80; Kenneth Stewart, "Press Rx," *Saturday Review*, Apr. 5, 1947, 14.

Chapter Nine. Resurrecting Free Speech

1. Archibald MacLeish, *A Continuing Journey* (Boston: Houghton Mifflin, 1967), v.

2. Linda Soest, interview with Archibald MacLeish, Mar. 18, 1966, 3, 10 (punctuation corrected), Ames Papers; Stephen Bates, "Public Intellectuals as Press Critics," *Society* 46 (2009): 124, 126; RMH to John U. Nef, Nov. 1, 1937, Ashmore Collection, box 13; MacLeish to RMH, May 16, 1938, RMH Chicago, box 158.

3. Scott Donaldson, *Archibald MacLeish: An American Life* (Boston: Houghton Mifflin, 1992), 5, 13, 63, 71, 87, 100, 114; Archibald MacLeish, *Archibald MacLeish: Reflections*, ed. Bernard A. Drabeck and Helen E. Ellis (Amherst: University of Massachusetts Press, 1986), 17, 78, 17; MacLeish to Felix Frankfurter, May 15, 1939, in *Letters of Archibald MacLeish, 1907 to 1982*, ed. R. H. Winnick (Boston: Houghton Mifflin, 1983), 299.

4. Donaldson, *Archibald MacLeish*, 105–107, 109, 125, 142–150, 167, 179, 234; Eric Hodgins, *Trolley to the Moon: An Autobiography* (New York: Simon and Schuster, 1973), 433; Archibald MacLeish to Dean Acheson, Dec. 30, 1919, in *Letters of Archibald MacLeish*, 63, 65 (punctuation corrected); MacLeish to Frankfurter, May 15, 1939, 299; William H. MacLeish, *Uphill with Archie: A Son's Journey* (New York: Simon and Schuster, 2001), 45; A. MacLeish, *Archibald MacLeish*, 17; Richard Meryman, "Archibald MacLeish: The Enlarged Life," *Yankee* 45 (Jan. 1981): 116.

5. A. MacLeish, *Archibald MacLeish*, 78; Donaldson, *Archibald MacLeish*, 192–194; W. A. Swanberg, interview with Archibald MacLeish, July 26, 1968, 1, Swanberg Papers; Alan Brinkley, *The Publisher: Henry Luce and His American Century* (New York: Knopf, 2010), 153, 160–161; MacLeish to HRL, Sept. 8, 1943, Time Inc. Archives; HRL to MacLeish, Nov. 6, 1933, 1, MacLeish Papers, box 8; Robert Vanderlan, *Intellectuals Incorporated: Politics, Art, and Ideas inside Henry Luce's Media Empire* (Philadelphia: University of Pennsylvania Press, 2010), 28, 38, 92, 100, 179; Hodgins, *Trolley to the Moon*, 383. Although MacLeish later maintained that the part-time arrangement was in place from the start, Luce's letter outlining it is dated 1933.

6. Michael Denning, *The Cultural Front: The Laboring of American Culture in the Twentieth Century* (New York: Verso, 1996), 389–390; HRL to Archibald MacLeish, Aug. 18, 1949, 1, Time Inc. Archives; Stephen Bates, "Is This the Best Philosophy Can Do? Henry R. Luce and *A Free and Responsible Press*," *Journalism & Mass Communication Quarterly* 95, no. 3 (2018): 818; Swanberg, interview with MacLeish, 2; Donaldson, *Archibald MacLeish*, 252; Ralph G. Martin, *Henry and Clare: An Intimate Portrait of the Luces* (New York: Putnam, 1991), 141.

7. Archibald MacLeish, "Preface to an American Manifesto," *Forum*, Apr. 1934, 195; Donaldson, *Archibald MacLeish*, 237, 262–265, 284–285; MacLeish, "The Poetry of Karl Marx," *Saturday Review*, Feb. 17, 1934, 486.

8. W. A. Swanberg, interview with Ralph Ingersoll, Aug. 16, 1968, 1, Swanberg Papers, box 18; Brinkley, *Publisher*, 160–162, 164–167, 265–267, 417; HRL to Dwight Macdonald, July 31, 1934, 2, Macdonald Papers, box 29; Macdonald, "Masscult and Midcult (II)," *Partisan Review*, Fall 1960, 613; Macdonald, "The Triumph of the Fact: An American Tragedy," *Anchor Review* 2 (1957): 120; Archibald MacLeish to HRL, ca. Sept. 8, 1938, in *Letters of Archibald MacLeish*, 297; MacLeish to HRL, Sept. 8, 1943.

9. Robert van Gelder, "An Interview with Archibald MacLeish," *New York Times*, May 10, 1942, 2; Swanberg, interview with MacLeish; Soest, interview

with MacLeish, 10; MacLeish, *Archibald MacLeish*, 68, 78, 120–121; Donaldson, *Archibald MacLeish*, 213, 192; W. MacLeish, *Uphill with Archie*, 124; Brinkley, *Publisher*, 164–165; Vanderlan, *Intellectuals Incorporated*, 26, 29, 98, 317n54; William H. MacLeish, "The Silver Whistler," *Smithsonian*, Oct. 1983, 61.

10. Donaldson, *Archibald MacLeish*, 212, 224–225; van Gelder, "Interview with Archibald MacLeish," 2; Frederick J. Stielow, "Librarian Warriors and Rapprochement: Carl Milam, Archibald MacLeish, and World War II," *Libraries and Culture* 25, no. 4 (Fall 1990): 513–514.

11. Donaldson, *Archibald MacLeish*, 310, 329, 337; Robert Lee Bishop, "The Overseas Branch of the Office of War Information" (PhD diss., University of Wisconsin, 1966), 2; Archibald MacLeish, "Libraries in the Contemporary Crisis," *Library Journal*, Nov. 15, 1939, 880; Vanderlan, *Intellectuals Incorporated*, 129–134; MacLeish, *The Irresponsibles: A Declaration* (New York: Duell, Sloan and Pearce, 1940); Ruth McKenney, "In 'Unity' There Is MacLeish," *New Masses*, Apr. 22, 1941, 19; Morton Dauwen Zabel, "The Poet on Capitol Hill," *Partisan Review* 8 (1941): 3; "On the 'Brooks-MacLeish Thesis,'" *Partisan Review* 9, no. 1 (Jan. 1942): 46 (James T. Farrell); Dwight Macdonald, "Kulturbolschewismus Is Here," *Partisan Review* 8, no. 6 (Nov. 1941): 450; Malcolm Cowley, "Poets and Prophets," *New Republic*, May 5, 1941, 639.

12. Harold L. Ickes, *The Secret Diary of Harold L. Ickes: The Lowering Clouds, 1939–1941* (New York: Simon and Schuster, 1954), 506–507; Executive Order 8922, Establishing the Office of Facts and Figures, Oct. 24, 1941, http://www.presidency.ucsb.edu/ws/index.php?pid=16024#ixzz1tOa CMG3d; John Morton Blum, *V Was for Victory: Politics and American Culture during World War II* (New York: Harvest/HBJ, 1976), 22–31; Sydney Weinberg, "What to Tell America: The Writers' Quarrel in the Office of War Information," *Journal of American History* 55, no. 1 (June 1968): 76.

13. GGT [Grace Tully] to President Roosevelt, June 29, 1944, PPF 6295, Franklin D. Roosevelt Library; Brett Gary, *The Nervous Liberals: Propaganda Anxieties from World War I to the Cold War* (New York: Columbia University Press, 1999), 154–155; Archibald MacLeish, *Champion of a Cause: Essays and Addresses on Librarianship* (Chicago: American Library Association, 1971), 68–70; MacLeish to J. Edgar Hoover, Feb. 3, 1942, MacLeish Papers, box 11.

14. Brinkley, *Publisher*, 290; Archibald MacLeish to HRL, Feb. 13, 1942, 1, Time Inc. Archives; HRL to MacLeish, Feb. 16, 1942, Time Inc. Archives; " 'Strategy of Truth,' " *Time*, Feb. 23, 1942, 17.

15. Archibald MacLeish, *A Time to Act: Selected Addresses* (New York: Houghton Mifflin, 1943), 16, 18, 133; Richard Norton Smith, *The Colonel: The Life and Legend of Robert R. McCormick, 1880–1955* (Boston: Houghton Mifflin, 1997), 404; William Fulton, "A Woman Editor Prints a Story about MacLeish," *Chicago Tribune*, July 8, 1942, 2 (spelling corrected).

16. Archibald MacLeish to President Roosevelt, n.d., PPF 6295, Franklin D. Roosevelt Library.

17. President Roosevelt to Archibald MacLeish, July 13, 1942, PPF 6295, Franklin D. Roosevelt Library.

18. Archibald MacLeish, *The Love of This Land* (New York: Anti-Defamation League, 1954), 16, 18–19; MacLeish, "We Have Purpose. We Know It," *Life*, May 30, 1960, 86, 93; MacLeish, *Continuing Journey*, 141; MacLeish, "Loyalty and Freedom," *American Scholar* 22, no. 4 (Autumn 1953): 393.

19. Doc. 75, 55–56 (emphasis in original); Doc. 112, 3.

20. Archibald MacLeish to RMH, Aug. 5 [1946], RMH Chicago, box 8; Doc. 99, 9–10, 24–25, 69–70; Doc. 119, 13–17, 19; Doc. 83, 5–6, 17; Doc. 111-1, 10–11; Doc. 112, 2; MacLeish, footnote in WEH, *Freedom of the Press: A Framework of Principle* (Chicago: University of Chicago Press, 1947), 99n4.

21. Doc. 90, 9–10, 133; Doc. 91, 13; Doc. 91C, 2; Frank Luther Mott, review of *FRP, Political Science Quarterly* 62, no. 3 (Sept. 1947): 443; Fred S. Siebert to Howard Ellis, May 22, 1947, Hughes Papers, box 26; Joseph S. Roucek and George B. De Huszar, *Introduction to Political Science* (New York: Thomas Y. Crowell, 1950), 526–529.

22. Doc. 99, 7–13, 36–37.

23. Jerome A. Barron, "Access to the Press—A New First Amendment Right," *Harvard Law Review* 80 (1967): 1641–1678; Stephen Bates, "Regulating Gatekeepers of Information: The Associated Press as Common Carrier," *UB Journal of Media Law and Ethics* 3, nos. 1–2 (Winter–Spring 2012): 90–106; Victor Pickard, *America's Battle for Media Democracy: The Triumph of Corporate Libertarianism and the Future of Media Reform* (New York: Cambridge University Press, 2015), 162–163, 168–169, 207–208. See generally Jerome A. Barron, *Freedom of the Press for Whom? The Right of Access to Mass Media* (Bloomington: Indiana University Press, 1973); Benno C. Schmidt Jr., *Freedom of the Press vs. Public Access* (New York: Praeger, 1976).

24. *FRP*, 23–25, 90–93, 104, 124; Doc. 90, 104; Doc. 108B, 108.

25. Doc. 48, 49; Doc. 119, 173.

26. Doc. 48, 48–58.

27. *FRP*, 23 and n1.

28. *FRP*, 24; Doc. 99, 4–5.

Chapter Ten. Is Bigness Badness?

1. "Let Freedom Ring True," *Time*, Mar. 31, 1947, 67; Oswald Garrison Villard, *The Disappearing Daily: Chapters in American Newspaper Evolution* (New York: Knopf, 1944), 3, 6–7; Bryce W. Rucker, *The First Freedom* (Carbondale: Southern Illinois University, 1968), 7; Morris L. Ernst, *The First Freedom* (New York: Macmillan, 1946), xii, 245. Ernst's *First Freedom*

and, to a lesser extent, the commission's *Free and Responsible Press* relied on studies by Raymond B. Nixon, but Nixon maintained that both books drew unwarranted conclusions from his data. Nixon, "Implications of the Decreasing Numbers of Competitive Newspapers," in *Communications in Modern Society,* ed. Wilbur Schramm (Urbana: University of Illinois Press, 1948), 43.

2. Doc. 90, 9; Sam Lebovic, *Free Speech and Unfree News: The Paradox of Press Freedom in America* (Cambridge, MA: Harvard University Press, 2016), 141. On economic concentration and the commission, see also David Goodman, *Radio's Civic Ambition: American Broadcasting and Democracy in the 1930s* (New York: Oxford University Press: 2011), 301–305; Victor Pickard, *America's Battle for Media Democracy: The Triumph of Corporate Libertarianism and the Future of Media Reform* (New York: Cambridge University Press, 2015), 169–174.

3. Doc. 34, 151 (emphasis omitted); *FRP,* 85 (published in 1947, the report was written in 1946); Doc. 119, 43.

4. Alva Johnston, "Profiles: The National Idea Man—I," *New Yorker,* Feb. 10, 1945, 28; FBI file on Beardsley Ruml (obtained under Freedom of Information Act); "Beardsley Ruml," in *The Rockefeller Foundation: A Digital History,* accessed Feb. 7, 2020, https://rockfound.rockarch.org/biographical/-/asset_publisher/6ygcKECNI1nb/content/beardsley-ruml; Johnston, "Profiles: The National Idea Man—II," *New Yorker,* Feb. 17, 1945, 31, 33; William L. Laurence, "Patriotism Viewed as Mild Nostalgia," *New York Times,* Sept. 8, 1933, 15; Johnston, "Profiles: The National Idea Man—III," *New Yorker,* Feb. 24, 1945, 33; Everett M. Rogers, *A History of Communication Study: A Biographical Approach* (New York: Free Press, 1994), 145.

5. Johnston, "National Idea Man—I," 28, 30; Johnston, "National Idea Man—III," 38–41; "Beardsley Ruml," *Fortune,* Mar. 1945, 174.

6. Johnston, "National Idea Man—I," 31–32, 35; Johnston, "National Idea Man—II," 28–29; "Beardsley Ruml," 135; Kate Holliday, "Mrs. Ruml Talks about 'Bee'; 'Was Always Outstanding,'" *Washington Post,* Mar. 29, 1943, B4; "Small Business and the Problem of Capital Formation," May 31, 1985, 16, Center for the Study of Democratic Institutions Collection, box 678.

7. Beardsley Ruml, *Tomorrow's Business* (New York: Farrar and Rinehart, 1945), 1; Doc. 119, 130; Doc. 90, 21; Doc. 108B, 61; Doc. 4, 6; Doc. 48, 26, 55–58, 63; Doc. 108C-D, 260–269.

8. Doc. 91C, 3; Doc. 21, 21–22; Doc. 94A, 45.

9. RMH to Archibald MacLeish, Jan. 22, 1946, 6, RMH Chicago, box 8; [Charles E. Merriam], comments on draft report, n.d., 1, att'd to Merriam to Robert D. Leigh, Sept. 7, 1946, Merriam Papers, box 65; Doc. 99, 84; *FRP,* 5, 80.

10. George L. Haskins, "John Dickinson, 1894–1952," *University of Pennsylvania Law Review* 101, no. 1 (Oct. 1952): 3–6; John Dickinson, "Legal

Change and the Rule of Law," *Dickinson Law Review* 44, no. 3 (Mar. 1940): 149n; "Post Resigned by Dickinson," *Los Angeles Times*, Dec. 25, 1936, 5. Two unpublished dissertations give the fullest discussions of Dickinson's role on the commission: Paul Mark Fackler, "The Hutchins Commissioners and the Crisis in Democratic Theory, 1930–1947" (PhD diss., University of Illinois at Urbana-Champaign, 1982), 246–252; Frederick Blevens, "Gentility and Quiet Aggression: A Cultural History of the Commission on Freedom of the Press" (PhD diss., University of Missouri, Columbia, 1995), 214–217.

11. Haskins, "John Dickinson," 3, 7–8, 22, 24; Felix Frankfurter to Stanley Reed, Mar. 25, 1936, Frankfurter Papers, folder 001757-002-0700; Peter H. Irons, *The New Deal Lawyers* (Princeton, NJ: Princeton University Press, 1982), 12; Robert L. Stern, "Reminiscences of the Solicitor General's Office," *Journal of Supreme Court History* (1995): 126; Paul W. Ward, "Washington Weekly," *Nation*, Mar. 25, 1936, 372; A Real Democrat, "Dickinson Chided," *Washington Post*, May 27, 1934, B5.

12. Raymond Moley, *The First New Deal* (New York: Harcourt, Brace and World, 1966), 290–291; Haskins, "John Dickinson," 9–10; Kenneth S. Davis, *FDR: The New Deal Years, 1933–1937—A History* (New York: Random House, 1986), 102–103, 115–122; Adam Cohen, *Nothing to Fear: FDR's Inner Circle and the Hundred Days That Created Modern America* (New York: Penguin, 2009), 231–232; T. H. Watkins, *The Hungry Years: A Narrative History of the Great Depression in America* (New York: Holt, 1999), 185–188; John T. Flynn, "Whose Child Is the NRA?," *Harper's*, Sept. 1934, 388, 391, 393–394; "Assails Rugged Individualism," *New York Times*, June 21, 1935, 38; "Holds Roosevelt Averted Dictator," *New York Times*, Feb. 18, 1934, 29; "The President's Good Fortune," *Washington Post*, July 9, 1935, 8.

13. John Dickinson, "Social Order and Political Authority," *American Political Science Review* 23, no. 2 (May 1929): 293; Dickinson, "The Anti-trust Laws and the Self-Regulation of Industry," *American Bar Association Journal* 18 (1932): 601; Irons, *New Deal Lawyers*, 12–13; Haskins, "John Dickinson," 9, 11; Arthur Krock, "Dickinson Appointment Is Viewed as an Anomaly," *New York Times*, July 26, 1935, 14; John T. Flynn, "Other People's Money," *New Republic*, July 24, 1935, 307.

14. *Annual Report of the Attorney General* (Washington, DC: Government Printing Office, 1937), 21–22, 28–29; *Annual Report of the Attorney General* (Washington, DC: Government Printing Office, 1938), 10–11; Karl Adolph Boedecker, "A Critical Appraisal of the Antitrust Policy of the United States Government from 1933 to 1945" (PhD diss., University of Wisconsin, 1947), 205; Ellis Wayne Hawley, "The New Deal and the Problem of Monopoly, 1934–1938: A Study in Economic Schizophrenia" (PhD diss., University of Wisconsin, 1958), 746–747; Spencer Weber Waller, "The Antitrust Legacy of Thurman Arnold," *St. Johns Law Review*

78 (2004): 572; "Nation Warned Trusts Ignore Federal Curbs," *Christian Science Monitor*, Dec. 31, 1936, 1.

15. "Dickinson Resigns as Cummings Aide," *New York Times*, Dec. 25, 1936, 1, 8; Arthur M. Schlesinger Jr., *The Age of Roosevelt: The Politics of Upheaval* (Boston: Houghton Mifflin, 1960), 581; Homer Cummings to John Dickinson, Dec. 18, 1936, Cummings Papers; Haskins, "John Dickinson," 12. Dickinson also endured a slap-down from J. Edgar Hoover for having given a campaign speech titled "Crime, Criminals, and G-Men." Hoover to Cummings, Aug. 28, 1936, Cummings Papers.

16. Boedecker, "Critical Appraisal," 205, 211–212; Gene M. Gressley, introduction to *Voltaire and the Cowboy: The Letters of Thurman Arnold*, ed. Gressley (Boulder: Colorado Associated University Press, 1977), 39–44; Hawley, "New Deal," 807–831; Tony A. Freyer, *Antitrust and Global Capitalism, 1930–2004* (New York: Cambridge University Press, 2006), 14–15; Waller, "Antitrust Legacy," 581–584, 588–590, 592–597, 600–603; Raymond Moley, *After Seven Years* (New York: Harper, 1939), 189; Jonathan Alter, *The Defining Moment: FDR's Hundred Days and the Triumph of Hope* (New York: Simon and Schuster, 2006), 323. See generally Spencer Weber Waller, *Thurman Arnold: A Biography* (New York: New York University Press, 2005).

17. George E. Sokolsky, "The Gospel of Humanitarian Slavery," *Deseret (UT) News*, Dec. 1, 1943, 3; George Sokolsky–John Dickinson correspondence, Sokolsky Papers, box 42; Dickinson, "The Common Man and the Common Law," *Vital Speeches* 10, no. 8 (Feb. 1, 1944): 242; Dickinson, "Planned Society," *Bulletin of the College of William and Mary* 37, no. 4 (June 1943): 33; Dickinson, "The Old Political Philosophy and the New," *Proceedings of the American Philosophical Society* 87, no. 3 (July 1943): 251, 253, 258, 259.

18. Haskins, "John Dickinson," 25; Doc. 90, 144; Doc. 108C-D, 234.

19. Dickinson, "Planned Society," 19; Doc. 108B, 57.

20. Donald L. Smith, *Zechariah Chafee Jr.: Defender of Liberty and Law* (Cambridge, MA: Harvard University Press, 1986), 102; "Dramatis Personae," att'd to Zechariah Chafee Jr. to Robert D. Leigh, Jan. 4, 1947, CFP Brown, box 2; Chafee to John Dickinson, June 3, 1944, CFP Brown, box 1; Dickinson, "Comments and Suggestions for Preparing a Preliminary Report of the Law and Government Committee," May 9, 1944, 8–9, CFP Brown, box 1; Doc. 90, 18; Doc. 91B, 7; Doc. 108B, 61.

21. Doc. 104, 130 (capitalization and punctuation altered); Doc. 108C-D, 141.

22. Doc. 108C-D, 143, 229; Doc. 108B, 60.

23. Doc. 108C-D, 149, 150.

24. Doc. 108B, 54; Doc. 108C-D, 150.

25. Doc. 108C-D, 150–151, 156–157.

26. Doc. 119, 43–44.

27. Doc. 119, 46–47; Doc. 111, chap. 6, 4–5.
28. Doc. 119, 49 (punctuation altered).
29. Doc. 119, 131.
30. *FRP*, 85, 2; Doc. 108C-D, 146.
31. Edward A. Purcell Jr., *The Crisis of Democratic Theory: Scientific Naturalism and the Problem of Value* (Lexington: University Press of Kentucky, 1973), 159; HRL to RMH, Oct. 25, 1943, Time Inc. Archives; [Thurman Arnold], manuscript att'd to Arnold to Irita Van Doren, n.d. [1946], 5, Arnold Papers, box 4.

Chapter Eleven. Gadgeteer

1. Doc. 48, 55.
2. Doc. 83, 42; WEH, *Freedom of the Press: A Framework of Principle* (Chicago: University of Chicago Press, 1947), 147; Doc. 16, 21; Doc. 4, 1 (punctuation altered).
3. Barry D. Karl, *Charles E. Merriam and the Study of Politics* (Chicago: University of Chicago Press, 1974), 89–95, 99; Thomas E. Blantz, *George N. Shuster: On the Side of Truth* (Notre Dame, IN: University of Notre Dame Press, 1993), 154; Harold D. Lasswell, *Propaganda Technique in World War I* (New York: Knopf, 1927).
4. Harold D. Lasswell, "The Person: Subject and Object of Propaganda," *Annals of the American Academy of Political and Social Science* 179 (May 1935): 189; Lasswell, *Democracy through Public Opinion* (Menasha, WI: George Banta and Chi Omega Service Fund Studies, 1941), 40.
5. Doc. 10, 2–3.
6. Arnold A. Rogow, "Toward a Psychiatry of Politics," in *Politics, Personality, and Social Science in the Twentieth Century: Essays in Honor of Harold D. Lasswell*, ed. Rogow (Chicago: University of Chicago Press, 1969), 127; Gabriel A. Almond, *Harold Dwight Lasswell, 1902–1978: A Biographical Memoir* (Washington, DC: National Academy of Sciences, 1987), 265; Everett M. Rogers, *A History of Communication Study: A Biographical Approach* (New York: Free Press, 1994), 203, 228–230; Irving Horowitz, *Tributes: Personal Reflections on a Century of Social Research* (New Brunswick, NJ: Transaction, 2004), 167; Harold D. Lasswell, "On the Policy Sciences in 1943," *Policy Science* 36 (Mar. 2003): 74; William Benton to HRL, Nov. 21, 1939, 1, Benton Papers, box 67.
7. Almond, *Harold Dwight Lasswell*, 249–250; Karl, *Charles E. Merriam*, 145; Rogers, *History of Communication Study*, 207; Yale Law School, Policy Sciences Center, and Ogden Foundation, *Harold Dwight Lasswell, 1902–1978* (New Haven, CT: Yale Law School, Policy Sciences Center, and Ogden Foundation, 1979), 42; Lasswell, *Propaganda Technique*, 220.
8. Lasswell, *Propaganda Technique*, 4; Harold D. Lasswell, review of *The Phantom Public*, by Walter Lippmann, *American Journal of Sociology* 31, no.

4 (Jan. 1926): 535; Lasswell to Charles E. Merriam, n.d., 2, Merriam Papers, box 51; [Lasswell], "Provisional List of Questions for Psychiatric Interview Designed to Explain Political Opinions and Practices," n.d., Merriam Papers, box 51; Lasswell, *Democracy through Public Opinion*, 1, 108 (emphasis added), 110. On Lasswell's views on democracy, see Raymond Seidelman with Edward J. Harpham, *Disenchanted Realists: Political Science and the American Crisis, 1884–1984* (Albany: State University of New York Press, 1985), 133–148; Brett Gary, *The Nervous Liberals: Propaganda Anxieties from World War I to the Cold War* (New York: Columbia University Press, 1999), 55–84.

9. RMH, "The Issue in the Higher Learning," *International Journal of Ethics* 44, no. 2 (Jan. 1934): 178; RMH to W. H. Ferry, Jan. 25, 1965, RMH UCSB, box 2; Leo Rosten, "Harold D. Lasswell," in *Remembering the University of Chicago: Teachers, Scientists, and Scholars*, ed. Edward Shils (Chicago: University of Chicago Press, 1991), 284. See also Leo Rosten, "Harold Lasswell: A Memoir," *Saturday Review*, Apr. 15, 1967, 65–67. Accounts differ somewhat on factors behind Lasswell's decision to leave Chicago. Rogers, *History of Communication Study*, 216–219.

10. William Benton to Harold D. Lasswell, Oct. 3, 1939, Time Inc. Archives; record of Time Inc. payment to Lasswell, Dec. 6, 1939, Time Inc. Archives; Lasswell, "Time Analysis," n.d., 2–3, Benton Papers, box 67; Almond, *Harold Dwight Lasswell*, 261; Lasswell, "On the Policy Sciences," 76.

11. Rosten, "Harold D. Lasswell," 276–286; Rosten, "Harold Lasswell: A Memoir," 65–67; *Harold Dwight Lasswell, 1902–1978*, 73; Bruce Lannes Smith, "The Mystifying Intellectual History of Harold D. Lasswell," in Rogow, *Politics, Personality, and Social Science in the Twentieth Century*, 46.

12. Walter Lincoln Whittlesey, review of *World Politics and Personal Insecurity*, by Harold D. Lasswell, *American Political Science Review* 29, no. 3 (June 1935): 501; Lasswell, *Democracy through Public Opinion*, xi; Lasswell, *World Politics and Personal Insecurity* (New York: McGraw-Hill, 1935), v.

13. Gary, *Nervous Liberals*, 249; Rodney Muth, "Harold Dwight Lasswell: A Biographical Profile," in *Harold D. Lasswell: An Annotated Bibliography*, by Rodney Muth, Mary M. Finley, and Marcia F. Muth (New Haven, CT: New Haven Press, 1990), 14; "Solve Red Angle in Crash Death; Papers Traced," *Chicago Tribune*, Oct. 24, 1938, 20.

14. Gary, *Nervous Liberals*, 168; Muth, "Harold Dwight Lasswell," 15; Almond, *Harold Dwight Lasswell*, 262; *Harold Dwight Lasswell, 1902–1978*, 79–80; Harold D. Lasswell and Abraham Kaplan, *Power and Society: A Framework for Political Inquiry* (New Haven, CT: Yale University Press, 1950), v; "An Investigator of 'Glamor' Digs into Nazi 'News,'" *Chicago Tribune*, May 21, 1942, 13; Robert D. Leigh, testimony, June 13, 1944, *Study and Investigation of the Federal Communications Commission: Hearings before the Select Committee to Investigate the Federal Communications Commission, House of Representatives, Seventy-Eighth Congress, First Session*

(Washington, DC: Government Printing Office, 1943–1944), 3792; FBI file on Harold D. Lasswell (obtained under Freedom of Information Act).

15. Gary, *Nervous Liberals*, 215; Rogers, *History of Communication Study*, 225n; *United States v. Pelley*, 132 F.2d 170, 171, 176 (7th Cir. 1942), *cert. denied*, 318. U.S. 764 (1943).

16. Richard W. Steele, *Free Speech in the Good War* (New York: St. Martin's, 1999), 168; "Content Analysis of the *Chicago Daily Tribune*," May 19, 1942, 1–2, Biddle Papers, box 2; "Domestic Propaganda," n.d., 1, Biddle Papers, box 2; Willard Edwards, "Inquiry Bares New Deal Plot to Rule Press," *Chicago Tribune*, June 18, 1944, 7.

17. Harold D. Lasswell to William Benton, Apr. 10, 1942, Benton Papers, box 75.

18. Frederick Blevens, "Gentility and Quiet Aggression: A Cultural History of the Commission on Freedom of the Press" (PhD diss., University of Missouri, Columbia, 1995), 256; RMH to HRL and Eric Hodgins, Feb. 8, 1944, 1, Lasswell Papers, box 26; Doc. 3; Zechariah Chafee Jr. to Lasswell, Feb. 1, 1944, 2–3, Lasswell Papers, box 26.

19. Doc. 94A, 94; Doc. 108C-D, 155, 157; Doc. 108B, 113 (spelling corrected); Doc. 3, 24, 33–34.

20. Doc. 21, 12–13 (document paraphrases rather than quotes remarks); Bill Chamberlin, interview with Harold D. Lasswell, Mar. 31 [1966], 21, Ames Papers; Doc. 91F, 2; Doc. 3, 8, 12 (emphasis omitted), 45. Lasswell's guiding question became well known in the literature on communications study. Scholars often credit him for coining it, though according to Jefferson Pooley, it may have first appeared in a collaborative work. Pooley, "The New History of Mass Communication Research," in *The History of Media and Communication Research: Contested Memories*, ed. David W. Park and Pooley (New York: Peter Lang, 2008), 53.

21. George A. Lundberg to Ruth Inglis, July 26, 1944, Lundberg Papers, box 7; Inglis, "An Objective Approach to the Relationship between Fiction and Society," *American Sociological Review* 3, no. 4 (Aug. 1938): 526–533; Milton D. Stewart, "Importance in Content Analysis: A Validity Problem," *Journalism Quarterly* 20, no. 4 (Dec. 1943): 286–293.

22. Doc. 26, 5; Doc. 101A, 1; Ruth Inglis to George A. Lundberg, June 28, 1946, Matthews Papers, box 709; Inglis to Stuart Dodd, Dec. 12, 1945, Matthews Papers, box 705; [Inglis], "The Myth of Monopoly in Radio and the Press," n.d., 2, Lundberg Papers, box 7.

23. Doc. 90, 1.

24. Doc. 90A, 181.

25. Doc. 90A, 184–186.

26. Doc. 90A, 187, 189, 193, 195.

27. Doc. 90A, 201–204.

28. Robert D. Leigh to Archibald MacLeish, Dec. 24, 1945 (punctuation altered), MacLeish Papers, box 13; *FRP*, 97, 99.

29. Doc. 108C-D, 254.

Chapter Twelve. Beguiling the Dragon

1. Doc. 99, 85; Doc. 90, 95 (spelling corrected).

2. Doc. 26, 14; Doc. 48, 39; Doc. 108B, 137; Doc. 108C-D, 274–281 (punctuation altered); *FRP*, 62, 93, 97–99.

3. *FRP*, 88–89; Llewellyn White and Robert D. Leigh, *Peoples Speaking to Peoples: A Report on International Mass Communication from the Commission on Freedom of the Press* (Chicago: University of Chicago Press, 1946); Doc. 94A, 95.

4. Upton Sinclair, *The Brass Check* (n.p.: self-published, n.d. [1919]), 408–409; Alice M. Holden, "Current Municipal Affairs," *American Political Science Review* 7, no. 3 (Aug. 1913): 455; Alan J. Stavitsky, "New York City's Municipal Broadcasting Experiment: WNYC, 1922–1940," *American Journalism* 9, nos. 3–4 (1992): 84–96; Michael J. Socolow, " 'News Is a Weapon': Domestic Radio Propaganda and Broadcast Journalism in America, 1939–1944," *American Journalism* 24, no. 3 (2007): 109–131; WEH, *Freedom of the Press: A Framework of Principle* (Chicago: University of Chicago Press, 1947), 188; Doc. 99, 177; Doc. 48, 137; Doc. 106; Zechariah Chafee Jr., *Government and Mass Communications* (Chicago: University of Chicago Press, 1947), 774. Before 1860, in addition, many presidential administrations had designated de facto official newspapers by conferring patronage largesse on printers. Timothy E. Cook, *Governing with the News: The News Media as a Political Institution* (Chicago: University of Chicago Press, 1998), 25–32.

5. "Is the American Press Really Free?," *Town Meeting* 12, no. 25 (Oct. 17, 1946): 6–7; Doc. 48, 26, 59–69; John Dickinson, "Comments and Suggestions for Preparing a Preliminary Report of the Law and Government Committee," May 9, 1944, 6, CFP Brown, box 1; Chafee, *Government and Mass Communications*, 667, 701; Victor Pickard, *America's Battle for Media Democracy: The Triumph of Corporate Libertarianism and the Future of Media Reform* (New York: Cambridge University Press, 2015), 163–164.

6. *FRP*, 5–6n1, 81, 84.

7. Doc. 99, 148; John M. Clark to RMH, Nov. 6, 1946, RMH Chicago, box 8; Pickard, *America's Battle for Media Democracy*, 173; Doc. 91F, 2; Doc. 91, 12; Doc. 90A, 186, 188.

8. Doc. 106, 98; *FRP*, 85, 91–92; Pickard, *America's Battle for Media Democracy*, 182.

9. Doc. 90, 55, 59; Archibald MacLeish to the Commission, n.d., included in Doc. 89, 93.

10. *FRP*, 69–76; Doc. 90, 7.

11. Doc. 90, 21, 59; Llewellyn White to Max Ascoli, Jan. 24, 1950, 1, Ascoli Collection, box 87.

12. Doc. 111(1), 6; Louis D. Brandeis, "Business—The New Profession," *System*, Oct. 1912, 365. See generally Thomas L. Haskell, "Professionalism versus Capitalism: R. H. Tawney, Emile Durkheim, and C.S. Peirce on the Disinterestedness of Professional Communities," in *The Authority of*

Experts: Studies in History and Theory, ed. Haskell (Bloomington: Indiana University Press, 1984), 180–225.

13. *FRP,* 69, 76–78, 91–92.

14. Doc. 109, chap. 5, 6; Doc. 119, 158–159.

15. Doc. 119, 158–167 (spelling corrected).

16. *FRP,* 78, 95, 99, 105.

17. Doc. 41, 4; Doc. 99, 157; *FRP* manuscript with annotations by HRL (Doc. 120), 84, Time Inc. Archives. See also Chafee, *Government and Mass Communications,* 717–719.

18. Doc. 4A, 1–2; Doc. 26, 18; Doc. 16, 5; Doc. 36, discussion of chap. 11, 15.

19. Doc. 83, 11–12, 66–68, 89–91.

20. Doc. 47, 4; RMH to George Seldes, Mar. 3, 1944, RMH Chicago, box 8; Seldes to Zechariah Chafee Jr., Feb. 5, 1946, CFP Brown, box 2; Robert D. Leigh to Chafee, Feb. 11, 1946, 2; "Seldes Hits and Runs after Talk to SDX," *Editor & Publisher,* Apr. 26, 1947, 26.

21. Doc. 91B, J6; Doc. 119, 150–151; Archibald MacLeish, *A Time to Act: Selected Addresses* (New York: Houghton Mifflin, 1943), 13–18; *FRP,* 65–66, 94, 103.

22. Doc. 9, 2; Ruth Inglis to Robert D. Leigh, Nov. 5, 1945, 2, CFP UW, box 1; Inglis to Leigh, Mar. 28, 1946, CFP UW, box 1; Inglis, "Need for Voluntary Self-Regulation," *Annals of the American Academy of Political and Social Science* 254 (1947): 159; Inglis, *Freedom of the Movies: A Report on Self-Regulation from the Commission on Freedom of the Press* (Chicago: University of Chicago Press, 1947), 125, 177, 190; Stephen Bates, "Case Half-Closed: The Hutchins Commission's Indictment of Pressure Groups for Media Manipulation," *Media History,* forthcoming.

23. *FRP,* 58–59, 96, 100, 104.

24. Doc. 75, 121; RMH to Martin L. Gibson, Mar. 25, 1970, RMH UCSB, box 2; Doc. 97, 89; William Hesse, interview with RMH, Mar. 8, 1966, 20, Ames Papers; Roger Simpson, " 'Our Single Remedy for All Ills': The History of the Idea of a National Press Council," *American Journalism* 12, no. 4 (Fall 1995): 477–495; Stephen Bates, "The Commission and Its Lessons," *Communication Law & Policy* 3 (1998): 142. Niebuhr thought the government might ultimately take over the organization. Reinhold Niebuhr to WEH, n.d., CFP Columbia, box 9.

25. *FRP,* 103; Doc. 76, 6; Robert D. Leigh to WEH, Aug. 22, 1945, 2, CFP Brown, box 1; Doc. 75, 24, 54–55; Doc. 79A, 1; Doc. 48, 94; Doc. 79, 6.

26. *FRP,* 101–102; Doc. 75, 70, 124.

27. Doc. 90, 9; *CBS Views the Press,* Dec. 4, 1948, 5, Hollenbeck Broadcast Papers, box 5; Doc. 75, 68, 70; Doc. 17, 28–29.

28. Ruth Inglis to Robert D. Leigh, Nov. 5, 1945, 1–2, CFP UW, box 1; Inglis to George A. Lundberg, Nov. 5, 1945, Inglis Papers.

29. Doc. 26, 7; Zechariah Chafee Jr., "Comment on Report of Sub-Committee on Remedies for Press-Lying," Sept. 10, 1945, 10, CFP Brown, box 1; Chafee, *Government and Mass Communications,* 713–714.

30. Doc. 111A; Reinhold Niebuhr, *Moral Man and Immoral Society: A Study in Ethics and Politics* (New York: Scribner, 1936), xv; Niebuhr, "The Revival of Feudalism," *Harper's*, Mar. 1935, 485; Doc. 90, 48; Doc. 75, 57, 121; Doc. 17, 24; Doc. 17A, 3; Doc. 99, 176–177, 189; Doc. 49, 2.

31. Doc. 90, 24, 63; Doc. 99, 22; Reinhold Niebuhr, *The Children of Light and the Children of Darkness: A Vindication of Democracy and a Critique of Its Traditional Defence* (New York: Scribner, 1944), 118.

32. RMH to Robert D. Leigh, Apr. 7, 1945, Redfield Papers, box 7; Doc. 90, 24; Doc. 91, 2; Charles E. Merriam to Leigh, Apr. 6, 1946, Merriam Papers, box 65; RMH, "Comments on Document 100," June 18, 1946, RMH Chicago, box 8.

33. RMH, "The American Press," *Spectator*, Apr. 25, 1947, 455.

Chapter Thirteen. Consider Yourself Pedestaled

1. Milton Mayer, *Robert Maynard Hutchins: A Memoir* (Berkeley: University of California Press, 1993), 173, 294, 306–307, 332, 358–359; RMH, "The State of the University [1946]" (pamphlet), University of Chicago, Nov. 25, 1946, 14, HathiTrust Digital Library, https://www.hathitrust.org; James Sloan Allen, *The Romance of Commerce and Culture: Capitalism, Modernism, and the Chicago-Aspen Crusade for Cultural Reform*, rev. ed. (Boulder: University Press of Colorado, 2002), 84; RMH to Eric Hodgins, July 12, 1944, RMH Chicago, box 9; RMH, *Education for Freedom* (Baton Rouge: Louisiana State University Press, 1943), 13; RMH to Thornton Wilder, Feb. 22, 1941, 2, Wilder Papers, box 43; RMH to Wilder, May 17, 1946, 3, Wilder Papers, box 43.

2. Frank K. Kelly, "Trees Grew in Brooklyn," *Center Magazine*, Nov. 1968, 21, 22.

3. RMH to Ernest Kirschten, Aug. 7, 1945, RMH Chicago, box 7; "Atomic Force: Its Meaning for Mankind," *University of Chicago Round Table*, no. 386, Aug. 12, 1945, 2; RMH, "The Atomic Bomb versus Civilization," *Human Events Pamphlet* 1 (Dec. 1945): 11; RMH, "The Bomb Secret Is Out!," *American Magazine*, Dec. 1947, 136; Dwight Macdonald, "Small Talk," *Politics*, Winter 1948, 57.

4. "Brief History of the Committee," *Common Cause* 1, no. 1 (July 1947): 14, 16; "Index of Committee Documents," *Common Cause* 1, no. 1 (July 1947): 23–27. Hutchins was president of the committee; Richard P. McKeon was chair. On the committee and its draft constitution, see Robert L. Tsai, *America's Forgotten Constitutions: Defiant Visions of Power and Community* (Cambridge, MA: Harvard University Press, 2014), 185–217; Or Rosenboim, *The Emergence of Globalism: Visions of World Order in Britain and the United States, 1939–1950* (Princeton, NJ: Princeton University Press, 2017), 168–208.

5. "Preliminary Draft of a World Constitution," *Common Cause* 1, no. 9 (Mar. 1948): 325–346; "From the Parliament of Man," *Common Cause* 1,

no. 9 (Mar. 1948): 322–324; "Dedication to Gandhi," *Common Cause* 1, no. 9 (Mar. 1948): 321; "Brief History of the Committee," 14.

6. "Preliminary Draft of a World Constitution"; Tsai, *America's Forgotten Constitutions*, 195–205; "To the Reader," *Common Cause* 1, no. 9 (Mar. 1948): 326; "Of Symbols and Emblems," *Common Cause* 1, no. 9 (Mar. 1948): 360.

7. Paul Boyer, *By the Bomb's Early Light: American Thought and Culture at the Dawn of the Atomic Age* (New York: Pantheon, 1985), 33–45; Tsai, *America's Forgotten Constitutions*, 205–215; Reinhold Niebuhr, "The Myth of World Government," *Nation*, Mar. 16, 1946, 312, 313.

8. Tsai, *America's Forgotten Constitutions*, 211–212; "Comment by Reinhold Niebuhr," *Public Opinion Quarterly* 17, no. 4 (Winter 1953–1954): 437; Henry Regnery, *Memoirs of a Dissident Publisher* (New York: Harcourt Brace Jovanovich, 1979), 58.

9. RMH, "Bomb Secret Is Out," 136–138; RMH, "The State of the University, 1929–1949" (pamphlet), University of Chicago, Sept. 21, 1949, 31, HathiTrust Digital Library, https://www.hathitrust.org; RMH, "Let's Split the Education Atom," *Collier's*, Dec. 7, 1946, 80; RMH, *The Great Conversation: The Substance of a Liberal Education* (Chicago: Encyclopædia Britannica / Great Books of the Western World, 1952), 18; RMH, "Comments," in *Challenges to Democracy: The Next Ten Years*, ed. Edward Reed (New York: Praeger, 1963), 220.

10. Allen, *Romance of Commerce and Culture*, 106–107; Mortimer J. Adler, *Philosopher at Large: An Intellectual Autobiography* (New York: Macmillan, 1977), 262–267; Alex Beam, *A Great Idea at the Time: The Rise, Fall, and Curious Afterlife of the Great Books* (New York: PublicAffairs, 2008), 62; RMH, "The State of the University [1945]" (pamphlet), University of Chicago, Sept. 25, 1945, 13–14, HathiTrust Digital Library, https://www.hathitrust.org; RMH, "State of the University, 1929–1949," 33; "Worst Kind of Troublemaker," *Time*, Nov. 21, 1949. On the Great Books, see also Tim Lacy, *The Dream of a Democratic Culture: Mortimer J. Adler and the Great Books Idea* (New York: Palgrave Macmillan, 2013); Joan Shelley Rubin, *The Making of Middlebrow Culture* (Chapel Hill: University of North Carolina Press, 1992), 148–197.

11. Adler, *Philosopher at Large*, 30, 237–239; RMH, "State of the University, 1929–1949," 31–32; Beam, *Great Idea*, 80; RMH, *Great Conversation*, xvi.

12. Dwight Macdonald, "The Book-of-the-Millennium Club," *New Yorker*, Nov. 29, 1952, 175, 179–182; RMH, *Great Conversation*, xx, 47, 52, 75, 80.

13. Macdonald, "Book-of-the-Millennium Club," 172, 175, 178–179, 182, 185–187; Zachary Leader, *The Life of Saul Bellow: To Fame and Fortune, 1915–1964* (New York: Knopf, 2015), 253–254; Dwight Macdonald, "Masscult and Midcult (II)," *Partisan Review*, Fall 1960, 615n7; Macdonald to editor of *Manas*, n.d. [Jan. 1953], in *A Moral Temper: The Letters of Dwight Macdonald*, ed. Michael Wreszin (Chicago: Ivan R. Dee, 2001), 232.

14. Macdonald, "Book-of-the-Millennium Club," 171, 180–181; "Walter Black, 64, Book Publisher," *New York Times*, Apr. 17, 1958, 31; "Books Published Today," *New York Times*, May 23, 1952, 19; Penguin Books ad, *New York Times*, Mar. 25, 1951; Eugene O'Neill Jr., "Famous Voyage, Cut-Rate," *New York Times Book Review*, Dec. 8, 1946, 18.

15. Regnery ad, *New York Times Book Review*, Oct. 9, 1949, 20; Regnery, *Memoirs of a Dissident Publisher*, 171–173; Henry Regnery to RMH, Aug. 21, 1952, 1, Regnery Papers, box 33.

16. Lacy, *Dream of a Democratic Culture*, 75–80; RMH, "Education for Freedom," *Harper's*, Oct. 1941, 522; Great Books ad, *Chicago Tribune*, Sept. 16, 1956, H7.

17. RMH to HRL, Mar. 1, 1939, Time Inc. Archives; RMH to Hodgins, July 12, 1944; RMH to Thornton Wilder, July 1, 1942, 2–3, Wilder Papers, box 43; Harry S. Ashmore, *Unseasonable Truths: The Life of Robert Maynard Hutchins* (Boston: Little, Brown, 1989), 225; RMH, "State of the University [1945]," 3; Mayer, *Robert Maynard Hutchins*, 238–239; RMH to Wilder, Aug. 28, 1949, 2, Wilder Papers, box 43; RMH, "State of University, 1929–1949," 37.

18. RMH, "State of the University [1945]," 27; Mayer, *Robert Maynard Hutchins*, 131, 244; RMH, "State of the University, 1929–1949," 42; John W. Boyer, *The University of Chicago: A History* (Chicago: University of Chicago Press, 2015), 316, 332; Mary Ann Dzuback, *Robert M. Hutchins: Portrait of an Educator* (Chicago: University of Chicago Press, 1991), 154–155.

19. RMH to John [Nef], Dec. 8, 1944, 1, Ashmore Collection, box 13; Mayer, *Robert Maynard Hutchins*, 377–378; Harold D. Lasswell to William Benton, Jan. 28, 1948, 2, Benton Papers, box 102; Ashmore, *Unseasonable Truths*, 189, 225; HRL to RMH, Apr. 10, 1942, RMH Chicago, box 157; RMH to HRL, May 23, 1946, 2, Time Inc. Archives; RMH to Wilder, July 1, 1942, 4.

20. "Hutchins Fragments," *Newsweek*, Nov. 8, 1943, 98; Lloyd Wendt, "The Midway's Versatile First Lady," *Chicago Tribune*, June 21, 1942, H2; Maxwell Geismar, introduction to *The Elevator*, by Maude Hutchins (New York: William Morrow, 1962), viii; Terry Castle, introduction to *Victorine* (1959), by Maude Hutchins (New York: New York Review Books, 2008), xv.

21. Dzuback, *Robert M. Hutchins*, 204–205; RMH to Thornton Wilder, Feb. 2, 1931, 1, Wilder Papers, box 43; Ashmore, *Unseasonable Truths*, 287; Mayer, *Robert Maynard Hutchins*, 360–361.

22. Maude Phelps Hutchins, "From Morning Till Night," *Foreground* 1, no. 1 (Winter 1946): 3–15.

23. "Died of Grief for His Wife," *New York World*, Feb. 7, 1900; "Why Paul Wilkes Fought a Duel" and "The Wounded Duelists," *San Francisco Chronicle*, Nov. 14, 1895, 1; "Married," *South Side Signal* (Babylon, NY), Oct. 17, 1896, 2; "Obituary Notes," *Fourth Estate*, Feb. 10, 1900, 5; Ashmore, *Unseasonable Truths*, 64.

24. William Seabrook, "Hutchins Family Portrait Gallery," *Town and Country*, Sept. 1938, 51; Maude Hutchins, *Blood on the Doves* (New York: William Morrow, 1965), book jacket; M. Hutchins, *Love Is a Pie* (n.p.: New Directions, n.d. [1952]), 157, 158; M. Hutchins, *Georgiana* (n.p.: New Directions, 1948), 67–68. The novel *Georgiana* incorporates sections of a memoir she began writing. [M. Hutchins], notes on childhood, M. Hutchins Papers, box 22.

25. [Maude Phelps Hutchins], "Society," n.d., M. Hutchins Papers, box 21; Clifton Fadiman to M. Hutchins, Mar. 7, 1938, M. Hutchins Papers, box 30; M. Hutchins to Fadiman, Mar. 14, 1938, M. Hutchins Papers, box 30; C. A. Pearce to M. Hutchins, Dec. 24, 1942, Geismar Papers, box 217; M. Hutchins to Pearce, Dec. 29, 1942, Geismar Papers, box 217.

26. Wendt, "Midway's Versatile First Lady"; Maude Phelps Hutchins to A. N. Marquis Co., May 22, 1945, M. Hutchins Papers, box 31; [M. Hutchins], annotation on RMH to Paul L. Blakely, Nov. 10, 1936, M. Hutchins Papers, box 30; Seabrook, "Hutchins Family Portrait Gallery," 51; "University President's Wife Makes Name as Artist, Poet," *Yonkers (NY) Herald Statesman*, Aug. 12, 1944, 7; "Not an Optimist," *Time*, May 18, 1942, 44; M. Hutchins, letter to the editor, *Time*, June 1, 1942; M. Hutchins to HRL, May 14, 1942, Time Inc. Archives.

27. Carroll Mason Russell, *The University of Chicago and Me, 1901–1962* (Chicago: University of Chicago Printing Dept., 1982), 47, 94; Dzuback, *Robert M. Hutchins*, 204; lists of invitations and responses, 1929–1932, M. Hutchins Papers, box 37; [Maude Phelps Hutchins], "What Is Stage Fright," n.d., M. Hutchins Papers, box 23; [M. Hutchins], notes on professors for possible newspaper column, n.d., M. Hutchins Papers, box 23; "Maude Phelps Hutchins Finds Today's Student a 'Complete Conservative,' " *Daily Maroon*, June 9, 1932.

28. Mayer, *Robert Maynard Hutchins*, 362–363; Russell, *University of Chicago and Me*, 54; Dzuback, *Robert M. Hutchins*, 204–205; Pearl C. Rubins and Dick Himmel, "Fadeout," *Cap and Gown*, 1940, 241; Ashmore, *Unseasonable Truths*, 287–288; RMH to Mr. and Mrs. William J. Hutchins, Sept. 12, 1941, Ashmore Collection, box 13; Milton Mayer interview, Dec. 29, 1976, 20, RMH Oral History, box 2; RMH to Marshall Field, Sept. 16, 1943, RMH Chicago, box 125.

29. [Maude Phelps Hutchins], "Little Oddity," n.d., 6, M. Hutchins Papers, box 9; [M. Hutchins], "The Man Next Door," n.d., M. Hutchins Papers, box 9; M. Hutchins to Cardinal [Samuel] Stritch, n.d., M. Hutchins Papers, box 34; [M. Hutchins], untitled poem ms., n.d., M. Hutchins Papers, box 2; "Hutchins Fragments"; [M. Hutchins], "Renunciation," n.d., M. Hutchins Papers, box 2; M. Hutchins, "Conversation Piece," in *The Elevator* (New York: William Morrow, 1962), 87–92; Stephen Bates, "From Blue Book to White Book: The Hutchins Commission and Llewellyn White's *The American Radio*," *Historical Journal of Film, Radio and Television* (forthcoming).

30. Thornton Wilder to Gertrude Stein and Alice Toklas, Jan. 28, 1940, in *The Letters of Gertrude Stein and Thornton Wilder*, ed. Edward M. Burns and Ulla E. Dydo (New Haven, CT: Yale University Press, 1996), 255; Wilder to Stein and Toklas, "Middle of March" (1940), in *Letters of Gertrude Stein and Thornton Wilder*, 258; Wilder to Stein and Toklas, Oct. 30, 1940, in *Letters of Gertrude Stein and Thornton Wilder*, 271–272; RMH to Wilder, May 17, 1946, 2, Wilder Papers, box 43; RMH to Wilder, Sept. 23, 1966, 2, Wilder Papers, box 43; Ashmore, *Unseasonable Truths*, 106–107.

31. Alfred de Grazia, *The Student at Chicago in Hutchins' Hey-Day* (Princeton, NJ: Quiddity, 1991), 166, 255; Mayer interview, 20.

32. "Wife Granted Divorce from Dr. Hutchins," *Chicago Tribune*, July 9, 1948, 1; Mayer, *Robert Maynard Hutchins*, 364–366; Ashmore, *Unseasonable Truths*, 291; Maude Phelps Hutchins to James Laughlin, n.d., 1, New Directions Publishing Corp. Records, file 830; M. Hutchins to Charles Lindbergh, May 20, 1947, Lindbergh Papers, box 17.

33. "Wife Granted Divorce"; Mayer, *Robert Maynard Hutchins*, 365; Dzuback, *Robert M. Hutchins*, 205–206; Irwin Ross, "Robert M. Hutchins," *New York Post*, Feb. 22, 1956, 14.

34. Paul Mark Fackler, "The Hutchins Commissioners and the Crisis in Democratic Theory, 1930–1947" (PhD diss., University of Illinois at Urbana-Champaign, 1982), 364, table 1; Doc. 4A, 1; RMH to Will H. Hays, Jan. 26, 1945, RMH Chicago, box 11; RMH to Robert D. Leigh, Apr. 7, 1945, Redfield Papers, box 7; Leigh to RMH, Mar. 1, 1945, RMH Chicago, box 7; Leigh to Ruth Inglis, Aug. 15, 1946, CFP UW, box 1.

35. Charles E. Merriam to Harold D. Lasswell, May 17, 1944, Merriam Papers, box 65; Merriam to Robert D. Leigh, Dec. 6, 1945, 1, Merriam Papers, box 65; WEH to Reinhold Niebuhr, Apr. 1, 1946, Hocking Papers, file 4509; unedited transcript of Sept. 1945 CFP meeting, 256, CFP UW, box 1.

36. Doc. 36, pt. 1, 3–4; HRL to RMH, Nov. 12, 1945, RMH Chicago, box 157.

Chapter Fourteen. All Great Problems Are Insoluble

1. Llewellyn White to Max Ascoli, Jan. 24, 1950, 1–3, Ascoli Collection, box 87 (spelling corrected). White was a founding editor of Ascoli's political magazine the *Reporter*. Elke van Cassel, "A Cold War Magazine of Causes: A Critical History of *The Reporter*, 1959–1968" (PhD diss., Radboud University, Nijmegen, Netherlands, 2007), 349.

2. Doc. 99, 108; RMH to Ernest Kirschten, Aug. 7, 1945, RMH Chicago, box 7.

3. Doc. 37, pt. 37A, 4 (emphasis in original); Doc. 90, 116–117; Doc. 37, pt. 37C, 9; Doc. 85, 2; Doc. 3, 2; Doc. 21, 7; Doc. 111-1, 13; RMH, foreword to *FRP*, viii; [HRL], "General Commentary I," Dec. 15 (?), 1946,

1–5, Time Inc. Archives; HRL to C. D. Jackson, Sept. 10, 1945, Time Inc. Archives; Doc. 4A, 3; [HRL], "General Commentary II," Dec. 15 (?), 1946, 9, Time Inc. Archives.

4. Doc. 26, 18–19; Doc. 75, 93, 94 (capitalization altered); Doc. 21, 11–15; Doc. 101A, 4 (punctuation corrected); Doc. 119, 3, 121; Doc. 94A, 13–14; Ruth A. Inglis, *Freedom of the Movies* (Chicago: University of Chicago Press, 1947).

5. Doc. 90, 11. See also Doc. 91, 13.

6. Doc. 90, 7, 99, 117; Doc. 48, 89; Doc. 89, 75; Doc. 21, 6; *FRP*, 18.

7. [Eric Hodgins], "P&O," July 26, 1944, 3, Time Inc. Archives; Hodgins to John K. Jessup, Dec. 1968, 3, Time Inc. Archives.

8. Thomas P. Brockway, *Bennington College: In the Beginning* (Bennington, VT: Bennington College Press, 1981), 213–217; Robert D. Leigh, testimony, May 19, 1944, *Study and Investigation of the Federal Communications Commission: Hearings before the Select Committee to Investigate the Federal Communications Commission, House of Representatives, Seventy-Eighth Congress, First Session* (Washington, DC: Government Printing Office, 1943–1944), 3439. See generally Stephen C. Mercado, "FBIS against the Axis, 1941–1945: Open-Source Intelligence from the Airwaves," *Studies in Intelligence*, Fall–Winter 2001, https://www.cia.gov/library/center-for-the-study-of-intelligence/csi-publications/csi-studies/studies/fall_winter_2001/article04.html; Susan L. Brinson, *The Red Scare, Politics, and the Federal Communications Commission, 1941–1960* (Westport, CT: Praeger, 2004).

9. Robert D. Leigh, testimony, June 8, 1944, *Study and Investigation of the Federal Communications Commission*, 3745; Archibald MacLeish to RMH, Feb. 7, 1946, RMH Chicago, box 9. Leigh later acknowledged having had "difficulties . . . especially with Johnny White, as regards the location of authority and responsibility." Leigh to Ruth Inglis, Feb. 14, 1947, 2, CFP UW, box 1.

10. Llewellyn White and Robert D. Leigh, *Peoples Speaking to Peoples* (Chicago: University of Chicago Press, 1946), 116; Leigh to RMH, Dec. 12, 1944, RMH Chicago, box 7; Leigh to RMH, Oct. 4, 1945, 2, RMH Chicago, box 7; Charles E. Merriam to Leigh, Oct. 19, 1945 (spelling corrected), Merriam Papers, box 65; Merriam to Leigh, Oct. 24, 1945, Merriam Papers, box 65; White to Leigh, Nov. 14, 1946, 8, Clark Papers, box 31; Loyalty of Government Employees, Investigation of Milton David Stewart, Oct. 10, 1951, 2–3, FBI file on Milton David Stewart (obtained under Freedom of Information Act); Ruth Inglis to George A. Lundberg, May 16, 1946, 2, Matthews Papers, box 709.

11. George A. Lundberg to Ruth Inglis, July 26, 1944, Lundberg Papers, box 7; [Robert D. Leigh], "Minimum Field Research for Verification of Commission Assumptions," Aug. 25, 1944, 2, RMH Chicago, box 9; Leigh to RMH, July 28, 1944, 3, RMH Chicago, box 9; Leigh to Harold D. Lasswell, Aug. 2, 1944, Lasswell Papers, box 27; Doc. 21, 7–8; Doc. 36, pt. I, 4–5.

12. Robert D. Leigh to RMH, Feb. 8, 1946, 2, RMH Chicago, box 9; RMH, foreword to *FRP,* ix; RMH to Leigh, Feb. 18, 1946, 1, RMH Chicago, box 9 (decimal and zeroes omitted).

13. "The Reports," n.d., att'd to Robert D. Leigh to Llewellyn White and others, Dec. 11, 1945, CFP UW, box 1; Milton D. Stewart to Leigh and others, Apr. 2, 1945, CFP UW, box 1; Stewart to Commission members, July 6, 1946 (cover letter to Doc. 107); Leigh to Commission members, Feb. 6, 1947 (cover letter to Doc. 98I); Leigh to RMH, Feb. 8, 1946, 2; Stewart to Harold D. Lasswell, Mar. 26, 1946, Lasswell Papers, box 90; Lasswell to Stewart, Oct. 31, 1946, Lasswell Papers, box 90; University of Chicago Press to *Chicago Tribune* Library, Aug. 6, 1948, Hughes Papers, box 27; U.S. Senate, Select Committee on Small Business, "Nomination of Milton D. Stewart to Be Chief Counsel for Advocacy of the Small Business Administration," 85th Cong., 2d sess., May 25, 1978, 2–3; Loyalty of Government Employees, Investigation of Milton David Stewart, interview with Morris Ernst, Oct. 18, 1951, FBI file on Milton David Stewart (obtained under Freedom of Information Act).

14. "Demise of the Center," *Time,* May 26, 1975, 70; RMH to Eric Hodgins, Feb. 26, 1944, RMH Chicago, box 9; Hodgins to Robert D. Leigh, Sept. 14, 1944, Time Inc. Archives; Stephen Bates, "Is This the Best Philosophy Can Do? Henry R. Luce and *A Free and Responsible Press,*" *Journalism & Mass Communication Quarterly* 95, no. 3 (2018): 818; Frank Hughes, *Prejudice and the Press: A Restatement of the Principle of Freedom of the Press with Specific Reference to the Hutchins-Luce Commission* (New York: Devin-Adair, 1950), 21; [Hodgins], "P&O," 3; Hodgins to HRL and Roy Larsen, July 12, 1944, and HRL handwritten response, Time Inc. Archives.

15. "Explanation of Items of Expenditure," Aug. 9, 1944, 2, Time Inc. Archives; "Draft Budget for Fiscal Year, July 1, 1944–June 30, 1945," July 1, 1944, 2, RMH Chicago, box 9; RMH to Robert D. Leigh, June 4, 1945, RMH Chicago, box 9; Raymond Fosdick to RMH, Feb. 8, 1944, RMH Chicago, box 7.

16. Leigh to RMH, Oct. 4, 1945, 2; RMH to Archibald MacLeish, Dec. 27, 1945, RMH Chicago, box 9; RMH to Leigh, Feb. 18, 1946, 1; Leigh to RMH, Feb. 8, 1946, 2–3; Leigh to RMH, Mar. 6, 1946, RMH Chicago, box 9; HRL to RMH, Mar. 8, 1946, Time Inc. Archives; RMH, foreword to *FRP,* v; Doc. 94, 1; Ruth Inglis to Marion Miller, Aug. 7, 1946, CFP UW, box 1; Inglis to Leigh, Aug. 5, 1946, CFP UW, box 1; Inglis to Leigh, July 20, 1946, CFP UW, box 1; Leigh to RMH, Sept. 9, 1946, 2, RMH Chicago, box 8; Leigh to RMH, Sept. 27, 1946, 2, RMH Chicago, box 8; University of Chicago Comptroller, "Report on the Commission on Freedom of the Press," Jan. 24, 1947, RMH Chicago, box 9; Leigh to Zechariah Chafee Jr., Mar. 5, 1947, CFP Brown, box 2.

17. RMH to HRL, Nov. 15, 1945, Time Inc. Archives; Bates, "Is This the Best Philosophy Can Do?," 818.

18. Archibald MacLeish to RMH, Dec. 28, 1944, RMH Chicago, box 7; Scott Donaldson, *Archibald MacLeish: An American Life* (Boston: Houghton Mifflin, 1992), 379, 390.

19. RMH to Archibald MacLeish, Aug. 30, 1945, RMH Chicago, box 7; Doc. 90, 2; Stephen Bates, *Realigning Journalism with Democracy: The Hutchins Commission, Its Times, and Ours*, Annenberg Washington Program Monograph (Washington, DC: Annenberg Washington Program in Communications Policy Studies, Northwestern University, 1995), 18; Robert D. Leigh to W. T. Couch, Dec. 11, 1945, University of Chicago Press Records, box 287; Doc. 75, 120, 123.

20. [Robert D. Leigh], "Notes on Procedure," n.d., 2, RMH Chicago, box 9; Doc. 104, 166–167 (capitalization altered); Doc. 34, 114, 160.

21. Robert D. Leigh to Zechariah Chafee Jr., Oct. 16, 1945, CFP Brown, box 2; MacLeish to RMH, Feb. 7, 1946; Doc. 83, 1–3, 31, 66–67.

22. RMH to Archibald MacLeish, Jan. 22, 1946, 1, RMH Chicago, box 8.

23. RMH to MacLeish, Jan. 22, 1946, 1; Doc. 90, 19, 22, 91, 94, 97, 105, 117–118, 129, 138–139.

24. Doc. 90, 19 (emphasis added), 24–26.

25. Archibald MacLeish to RMH, Feb. 15, 1946, RMH Chicago, box 11; Doc. 91, 1–16; MacLeish to RMH, Mar. 31 [1946], RMH Chicago, box 8.

26. Doc. 89, 93; Doc. 94, 5; Zechariah Chafee Jr., "Memorandum on Papers of the Commission on Freedom of the Press Deposited in the Library of Brown University," Oct. 1947, 18, RMH Chicago, box 8; Doc. 94A, 7; RMH to Archibald MacLeish, Apr. 5, 1946 (capitalization altered), RMH Chicago, box 8.

27. Eric Hodgins, *Trolley to the Moon: An Autobiography* (New York: Simon and Schuster, 1973), 432.

28. Doc. 99, ii, 1–3, 6, 53, 82, 102, 202.

29. Doc. 108B, 50.

30. Doc. 108B, 61, 66, 68; Doc. 108C-D, 156, 240–242; Ruth Inglis to George A. Lundberg, July 13, 1946, Matthews Papers, box 709.

31. Doc. 108B, 70 (capitalization altered); Robert D. Leigh to Charles E. Merriam, n.d., 2, Merriam Papers, box 65.

32. Doc. 108B, 75.

33. Doc. 108B, 53; Doc. 108, 1; Chafee, "Memorandum on Papers," 23.

Chapter Fifteen. Jefferson's Epitaph

1. Archibald MacLeish to RMH, July 20, 1946, 6, RMH Chicago, box 8; Doc. 104, 138–142; Doc. 48, 35; Doc. 119, 61.

2. Zechariah Chafee Jr., "Comments on Hutchins' Chapter III (Doc. 109)," July 26, 1946, 2, CFP Brown, box 2; MacLeish to RMH, July 20 [1946], 1–2, 6.

3. Robert D. Leigh to Ruth Inglis, Nov. 13, 1946, 2–3, CFP UW, box 1; *FRP*, 19–20, 82–83; Llewellyn White to Leigh, Dec. 3, 1946, 5, Clark Papers, box 31; Doc. 119, 67, 71; Archibald MacLeish to RMH, Aug. 5 [1946], RMH Chicago, box 8 (spelling corrected); Victor Pickard, *America's Battle for Media Democracy: The Triumph of Corporate Libertarianism and the Future of Media Reform* (New York: Cambridge University Press, 2015), 170.

4. Doc. 91, 3, 13; Doc. 111C; John M. Clark to WEH, Oct. 21, 1946, Clark Papers, box 32; Doc. 119, 120, 122, 125; *FRP*, 82; Charles E. Merriam to Harold L. Ickes, Jan. 27, 1947, Merriam Papers, box 64.

5. "Radio, Film Reports Absorb All of Luce's 200G; Mag, Press Probes Off?," *Variety*, Aug. 14, 1946, 21; Doc. 55, 2; "Canada's John Grierson Gives Ideas on Propaganda Functions of Govt. Pix," *Variety*, Aug. 26, 1942, 27.

6. Doc. 119, 1; Zechariah Chafee Jr. to Robert D. Leigh, Sept. 20, 1946, CFP Brown, box 2.

7. Doc. 119, 12, 29–31; Doc. 111-1, 2 (punctuation altered).

8. Doc. 119, 7–8, 16, 41–42, 46–47, 64–65, 68–70, 85, 145.

9. Doc. 119, 63 (spelling altered), 171–175; Zechariah Chafee Jr., "Comment on Report of Sub-Committee on Remedies for Press-Lying," Sept. 10, 1945, 10, CFP Brown, box 1.

10. Doc. 119, 19, 39–40, 92, 136, 144, 184, 193 (punctuation corrected).

11. Robert D. Leigh to John M. Clark, Sept. 20, 1946, 1, Clark Papers, box 31.

12. Doc. 120, iii; Doc. 99, 208; John Nerone, "Journalism," in *The Handbook of Communication History*, ed. Peter Simonson, Janice Peck, Robert T. Craig, and John P. Jackson Jr. (New York: Routledge, 2013), 202; Robert D. Leigh to Commissioners, Nov. 4, 1946, cover note to Doc. 120A.

13. Cynthia B. Meyers, "From Radio Adman to Radio Reformer: Senator William Benton's Career in Broadcasting, 1930–1960," *Journal of Radio & Audio Media* 16, no. 1 (May 2009): 17–29; Sidney Hyman, *The Lives of William Benton* (Chicago: University of Chicago, 1969); RMH to Thornton Wilder, Feb. 8, 1957, Wilder Papers, box 43.

14. William Benton to John Howe, May 27, 1959, Benton Papers, box 426; Benton to Howe, Dec. 20, 1963, Benton Papers, box 426; Hyman, *Lives of William Benton*, 396; Doc. 120, iii, 48, 57, 81, 84; Doc. 120A, 48, 81, 84; *FRP* manuscript, iii, 57, Time Inc. Archives; Robert D. Leigh to W. T. Couch, Nov. 6, 1946, 1, University of Chicago Press Records, box 118; Stephen Bates, "Reluctant to Criticize: Media, Academia, and the Press Council without a Home," *Journalism and Mass Communication Quarterly* (forthcoming).

15. Archibald MacLeish to RMH, Nov. 8, 1946, 1–2, RMH Chicago, box 8.

16. Doc. 120, 48, 81; *FRP*, 55; Hyman, *Lives of William Benton*, 335.

17. John Dickinson to RMH, Feb. 10, 1947, University of Chicago Press Records, box 287; Dickinson to RMH, Feb. 25, 1947, and encl.; jacket copy, *FRP*, University of Chicago Press Records, box 287.

18. RMH, foreword to *FRP*, v–vi, viii; A. J. Liebling, "Some Reflections on the American Press," *Nation*, Apr. 12, 1947, 427.

19. *FRP*, 2, 6, 7, 9.

20. *FRP*, 3, 17–18, 93, 96; Doc. 91, 27.

21. *FRP*, 14–18, 23, 57, 104.

22. Doc. 3, 4–6; Doc. 34, 159–161; Doc. 41, 1–6; Doc. 70, 3–11; Doc. 87, 15; Doc. 104, 37–38; *FRP*, 20–21. See also Harold D. Lasswell, "The Achievement Standards of a Democratic Press," in *Freedom of the Press Today: A Clinical Examination by 28 Specialists*, ed. Harold L. Ickes (New York: Vanguard, 1941), 172–177.

23. *FRP*, 5 (footnote omitted), 8, 80, 100.

24. RMH to Archibald MacLeish, Jan. 22, 1946, 4 (emphasis added), RMH Chicago, box 8; Zechariah Chafee Jr., *Government and Mass Communications* (Chicago: University of Chicago Press, 1947), 18; Doc. 90, 108, 118–121; Doc. 99, 106; *FRP*, 96.

25. *FRP*, 96–97.

26. *FRP*, 79–96; Doc. 108C-D, 237.

27. *FRP*, 96–106. The commission did endorse citizen activism in seeking better radio programming. *FRP*, 104; "Statement by the Commission," in *The American Radio*, by Llewellyn White (Chicago: University of Chicago Press, 1947), ix.

28. Mortimer Adler to RMH, "Saturday afternoon," 1, RMH Chicago, box 8; Laird Bell to RMH, Nov. 3, 1946, 2, RMH Chicago, box 8; Sims Carter, "Observations on the Report of the Commission on the Freedom of the Press," Sept. 10, 1946, 1–2, filed with Doc. 120, CFP UW; Pickard, *America's Battle for Media Democracy*, 175–176. Commission members largely ignored Carter's comments. Hutchins said he hadn't read the draft with care. Doc. 119, 2, 62.

29. Walter Lippmann to RMH, n.d., Lippmann Papers, folder 1113; RMH to Lippmann, Oct. 29, 1946, Lippmann Papers, folder 1113; Lippmann to RMH, Nov. 2, 1946, 1–2, Lippmann Papers, folder 1113; Pickard, *America's Battle for Media Democracy*, 175; RMH to Lippmann, Nov. 5, 1946, Lippmann Papers, folder 1113.

30. Ruth Inglis to RMH, n.d., att'd to Inglis to RMH, Jan. 22, 1947, Matthews Papers, box 706.

31. RMH to Ruth Inglis, Jan. 28, 1947, Matthews Papers, box 706. The commission had thirteen American members, who signed the report, and, at the end, two foreign advisers, who were not asked to sign it.

Chapter Sixteen. Gentleman's "C"

1. WEH to HRL, Aug. 3, 1946, 1, 2, Time Inc. Archives; Stephen Bates, "Is This the Best Philosophy Can Do? Henry R. Luce and *A Free and Responsible Press*," *Journalism & Mass Communication Quarterly* 95, no. 3 (2018): 819.

2. Doc. 119, 42; HRL to RMH, Sept. 16, 1946, Time Inc. Archives.

3. *FRP* manuscript with annotations by HRL (Doc. 120), iii, Time Inc. Archives.

4. *FRP* manuscript, 1–3, 8–9, 12–13, 15–16, 32–33; Bates, "Is This the Best Philosophy Can Do?," 819.

5. *FRP* manuscript, 32, 47–48, 67, 71–72, 81, 83; *FRP* manuscript appendix, 21; Bates, "Is This the Best Philosophy Can Do?," 820.

6. T. S. Matthews to HRL, Nov. 30, 1946, 1, Time Inc. Archives; John K. Jessup to Roy E. Larsen, Nov. 13, 1946, 1, Time Inc. Archives; Calvin Fixx to Larsen, Nov. 9, 1946, 1, Time Inc. Archives; Bernard Barnes to Larsen, Oct. 29, 1946, 1, Time Inc. Archives; Eric Hodgins to Jessup, Dec. 1968, 5, Time Inc. Archives; Bates, "Is This the Best Philosophy Can Do?," 820.

7. RMH to CFP members, Oct. 18, 1946, cover note to Doc. 120; Bates, "Is This the Best Philosophy Can Do?," 820; Robert Redfield to RMH, Oct. 25 [1946], RMH Chicago, box 8; John M. Clark to RMH, Oct. 21, 1946, Clark Papers, box 32; *FRP*, 52; RMH to Zechariah Chafee Jr., Nov. 8, 1946, RMH Chicago, box 8.

8. RMH to Roy E. Larsen, Oct. 29, 1946, RMH Chicago, box 8; Bates, "Is This the Best Philosophy Can Do?," 820.

9. HRL to RMH, Nov. 29, 1946, 1, Time Inc. Archives; Bates, "Is This the Best Philosophy Can Do?," 821.

10. Doc. 4A, 5; RMH to Junius B. Wood, June 1, 1944, RMH Chicago, box 8; HRL to RMH, Nov. 29, 1946, 1–2; Bates, "Is This the Best Philosophy Can Do?," 821.

11. Reinhold Niebuhr to RMH, Dec. 5, 1946, RMH Chicago, box 8; WEH to Niebuhr, Dec. 17, 1946, Niebuhr Papers, box 3; WEH to RMH, Dec. 7, 1946, WEH Papers, folder 2973; WEH to HRL (full draft), Dec. 7, 1946, WEH Papers, folder 3762; WEH to HRL (partial draft), Dec. 7, 1946, WEH Papers, folder 3762; Bates, "Is This the Best Philosophy Can Do?," 821–822.

12. RMH to Reinhold Niebuhr, Dec. 10, 1946, Merriam Papers, box 64; Doc. 90, 3–4; Bates, "Is This the Best Philosophy Can Do?," 822.

13. HRL to RMH, Dec. 15, 1946, Time Inc. Archives; Bates, "Is This the Best Philosophy Can Do?," 822.

14. [HRL], "General Commentary I" and "General Commentary II," Dec. 15 (?), 1946, Time Inc. Archives; RMH to William Benton, Dec. 27, 1946, Benton Papers, box 490. Part 2 of Luce's memo appears as HRL, "Critique of a Commission," in *The Ideas of Henry Luce*, ed. John K. Jessup (New York: Atheneum, 1969), 61–69, but not part 1.

15. [HRL], "General Commentary I," 2–3; Bates, "Is This the Best Philosophy Can Do?," 823.

16. [HRL], "General Commentary I," 5–8; [HRL], "General Commentary II," 4–5, 7–8; Bates, "Is This the Best Philosophy Can Do?," 823; HRL, "Critique of a Commission," 64.

17. [HRL], "General Commentary I," 3–4; Bates, "Is This the Best Philosophy Can Do?," 823.
18. [HRL], "General Commentary II," 6, 10–13; Bates, "Is This the Best Philosophy Can Do?," 823–824.
19. Doc. 108B, 78, 84.
20. HRL to RMH, Dec. 11, 1946, Time Inc. Archives; attachments to RMH to Benton, Dec. 27, 1946; *FRP*, 78; RMH, foreword to *FRP*, v–ix; RMH to HRL, Dec. 26, 1946, Time Inc. Archives; Bates, "Is This the Best Philosophy Can Do?," 824.
21. William Benton to RMH, Jan. 1, 1947, Benton Papers, box 490; Bates, "Is This the Best Philosophy Can Do?," 824.

Chapter Seventeen. The Luce That Laid the Golden Egg

1. RMH to HRL, Feb. 3, 1947, Time Inc. Archives; Robert R. McCormick to Ralph D. Paine Jr., Feb. 24, 1947, Matthews Papers, box 706; Stephen Bates, "Prejudice and the Press Critics: Colonel Robert McCormick's Assault on the Hutchins Commission," *American Journalism* 36, no. 4 (2019): 429.
2. "Outlines Plot to Destroy U.S. Press Freedom," *Chicago Tribune*, Mar. 5, 1947, 4; "Text of Address," *Chicago Tribune*, Mar. 5, 1947, 4; "McCormick Flays N.Y. Dailies and Press Report," *Advertising Age*, Apr. 14, 1947; Charles Gotthart, "Col. M'Cormick Hits Ignorant Press Critics," *Chicago Tribune*, Jan. 30, 1948, 3.
3. Charles E. Merriam to RMH, Mar. 11, 1947, Merriam Papers, box 64.
4. Bernie Auer to RMH and others, Feb. 25, 1947, 1, University of Chicago Press Records, box 118; "Final Publicity Report and Analysis of A FREE AND RESPONSIBLE PRESS," n.d., 1, Time Inc. Archives; Ralph D. Paine Jr., letter accompanying *Fortune* editorial, Mar. 15, 1947, Time Inc. Archives.
5. "Editorial—Solow (3rd Revision)," Feb. 28, 1947, 1–2, CFP Brown, box 2; RMH to William Benton, Mar. 2, 1947, 1, Benton Papers, box 490; Stephen Bates, "Is This the Best Philosophy Can Do? Henry R. Luce and *A Free and Responsible Press*," *Journalism & Mass Communication Quarterly* 95, no. 3 (2018): 825; Herbert Solow to John M. Clark, Mar. 5, 1947, Clark Papers, box 31; Zechariah Chafee Jr. to Arthur M. Schlesinger, Mar. 4, 1947, CFP Brown, box 2; Chafee, "Comments on the Draft of Fortune Editorial," n.d., Time Inc. Archives; Solow to Bernard Barnes, Dec. 6, 1948, Time Inc. Archives.
6. Eric Hodgins to RMH, June 28, 1944, RMH Chicago, box 7; RMH to Hodgins, June 30, 1944, RMH Chicago, box 7; "Commission on the Freedom of the Press Work Program," n.d., 1–2, Time Inc. Archives.
7. "Daily Appointments of Harry S. Truman: Mar. 25, 1947," Harry S. Truman Library and Museum, http://www.trumanlibrary.org/calendar/main

.php?currYear=1947&currMonth=3&currDay=25; "Final Publicity Report," 1; RMH to Benton, Mar. 2, 1947, 2; Robert D. Leigh, invitation to news conference, Mar. 19, 1947, Time Inc. Archives; Frank S. Adams, "Commission on Freedom of the Press Issues Report," *New York Times,* Mar. 27, 1947, 24.

8. [RMH], statement on release of *FRP,* 2, RMH Chicago, box 8; "Report Aimed Directly at Owners—Hutchins," *Editor & Publisher,* Mar. 29, 1947, 8; "Commission Finds Press Fails to Meet People's Needs," *PM,* Mar. 27, 1947.

9. *FRP,* 43–44n4; Bernie Auer to Bernard Barnes, Mar. 18, 1947, 1, Time Inc. Archives; Auer to Barnes, Mar. 22, 1947 (first of two memos with that date), Time Inc. Archives; Robert D. Leigh to William T. Couch, Mar. 21, 1947, University of Chicago Press Records, box 287; Ralph D. Paine Jr. to Elizabeth Wright, Feb. 7, 1947, University of Chicago Press Records, box 287.

10. Doc. 119, 192; RMH, foreword to *FRP,* ix; Robert D. Leigh to Elizabeth Wright, Nov. 18, 1946, University of Chicago Press Records, box 287; Leigh to Zechariah Chafee Jr., Apr. 23, 1947, 1–2, CFP Brown, box 2; Chafee, *Government and Mass Communications* (Chicago: University of Chicago Press, 1947), xii–xiii.

11. "Let Freedom Ring True," *Time,* Mar. 31, 1947, 68; Bernard Barnes to John Billings, Mar. 27, 1947, Time Inc. Archives; T. S. Matthews to HRL, Mar. 28, 1947, Time Inc. Archives; John Sousa to James A. Linen, Apr. 24, 1947, Time Inc. Archives; HRL to RMH, Apr. 1, 1947, Time Inc. Archives. The commission's official index of documents lists nine drafts, but a series of lectures by Leigh was also treated as a draft. "Complete Index of Documents," n.d., 10, CFP UW, box 2; Zechariah Chafee Jr., "Memorandum on Papers of the Commission on Freedom of the Press Deposited in the Library of Brown University," Oct. 1947, 18, RMH Chicago, box 8.

12. "Dangers to Press Freedom," *Fortune,* Apr. 1947, 2–5; Archibald MacLeish to HRL, Apr. 30, 1947, Time Inc. Archives; Bates, "Is This the Best Philosophy Can Do?," 822.

13. T.W., "Freedom for What," *New Republic,* Mar. 31, 1947, 34; "The Press and Criticism," *Los Angeles Times,* Apr. 13, 1947, 4; Kenneth Stewart, "Press Rx: Faith Healing?," *Saturday Review,* Apr. 5, 1947, 14; review of *FRP, New Yorker,* Apr. 26, 1947, 99; R. L. Duffus, "An Analysis of Our Mass Media," *New York Times Book Review,* Mar. 30, 1947, 42; John M. Clark to HRL, Apr. 2, 1947, Clark Papers, box 31.

14. Harry S. Ashmore, *Unseasonable Truths: The Life of Robert Maynard Hutchins* (Boston: Little, Brown, 1989), xviii; "Pulitzer Prize Editor Urges Citizens Group to Serve as Mass Communications Conscience," news release, Center for the Study of Democratic Institutions, Apr. 25, 1966, 3–4, Center for the Study of Democratic Institutions Collection, box 89;

Harold Evans, *My Paper Chase: True Stories of Vanished Times* (New York: Little, Brown, 2009), 197; Norman E. Isaacs, *Untended Gates: The Mismanaged Press* (New York: Columbia University Press, 1986), 101.

15. A. J. Liebling, "Some Reflections on the American Press," *Nation*, Apr. 12, 1947, 427; George Seldes, *One Thousand Americans* (New York: Boni and Gaer, 1947), 235, 237; Seldes, *The People Don't Know: The American Press and the Cold War* (New York: Gaer Associates, 1949), 23, 53; Seldes, *Witness to a Century: Encounters with the Noted, the Notorious, and the Three SOBs* (New York: Ballantine Books, 1987), 395–396; Bernie Auer to Bernard Barnes, Mar. 11, 1947, 1, Time Inc. Archives; Morris L. Ernst, "Guest Review of the Week," *Winston-Salem (NC) Journal*, Mar. 30, 1947 (punctuation altered), University of Chicago Press Records, box 287; Loren Ghiglione, *CBS's Don Hollenbeck: An Honest Reporter in the Age of McCarthyism* (New York: Columbia University Press, 2008), 124 (quoting I. F. Stone, interviewed in 1975).

16. "Free Means Free," *Wall Street Journal*, Apr. 7, 1947; "Controlled Press Opposed by Cooper," *New York Times*, Aug. 2, 1947; Frank Thayer, "Right to Own Press Can't Be Denied Legally," *Editor & Publisher*, Aug. 16, 1947, 54; American Society of Newspaper Editors, *Proceedings of the Twenty-Fifth Anniversary Convention*, Apr. 17–19, 1947, Washington, DC (Columbia, MO: American Society of Newspaper Editors, 1947), 208–232; Harry S. Ashmore, "The Mournful Numbers," address to "The Meaning of Commercial Television" conference, Apr. 24, 1966, Asilomar, California, 24, Center for the Study of Democratic Institutions Collection, box 89. See also Herbert Brucker, *Communication Is Power: Unchanging Values in a Changing Journalism* (New York: Oxford University Press, 1973), 202–205.

17. Frank Hughes, " 'A Free Press' (Hitler Style) Sought for U.S.," *Chicago Tribune*, Mar. 27, 1947, 38; "Text of Address"; Hughes, *Prejudice and the Press: A Restatement of the Principle of Freedom of the Press with Specific Reference to the Hutchins-Luce Commission* (New York: Devin-Adair, 1950). See generally Bates, "Prejudice and the Press Critics."

18. Frank Tripp, "The Movies Join the Press," *Editor & Publisher*, Mar. 29, 1947, 9.

19. George E. Sokolsky, "Stick to Your Last," *New Philadelphia (OH) Times*, Apr. 9, 1947 (spelling corrected); "Free-for-All: Freedom of the Press," *Fortune*, June 1947, 24 (quoting *Printer's Ink*); *FRP*, 55; "The Press Is Indicted," *Editor & Publisher*, Mar. 29, 1947, 38; "Forrest Says Report Helps Destroy Prestige of Press," *Editor & Publisher*, Mar. 29, 1947, 59 (spelling corrected); Walter Winchell, "Notes of a New Yorker," *Cincinnati Enquirer*, May 16, 1947, 6A; Sokolsky, "Readers Criticize Freely, 'Expert' Hutchins Told," *Chicago Herald-American*, May 14, 1947; Stewart, "Press Rx," 28.

20. "U.S. Press Hailed as Best in World," *New York Times*, Apr. 7, 1947, 25; "Press Is Indicted," 38; Duffus, "Analysis of Our Mass Media," 1; Walter

Lippmann, "On Criticism of the Press," *Washington Post*, Mar. 27, 1947, 9; Liebling, "Some Reflections."

21. Llewellyn White to WEH, Dec. 16, 1947, WEH Papers, folder 651; RMH to Zechariah Chafee Jr., Apr. 9, 1947, RMH Chicago, box 8; "Publicity Analysis of A FREE AND RESPONSIBLE PRESS," Apr. 15, 1947, 3, Time Inc. Archives.

22. HRL to John Shaw Billings and Roy E. Larsen, n.d., Time Inc. Archives; Bates, "Is This the Best Philosophy Can Do?," 825–826.

23. HRL to Commission on Freedom of the Press members, n.d. (unsent; spelling corrected and capitalization altered); HRL to WEH, Apr. 1, 1947, Time Inc. Archives; Bates, "Is This the Best Philosophy Can Do?," 825; Robert D. Leigh to Charles Merriam, Apr. 7, 1947, Merriam Papers, box 65.

24. RMH to HRL, Apr. 7, 1947, Time Inc. Archives; Bates, "Is This the Best Philosophy Can Do?," 825.

25. Bernie Auer to Bernard Barnes, Mar. 22, 1947 (second of two memos with that date), Time Inc. Archives; Bates, "Is This the Best Philosophy Can Do?," 825.

26. Margaret A. Blanchard, "The Hutchins Commission, the Press and the Responsibility Concept," *Journalism Monographs* 49 (May 1977): 52; Victor Pickard, *America's Battle for Media Democracy: The Triumph of Corporate Libertarianism and the Future of Media Reform* (New York: Cambridge University Press, 2015), 187; Louis Menand, *The Metaphysical Club* (New York: Farrar, Straus and Giroux, 2001), 438.

27. Archibald MacLeish, "Victory without Peace," *Saturday Review*, Feb. 9, 1946, 5; Doc. 106, 97 (punctuation altered); Garry Wills, introduction to *Scoundrel Time*, by Lillian Hellman (Boston: Little, Brown, 1976), 9–11; "Hutchins Defends the 'Brains Trust,'" *New York Times*, May 18, 1933; N.C. [Norman Cousins], "The Retreat from Washington," *Saturday Review*, Dec. 6, 1947, 28.

28. "A Free and Responsible Press," *University of Chicago Round Table* 472 (Apr. 6, 1947): 12; Michael Kazin, *The Populist Persuasion: An American History* (New York: Basic Books, 1995), 165; Aaron Lecklider, *Inventing the Egghead: The Battle over Brainpower in American Culture* (Philadelphia: University of Pennsylvania Press, 2013), 197.

29. Hughes, *Prejudice and the Press*, 33.

30. M. A. Jones to L. B. Nichols, Dec. 13, 1947, FBI file on Llewellyn White (obtained under Freedom of Information Act); [J. Edgar Hoover] to Nichols, n.d. [1947], FBI file on Llewellyn White; [Hoover], note appended to H. D. Smoot to M. A. Jones, Jan. 7, 1948, 3, FBI file on Llewellyn White; George F. Bergeron, Report on Llewellyn Brooke White, Special Inquiry—State Department, 10, FBI file on Llewellyn White; A. H. Belmont to D. M. Ladd, Aug. 27, 1952, 6, FBI file on Beardsley Ruml (obtained under Freedom of Information Act).

31. Doc. 111F, 1; Inglis to John M. Clark, Aug. 7, 1946, Matthews Papers, box 705; Arthur Herman, *Joseph McCarthy: Reexamining the Life and Legacy of America's Most Hated Senator* (New York: Free Press, 2000), 200; Anne C. Heller, *Ayn Rand and the World She Made* (New York: Doubleday, 2009) 245–246; J. B. Matthews file, Buckley Papers, box 3; Inglis, entry for Mar. 30, 1954, *Daily Reminder 1954*, Inglis Papers; J. B. Matthews, "Did the Movies Really Clean House?," *American Legion Magazine*, Dec. 1951, 12–13, 49–56; Inglis to Paul F. Lazarsfeld, June 26, 1948, with notation "not sent," 3, Matthews Papers, box 706; [Inglis], "Subversion in the Foundations," n.d., 24, Matthews Papers, box 226. See generally Robert M. Lichtman, "J. B. Matthews and the 'Counter-subversives': Names as a Political and Financial Resource in the McCarthy Era," *American Communist History* 5, no. 1 (2006): 1–36.

32. Donald E. Barnes to David P. Busse, Feb. 21, 1947, University of Chicago Press Records, box 287; memo on *A Free and Responsible Press*, n.d., 2, University of Chicago Press Records, box 118; memo on Commission on Freedom of the Press books, Mar. 15, 1956, University of Chicago Press Records, box 118.

Chapter Eighteen. From Target to Canon

1. "Dr. Ralph D. Casey, 87, Communications Scholar," *New York Times*, July 17, 1977, 42; Robert D. Leigh to RMH, July 8, 1944, RMH Chicago, box 7; Everett M. Rogers and Steven H. Chaffee, "Communication and Journalism from 'Daddy' Bleyer to Wilbur Schramm: A Palimpsest," *Journalism Monographs* 148 (1994): 21–25; Ralph D. Casey, "The Press, Propaganda, and Pressure Groups," *Annals of the American Academy of Political and Social Science* 219 (1942): 66–75; Harold D. Lasswell, Casey, and Bruce Lannes Smith, *Propaganda and Promotional Activities: An Annotated Bibliography* (Minneapolis: University of Minnesota Press, 1935); "Report of Expenditures: July 1, 1944 to June 30, 1945," RMH Chicago, box 9; Doc. 55, 2.

2. Doc. 75, 32–33; Ralph D. Casey to Robert D. Leigh, Mar. 22, 1947, 2, Lasswell Papers, box 27; Doc. 119, 163; Frank Hughes to Pat Maloney, Jan. 26, 1948, 2, Hughes Papers, box 27. See also Hughes, *Prejudice and the Press: A Restatement of the Principle of Freedom of the Press with Specific Reference to the Hutchins-Luce Commission* (New York: Devin-Adair, 1950), 341–342.

3. Casey to Leigh, Mar. 22, 1947, 1–2; *FRP*, 78; Dwight Bentel, "Journalism Educators Decry Lack of Facts," *Editor & Publisher*, Mar. 29, 1947, 12; Bentel, "Journalism Teachers Parry with Hutchins," *Editor & Publisher*, Jan. 3, 1948, 10.

4. Bentel, "Journalism Teachers Parry with Hutchins," 10; RMH, speech ms. for delivery Dec. 30, 1947, 3, Center for the Study of Democratic Institutions Collection, box 89.

5. Fred S. Siebert, "My Experiences with the First Amendment," *Journalism Quarterly* 56 (1979): 447; Jeffery A. Smith, "Fredrick Siebert's Absolute, Adjustable First Amendment," *Communication Law and Policy* 7 (2002): 385–388; Margaret A. Blanchard, "The Associated Press Antitrust Suit: A Philosophical Clash over Ownership of First Amendment Rights," *Business History Review* 61, no. 1 (Spring 1987): 77; Siebert to Howard Ellis, May 22, 1947, Hughes Papers, box 26.

6. Frederick S. Siefert [*sic*], "The Historical Pattern of Press Freedom," *Vital Speeches of the Day* 19 (Aug. 15, 1953): 659–662; Siebert, "The Role of Mass Communication in American Society," in *Mass Media and Education: The Fifty-Third Yearbook of the National Society for the Study of Education*, ed. Nelson B. Henry (Chicago: National Society for the Study of Education, 1954), 13–14, 18–19; *FRP*, 126.

7. John M. Clark, *Social Control of Business* (1926; repr., New York: McGraw Hill, 1939); Beardsley Ruml, *Tomorrow's Business* (New York: Farrar and Rinehart, 1945); Howard R. Bowen, *Social Responsibilities of the Businessman* (1953; repr., Iowa City: University of Iowa Press, 2013), 6. See generally Archie B. Carroll, "A History of Corporate Social Responsibility: Concepts and Practices," in *The Oxford Handbook of Corporate Social Responsibility*, ed. Andrew Crane et al. (New York: Oxford University Press, 2008), 19–46.

8. Theodore Peterson, "*Four Theories:* A Brief History of Its Origins," *American Journalism* 10, nos. 1–2 (1993): 4–6; Reinhold Niebuhr, introduction to *Responsibility in Mass Communication*, by Wilbur Schramm (New York: Harper, 1957), xiv; Peterson to Nicholas J. Bruno, Sept. 18, 1986, 1, Peterson Papers, box 20.

9. Theodore Peterson, "The Social Responsibility Theory of the Press," in *Four Theories of the Press: The Authoritarian, Libertarian, Social Responsibility and Soviet Communist Concepts of What the Press Should Be and Do*, by Fred S. Siebert, Peterson, and Wilbur Schramm (Urbana: University of Illinois Press, 1956), 74–75, 100.

10. Peterson to Bruno, 2; Peterson, "Social Responsibility Theory," 103.

11. Theodore Peterson, "Social Responsibility Thirty Years after the Hutchins Commission," ms. dated Oct. 12, 1979, 2, Peterson Papers, box 21; Jerilyn S. McIntyre, "Repositioning a Landmark: The Hutchins Commission and Freedom of the Press," *Critical Studies in Mass Communication* 4 (1987): 137; John C. Merrill, Peter J. Gade, and Frederick R. Blevens, *Twilight of Press Freedom: The Rise of People's Journalism* (Mahwah, NJ: Lawrence Erlbaum, 2001), 104–105; Victor Pickard, *America's Battle for Media Democracy: The Triumph of Corporate Libertarianism and the Future of Media Reform* (New York: Cambridge University Press, 2015), 188; William E. Ames to HRL, Feb. 14, 1966, Time Inc. Archives; Joseph A. Mirando, "Lessons on Ethics in News Reporting Textbooks, 1867–1997," *Journal of Mass Media Ethics* 13, no. 1 (1998): 34; Timothy W. Gleason,

"Saving Journalism from Itself (and from Us): The Hutchins Commission Was Right Then, So What about Now?," *Communication Law & Policy* 3, no. 3 (1998): 412.

12. H. Eugene Goodwin to Harry S. Ashmore, Sept. 14, 1967, Center for the Study of Democratic Institutions Collection, box 89; transcript of "The Hutchins Commission Revisited," Association for Education in Journalism conference, University of Colorado, Aug. 30, 1967, 25, 35–36, Center for the Study of Democratic Institutions Collection, box 89; James Boylan, "The Hutchins Report: A Twenty-Year View," *Columbia Journalism Review* 6, no. 2 (Summer 1967): 5–8; "The Commission Recommendations," *Columbia Journalism Review* 6, no. 2 (Summer 1967): 9–20; Edward Engberg, " 'A Free and Responsible Press': Where Are They Now?," *Center Magazine* 1 (Oct.-Nov. 1967).

13. Hilda M. Bryant, "A Free and Responsible Press: A Three-Year Inquiry—An Intellectual History of the Hutchins Commission Study of the American Press, 1943–1946" (MA thesis, University of Washington, 1969), 12; Margaret A. Blanchard, "The Hutchins Commission, the Press and the Responsibility Concept," *Journalism Monographs* 49 (May 1977); Jerilyn S. McIntyre, "The Hutchins Commission's Search for a Moral Framework," *Journalism History* 6, no. 2 (Summer 1979): 54–57, 63; McIntyre, "Repositioning a Landmark"; Roger Simpson, " 'Our Single Remedy for All Ills': The History of the Idea of a National Press Council," *American Journalism* 12, no. 4 (Fall 1995): 477–495; Jane S. McConnell, "Choosing a Team for Democracy: Henry R. Luce and the Commission on Freedom of the Press," *American Journalism* 14, no. 2 (Spring 1997): 148–163; Brett Gary, "The Search for a Competent Public: The Hutchins Commission and Post–World War II Democratic Possibilities," in *Democracy and Excellence: Concord or Conflict?*, ed. Joseph Romance and Neal Riemer (Westport, CT: Praeger, 2005), 75–90, 143–147; Victor Pickard, " 'Whether the Giants Should Be Slain or Persuaded to Be Good': Revisiting the Hutchins Commission and the Role of Media in a Democratic Society," *Critical Studies in Media Communication* 27, no. 4 (Oct. 2010): 391–411; Pickard, *America's Battle for Media Democracy*, 124–189; Stephen Bates, *Realigning Journalism with Democracy: The Hutchins Commission, Its Times, and Ours*, Annenberg Washington Program Monograph (Washington, DC: Annenberg Washington Program in Communications Policy Studies, Northwestern University, 1995); Bates, "Public Intellectuals as Press Critics," *Society* 46 (2009): 124–128; Bates, "Is This the Best Philosophy Can Do? Henry R. Luce and *A Free and Responsible Press*," *Journalism and Mass Communication Quarterly* 95, no. 3 (2018): 811–834; Roy Peter Clark to Bates, May 28, 1993, 1, in author's possession. Margaret A. Blanchard, Randall Bezanson, Tim Gleason, Donald M. Gillmor, John E. Nowak, Sandra Davidson, Ronald Rotunda, Rodney A. Smolla, Kaarle Nordenstreng, and I, among others, presented papers at the Illinois symposium in 1997, which

were published in *Communication Law and Policy*. Steven Helle, introduction to *Communication Law and Policy* 3, no. 2 (Spring 1998): 133–139.

14. Everette E. Dennis and Melvin L. DeFleur, *Understanding Media in the Digital Age: Connections for Communication, Society, and Culture* (New York: Allyn and Bacon, 2010), 387; Edmund B. Lambeth, *Committed Journalism: An Ethic for the Profession* (Bloomington: Indiana University Press, 1986), 9; C. Edwin Baker, *Media, Markets, and Democracy* (New York: Cambridge University Press, 2002), 154; James Curran, *Media and Democracy* (New York: Routledge, 2011), 9 (footnote omitted); J. Edward Gerald, *The Social Responsibility of the Press* (Minneapolis: University of Minnesota Press, 1963), 103; Curran, "What Democracy Requires of the Media," in *The Press*, ed. Geneva Overholser and Kathleen Hall Jamieson (New York: Oxford University Press, 2005), 135; Thomas Patterson, "If Clinton Loses, Blame the Email Controversy and the Media," *Los Angeles Times*, Sept. 21, 2016, http://www.latimes.com/opinion/op-ed/la-oe-patterson-clinton-press-negative-coverage-20160921-snap-story.html; Jack Snyder, "Bring Back the Visible Hand," *British Journal of Politics and International Relations* 21, no. 1 (2019): 75; Jessica Roberts, "From the Streets to Public Service: 'Humans of New York' Photographer's Journey to Journalism," *Journalism* 20, no. 11 (2019): 1483, 1492; Wiebke Lamer, *Press Freedom as an International Human Right* (New York: Palgrave-Macmillan, 2018), 29.

15. *FRP*, 34–35, 45–46; Curran, *Media and Democracy*, 206n1.

16. *FRP*, 58–62, 96, 100, 104, 128–129; WEH, *Freedom of the Press: A Framework of Principle* (Chicago: University of Chicago Press, 1947), 135–141; Lee C. Bollinger, *Uninhibited, Robust, and Wide-Open: A Free Press for a New Century* (New York: Oxford University Press, 2010), 62.

17. Pickard, *America's Battle for Media Democracy*, 189, 195; John C. Merrill, "Communitarianism's Rhetorical War against Enlightenment Liberalism," in *Mixed News: The Public/Civic/Communitarian Journalism Debate*, ed. Jay Black (Mahwah, NJ: Lawrence Erlbaum, 1997), 58; Gleason, "Saving Journalism from Itself," 411; Andie Tucher, "Hutchins Commission Half a Century On—I," in *What's Fair? The Problem of Equity in Journalism*, ed. Robert Giles and Robert W. Snyder (New Brunswick, NJ: Transaction, 2000), 54; Gary, "Search for a Competent Public," 76–78; Gerald J. Baldasty and Roger A. Simpson, "The Deceptive Right to Know: How Pessimism Rewrote the First Amendment," *Washington Law Review* 56 (1981): 368–370; Peterson, "Social Responsibility Theory," 100–101; Baker, *Media, Markets, and Democracy*, 155–156; RMH, "Freedom Requires Responsibility," *Vital Speeches of the Day*, Jan. 1, 1949, 175.

18. Herbert Solow to Bernard Barnes, Dec. 6, 1948 (punctuation altered), Time Inc. Archives.

19. Frank K. Kelly, *Court of Reason: Robert Hutchins and the Fund for the Republic* (New York: Free Press, 1981), 132–144; William Benton to RMH, May 19, 1959, 1–2, Benton Papers (paraphrasing Luce).

20. Nicholas von Hoffman, "Remembering Robert Hutchins, a Remarkable University President," *Washington Post*, May 31, 1977, B4.

21. Lee B. Becker, Tudor Vlad, and Oana Stefanita, "Professionals or Academics? The Faculty Dynamics in Journalism and Mass Communication Education in the United States," paper presented at International Conference on Media and the Public Sphere, Lyon, France, 2015, http://www.grady .uga.edu/annualsurveys/Supplemental_Reports/BeckerVladStefanita_ Lyon062015.pdf, 30 (charts 3 and 4), 32 (chart 7); Albert Alton Sutton, *Education for Journalism in the United States from Its Beginning to 1940* (Evanston, IL: Northwestern University, 1945), 52 (1940 figure for accredited schools); John Maxwell Hamilton, "Journalism Education: The View from the Provost's Office," *Journalism and Mass Communication Educator* 69, no. 3 (2014): 294, fig. 1; William Hesse, interview with RMH, Mar. 8, 1966, 23, Ames Papers; RMH to William Benton, Aug. 29, 1961, Fund for the Republic Records, box 189; Rogers and Chaffee, "Communication and Journalism," 11–12; Wilbur L. Schramm, "Education for Journalism: Vocational, General, or Professional?," *Journal of General Education* 1, no. 2 (Jan. 1947): 94. On the development of journalism education, see Jean Folkerts, "History of Journalism Education," *Journalism and Communication Monographs* 16, no. 4 (Winter 2014): 227–299; Everette E. Dennis, "Whatever Happened to Marse Robert's Dream? The Dilemma of American Journalism Education," *Gannett Center Journal* 2 (Spring 1988): 2–22; Wm. David Sloan, "In Search of Itself: A History of Journalism Education," in *Makers of the Media Mind: Journalism Educators and Their Ideas*, ed. Sloan (Hillsdale, NJ: Lawrence Erlbaum, 1990), 3–22; Michael Bromley, "The 'New Majority' and the Academization of Journalism," *Journalism* 14, no. 5 (2012): 569–586; Theodore Peterson, "The Changing Role of Journalism Schools," *Journalism Quarterly* 37 (1960): 579–585.

22. RMH to Ernest Kirschten, June 2, 1947, RMH Chicago, box 6; RMH, *The Higher Learning in America* (New Haven, CT: Yale University Press, 1936), 109–110; Everett M. Rogers, *A History of Communication Study: A Biographical Approach* (New York: Free Press, 1994), 26–27; Steven H. Chaffee, "In Memoriam: Wilbur Schramm, 1907–1987," *Public Opinion Quarterly* 52, no. 3 (Autumn 1988): 373; Everette E. Dennis and David L. Stebenne, "Requiem for a Think Tank: The Life and Death of the Gannett Center at Columbia, 1984–1996," *Press/Politics* 8, no. 2 (Spring 2003): 11–35.

23. *FRP*, 78; Dwight Bentel, "Schools Restrained from Press Criticism," *Editor & Publisher*, Apr. 12, 1947; Herbert Strentz, Kenneth Starck, David L. Anderson, and Loren Ghiglione, "The Critical Factor: Criticism of the News Media in Journalism Education," *Journalism Monographs* 32 (Feb. 1974): preface, 9–10, 13.

24. Barbara W. Hartung, "Attitudes Toward the Applicability of the Hutchins Report on Press Responsibility," *Journalism Quarterly* 58, no. 3 (1981):

431–432, table 2; David Weaver and G. Cleveland Wilhoit, "A Profile of JMS Educators: Traits, Attitudes and Values," *Journalism Educator* 43, no. 2 (Summer 1988): 37. See also Michael Ryan, "How Educators, Editors View Aspects of J School's Role in Press Criticism," *Journalism Quarterly* 55, no. 2 (1978): 297–298, table 1.

25. Pickard, *America's Battle for Media Democracy,* 15, 188–195.
26. Simpson, "'Our Single Remedy for All Ills,'" recounts the major Hutchins and Benton efforts through 1955.
27. William Benton to RMH, July 11, 1949, Hutchins Administration Records, box 91; Benton, "My Current Reading," *Saturday Review,* Mar. 27, 1948, 12; Sidney Hyman, *The Lives of William Benton* (Chicago: University of Chicago, 1969), 408–409, 468–469, 480; Cynthia B. Meyers, "From Radio Adman to Radio Reformer: Senator William Benton's Career in Broadcasting, 1930–1960," *Journal of Radio & Audio Media* 16, no. 1 (May 2009): 26–27; Benton to Harry S. Ashmore, Sept. 18, 1967, 2, Center for the Study of Democratic Institutions Collection, box 89; Stephen Bates, "Reluctant to Criticize: Media, Academia, and the Press Council without a Home," *Journalism and Mass Communication Quarterly* (forthcoming).
28. Gabe Kaimowitz to RMH, June 7, 1964, 1–2, WEH Papers, folder 7727; WEH to RMH, June 11, 1964, Time Inc. Archives; Harry S. Ashmore to RMH, Sept. 1, 1964, 1–2, 5, Time Inc. Archives; RMH to HRL, Oct. 21, 1964, Time Inc. Archives.
29. RMH to HRL, Oct. 21, 1964.
30. HRL to RMH, Oct. 26, 1964, Time Inc. Archives.
31. "Possible Candidates, Commission on the Mass Media," n.d., Benton Papers, box 426; William Benton to J. M. Kaplan, Mar. 5, 1957, 1, Benton Papers, box 274; Harry S. Ashmore to Benton, Sept. 28, 1961, 3, Benton Papers, box 426; Adlai Stevenson to John B. Elliott, Oct. 23, 1957, Benton Papers, box 100; Ashmore to Benton, May 15, 1961, 3, Benton Papers, box 426; Ashmore to Benton, Dec. 21, 1962, 1–2, Benton Papers, box 426; Ashmore to Benton, Jan. 29, 1963, 1, Benton Papers, box 426; RMH to Benton, Oct. 2, 1971, RMH UCSB, box 3; RMH to Benton, Apr. 20, 1971, RMH UCSB, box 2; Benton to RMH and Ashmore, Sept. 22, 1960, 1, Murrow Papers, box 32.
32. William Benton to Harry S. Ashmore, Mar. 6, 1962, 2, Benton Papers, box 426; Nathan M. Pusey to Ashmore, Feb. 1, 1961, Benton Papers, box 426; Robert F. Goheen to Ashmore, Sept. 18, 1961, 1, Benton Papers, box 426; Benton to Harold D. Lasswell, Dec. 13, 1960, Benton Papers, box 175; John Howe to Ashmore, Sept. 10, 1965, 1, Benton Papers, box 426; RMH to Benton, Nov. 9, 1961, 1–2, Benton Papers, box 426; Benton to Ashmore and Frank Kelly, Jan. 29, 1962, 1–3, Benton Papers, box 426; Benton to Edward Barrett, May 25, 1965, 1, Benton Papers, box 123; Barrett to Benton, July 3, 1962, 1, Benton Papers, box 426; transcript of "Hutchins Commission Revisited," 12–13; Bates, "Reluctant to Criticize."

33. George Shuster to RMH, Apr. 11, 1961, Fund for the Republic Records, box 191; Shuster to Harry S. Ashmore, Aug. 30, 1961, 1, Benton Papers, box 426; Ashmore to William Benton, Dec. 20, 1961, 4, Fund for the Republic Records, box 189; John Howe to Benton, Feb. 24, 1964, 1, Benton Papers, box 426; Ashmore to Newton N. Minow, May 14, 1964, Benton Papers, box 426; Bates, "Reluctant to Criticize."

34. Patrick Brogan, *Spiked: The Short Life and Death of the National News Council* (New York: Twentieth Century Fund / Priority, 1985), 6–7, 27, 90–92, 109; transcript of "The National News Council—A Solution?," Jan. 30–31, 1973, Center for the Study of Democratic Institutions Collection, box 568; Stanley H. Fuld to Jack Howard, May 29, 1974, 1, National News Council Records.

35. Donald McDonald to Jerry, July 30, 1986, Center for the Study of Democratic Institutions Collection, box 487; James W. Carey, "The Press and the Public Discourse," *Center Magazine*, Mar.–Apr. 1987, 4–15; Carey, "In Defense of Public Journalism," in *The Idea of Public Journalism*, ed. Theodore L. Glasser (New York: Guilford, 1999), 58; Renita Coleman, "The Intellectual Antecedents of Public Journalism," *Journal of Communication Inquiry* 21, no. 1 (Spring 1997): 61, 64–65; Baker, *Media, Markets, and Democracy*, 158–163; Pickard, *America's Battle for Media Democracy*, 187–188.

36. Jonathan Wai and Kaja Perina, "Expertise in Journalism: Factors Shaping a Cognitive and Culturally Elite Profession," *Journal of Expertise* 1, no. 1 (2018): 64–65, https://www.journalofexpertise.org/articles/volume1_issue1/Jo-E_2018_1_1_Wai_Perina.pdf.

37. *Miami Herald Publishing Co. v. Tornillo*, 418 U.S. 241 (1974); *Red Lion Broadcasting Co. v. FCC*, 395 U.S. 367, 390 (1969); Pickard, *America's Battle for Media Democracy*, 207–208.

38. *Miami Herald Publishing Co. v. Tornillo*, oral argument, Apr. 17, 1974, https://www.oyez.org/cases/1973/73-797.

39. *Tornillo*, 418 U.S. at 248–251 and nn.11, 17; Samantha Barbas, "Creating the Public Forum," *Akron Law Review* 44 (2011): 849.

40. *Tornillo*, 418 U.S. at 256.

41. Jerome A. Barron, "Access Reconsidered," *George Washington Law Review* 76 (2008): 837.

Chapter Nineteen. Democracy on the Skids

1. "Text of Hutchins Speech before Society of Newspaper Editors," *New York Times*, Apr. 22, 1955, 16.

2. Doc. 106, 98; WEH, *Freedom of the Press: A Framework of Principle* (Chicago: University of Chicago Press, 1947), 43, 110; Doc. 1, 9; WEH to RMH, July 24, 1946 (typo corrected), RMH Chicago, box 8.

3. Zechariah Chafee Jr., "Comments on Chapter IV—Hutchins Draft," July 29, 1946, 2, CFP Brown, box 2; Doc. 16, 21; Doc. 108A, 37; David

Goodman, *Radio's Civic Ambition: American Broadcasting and Democracy in the 1930s* (New York: Oxford University Press, 2011), 307. See also Reinhold Niebuhr, introduction to *Responsibility in Mass Communication*, by Wilbur Schramm (New York: Harper, 1957), xx–xxii.

4. Doc. 89, 36; WEH, *Freedom of the Press*, 168; *FRP*, 20.

5. Timothy Garton Ash, *Free Speech: Ten Principles for a Connected World* (New Haven, CT: Yale University Press, 2016), 47; Gertrude Stein, *Everybody's Autobiography* (New York: Random House, 1937), 206.

6. C. W. Anderson, Emily Bell, and Clay Shirky, "Post Industrial Journalism: Adapting to the Present," Tow Center for Digital Journalism, Columbia Journalism School, n.d. [2012], 3; Pew Research Center, "Newspapers Fact Sheet," July 9, 2019, https://www.journalism.org/factsheet/newspapers/; Eric Hodgins, "A Definition of News for the World of Tomorrow," *Journalism Quarterly* 20, no. 4 (Dec. 1943): 273.

7. Victor Pickard, "Media Failures in the Age of Trump," *Political Economy of Communication* 4, no. 2 (2016): 120; Pickard, "Confronting Market Failure: Past Lessons Toward Public Policy Interventions," in *The Communications Crisis in America and How to Fix It*, ed. Lewis Friedland and Mark Lloyd (New York: Palgrave Macmillan, 2016), 127–142; Robert W. McChesney, "Journalism Is Dead! Long Live Journalism? Why Democratic Societies Will Need to Subsidise Future News Production," *Journal of Media Business Studies* 13, no. 3 (2016): 128–135; Lee C. Bollinger, "News for the World," *Columbia Journalism Review*, July–Aug. 2011, https://archives.cjr.org/cover_story/news_for_the_world.php.

8. WEH, *Freedom of the Press*, 188 (emphasis omitted); Richard J. Tofel, *Why American Newspapers Gave Away the Future* (Now and Then Reader ebook, 2012).

9. Doc. 17, 29 (paraphrasing remarks). See also Doc. 16, 20–21.

10. Doc. 108B, 108; Doc. 17, 29; Doc. 4, 4; Doc. 90, 145; Zechariah Chafee Jr., *Government and Mass Communications* (Chicago: University of Chicago Press, 1947), 11; Doc. 16, 20.

11. John Maurice Clark, *Alternative to Serfdom* (New York: Knopf, 1948), 136–142; Reinhold Niebuhr, *Moral Man and Immoral Society: A Study in Ethics and Politics* (New York: Scribner, 1936), xi–xii, xxii–xxiv, 9; WEH, *Freedom of the Press*, 92–93; Doc. 34, 4–5; Chafee, *Government and Mass Communications*, 15, 22; Zechariah Chafee Jr. to Robert D. Leigh, Nov. 21, 1947, CFP Columbia, box 10; Doc. 16, 13–14.

12. George Shuster to RMH, Feb. 6, 1946, 1–2, MacLeish Papers, box 11; Doc. 52, 15; Doc. 16A, 2; WEH, *Freedom of the Press*, 119; Doc. 19, 3; Llewellyn White, "Seven Keys to Addlepate," *Harper's*, Oct. 1945, 337.

13. Doc. 34, 55; Milton D. Stewart, "Twentieth Century Pressure Group Techniques in the United States," July 1944, 57–62, Communications Collection, Columbia University Libraries, New York, NY.

14. Doc. 106, 117; Stewart, "Twentieth Century Pressure Group Techniques"; Doc 104, Robert D. Leigh, ed., "Draft of the General Report: Sixth Revision," June 26, 1946, 46; Doc. 108B, 121; Doc. 36, discussion of chap. 11, 23; Doc. 19, 4; Doc. 34, 54–55; Llewellyn White and Robert D. Leigh, *Peoples Speaking to Peoples* (Chicago: University of Chicago Press, 1946), 108; Doc. 21, 20; Doc. 70, 4–5.

15. Doc. 16, 13; "Statement by the Commission," in Chafee, *Government and Mass Communications*, viii; WEH, *Freedom of the Press*, 203; Reinhold Niebuhr, "Pawns for Fascism: Our Lower Middle Class," *American Scholar*, June 1937, 145–152; Niebuhr, *The Nature and Destiny of Man: A Christian Interpretation*, vol. 1, *Human Nature* (London: Nisbet, 1941), 225–226; Niebuhr, *The Children of Light and the Children of Darkness: A Vindication of Democracy and a Critique of Its Traditional Defense* (New York: Scribner, 1944), 146.

16. WEH, *Freedom of the Press*, 148–149, 187, 202, 205; Harold D. Lasswell, *Democracy through Public Opinion* (Menasha, WI: George Banta, 1941), 40, 104; Doc. 19, 2; RMH, *The Great Conversation: The Substance of a Liberal Education*, Great Books of the Western World 1 (Chicago: Encyclopædia Britannica, 1952), 80.

17. Doc. 70, 4–5; Doc. 21, 20; Doc. 108B, 121; *FRP*, 25; Doc. 48, 106; "Comments by Llewellyn White on Proposed Report of Subcommittee on Truth," n.d., 1, CFP Columbia, box 9; WEH, *Freedom of the Press*, 187–188; Chafee, *Government and Mass Communications*, 129–130.

18. WEH, *Freedom of the Press*, 199.

19. *FRP*, 25, 27; Doc. 91, 27.

20. John Dickinson, "Planned Society," James Goold Cutler Lecture, College of William and Mary, Apr. 21, 1943, *Bulletin of the College of William and Mary* 37, no. 4 (June 1943): 19; Doc. 108B, 107.

21. Doc. 48, 114; WEH, *Freedom of the Press*, 184–186.

22. *FRP*, 20, 23–25; Doc. 48, 49; Doc. 99, 4–5, 42; RMH, foreword to *FRP*, viii.

23. Niebuhr, introduction to *Responsibility in Mass Communication*, xix.

24. Yochai Benkler, Robert Faris, and Hal Roberts, *Network Propaganda: Manipulation, Disinformation, and Radicalization in American Politics* (New York: Oxford University Press, 2018), 314, 381, 383, 387.

25. Knight Commission on Trust, Media and Democracy, *Crisis in Democracy: Renewing Trust in America* (Washington, DC: Aspen Institute, 2019).

26. Doc. 16, 21.

27. HRL to WEH, Dec. 1, 1943, 1–2, Time Inc. Archives. For a brief review of scholarly assertions that self-interest guided Luce, see Stephen Bates, "Is This the Best Philosophy Can Do? Henry R. Luce and *A Free and Responsible Press*," *Journalism & Mass Communication Quarterly* 95, no. 3 (2018): 813–814.

28. Russell Jacoby, *The Last Intellectuals: American Culture in the Age of Academe* (New York: Basic Books, 1982); Jacoby, "Last Thoughts on *The Last Intellectuals*," *Society* 46 (2009): 38–44.

Acknowledgments

I FIRST LOOKED INTO the Commission on Freedom of the Press in the 1990s, as a fellow at the Annenberg Washington Program of Northwestern University. The Annenberg Program published my monograph on the commission in 1995. I'm indebted to the director of the program, Newton N. Minow, for supporting my research and for connecting me with Michael Beschloss, Sissela Bok, Fred H. Cate, Elizabeth Drew, Reuven Frank, Georgie Anne Geyer, Lawrence K. Grossman, Rodney A. Smolla, and Frank Stanton, with whom I discussed my research in conversation or correspondence. Edwin Diamond, Jonathan B. Imber, Martin A. Linsky, Seymour Martin Lipset, James T. Patterson, David A. Stephens, Abigail Thernstrom, and Stephan Thernstrom provided incisive comments on drafts of the monograph.

Archival research was made possible by an AEJMC Senior Scholar Grant and a Faculty Opportunity Award from the University of Nevada, Las Vegas. Gaining access to the Time Inc. archives required a sustained campaign on many fronts; I'm grateful to Jack Shafer, Richard J. Tofel, William Powers, James R. Gaines, Ann S. Moore, Dan Okrent, Roy Peter Clark, Peter Costiglio, Nancy Gibbs, John Huey, and David von Drehle, for helping me get in, and to Bill Hooper, for his assistance with the archival materials. (The Time Inc. files now are housed at the New-York Historical Society.) I'm indebted to Barbara Hutchins Gourley, who authorized me to quote the letters of her stepfather, Robert Maynard Hutchins; Martin Matthews, who gave me access to the papers and insights into the character of his stepmother, Ruth Inglis Matthews, one of the commission's staff researchers; Christopher Buckley, who let me consult the Ruth Inglis Matthews materials in the William F. Buckley Jr. Papers at Yale; Virginia Trippi, who shared her knowledge of another staff researcher, Llewellyn White; Peter Ascoli, who authorized me to quote White's reflections on his experience with the commission; and Timothy Stewart-Winter, Abigail J. Stewart, David O. Stewart, and Joan

Stewart, who helped fill in my understanding of the third researcher, Milton D. Stewart.

Hannah Birch provided invaluable help with archival research at the University of Washington. Ami E. Cutler and Christopher Gross also provided extensive aid. I received additional research assistance from Alexandre Baude, Andy Donahue, Jessica Wheeler, and Jessica Zimmerman. Susie Skarl and Yuko Shinozaki of Lied Library at UNLV helped me chase down materials, and Julie Grahame of the Yousuf Karsh Estate guided me through the process of photo research.

I exchanged ideas about the Hutchins Commission at a commemoration of the commission's fiftieth anniversary at the University of Illinois. I'm grateful to Steven Helle for inviting me to speak. The Poynter Institute included me in a seminar on the Hutchins and Kerner Commissions. I also presented my work at the MacBride Round Table on Communication Access at the University of Colorado, Boulder; the Boston University Institute on Culture, Religion, and World Affairs Conference on Public Intellectuals; and several other academic conferences.

I benefited from conversation and correspondence with many scholars and authors, including Theodore Peterson, who starting in the late 1950s was largely responsible for the revival of attention to the Commission on Freedom of the Press, as well as Douglas Anderson, Jerome A. Barron, Margaret A. Blanchard, Lee C. Bollinger, Alan Brinkley, Hilda Bryant, Dane Claussen, Mary Ann Dzuback, Sir Harold Evans, Stanley E. Flink, Peggy Lee Fox, Richard Wightman Fox, Loren Ghiglione, Stephen Hess, Donna Ippolito, Michael Janeway, Nicholas Johnson, John J. Kaag, Richard Kaye, Michael J. Lacey, Laurel Leff, Robert H. McGaughey III, Jerilyn S. McIntyre, Ian S. MacNiven, Robert Merry, Kaarle Nordenstreng, Jaroslav Pelikan, Stephanie Perry, Elaine Walls Reed, Jay Rosen, Roger Simpson, John Smith, Mitchell Stephens, Sam Tanenhaus, Elke van Cassel, Robert Vanderlan, Spencer Weber Waller, and Barbara E. Will, plus my colleagues in the Hank Greenspun School of Journalism and Media Studies at UNLV.

For comments on drafts of the manuscript, I'm profoundly grateful to Hal Berghel, Dillon Teachout Burns, Everette E. Dennis, Sally Denton, Amanda Fortini, David Fott, Michael Green, Brian Gross, Steve Lagerfeld, Ann Jamison Loftin, Christina Peters, Victor Pickard, William Powers, William Todd Schultz, Jack Shafer, and Arnon Siegel. My agents, Lynn Chu and Glen Hartley, and my editor, William Frucht, sharpened the manuscript and saw it through to publication.

Closer, much closer, to home, my daughters, Charlotte and Clara, brighten the days beyond measure, and my wife, Polly, is my greatest good fortune. Some debts can't fit on a page.

Index

academia: division of labor between media and academia, 15; and journalism education, 196, 203; as model for media, 133, 222. *See also* journalism schools; *specific schools*

accountability, 58, 130, 165, 172, 174, 182

activists, 33, 51–52, 84, 215, 221, 281n27

Addams, Jane, 30

Adler, Mortimer: commentary on Commission publications by, 7, 175; *Diagrammatics* (art project and book with Maude Hutchins), 18–19; Great Books curriculum taught by, 12, 140, 143–145; Hutchins and, 143–145, 147, 150; as potential Commission member, 51

advertising: for electoral campaigns, 100; free expression and, 53; internet's impact on, 214–215; MacLeish's objections to, 64; news coverage influenced by, 127, 201; presented as news, 86, 172, 222; press's responsibility priorities and, 183; social responsibility theory and, 199

AEJ (Association for Education in Journalism), 200, 204

affirmative First Amendment. *See* positive First Amendment

Agee, James, 23

America First Committee, 17, 149

American Legion, 217

American Newspaper Publishers Association, 40–41, 130

American Political Science Association, 33, 35

Americans for Democratic Action, 51

American Society of Newspaper Editors, 15, 41, 130, 189, 212–213

American Tailors Guild, 11

Ames, William E., 199–200

antitrust law and enforcement: Associated Press case, 46, 49, 51, 75, 87, 111, 114–115, 167; Commission's debates on, 5, 51, 105–115, 174; common carrier model and, 102; Dickinson and, 109–114, 170; MacLeish on, 167; McCormick and, 43, 46; Niebuhr and, 138; positive First Amendment and, 75; press critics and, 85

Aristotle: *Politics*, 167

Arnold, Thurman, 46–48, 51, 110–111, 114–115

Arts Club (Chicago), 19

Ascoli, Max, 153, 276n1